"The church loses a healthy connection to her past at great peril for her future. This book is a superb remedy to this danger. *Historical Theology for the Church* is both informative and well written. It proves theology can be instructive and interesting at the same time. I like this work. I will be quick to commend this book for scholar and layperson alike."

—**Daniel L. Akin**, president, Southeastern Baptist Theological Seminary

"Drs. Jason Duesing and Nathan Finn have done the church a remarkable service by assembling *Historical Theology for the Church*. They, together with fourteen other top-tier contributors, give the reader an informative overview of the development of essential Christian doctrines throughout the history of church. All who love theology, church history, and the church itself will want this book and benefit from it. I'm thankful for this volume and hopeful that it gets a broad readership."

—**Jason K. Allen**, president, Midwestern Baptist Theological Seminary

"Jaroslav Pelikan once said that tradition is the living faith of the dead. That being so, we need to know the theology of the dead if the church is to preserve the living faith handed down through the centuries. In *Historical Theology for the Church*, Duesing and Finn have provided a helpful doorway into our great tradition. This volume is full of wisdom in how to apply the riches of church history to our modern context. I hope this book will awaken many in the church to the life-giving study of historical theology."

—**Brian J. Arnold**, president, Phoenix Seminary

"In modern Christianity's rush to reject traditions as unhelpful ties to the past, the church risks surrendering the past altogether. Rather than recognizing that the 'faith once for all handed down to the saints' comes to us by way of 2000 years of church history, today's believers find themselves trying to reinvent the theological wheel over and over again without the benefit of the experience and tools of those who've gone before. Thus, after two millennia many Christians continue to fight age-old battles or deprive themselves of the soul-satisfying fruit of their predecessors' labors. This book makes great strides to correct these woeful errors. Duesing, Finn, and all the rest give the reader a thorough yet winsome look at the development of key ideas through the sands of time, handing them down to today's believer in a manner that is readable and relevant. *Historical Theology for the Church* breathes life once again into the past and revives it for a new generation."

—**Peter Beck**, professor of Christian studies and Ott Chair of Theology, Charleston Southern University

"*Historical Theology for the Church* is rooted in Scripture yet aware of tradition; encompasses the church universal while providing application for the church local; is evangelical in its orientation and evangelistic in its presentation; and is academically sound with an edifying tone. Each chapter contains substantive historical overviews, significant case studies, and salient church practices, thus providing the reader with a unique resource detailing what the church has believed, why the church has believed, and what the church should believe."

—**Anthony Chute**, professor of church history and associate dean of the school of Christian ministries, California Baptist University

"*Historical Theology for the Church* will serve as a wonderful gift to pastors, church leaders, students, and theologians alike. Jason Duesing and Nathan Finn have assembled a talented cohort of Baptist thinkers to serve as thoughtful and engaging guides to help us better understand the development of key theological concepts as they have been articulated and debated through the centuries. Bringing their Baptist commitments to bear on this praiseworthy work, the contributors enable us to gain a greater appreciation for a knowledge of the past, the value of tradition, and the importance of catholicity. In all of these things, the authors desire to spur us toward retrieval for the sake of renewal in our personal discipleship as well as in our worship, preaching, teaching, and service in and for the church. It is a delight to recommend this fine resource."

—**David S. Dockery**, distinguished professor of theology, Southwestern Baptist Theological Seminary, and president, International Alliance for Christian Education

"We have been waiting for a book like this for a long time—well-crafted essays, written by first-rate scholars, tracking the course of Christian belief across the centuries. Rooted in faith and aimed to build up the church, this volume is a prime example of what I have called retrieval for the sake of renewal. Warmly welcomed!"

—**Timothy George**, distinguished professor of divinity, Beeson Divinity School of Samford University

"The historical development of Christian theology is one of the most important dimensions of our theological task today, and it is especially urgent in this time of doctrinal and theological amnesia. This volume combines much-needed scholarship and deep concern for the church, and it represents a hope for theological recovery in this age. Thus, it is a genuine achievement that will serve the church for years to come."

—**R. Albert Mohler Jr.**, president, The Southern Baptist Theological Seminary

HISTORICAL THEOLOGY FOR THE CHURCH

HISTORICAL THEOLOGY FOR THE CHURCH

edited by

JASON G. DUESING *and* NATHAN A. FINN

B&H ACADEMIC
BRENTWOOD, TENNESSEE

Historical Theology for the Church

Published by B&H Academic
Brentwood, Tennessee

ISBN: 978-143364915-8
Dewey Decimal Classification: 230
Subject Heading: DOCTRINAL THEOLOGY / THEOLOGY--HISTORIOGRAPHY / THEOLOGY--HISTORY OF DOCTRINES

Cover credit line: Cover design by Mark Karis.
Cover illustration by rashpil/iStock.

Printed in the United States of America

3 4 5 6 7 8 9 10 VP 27 26 25 24 23

To our students
and
To local churches
that are living and creating
the historical theology of the future

CONTENTS

INTRODUCTION

Jason G. Duesing

> "Therefore," he said to them, "every teacher of the law who has become a disciple in the kingdom of heaven is like the owner of a house who brings out of his storeroom treasures new and old."
>
> —Matthew 13:52

The Lord's Remembrancer

When David Levin set out to describe the early years of Cotton Mather's life (1663–1703), he dubbed him "the Lord's Remembrancer."[1] This title is taken from the oldest functioning judicial position in England, the King's Remembrancer. Established in the twelfth century, this clerk serves the monarchy by reminding of previous business recorded. Yet, bestowing Mather with this honorific comes with some controversy given his role in the Salem witch trials. That chapter in Mather's life often overshadows

[1] David Levin, *Cotton Mather: The Young Life of the Lord's Remembrancer, 1663–1703* (Cambridge, MA: Harvard University Press, 1978).

his prodigious work as historian, biographer, and biblical commentator. Mather's *magnum opus*, the *Magnalia Christi Americana*, is an example of his careful work and the primary reason why Levin gives Mather the title of the Lord's Remembrancer. Written to provide an ecclesiastical history of New England, Levin praises Mather for his faithful historical work. He states that his "strength as a historian grows out of the range and number of his examples, and the persistence of his theme—the piety, the faith, the struggle, the perplexity, and the resignation in dozens of actual lives."[2]

Such is a fitting description of the task of the historical theologian—a servant of the church who reminds present and future readers of previous actions and theological developments from earlier eras in Christianity's history. As the Lord's remembrancers, faithful historical theologians are able to serve the church present and future, but what does that entail? How is this work done? This chapter presents a retrospective survey of historical theologies and casts the vision for crafting a historical theology for the church.

What Is Historical Theology?

Before examining the past or considering the future, one must first ask whether it is even possible to arrive at an evaluation of theology in history? C. S. Lewis, in answering this question, remarked that most history cannot be known. He asserted that "a single second of lived time contains more than can be recorded." Lewis was not saying everything from history is unknown, for he recognized that "important parts of the past survive."[3] What is recorded is worth knowing and analyzing, from which we can discern truths about the past to the degree that comparisons to other eras can be made. One can also track the manner in which authors understood various doctrines in their own time and context.

---

[2] Levin, 262.

[3] C. S. Lewis, "Historicism," in Lewis, *Christian Reflections* (Grand Rapids: Eerdmans, 1967; New York: HarperCollins, 2014), 132, 134.

If studying the past has value, and truth from the past can be ascertained to formulate a field of study called history, what then is historical theology? The next section will examine the history of historical theology, how long historians have been studying the development of theology in history, and who are the primary figures. For now, this section aims to arrive at a common definition.

Essentially, historical theology is a process of historical inquiry that serves and supports other distinct but compatible disciplines. A helpful approach to arriving at a definition of historical theology is to set historical theology in relief against these other disciplines. First, historical theology complements systematic and biblical theology by providing a historical context for classical doctrines. This is true whether historians find their organization by a collection of biblical references across the Bible (systematic) or through each book and from the canon as a facet of the story of the Bible (biblical). Second, historical theology complements church history by providing a repository for the historical development of doctrines alongside the development of the people, places, events, and social factors that comprise the story of Christianity's history. Church history reviews the history of the theologians; historical theology investigates the theologians' ideas.

Another way to examine the relationship of historical theology to other disciplines is to consider the role of tradition in the history of Christianity. As Rowan Williams explains in his recently revised *Why Study the Past?*, "Churches have always been 'conserving' communities: that is, they have always been concerned about the past and about whether they were in some sense doing the same thing as the previous generation had done."[4] Although Christians have often debated the relationship of tradition to the Bible or one tradition to another, the history of Christianity makes clear that Christians have intentionally sought to stay connected to the past and have placed value on how other Christians have sought to live out their faith

---

[4] Rowan Williams, *Why Study the Past? The Quest for the Historical Church* (London: Darton, Longman, and Todd, 2005, 2014), 91–92.

individually and in community. So, how are Christians of the present and future to understand the traditions of the past? How are Christians to find help or correction from those who have lived the Christian life? Historical theology provides answers by documenting doctrinal development of Christians through the ages and how they have transferred their tradition to the next generation.

Alister McGrath notes that this teaching function of historical theology as a pedagogical tool is unique to the field. The study of historical theology allows Christians and churches to make sense of what they have inherited as well as to receive instruction from those who have lived in other times and persevered through other trials. McGrath explains, "It is virtually impossible to do theology as if it had never been done before. There is always an element of looking over one's shoulder, to see how things were done in the past, and what answers were then given. Part of the notion of 'tradition' is a willingness to take seriously the theological heritage of the past."[5]

To illustrate this function, consider what happens when a person walks up to observe two people playing chess. The two opponents have already started the game, and thus the onlooker is forced to survey the chessboard and make an assessment of what has happened, who is winning, whose turn is next, and who has the advantage. The onlooker observes the game in progress and, using her knowledge of the game, evaluates the strategies in play to appreciate what is happening. The better one knows the game, the more quickly one can adapt to this, but anyone would prefer to have observed the game from the beginning to appreciate the match in full. Second to that, the onlooker would be helped if the opponents paused to explain to her how many moves had occurred, what mistakes had been made, and what each player was thinking at the time. A third level of intrigue and complexity could occur should one of the players leave his game and ask the onlooker to take over and play for him. At this point, for the onlooker to have a chance,

[5] Alister E. McGrath, *Historical Theology: An Introduction to the History of Christian Thought* (London: Blackwell, 1998; Wiley, 2012), 12.

she would need to have knowledge, experience, and a sense of not only what she has inherited but also what she should do next.

Such it is with the study of historical theology. Christians of the present and future, once they start their journey in the Christian life, either as individuals or in local churches, are put in the position of the onlooker. Christians before them are playing or have played many chess games with the Christian tradition. Each develops his or her skills with the doctrines of the Bible and also contributes new understanding to how the Christian life is lived in each era and under unique circumstances. The onlooker is helped if she has the opportunity not only to study and learn in community the rules of the game that comes through the study of the Bible, but also to learn from and observe other Christians, nearby and in previous ages, how they have done the same. Further, often in local churches or in families, the onlooker is asked to take over a game when she is brought into a church tradition, moves to a new community, or joins a new Christian family. The discipleship that comes through the study of historical theology can aid the onlooker in understanding her new surroundings, what has taken place before, and how to know what should take place next. Historical theology is the pedagogical tool to aid Christians with these situations they will encounter.

With respect to formal definitions of *historical theology* as a discipline, this chapter presents three of the most common meanings of the term, to show a mutual understanding before concluding with an original definition. Jaroslav Pelikan (1969) defined historical theology as "the study of what the church of Jesus Christ believes, teaches, and confesses on the basis of the Word of God."[6] Alister McGrath (1998) defined historical theology as "the branch of theological inquiry which aims to explore the historical development of Christian doctrines, and identify the factors which were influential

[6] Jaroslav Pelikan, *Development of Christian Doctrine* (New Haven, CT: Yale University Press, 1969), 143.

in their formulation."[7] Gregg Allison (2011) defined historical theology as "the study of the interpretation of Scripture and the formulation of doctrine by the church of the past."[8] This section concludes with the following working definition: historical theology is the study of the development of Christian doctrine and tradition from the Bible by the church and for the church.

Retrospect: The History of Historical Theology

In his meditation on Rom 8:28 and whether and how God can work good out of sinful situations, the Puritan Thomas Watson thought of the Bible's Samson, saying, "It is a matter of wonder that any honey should come out of this lion."[9] When one reviews the work of historical theology in history, with all the flaws and faults that humans bring to bear in every era, it is a marvel that any honey has been found. Yet historical theology has shaped historical movements for good. Stratford Caldecott reminds, "For every great change, every rebirth or *renaissance* in human culture, has been triggered by the retrieval of something valuable out of the past, making new, creative developments possible."[10] Whereas the previous section examined the "what" of historical theology, this section aims to present the "who" and the "how" of historical theology. This retrospective survey functions as an additional layer of foundation on which the final section aims to build for the present and future understanding of a historical theology for the church.

---

[7] McGrath, *Historical Theology*, 9.

[8] Gregg R. Allison, *Historical Theology* (Grand Rapids: Zondervan, 2011), 23.

[9] Thomas Watson, *All Things for Good* (1663; repr., n.p.: Banner of Truth, 2013), 44.

[10] Stratford Caldecott, *Beauty for Truth's Sake* (Grand Rapids: Brazos, 2009), 12.

The History of Historical Theologians

In 1986, Timothy George presented his faculty address in the Alumni Chapel of the Southern Baptist Theological Seminary. In his address titled "Dogma beyond Anathema: Historical Theology in the Service of the Church," George said that historical theology "is a relative newcomer to the body of divinity."[11] By that he meant that while the classical Christian tradition had undergone transmission and evaluation since the early church, it was not until the Reformers returned to the sources to critique Rome that the practice of historical theology developed.[12] To put it another way, with the Reformation, the need for a reevaluation of the tradition of the church emerged as Protestants sought to understand where the Roman Catholic Church erred in history. Martin Luther (1483–1546) and Philipp Melanchthon (1497–1560), in particular, emphasized a distinction between a history of the church and a history of the state, focusing almost solely on the former.[13] Thus, historical theology began with the Reformation and served as a vital tool to aid each Reformer as they carried out the work of rebuilding the church.

Although the Reformers used historical theology to recover the Christian tradition, the Enlightenment theologians used historical theology to harvest from the Christian tradition for reinvention. George identifies Friedrich Schleiermacher (1768–1834) as one who "revolutionized modern theology by radically reinterpreting traditional doctrines in light of the Christian self-consciousness."[14] F. C. Baur (1792–1860) applied the logic of Georg W. F. Hegel (1770–1831) to the development of doctrine and, thereby, discarded the value of much of the Christian tradition. The Enlightenment approach

---

[11] Timothy George, "Dogma beyond Anathema: Historical Theology in the Service of the Church," *Review & Expositor* 4 (Fall 1987): 693.

[12] McGrath, *Historical Theology*, 10–11, agrees, noting that both Protestants and Catholics "found they had to become familiar with both patristic theology and the modification of these ideas in the Middle Ages."

[13] Ernst Breisach, *Historiography*, 3rd ed. (Chicago: University of Chicago Press, 2007), 166–68.

[14] George, "Dogma," 697.

to historical theology culminated with Adolf von Harnack (1851–1930). Harnack's *History of Dogma*, George notes, "was itself the most suitable means for liberating the church from dogmatic Christianity."[15] By this, George explains that Harnack saw the development of Christian doctrine at Nicea and Chalcedon as corruptions of the simple teaching of Jesus. Thus, for Harnack, historical theology is the task of harvesting history to return to the kernel of simple truth. The challenge with this approach, however, as history has revealed, is that much like the Narnian adventures of Eustace Scrubb seeking to "undragon" himself by scraping off his scales, when one harvests the Christian tradition to uncover the core of the tradition, one finds that the scales are what makes the dragon. That is, once undragoned, one is no longer a dragon.

Following the Enlightenment, there were other theologians who did not follow the "reductionism" of Harnack. John Henry Newman (1801–1890) and Philip Schaaf (1819–1893) from the nineteenth century are two whom George sees as having "stressed the organic character of doctrinal development, its rootedness in the wider life of the church."[16] In the twentieth century, several theologians from various branches of the Christian tradition also would craft works of historical theology from a traditional perspective of doctrinal development. Louis Berkhof (1873–1957) wrote *The History of Christian Doctrines* (1937) from the Reformed tradition. Jaroslav Pelikan (1923–2006) wrote his five-volume *The Christian Tradition* from the Lutheran tradition but included surveys of Roman Catholicism and Eastern Orthodoxy. Justo L. Gonzalez (1937–) wrote *A History of Christian Thought* (1970–1974) as a Methodist theologian. Geoffrey Bromiley (1915–2009) wrote *Historical Theology* (1978) from the Anglican tradition. In the late twentieth and early twenty-first centuries, several evangelical theologians contributed works of historical theology. Alister McGrath, an Anglican, wrote *Historical Theology* (1998, 2012); Roger E. Olson, an Arminian

[15] George, 698.

[16] George, 699.

Baptist, wrote *The Story of Christian Theology* (1999); Gregg R. Allison, a Calvinistic Baptist, wrote *Historical Theology* (2011); and Gerald Bray, an Anglican, wrote *God Has Spoken: A History of Christian Theology* (2014).

The Historiography of Historical Theology

Although this survey gives some insight into how historical theology has been done since the Reformation in a broad sense, others have reviewed the historiography of church history and historical theology in greater detail. Not without surprise, there is a good deal of debate among scholars over how correctly to review the development of doctrine in history. Like C. S. Lewis's "Wood between the Worlds," wherein there are several ponds that serve as portals to different places, there is a group of scholars discussing not only what is historical theology, but also the best and right way to develop historical theology. That is, what pond is the best to jump into for the task of evaluating the history of Christian theology? As one helpful tool, Jay Green's *Christian Historiography: Five Rival Versions* establishes and evaluates at least five approaches to the task. Given this chapter's attempt to establish a broad orientation or disposition of doing historical theology for the church rooted in the Bible and consistent with the Christian tradition recovered by the Reformers, further discussion of the role of providence in history, the implications of historical approaches for ethics and apologetics, and the like, will have to receive further treatment at another time. For now, this chapter seeks to establish simply that honey can come from the lion. Historical theology can be done for the church.

Prospect: Historical Theology for the Church

What are the prospects for the present and future of historical theology, and what would it look like to develop a historical theology for the church? We conclude with the start of a list of characteristics of historical theology for the church. Following are examples from works that exhibit these characteristics, as well as descriptions of future needs for more work. By no means is this list final or comprehensive. The purpose here is to conclude with a tangible blueprint as an outline for future and ongoing construction.

1. Historical theology for the church upholds the primacy of the Bible over tradition and history but recognizes the value of tradition and history.

On the one hand, this statement is meant as a simple affirmation of the common understanding that at the Reformation's core was a call to *sola scriptura* as a critique and corrective against Rome's elevation of the authority of tradition to that of equal and superior to biblical authority. Historical theology for the church operates from the position of seeing the Bible as the only inerrant authority given to the church. This doesn't rule out there being other authorities vital for the task of historical theology. Indeed, the creeds and confessions of historic Christianity are the baseline, following Scripture, for establishing the development of doctrine in history. Yet historical theology for the church recognizes, with the Reformers, that the Bible alone is supreme and thus the authority by which all other authorities are judged and to which they are to be understood and conformed.

On the other hand, the above statement is a recognition of the ongoing conversations among biblical and theological scholars related to the Theological Interpretation of Scripture (TIS) movement. Discussions regarding the TIS have occurred formally since the start of the twenty-first century. These largely arose out of a desire to recover an understanding of the interpretation of Scripture that is connected to the history of the church before the widespread influence of the Enlightenment's historical-critical methods. In some ways, Timothy George, in his 1986 faculty address, anticipated the concerns expressed by the TIS when he said, "We must ask of the text not only what it meant in its original setting (the special task of Old and New Testament study) and what it means today (the combined task of biblical, systematic, and practical theology), but also what it *has meant* throughout the vast continuum of the Christian experience."[17] The key is how exactly historical theology for the church holds these two meanings together. In 2011, D. A. Carson provided a helpful analysis of the TIS movement with his chapter "Theological Interpretation of Scripture, Yes, But . . . ," which summarized the state of the discussion in six propositions, recognized where the TIS proponents were asking the right questions, and then raised helpful questions of his own.[18] This corrective essay helps to show "that what is most valuable in TIS (and much is), is not new" and "what is new in TIS varies from ambiguous to mistaken."[19] Alongside Carson, theologians Michael Allen and Scott Swain started the New Studies in Dogmatics series aimed at constructing theology "in a program of renewal through retrieval." That is, the pursuit of theology by "drawing more deeply upon the resources of Holy Scripture in conversation with the church's most trusted teachers (ancient, medieval, and modern) who have sought to fathom Christ's unsearchable riches."[20] More recently, Craig Carter's *Interpreting Scripture with the Great Tradition* also endeavors to follow the balance, seeing value in the fact that "ancient reading practices, which have never died out completely in the church, can help us hear God's Word in less subjective and more ruled ways than modern hermeneutics makes available to us."[21] Historical theology for the church should lean on and listen to these contemporary guides who are seeking to uphold the primacy of the Bible as the sole authority while recognizing the value of the Christian tradition for reading and interpreting the Bible.

---

[17] George, "Dogma," 701.

[18] D. A. Carson, "Theological Interpretation of Scripture: Yes, But . . ." in *Theological Commentary: Evangelical Perspectives*, ed. R. Michael Allen (London: T&T Clark, 2011), 187–207.

[19] Carson, 207.

[20] Michael Allen and Scott Swain, "Introduction to New Studies in Dogmatics," *Common Places,* April 16, 2015. https://zondervanacademic.com/blog/common-places-introduction-to-new-studies-in-dogmatics/.

[21] Craig A. Carter, *Interpreting Scripture with the Great Tradition* (Grand Rapids: Baker, 2018), x.

2. Historical theology for the church follows the two Greatest Commandments, as it is for the church catholic and church local.

Nathan Finn helpfully describes the task of the historian in light of the Greatest Commandments, indicating that what distinguishes the Christian historian is motive. Is one pursuing historical inquiry as "ultimately an act of worship done for the Lord" and seeking to "understand and appreciate why people in the past did what they did, even when the historian disagrees with the action itself"?[22] Historical theology for the church seeks to study the development of doctrine as an act of love for God and as an act of love for neighbor.[23] To love God is to love the church Jesus Christ loves and for whom he gave himself (Eph 5:25). Throughout the history of Christianity, the question, What is the church? has served as a source of debate and division, both small scale and large. Yet a simple understanding of what the church is, is needed to build a historical theology. The Niceno-Constantinopolitan Creed (381) describes the church in four attributes as one, holy, catholic, and apostolic. The idea of church catholicity or universality "came to be used synonymously with 'orthodox.'"[24] Todd Billings helpfully describes this sense of catholic as an "underground water table" of common ground wholeness that all traditions share at their depths.[25] Likewise, C. S. Lewis famously described the traditions as

> a hall out of which doors open into several rooms. If I can bring anyone into that hall I shall have done what I attempted. But it is in

---

[22] Nathan A. Finn, *History: A Student's Guide* (Wheaton, IL: Crossway, 2016), 21–22.

[23] Matthew 22:37–40: "He said to him, 'Love the Lord your God with all your heart, with all your soul, and with all your mind. This is the greatest and most important command. The second is like it: Love your neighbor as yourself. All the Law and the Prophets depend on these two commands.'"

[24] Mark Dever, *The Church* (Nashville: B&H Academic, 2012), 18.

[25] J. Todd Billings, "Rediscovering the Catholic-Reformed Tradition for Today," in *Reformed Catholicity*, Michael Allen and Scott R. Swain (Grand Rapids: Baker, 2015), 153.

> the rooms, not in the hall, that there are fires and chairs and meals. The hall is the place to wait in, a place from which to try the various doors, not a place to live in.[26]

Therefore, at one level the church in history shares a great hall of foundational confessional consensus expressed in various traditions with rooms off that hall allowing for fellowship and life in local churches while remaining connected to the larger Christian tradition.[27] Local churches need fellowship with other traditions within the larger church to, at one level, appreciate and develop the very things that make them distinct.

Even more, and for the same reasons, however, local churches need interaction with others in the church catholic who are no longer living. Robert Tracy McKenzie notes, "By one estimate, only 6 percent of all the human beings who have ever lived are alive right now, yet we write off the other 94 percent, jettisoning history from the curriculum in favor of purportedly more practical subjects."[28] As just two examples among many, what would we make of John Calvin's theology if he had not had the opportunity to interact with Augustine? How would the modern missions movement have accelerated if Andrew Fuller had not treasured the work of Jonathan Edwards? Historical theology for the church is done well when the church

---

[26] C. S. Lewis, *Mere Christianity* (1952; New York: HarperCollins, 2009), xv. George Marsden notes that this view has not been well received by Roman Catholics for, as one argues, "The Roman Catholic Church would have to insist that the envisaged house *is* the Roman Catholic Church, with the other communions as more or less attached to it as annexes or outbuildings," *C. S. Lewis's Mere Christianity: A Biography* (New Haven, CT: Princeton University Press, 2016), 130.

[27] For further commentary on this understanding, see Jason G. Duesing, "Baptist Contributions to the Christian Tradition," in *Baptists and the Christian Tradition*, ed. Matthew Y. Emerson, Christopher W. Morgan, and R. Lucas Stamps (Nashville: B&H Academic, 2020), 329–50.

[28] Robert Tracy McKenzie, *The First Thanksgiving: What the Real Story Tells Us about Loving God and Learning from History* (Downers Grove, IL: IVP, 2013), 11.

loves God and loves neighbor by valuing and learning from other expressions and traditions of the church catholic in history.

3. Historical theology for the church is done as a means to the end of fulfilling the Great Commission and glorifying God.

In 1 Pet 4:7, the apostle Peter explains that "the end of all things is near." By that he means he and his readers were living in the last days before the return of Jesus. Since that time until our very own, the church has been living on the verge of the end of the world. Peter explains that while believers in churches should have their eyes fixed and their hope set on the soon and certain return of Jesus, they should be using their spiritual gifts, whether they be serving or speaking, all for the glory of God. That is, until the end of time, whether one eats, drinks, preaches, trains, waters, reaps, types, writes, shares, or disciples, the church should be doing these things as the biblically prescribed means for carrying out the Great Commission to the glory of God. In short, historical theology for the church is done to enrich and strengthen churches for the sake of global evangelism and to see the knowledge of the glory of God among all peoples as the waters cover the sea (Hab 2:14).[29] Historical theology for the church functions as a tool to equip churches to learn and take their history of doctrinal development to those who do not have a historical theology.

4. Historical theology for the church is academic and edifying as it functions as friend to the work of systematic theology, biblical theology, and applied theology.

Historical theology for the church is helpful when it functions as a friend and not a rival to its companion disciplines. The idea of friendship is

---

[29] These ideas were first explored in similar wording in Jason G. Duesing, "A Denomination Always for the Church: Ecclesiological Distinctives as a Basis for Confessional Cooperation," *The SBC and the Twenty-First Century*, ed. Jason K. Allen, rev. ed. (Nashville: B&H Academic, 2019), 109–25.

both a metaphor and a necessary reality for academic work. As a metaphor, historical theology functions as a friend to other disciplines by filling the gap between history and biblical and theological analysis. Whereas systematic and biblical theologians might desire to construct theology without regard to history, the historical theologian serves a helpful function of ensuring his friends do not veer too far from the Christian tradition or the work of the church in history. Likewise, for those engaged in applied or pastoral theology who are prone to jettison tradition for the honorable sake of applicability or rhetorical relevance, the historical theologian helpfully reminds us of the relevance of knowing there is "nothing new under the sun" (Eccl 1:9). In this way, to return to the chess analogy, historical theology for the church functions as a friend to other disciplines. It does this by regularly seeking to hold their work "in check," triangulating around them, seeking to understand their movements, and keeping them tied to the work of other systematic, biblical, and practical theologians of other eras. That is, historical theologians, as friends, are helping theologians of the church present continue to do their work in connection to the church past and for the church future.

Historical theology for the church also functions as friend to these disciplines for mutual edification. As C. S. Lewis observed, significant friendship among believers doesn't come by chance. "Christ, who said to the disciples, 'Ye have not chosen me, but I have chosen you,' can truly say to every group of Christian friends, 'You have not chosen one another, but I have chosen you for one another.'"[30] Such it is also with the various theologian disciplines within the Christian tradition. Historical theology for the church is strengthened when challenged and sharpened by systematic theology, biblical theology, and applied theology. When these disciplines stick closer than brothers (Prov 18:24) for the church, they are modeling what the Lord Jesus modeled and provided for his disciples. He is the One who, when his church

---

[30] C. S. Lewis, "Friendship," in *The Four Loves* (New York: Harcourt Brace, 1960; New York: HarperCollins, 2017), 114. Citations refer to the HarperCollins edition.

was separated and far from him due to sin, brought her near at the price of his own blood (Eph 2:12–13). He loved the church, laid down his life, and called the church friends (John 15:13–15).

5. Historical theology for the church as an academic endeavor is done as a servant of the church, not as a master.

Timothy George recounts how Karl Barth (1886–1968) evaluated his theological contribution as "a relative of the donkey that went its way carrying an important burden." Just as the disciples were instructed by Jesus to retrieve the donkey, saying, "The Lord needs it" (Mark 11:3), before his triumphal entry, Barth saw himself as used by God as he "happened to be on the spot" when needed. He explained, "A theology somewhat different from the current theology was apparently needed in our time, and I was permitted to be the donkey that carried this better theology for part of the way, or tried to carry it as best I could."[31] Historical theology for the church helps the church when it understands that academic endeavor is the work of the donkey done in service to the master—the Lord Jesus and his church. This donkey work functions in two ways.

First, historical theologians doing historical theology for the church recognize, delight in, and remind others that the church is central to God's plan and not the academy, even while they are pursuing excellence in scholarship. A fine example of this is the recent volume by Scott Manetsch, *Calvin's Company of Pastors*, in the Oxford Studies in Historical Theology series. This work makes an original contribution by examining the pastoral theology of Geneva's ministers from 1536–1609. Therein, Manetsch states his primary concern is "not to employ a hermeneutic of suspicion when judging Geneva's ministers, but to exercise charity and critical subtlety in evaluating the pastoral behavior of Calvin and his colleagues in light of their unique

[31] George, "Dogma," 707.

historical and religious contexts."[32] To be sure, not all attempts at historical theology for the church will have a direct focus on ecclesiological analysis, but Manetsch's investigation into the life of pastors rightly tilts the exercise of academic inquiry toward that which serves the church. Throughout history, theologians and other church leaders have regularly strengthened the church of their age by discovery or representation of theological truth from the past with an eye toward the church, not merely the academy. This type of historical theology gives care to where it points, seeking to find the transcendental developments in history that are good, true, and beautiful for the church.[33] In this sense, again the idea of "retrieval for the sake of renewal" serves as a fitting mission statement for historical theology for the church.

Second, historical theologians doing historical theology for the church serve the church well when they also confront the church with the implications of its doctrinal development that the church might not want to see. To put it another way, historical theology for the church should regularly expose blind spots, sins, and inconsistencies of the church past and present. Although the Bible is perfect, the history of the Christian tradition is not. The historical theologian needs to carefully remind the church that it stands on the shoulders of many flawed giants in the past while pointing out the faults and failings of those giants. Stratford Caldecott, in his book *Beauty for Truth's Sake*, refers to Basil the Great's (330–379) practice of "following the bees" for finding the good in flawed history:

> For [the bees] neither approach all flowers equally, nor in truth do they attempt to carry off entire those upon which they alight, but

---

[32] Scott M. Manetsch, *Calvin's Company of Pastors: Pastoral Care and the Emerging Reformed Church, 1536–1609* (Oxford: Oxford University Press, 2013), 10.

[33] Roger Scruton, *Beauty: A Very Short Introduction* (Oxford: Oxford University Press, 2011), 3, reminds of Thomas Aquinas's transcendentals, those "features of reality possessed by all things, since they are aspects of being, ways in which the supreme gift of being is made manifest to the understanding."

> taking only so much of them as is suitable for their work, they suffer the rest to go untouched. We ourselves, too, if we are wise, having appropriated from this literature what is suitable to us and akin to the truth, will pass over the remainder. And just as in plucking the blooms from a rose-bed we avoid the thorns, so also in garnering from such writings whatever is useful, let us guard ourselves against what is harmful.[34]

Not every attempt by present historical theologians is without error; this requires other historical theologians to identify those errors for the sake of the church. As one example, John Fea, in his book *Why Study History?*, reminds that many "attempts to present American history to the church are often filled with basic errors of faith and interpretation, or they are used to manipulate the past for the purpose of promoting a religious or political agenda in the present."[35] Historical theology for the church, functioning as a donkey carrying the Master, serves his church well when it strives to provide correction of contemporary misapplications of the past for present and future churches.

The pursuit of scholarship for the church is not without cost. Robert Tracy McKenzie cautions scholars that "if we take this aspect of our calling seriously, however, we will likely run head-on against the values of an academic culture that is skeptical of overtly Christian reflection about the past, is dismissive of questions that tend to interest our faith communities, and is reflexively suspicious of scholarship geared toward a popular audience."[36]

---

[34] Basil the Great, "To Young Men," cited in Stratford Caldecott, *Beauty for Truth's Sake: On the Re-enchantment of Education* (Grand Rapids: Brazos, 2009), 16–17.

[35] John Fea, *Why Study History?* (Grand Rapids: Baker, 2013), 160.

[36] Robert Tracy McKenzie, "Don't Forget the Church: Reflections on the Forgotten Dimension of Our Dual Calling," in *Confessing History: Explorations in Christian Faith and the Historian's Vocation*, ed. John Fea, Jay Green, and Eric Miller (Notre Dame, IN: University of Notre Dame Press, 2010), 281.

Nevertheless, historical theologians doing historical theology for the church have the privilege of doing the humble work of a donkey for the Master by carefully guiding the church to the good, the true and the beautiful in history, while simultaneously pointing out the lack of theological clothes worn by many emperors of the academy.

As this work is for the church in our context, the authors selected for this work all affirm the Baptist Faith and Message (2000), which guides well the churches we seek to serve. Additionally, the authors selected have the appropriate academic credentials to teach this content. We hope the combined works demonstrate excellence in service to our churches. The original slate of authors included a few more voices, representing diverse ethnic minority perspectives, but for various personal or professional reasons, other matters prevented some from continued participation. We trust that God has directed the voices needed for this project to remain faithful to his Word and serve the churches with excellence.[37]

Conclusion: The Lord's Remembrancers

Benjamin Colman, preaching after Cotton Mather's funeral, noted that in his written work, Mather

> shone; being exceeding communicative, and bringing out of his *Treasury* things new and old, without measure. Here it was seen how his Wit, and Fancy, his Invention, his Quickness of thought, and ready Apprehension were all consecrated to God, as well as his Heart, Will, and Affections; and out of his Abundance within his *lips* overflowed, *dropt as the honeycomb*, fed all that came near him,

---

[37] The editors would like to extend a word of thanks to Thomas White and Cedarville University for hosting the early planning meetings for this project as well as providing helpful editorial advice and encouragement. *Historical Theology for the Church* arrives in print, in part, due to this valued support.

> and were as the *choice silver*, for richness and brightness, pleasure and profit.[38]

Jesus instructed that "every teacher of the law who has become a disciple in the kingdom of heaven is like the owner of a house who brings out of his storeroom treasures new and old." (Matt 13:52). Historical theology can be done for the church when historical theologians bring out the treasures from the doctrines of history and serve them as the Lord's remembrancers.

---

[38] Levin, *Cotton Mather*, ii.

UNIT ONE

THEOLOGY IN THE PATRISTIC ERA, AD 100–500

1

JESUS CHRIST

By Steven A. McKinion

Introduction

The question looming over Christianity from its inception was "Who is Jesus Christ?" When Jesus posed the question to his disciples, Peter answered correctly: "You are the Christ, the Son of the living God" (Matt 16:16 KJV). This confession identifying Jesus of Nazareth with the Old Testament Son of God was fundamental to Christian identity. Christians in antiquity understood this profession to be the essence of saving faith but nonetheless had to make sense of it. What did it mean for Jesus to be the "Son" of God? Christians in antiquity needed language that made sense of their liturgy, their proclamation of the gospel, and their ecclesial practices. The search for that language, and the formulations Christians agreed to, is Christology.

As Christianity emerged from the persecutions during the second and third centuries to acceptance as a major religion in the Roman Empire in the fourth century, theologians continued to distinguish Christianity from both Roman pagan religion and Judaism. Simultaneously, theologians increasingly contended with understandings of Jesus that were inconsistent with the "faith that was delivered to the saints once for all" (Jude 3). Apostolic Christianity understood Jesus in the context of the Old Testament, against other inaccurate interpretations of Jesus, such as those in Ebionism, Gnosticism, and Marcionism. This chapter will focus on developments related to language about Jesus Christ during the first five centuries of the Christian era.

Historical Overview

Second-Century Challenges to Christianity

In the early second century, Pliny the Younger (61–113) was governor of the Bithynia-Pontus province in the Roman Empire. He wrote a letter to Emperor Trajan (ruled 98–117), recounting his interrogation of Christians and requesting advice on how to deal with those Christians who refused to worship the Roman gods. Pliny's investigation revealed that when Christians gathered for worship, they sang hymns to Jesus Christ "as to a god." He noted that Christianity was little more than an excessive superstition, by which he meant that it was the worship of a strange god, Jesus.

The earliest Christian writings outside of the New Testament, collectively known as the *Apostolic Fathers*, confirm Pliny's contention that Christians worshipped Jesus as God. They also affirmed the biblical message that Jesus was a human being. The authors linked Jesus's work as Savior to his being both divine and human. During the late first and early second centuries, Christians defended the divinity and humanity of Christ against other groups that denied one or the other of these realities. These writers sought to preserve the Christian faith they had received from the apostles and to pass that gospel down without change or corruption.

Clement of Rome (35–99) represents those earliest Christian writers following the apostles. In his *Epistle to the Corinthians* (c. 96), Clement addressed the issue of pride in the church. He called on his readers to look to Jesus Christ as the ultimate picture of humility. Jesus existed as the eternal and preexistent Son of God who is worthy of all honor, majesty, and worship. Nevertheless, he humbled himself to join himself with humanity. Jesus is worthy of the same worship due the Father because Jesus is God just as the Father is God.

Clement stated that the Son of God became one with humanity to become the High Priest who would reconcile humanity to God. Although Clement did not examine this theme in detail, he was clear that Jesus identified fully and completely with humanity. As the High Priest, he gave "his flesh for our flesh, and his soul for our soul." For Clement, Jesus was worthy of worship because he was divine, but he offered himself for our salvation as a human. Both divine and human realities persisted in the one Lord Jesus Christ.

The *Shepherd of Hermas* was a text that many early Christians considered to be Scripture. It is a book of visions calling Christians to faithful living and right belief. The writer of *Shepherd* reminded his readers of the twofold confession in Philippians, that Jesus was both slave and God. The author further confessed that Jesus, as the Son of God, was preexistent. Because he was the agent of creation, the Son of God was before all created things, reminding the reader of Colossians 1 and John 1.

Another of the apostolic fathers is Ignatius of Antioch (35–108), who was martyred in Rome for the faith. As he traveled to Rome, he wrote seven letters to Christians along the way. In his *Epistle to the Trallians*, he remarked that "God appeared in human form to bring the fullness of life." Ignatius was clear that Jesus was both God and human. This profession was an unambiguous expression of the genuineness of the incarnation.

The first major threat to the Christian understanding of Jesus in the first and second centuries was Docetism. Docetism challenged the Christian affirmation that Jesus was the true incarnation of God by denying that Jesus was genuinely human. A number of different groups held this view, which finds early expression in those confronted by the biblical book of 1 John. Docetism comes from the Greek "to appear or to seem" and was the belief that Jesus was not fully human or did not identify with humanity fully and completely. In other words, Jesus only "appeared" to be a human being, when in reality he was only a divine being.

Against Docetism, Ignatius argued that denial of the true humanity of Jesus negated the salvation Jesus came to bring. For Ignatius and the other apostolic fathers, the reality of the human life in Jesus was necessary for salvation. Both types of being in Christ, the divine and human, were joined together to ensure eternal life for humanity. This gracious gift of life by the preexistent Son of God was at the heart of the Christian gospel.

A second major threat to the apostolic understanding of Jesus Christ as divine and human was Ebionism, a form of Judaizing Christianity such as that confronted by the apostle Paul in the book of Galatians. The Ebionites believed that Jesus was the Jewish Messiah but denied his divinity. They also denied the virgin birth and the redeeming death of Jesus. Instead, Jesus was seen as a righteous man who was adopted as the Son of God because of his faithfulness and obedience.

Second-century theologians responded to Ebionism with a renewed emphasis on Jesus as the eternal Son of God. Ebionism was based on a Jewish form of monotheism that believed only the Father was truly God. Justin Martyr (100–165), Athenagoras (130–190), and Tatian (120–180) opposed Ebionism and defended the divinity of Jesus by espousing the Christian view of a triune God, explaining that the eternal Son of God was the One who was incarnate. Jesus revealed God in the incarnation. The Christian practice of worshipping Jesus as God, going all the way back to the apostles, unambiguously demonstrates that Jesus was God. When Jesus acted, God himself acted.

Irenaeus of Lyons (130–202) wrote against Ebionite and Docetic Christologies, particularly those of the various Gnostic groups. The Gnostics viewed Christ as a semidivine figure who emanated from God. This being came to creation to announce a secret knowledge (Greek *gnosis*) by which salvation might be attainted. Marcion (85–160), who denied the Christian doctrine of God, claimed that Jesus was God clothed in the form of a human being. Denying the incarnation, Marcion posited a docetic Christ.

The second-century contribution to the development of Christology was the insistence that salvation is the union of God with humanity. As such, two fundamentally different and opposing ways of being must be united fully and completely in Jesus Christ. Moreover, while language that corresponded with those two ways of being must be maintained, that language was applied equally to Jesus Christ. It was fitting to speak of Jesus as God and equally as fitting to speak of him as a human being. There was a firm commitment to dual language about the one Christ.

Emerging from the second century, the question of the worship of Jesus was settled. It was also settled that Jesus was the same one who created the universe and became incarnate for the salvation of humanity. Fundamental language, even if not fully developed, already existed for Christians to proclaim Jesus as both God and a human being without diminishing or destroying either type of being.

Jesus Christ Is Fully God and Fully Human

The pagan philosopher Celsus was a formidable opponent of Christianity and claimed that the incarnation was irrational: either God changed into a human being or Jesus was just a man. Christians rejected Celsus's reasoning. Origen of Alexandria (184–253) responded by arguing that Jesus performed miracles and exhibited all of the attributes of God, including being all-knowing, all-powerful, and omnipresent. Because he possessed the divine attributes, he must be fully God. Hippolytus of Rome (170–235) countered Celsus's assertation by arguing that the eternal God was born of a woman while still remaining the eternal God.

Another threat to the consensus that Jesus is both divine and human came from Paul of Samosata (200–275). Paul's Christology is referred to as "dynamic Monarchianism," or "adoptionism." His view is that only the Father is God. Jesus is the Son of God in that he was adopted by God due either to his faithfulness or his righteousness. For Paul, Jesus was a man who became divine but was not God incarnate.

Paul of Samosata's adoptionism found its fullest expression in the Christology of Arius of Alexandria (256–336). Arius was a popular preacher in Alexandria who accused Alexander, the bishop of Alexandria (250–326), with Sabellianism. For Arius, Jesus was a semidivine figure who was God's Son but was not fully God. Arius believed that Jesus was not coeternal and coequal with God. This position was rooted in his understanding of salvation, in which Jesus was a human being who overcame sin and death by the grace of God, showing the way for humanity to be saved. Jesus identified with humanity, but was not God.

Alexander accused Arius of resuscitating the adoptionist heresies of Ebionism and Paul of Samosata. Like the earlier adoptionists, Arius recognized the full humanity of Jesus but denied his full divinity. The human Jesus was elevated, while God could be guarded from the limitations of humanity. Jesus was not God incarnate.

Alexander excommunicated Arius from the church in Alexandria. This conflict threatened to create chaos in the church even outside of Alexandria. The emperor Constantine (272–337) invited the bishops throughout the Roman Empire to gather in the city of Nicaea in what became the First Ecumenical Council in 325. At the Council of Nicaea, Arianism was condemned as a heresy because it denied the full divinity of Jesus as God incarnate. Arius was initially exiled for his heresy, but he submitted a confession that included simple statements from Scripture. He was reinstated to the church in 328.

Following the Council of Nicaea, Athanasius of Alexandria (296–373) became the leading defender of Nicaea's condemnation of Arianism. His work *On the Incarnation* stressed that only one who is truly God can give eternal life, and only one whose humanity is truly and completely like ours can save a sinful human race. Athanasius famously said, "He became what we are so we might become what he is." Athanasius insisted that the incarnation of God was the means to the salvation of humanity.

Another leading anti-Arian theologian was Apollinarius of Laodicea (310–390). Apollinarius was a friend of Athanasius whose Christological views were condemned at the Council of Constantinople in 381. Apollinarius believed that the biggest threat of Arianism was its adoptionist Christology. Arianism and adoptionism make Christ's death merely that of a human being, even if that human being is perfectly obedient by the grace of God.

Apollinarius's response to Arianism is famous: Apollinarius denied the presence of a human mind in Jesus. By replacing Christ's human mind with the eternal Son or Logos of God, Apollinarius believed he solved the problem of adoptionism. Apollinarius's Christology protects the full divinity of Jesus, and it ensures that salvation is solely the work of God, but it ends up diminishing the humanity of Jesus, rendering Christ as simply God with flesh.

Gregory of Nazianzus (329–390) was one of the Cappadocian fathers, along with brothers Basil of Caesarea (329–379) and Gregory of Nyssa (335–395). Against Apollinarianism, Gregory of Nazianzus offered his famous statement, "What is not assumed is not healed." Gregory contended that a genuine incarnation is the means to salvation. Whatever the Son of God takes up in the incarnation is what he redeems. If Jesus's humanity is merely the flesh, rather than the flesh and the soul, then only human flesh is saved. Salvation is possible only if Jesus is both fully God and fully human.

The fourth century was the period of firm commitment to the full divinity and full humanity of Jesus Christ. It was also a strong affirmation of the true divinity and true humanity of Jesus. Going forward, any Christology that diminished either of those constituent elements would be out of bounds.

The Fifth-Century Christological Controversy

What the Councils of Nicaea (325) and Constantinople (381) had been for the doctrine of the Trinity, the fifth-century Councils of Ephesus (431) and Chalcedon (451) were for the doctrine of Christ. Christians refined the language that helped them articulate how Jesus could be fully divine and fully human. Theologians spoke of one person and two natures. The language of person, fresh from the trinitarian discussions of the fourth century, meant an active subject or individual. In Jesus, that one person was the eternal Son of God. This one person possessed two full and complete natures, one divine and one human.

Two primary methods of understanding the relationship between these two natures emerged following the debates of the fourth century. One method was a tendency to emphasize that Jesus was God incarnate. This tendency, identified as Alexandrian Christology, identified one subject in Jesus Christ. The second tendency was Antiochene Christology, which identified two subjects in Christ. The zenith of the Christological controversies in the patristic period was the so-called Nestorian controversy of the fifth century. That controversy was rooted in the differences between Alexandrian and Antiochene Christologies, particularly in the rivalry between Diodore of Tarsus (d. 390) and Apollinarius of Alexandria. The ongoing opposition to Apollinarianism preceded the eventual conflict between the Alexandrians and the Antiochenes in the fifth century.

Diodore affirmed the full divinity of Christ against Arius and the full humanity of Christ against Apollinarius. Nevertheless, his Christology kept the two natures of Jesus distinct from one another. He identified each nature as a "Son"—one as the Son of God, the other as the son of David. There is one subject in Christ who is Son of God. There is also the subject who was born of Mary and died on the cross. By nature, the one born of Mary is the son of David and not the eternal Son of God.

Diodore's student Theodore of Mopsuestia (350–428) also rejected Apollinarianism, preferring a Christology in which the eternal Son of God dwells without the human person who was born from Mary. Eventually, he avoided adoptionism by affirming that only the eternal Son was active in the incarnation; the humanity was passive. The Son dwelled within the humanity to empower the human will to overcome sin and live obediently. Theodore's division of the humanity and divinity, however, still resulted in two subjects in Jesus.

In 412, Cyril (376–444) became the bishop of Alexandria. Cyril was a follower of Athanasius and was opposed to Theodore's division of the human and divine natures in Christ. At times, Cyril's language tended to be Apollinarian, even if his Christology was orthodox. His conflict with Nestorius of Constantinople (386–450) set the stage for the Third and Fourth Ecumenical Councils, resulting in the climax of Christological development found in the Definition of Chalcedon.

Nestorius became the bishop of Constantinople in 428 in what was an unremarkable ascension. Nestorius had the reputation of being a good preacher but had little experience in church politics. That inexperience probably contributed to his entering into the Christological fray with Cyril, who was a more experienced pastor and theologian.

The conflict between Nestorius and Cyril began with Nestorius's criticism of the traditional use of the term *Mother of God* for Mary, the mother of Jesus. Liturgically, the term (*Theotokos* in Greek) was used to highlight the incarnation of God. Nestorius, however, rejected the term because it made the eternal Son of God the subject of a human birth. He preferred to attribute the human birth to the humanity of Jesus, similarly to Theodore of Mopsuestia.

Cyril wrote to Nestorius to explain why it was important that the Son of God was born of Mary. This Christology was traditional, going back to Irenaeus and Athanasius. Additionally, if Jesus was just a human being, rather than the true incarnation of God, then the death of Jesus was just the death of a man. Cyril denied that the death of a mere man could provide salvation for humanity. Ultimately, Cyril alleged that Nestorius did not believe that Jesus was God. Cyril offered a list of twelve anathemas in his *Third Letter to Nestorius*, which he demanded Nestorius affirm. Nestorius believed most of the anathemas were fundamentally Apollinarian and rejected them outright.

To settle the controversy, the Third Ecumenical Council was called to meet in Ephesus in 431. When time came for the council to begin, a delegation led by a friend of Nestorius named John of Antioch (d. 442) was delayed due to the poor health of an elderly member of the group. Rather than waiting on that group to arrive, Cyril initiated the meeting. He and his supporters promptly condemned Nestorius as a heretic. When John of Antioch finally arrived, he and his supporters had their own meeting and condemned Cyril. In an effort to breach the impasse, both groups sent representatives to the emperor in Constantinople, looking for guidance.

The result was a compromise between Cyril of Alexandria and John of Antioch called the *Formula of Reunion*, authored by the Antiochene theologian Theodoret of Cyrus (393–458) and signed in 433 by the two theologians. Cyril agreed to abandon the effort to impose the Twelve Anathemas, and John agreed to the rejection of Nestorianism. Significantly, the *Formula* placed boundaries around Christological language that allowed Alexandrian and Antiochene models of Christology to be orthodox, while also rejecting the extremes of each model. The *Formula of Reunion* rejected both Apollinarius and Nestorius but affirmed Cyril of Alexandria and John of Antioch.

Jesus Christ Is the True Union of Humanity and Divinity

Following Cyril's death, many of his followers in the Alexandrian tradition became unhappy with the *Formula of Reunion* because it refused to condemn all Antiochene Christology. A notable opponent of the *Formula* was Dioscorus (d. 454), the bishop of Alexandria. Another key player in the conspiracy against the agreement was a monk in Constantinople named Eutyches (380–456). Along with Dioscorus, Eutyches believed Cyril had made too many concessions to John of Antioch, particularly in allowing language of two natures of Christ after the union of the humanity and divinity. Eutyches preferred to speak of only one nature in Christ. As a result, his followers were called Monophysites (one nature in Jesus).

Eutyches launched the plot by challenging the orthodoxy of the *Formula*, hoping to force a gathering of bishops to adjudicate the charge and defend the agreement. Bishop Flavian promptly fell into the trap by condemning Eutyches as a heretic based on the authority of the *Formula* itself. Dioscorus, in turn, accused Flavian of using a test of orthodoxy other than the Nicene-Constantinopolitan Creed, which had been banned at the Council of Ephesus in 431.

Due to the accusations and counteraccusations, Emperor Theodosius II (401–450) called a council of bishops to meet at Ephesus in 449. Dioscorus controlled the council, which condemned Theodoret of Cyrus and Domnus of Antioch as heretics. The bishops also condemned Flavian for appealing to the *Formula of Reunion* as a test of orthodoxy. Additionally, the council voted to acquit Eutyches of heresy. The Council of Ephesus (449) is commonly referred to as the Robber Synod and was rejected as a proper council at the Council of Chalcedon in 451.

A year after the Robber Synod, Emperor Theodosius died and was succeeded by his sister, Pulcheria (398–453). Pulcheria was opposed to the decision at Ephesus and rejected its rehabilitation of Eutyches. She exiled Eutyches and called a council of bishops to meet in Chalcedon in 451 in an effort to overturn the earlier synod.

The Council of Chalcedon deposed Dioscorus of Alexandria, restored Theodoret of Cyrus, and condemned Nestorius as a heretic. The bishops likewise condemned Apollinarianism and Eutychianism. The council produced a theological statement known as the Definition of Chalcedon, which outlines orthodox Christology. Notably, the Definition explicitly rejects each of the major Christological heresies.

Against Apollinarianism, the Definition states that Jesus Christ is of one nature (*homoousios*) with humanity. Against Arianism, Chalcedon holds that Jesus is of one nature (*homoousios*) with God the Father. The authors of the Definition then created parameters for understanding the union of the natures in Christ by employing four adverbs. The first two of those parameters refute Eutyches's Christology: "Christ is two natures united . . . without confusion and without change." Against Nestorianism, the Definition states that the two natures were united "without division and without separation." The Monophysites rejected Chalcedon, preferring to rely on the Council of Ephesus (431) and the Second Council of Ephesus (449) for their definitions of orthodox Christology. The Nestorians likewise rejected Chalcedon.

CASE STUDIES

Case Study 1: Gnostics and Gnosticism

Ignatius of Antioch countered Docetism by confessing that Jesus has two types of life, divine and human. Ignatius tied this theme of Christ's dual realities to his work of salvation. Salvation through union with Christ is possible only if there is both a divine reality and a human reality in Jesus. Because salvation is the reconciliation of humanity to God through union with the Son, Jesus must have been the perfect union of divine and human realities. Whereas Docetism denied the incarnation, Ignatius argued that the incarnation of God must be "perfect" or "genuine."

Ignatius's Christology emphasized the two genuine types of being present in Jesus: human and divine. Ignatius described these ways of being in his *Epistle to the Ephesians*: "There is one Physician who is possessed of flesh and spirit, both made and not made; God existing in the flesh; true life in death; of Mary and of God; first passible and then impassible, even Jesus Christ our Lord."

Moreover, Ignatius contended that both of these forms of reality were present in the *one* Lord Jesus Christ. To separate these types of being into two different subjects would make salvation impossible. Although the Gospels contain two distinct ways of speaking about Jesus, those statements simply correspond to the two types of being united in the one Lord Jesus Christ. Some statements in Scripture speak of Jesus as a human being. Other statements speak of him as the eternal Son of God. Both sets of statements are rightly attributed to the one Lord Jesus Christ.

Irenaeus of Lyons contributed to the development of Christological language in his defense of Christianity against the threat of Gnosticism. In his masterful work, *Against Heresies*, Irenaeus described Gnosticism as a collection of movements that claimed to be "Christian" but denied the apostolic faith. Central to Gnostic thought was the rejection of any material or physical aspect to salvation. Gnosticism denied that the human body would be saved. This was similar to the view Paul confronted in 1 Corinthians 15. Gnostics also rejected the Old Testament as Christian Scripture, so their doctrine of Jesus was not informed by the Old Testament idea of the Christ. When Gnostics spoke of Jesus as the "Son of God," they did not mean it in the same way the New Testament did.

Gnostics believed that the Son was a divine emanation, but not fully divine. Irenaeus anticipated the third- and fourth-century Christological debates by rejecting that Jesus was simply a semidivine being. The Gnostics likewise were docetic, denying the genuine humanity of Jesus. In opposition to orthodox Christology, Gnosticism proposed a Christ who was neither fully God nor truly human. Although earlier heresies denied either the humanity or the divinity in Christ, the Gnostics denied both of these realities. Irenaeus turned to the idea of recapitulation to explain the necessity of Jesus being both divine and human: Jesus was the final Adam who established a new beginning for humanity through his life, death, and resurrection. In Christ, humanity was renewed as it could share in the divine life of the Son of God who became incarnate in Jesus.

As the opponent of the Gnostics, Irenaeus had three primary theological goals. First, Jesus was God, not some semidivine figure who emanated from God. Second, Jesus was truly human, which was necessary for him to be the means of salvation. Third, there was only one subject in Jesus, meaning all of the human as well as divine statements about Jesus belong to the Son of God. The incarnation was the way the Son appropriated the human experiences of Jesus to himself for the salvation of humanity.

Case Study 2: The Schools of Alexandria and Antioch

The Councils of Nicaea (325) and Constantinople (381) established that Jesus Christ is truly God because he is *homoousios*, or of the same nature, as the Father. Christians developed their Christological language about both the divinity and the humanity of Jesus in opposition to Arianism but did so with two distinct models for understanding the relationship between the divine and human natures in Christ. These two Christological tendencies corresponded roughly to two major cities with significant Christian influence: Alexandria and Antioch. Both the Alexandrian and Antiochene Christological traditions confessed the full divinity and full humanity of Jesus Christ, though they differed with how to explain the union of those two natures. Understanding the Christological controversies that followed Nicaea requires awareness of these two Christological tendencies.

Alexandrian Christology corresponds roughly with the modern model of "Christology from above." Theologians within the Alexandrian school of theology tended to emphasize that the incarnation was the act of the Son of God. In this model, the Son united to himself a genuine human nature without ceasing to be God in any sense. All of the experiences of Jesus—even those human experiences such as birth and death—are attributable to the eternal Son incarnate. Most important for Alexandrian Christology was that God was the single active subject in Christ; when Jesus acts or speaks, God alone acts or speaks.

Major representatives of Alexandrian Christology include Athanasius of Alexandria, the Cappadocian Fathers, and Cyril of Alexandria. Although Athanasius is typically associated with his opposition to Arianism and defense of the Nicene faith, his work *On the Incarnation* was a foundational theological work on Alexandrian Christology. In that work, he offered his famous dictum that "the Son of God became human so that humans could become sons of God." Athanasius confessed the complete and genuine humanity of Jesus, but emphasized the single work of God in Christ. Jesus was God at work. The Cappadocians, particularly Gregory of Nazianzus, likewise acknowledged the true human nature in Christ but nonetheless tended toward theological language, making the humanity passive in the incarnation. Cyril of Alexandria (see next section) likewise spoke of the single person, or active agent, of Jesus being the eternal Son of God while also confessing the necessity of a complete human nature.

Apollinarius of Alexandria represents an extreme Alexandrian Christology. Apollinarius was a vocal anti-Arian theologian who is best remembered for denying the human mind of Christ. Apollinarius, like the other Alexandrians, emphasized the single subject of the Son of God acting in Jesus. Nevertheless, Apollinarius believed that two complete natures, the human and the divine, would be adoptionism. (See Paul of Samosata above.) He reasoned that if the human nature had its own human mind, it would be a human person who was taken up by God to be his "adopted" Son. Apollinarius's solution was to remove the part of the human nature that transformed it into a distinct and separate person. By removing the human mind, Apollinarius preserved God's activity in Christ, but he destroyed the salvation the Son came to provide. Against Apollinarius, Gregory of Nazianzus argued, "What is not assumed is not healed." Alexandrian Christology, as represented by Gregory, is clearly within the bounds of orthodoxy but had to guard against Apollinarius's diminishing the human nature of Christ.

Antiochene Christology likewise developed in opposition to Arius and Arianism. Antiochene theologians confessed that Jesus possessed a complete human nature and a complete divine nature. Their tendency was to emphasize the distinction of those two natures rather than their close union, and it corresponded closely with the modern "Christology from below" model. This distinction meant that Antiochene Christological language pointed toward two centers of activity in Christ. Whereas the Alexandrians attributed all of Jesus's experiences to the single subject of the Son of God, the Antiochenes attributed the human actions to the human nature and the divine actions to the divine nature. By keeping the natures distinct from one another, the Antiochene theologians avoided destroying one or both of the natures.

The major theologians associated with Antiochene Christology were Diodore of Tarsus, Theodore of Mopsuestia, John of Antioch, and Theodoret of Cyrus. Diodore is remembered for his "Two Sons" Christology, in which he spoke of the two centers of activity in Jesus as the "Son of God" and "Son of Man." His purpose was not to divide Jesus into two different persons but to emphasize the respective attribution of experiences to the two distinct natures in Christ. Theodore famously referenced the human nature of Jesus with relative pronouns, speaking of "he who was born of Mary," for example. This language was Theodore's attempt at acknowledging the union of the natures in Christ while simultaneously preserving the divinity from participation in the human actions and experiences of Christ.

Within Antiochene Christology the extreme position is represented by Nestorius of Constantinople. Following Diodore and Theodore, Nestorius emphasized the two natures in Christ over the one person of the Son of God. But Nestorius went further by giving the two natures their own unique identity or personhood. The Antiochene emphasis on two natures turned into the heresy of two persons. *Christ* became the term Nestorius used to name the juxtaposition of the eternal Son of God with the human being Jesus. Cyril of Alexandria recognized adoptionism in Nestorius's Christological formulation, and the Antiochenes agreed. Theodoret authored the *Formula of Reunion* between Cyril and John of Antioch, in which the Alexandrians and Antiochenes came together to reject the heresy of Nestorius. In that document, Theodoret emphasized the two natures of Christ over the single subject of his experiences. This language led some of the more extreme Alexandrians to reject the *Formula*, resulting in the ensuing Monophysite controversy and the Council of Chalcedon.

Both the single-subject Alexandrian Christology and the dual-subject Christology of the Antiochenes represented faithful expressions of the biblical message of the incarnation of God in Jesus Christ. The *Formula of Reunion* placed important parameters on both traditions. The Definition of Chalcedon ultimately allowed for the two schools of thought to operate within orthodoxy while preventing extremist Christologies. Both models were orthodox, but both could, and did, devolve into heresy. The Alexandrian model affirmed the two natures of Christ but emphasized the single divine person. The Antiochene model affirmed the union of the two natures but emphasized the distinction of those natures rather than the one person. Alexandrian Christology devolved into heresy when it diminished or devalued the humanity of Christ. Theologians within each tradition worked to avoid those heretical extremes without abandoning their own emphases regarding the two natures and one person of Jesus Christ.

Case Study 3: Cyril of Alexandria

Cyril of Alexandria engaged in a lengthy Christological conflict with Nestorius of Constantinople. Nestorius represented an extreme Antiochene Christology, while Cyril followed Athanasius and the Alexandrian emphasis on the single subject of the eternal Son of God in Christ. Although Cyril was a formidable opponent of Nestorius, he was also capable of compromise and flexibility, as demonstrated by the *Formula of Reunion* (433).

Cyril had been bishop of Alexandria for sixteen years when Nestorius became bishop of Constantinople in the year 428. The catalyst of the controversy between the two theologians was Nestorius's rejection of the title *Theotokos,* or "Mother of God," for the virgin Mary. Nestorius denied that God could be subject to a human birth. Cyril claimed that if God Incarnate did not experience a human birth, life, death, and resurrection, there could be no salvation for humanity. The controversy led to the Third Ecumenical Council at Ephesus in 431 and the Fourth Ecumenical Council at Chalcedon in 451. Ultimately, Nestorius was condemned as a heretic and deposed from his position. His teaching was rejected as heresy by both councils.

Along with Nestorianism, Cyril rejected Apollinarianism. Whereas Apollinarius had denied the human soul, or mind, of Christ, essentially diminishing or destroying the human nature, Cyril affirmed the existence of the human soul in Christ. Moreover, Cyril found a soteriological role for the human soul that made it indispensable in a way even the Cappadocians had not. The famous Cappadocian dictum "What is not assumed is not saved" ensured that Apollinarianism could not persist. But Cyril went beyond the simple ontological need for the human soul in Jesus and actually located the human sufferings of Jesus in the human soul. Without the presence of a genuine human soul, the sufferings of Jesus would have been attributed to the divine nature in Christ. Obviously, the divine nature cannot be subject to human sufferings. Therefore, a human soul allowed Jesus to experience true human suffering as a substitutionary sacrifice for humanity. The complete human nature of Jesus ensured the genuine human suffering of Jesus.

Cyril confessed the two complete natures of Christ but still emphasized the hypostatic union of those two natures.

Cyril's ultimate theological purpose in the Nestorian controversy was to protect the church from dividing the natures in Christ into two separate subjects, one human and one divine. Nestorian Christology was devastating to the confession that Jesus is God incarnate, so Cyril had to reject even a semblance of separation of the natures. At the same time, Cyril did acknowledge that the two natures were complete; he was no Apollinarian. His overriding concern, however, was not the diminishing of the human nature, which is expressly rejected, but the separation of Christ into two persons.

Nestorius, and even some other Antiochenes, still accused Cyril of being Apollinarian. But Cyril acknowledged the natures even after the union. It was important for Cyril to distinguish the natures, preserving their integrity without separating them into two independent persons. Cyril was constantly battling the extreme tendencies of the Alexandrian and Antiochene sides: the union must be genuine, and the natures must remain intact without two independent existences. Jesus Christ was God incarnate, the same person truly God and truly human.

Cyril contributed to the development of Christology by emphasizing that the Son of God was the single subject of all the actions, sayings, and experiences of Jesus Christ. The human experiences were not those of a human person, other than the human person who is God incarnate. Because God became a human, he was able to act humanly. Significantly, Cyril recognized the Christological importance of the human birth, human obedience, human death, and human resurrection of Christ. These human actions were not the actions of a mere man, but of God who became a man while remaining God.

Cyril's Christology anticipated the Definition of Chalcedon and set the stage for it. The Alexandrian model of Christology had fully matured into that of two natures, one person. Despite the fact that the later Monophysites still claimed Cyril's Christology from before the *Formula*, Chalcedon was the proper end of Cyril's Christological enterprise, emphasizing one subject acting in and through two complete natures.

Case Study 4: The Council of Chalcedon

Empress Pulcheria called the Council of Chalcedon (451) to deal with the Monophysite heresy espoused by Eutyches, the leader of a monastery in the capital city of Constantinople. Eutyches rejected two natures in Christ, claiming that Jesus merely had the form of a human being but not a genuine humanity taken from Mary. The Monophysites accepted the conclusions of the Council of Ephesus (431) but rejected Cyril of Alexandria's compromise with the Antiochenes in the *Formula of Reunion* (433). At the so-called Robber Synod of 449, the Monophysites condemned the *Formula*. Leo the Great, the bishop of Rome, had written to the synod his *Tome* rejecting the Christology of Eutyches and the Monophysites. Nevertheless, the letter was ignored and the synod rejected two natures in Christ.

Fundamental to the Council of Chalcedon was Leo's *Tome*. In it the two natures in Christ were preserved intact, coexisting in one person. The characteristics of both natures were shared by the eternal Son of God incarnate. There is a parallelism in Leo's Christology that most notably preserves the human nature in Christ against Eutychianism, which had denied that Jesus was homoousios with humanity. Being born of the virgin Mary ensured that Christ's humanity was genuine. Leo was clearly following the Cappadocian commitment to the soteriological significance of the assumed humanity.

Nevertheless, Leo also stated that the two natures functioned in a way that was proper or fitting to itself. This statement at first glance would appear to support a Nestorian separation of the natures. Nevertheless, Leo made clear that the natures functioned "in communion with the other." This union, or communion, of the natures was found within one person, the person of God incarnate. By this hypostatic union, Leo was able to preserve the natures without making them into separate persons, thereby avoiding Nestorianism. The Alexandrians were suspicious of Leo's *Tome*, concerned about its giving too much leeway for Nestorianism. But the purpose of the letter was to confront Eutychianism and to emphasize the reality of the human nature in Christ.

Leo's influence on the Definition of Chalcedon was enormous. He provided the bishops with a way to answer their fundamental Christological question: What language best reconciles belief in one Christ with the belief that Christ is both fully God and fully human? Leo's acknowledgment of two complete natures that were united to form a single person gave the bishops their answer to that question. Rather than producing another confession similar to the Nicene Creed, the Council crafted a *definition*, or statement, further explicating the Nicene Creed's confession of the one Lord Jesus Christ.

The Definition of Chalcedon began with the unambiguous statement that Jesus Christ is the Son of God incarnate. By confessing Jesus to be "one Lord," the Definition rejected any dualism that would separate Jesus into two persons, one human and one divine. The eternal Son of God is the single person in Christ. He alone is the subject of both the human and the divine experiences of Jesus.

The Definition acknowledged the distinction of the two natures in Christ. Jesus was complete in his divinity and complete in his humanity. He was truly God and truly human. He had a human soul as well as a human body. The one Jesus Christ was both *homoousios* with the Father and *homoousios* with humanity. Each of these statements ensured that neither nature was diminished or destroyed. Even though there was a stress on the duality of the natures, this stress follows the clear statement of a single subject made earlier in the Definition.

It was essential that the Definition preserve the natures intact while at the same time ensuring the integrity of the single person. To accomplish this twofold purpose, the Definition turned to the four Chalcedonian adverbs. The divine and human natures were preserved in the one person of Christ "without confusion, without change, without division, and without separation." By characterizing the union accordingly, the Definition put parameters on Christological language. The first two adverbs addressed Apollinarianism and Eutychianism—the extreme forms of Alexandrian Christology. To destroy or diminish one or both of the natures was out of bounds. The final two adverbs prevented Nestorianism and extreme Antiochene Christology. The natures were not merely connected to one another but were truly united to the one person of the Son. Chalcedon ensured that the eternal Son of God was the single subject of all the actions, sayings, and experiences of Jesus Christ.

For the Church

Jesus Christ is God. The earliest followers of Jesus recognized that he was God. They worshipped Jesus as God, prayed to him as God, and preached him to the world as God incarnate. Jesus told his disciples, "The one who has seen me has seen the Father" (John 14:9). He also told them, "I and the Father are one" (John 10:30). Any depiction of Christ that lessens his divinity is outside the bounds of the faith once for all delivered to the saints. The Baptist Faith and Message offers an unambiguous confession about Jesus: "Christ is the eternal Son of God. Jesus is more than merely a divine figure; as the eternal Son of God he is coeternal and coequal with the Father. Christians can confidently proclaim Jesus as God incarnate, who has come to bring eternal life to all who believe in him. He reveals God and works as God."

Jesus Christ is human. The incarnation is the apex and God's work of salvation. The virgin birth is the way in which God has become human for us and our salvation. In this incarnation, the Baptist Faith and Message reminds us that "Jesus perfectly revealed and did the will of God, taking upon himself human nature with its demands and necessities, and identifying himself complete with mankind yet without sin." Though the Son remained God in the incarnation, he took a human nature from Mary that is just like that of all other humans. When faced with the temptations which are common to all humanity, Jesus overcame those temptations and lived a perfectly obedient life as a substitute for humanity's sinfulness. He also died a substitutionary death on the cross in place of human beings so that those who believe in him might be saved. Christians can confidently trust in Jesus as their true substitute in life, in death, in resurrection, and in ascension. As the book of Hebrews notes, the eternal Son of God became a human to lead "many sons and daughters to glory" (Heb 2:10). He humbled himself to a genuine human life so that he could raise up humanity and ascend to heaven with that humanity.

Jesus Christ is the Mediator. The unity of the two natures in the one person of Christ results in a mediator who assures salvation for all who believe. The Baptist Faith and Message puts it this way: The crucified and risen Lord "is now exalted at the right hand of God where he is the one mediator, fully God, fully man, in whose person is effected the reconciliation between God and man." This statement captures well the patristic emphasis on the union of the two natures. God has reconciled humanity to himself by means of his own incarnation. In other words, Jesus is the reconciliation between God and humanity because he is, at one and the same time, fully God and fully human. Christians can have full assurance of their salvation because they are united to God in Christ. Salvation is not dependent on human effort or human righteousness. There is no works-based salvation. Jesus himself is the locus of God's work of salvation. The eternal Son of God assumed true humanity through the virgin birth and lived an obedient human life. The Son died a genuinely human death on the cross as a sacrifice for our sins, raised his humanity from the dead for our salvation, and exalted that humanity to his rightful place seated on the throne in heaven. Jesus remains God incarnate, assuring salvation for all who trust in him.

Contemporary challenges to Christianity are many. Those modern challenges, like those in antiquity, often concern inaccurate answers to the question "Who is Jesus Christ?" When modern heresies seek to diminish the deity of Christ, Christians must preach a gospel of God's true incarnation. God does not send a messenger to do his work; he becomes human himself to save his people. When modern heresies deny the humanity of

Christ, making him something of a superman, Christians must recognize the humiliation of the incarnation, in which God lived a genuine human life. Jesus is of the same nature as all other human beings, but he is without sin. It is essential that Jesus be fully God and fully human, with both natures belonging to the one person of the eternal Son of God, for him to save. This is the one Lord and Savior Jesus Christ whom we preach.

For Further Reading

Behr, John. *The Way to Nicaea.* The Formation of Christian Theology 1. New York: St. Vladimir's Press, 2001.

———. *The Nicene Faith.* The Formation of Christian Theology 2. New York: St. Vladimir's Press, 2004.

Clark, John, and Marcus Peter Johnson. *The Incarnation of God: The Mystery of the Gospel as the Foundation of Evangelical Theology.* Wheaton, IL: Crossway, 2015.

Crisp, Oliver D., and Fred Sanders. *Christology, Ancient and Modern: Explorations in Constructive Dogmatics.* Grand Rapids: Zondervan, 2013.

Hardy, Edward R., ed. *Christology of the Later Fathers.* Library of Christian Classics 3. Louisville: Westminster John Knox, 1954.

McGuckin, John A. *Saint Cyril of Alexandria and the Christological Controversy.* New York: St. Vladimir's Press, 2010.

McKinion, Steven A. *Words, Imagery, and the Mystery of Christ: A Reconstruction of Cyril of Alexandria's Christology.* Vigiliae Christianae Supplements 55. Leiden: Brill Academic, 2000.

Norris, Richard A., ed. *The Christological Controversy.* Sources of Early Christian Thought. Minneapolis: Fortress, 1980.

Sellers, R. V. *The Council of Chalcedon: A Historical and Doctrinal Survey.* London: SPCK, 1961.

Torrance, Thomas F. *Incarnation: The Person and Life of Christ.* Downers Grove, IL: IVP, 2013.

Wellum, Stephen. *God the Son Incarnate: The Doctrine of Christ*. Foundations of Evangelical Theology. Wheaton, IL: Crossway, 2016.

Young, Frances. *God's Presence: A Contemporary Recapitulation of Early Christianity*. Current Issues in Theology 12. Cambridge: Cambridge University Press, 2013.

Young, Frances M. *From Nicaea to Chalcedon: A Guide to the Literature and Its Background*. Grand Rapids: Baker Academic, 2010.

QUESTIONS FOR STUDY OR DISCUSSION

1. Why did the ancient church see Docetism as a threat to the Christian gospel?
2. Who were the key theologians of the Alexandrian school, and what did they contribute to the development of orthodox Christology?
3. What were the key differences between the Antiochene school and the Alexandrian school? Why were those differences important to the other side?
4. What did Gregory of Nazianzus mean by his statement "What is not assumed is not healed"?
5. What are the four "Chalcedonian adverbs," and how do they help explain the person of Jesus Christ?

2

THE TRINITY

By R. Lucas Stamps

Introduction

Is the doctrine of the Trinity biblical? There is a sense in which this is *the* central question of Christian identity and of the emerging theological culture that shaped the church over the first several centuries of Christian history. This question raises the further problem of what it even means for a doctrine to be biblical. In other words, it is a question of exegesis and theological method—issues that were hotly disputed throughout the patristic era. Through many fits and starts, and many complicated layers of controversy and development, the church eventually found its way to affirming what has become the standard, orthodox definition of the doctrine of the Trinity at the Council of Constantinople in 381. The Nicene Creed (more accurately termed the Niceno-Constantinopolitan Creed) affirmed that the Father and the Son are "of the same nature" (Greek *homoousios*) and that the Holy Spirit, as the "Lord and Giver of life," is to be "worshipped and glorified" together with the Father and the Son. The Creed thus affirms that the divine persons are coequal and coeternal, sharing in the numerically singular divine essence. They are to be distinguished only by their relations to one another, the eternal relations of origin: the Father is unbegotten, the Son is eternally begotten of the Father, and the Holy Spirit eternally proceeds from the Father (and the Son, as the Western church would later affirm). It is this triune God who is revealed in the gospel—the incarnation, life, death, burial, resurrection, ascension, and second coming of Christ—and in the outpouring of the Spirit on the church. God is as he reveals himself to be. If the Son is *sent from* the Father in the incarnation, it is only because he is *eternally from* the Father in his eternal generation. If the Spirit is *sent from* the Father and Son on the day of Pentecost, it is only because he is *eternally from* the Father and Son in his eternal procession. The Creed simply summarizes basic contours of the gospel and, foundationally, the God of the gospel.

But this doctrinal apparatus was not fully articulated in the immediate aftermath of the New Testament. To be sure, the triune God himself was definitively revealed in the saving missions of the Son and Spirit, which are infallibly attested to in the New Testament writings in fulfillment of the Old Testament promises. So, it is not a matter of later doctrinal developments improving on or even filling out God's definitive revelation of himself in Holy Scripture. Instead, the trinitarian developments of the earliest centuries tell the story of how the church sought to account for all that Scripture says about the triune God, in confrontation with heterodox teachings and in a manner that was conceptually coherent and faithful to the biblical gospel. This chapter recounts some (but by no means all) of the major persons and theological developments that take us from the New Testament revelation to the Nicene settlement and beyond into the fifth century.

Historical Overview

Pre-Nicene Developments

In the century after the New Testament, the basic building blocks of the doctrine of the Trinity were already being laid in the works of key thinkers in the Greek-speaking East and the Latin-speaking West. In the Greek-speaking East, the works of figures such as Justin Martyr and Irenaeus were especially important in laying this groundwork, though it must be noted that none of the second- and third-century authors were saying precisely the same thing as the fourth-century Nicene doctrine. The theologian must avoid anachronism and the notion that orthodoxy was a settled and unchanging norm. Both orthodoxy and heresy are developmental categories. This is not to say that the truth of the Trinity is a moving target. It is simply to admit that none of the theologians in question possessed the kind of infallibility which is only to be attributed to Scripture.

Justin Martyr (100–165) represented a movement that has come to be known as Logos Christology. In confrontation with pagan philosophy (especially Stoic philosophy), Justin and other theologians, such as Clement of Alexandria, emphasized the Johannine notion of the Son's identity as the Logos, the eternal Word of the Father. The Stoics maintained that there is a universal principle of reason, the Logos, that permeates all of reality and gives to it its rational shape and purpose. In an apologetic maneuver, the Logos Christologians emphasized that this Logos is a distinct divine power, which is revealed in Jesus of Nazareth. Justin maintained that the Logos is eternally inseparable from the Father. He writes, "This power [the Word] is indivisible and inseparable from the Father, just as they say that the light of the sun on earth is indivisible and inseparable from the sun in the heavens" (*Dialogue with Trypho* 128). There is reason to believe that, for Justin, the Logos is, in a sense, subordinate to the Father. Indeed, there are hints of subordinationism that run throughout the Fathers of the second and third centuries, tinges that would be erased and corrected in the fourth-century pro-Nicene doctrine. But for the present purposes, it is worth noting a principle that lays the groundwork for the more mature doctrine of the Trinity: the Father is never without his Word/Reason/Wisdom.

Irenaeus (c. 120–c. 200) likewise helped to shape the early trinitarian thought of the Eastern churches. In addition to his important criticism of second-century Gnosticism, *Against Heresies*, Irenaeus's only other extant work is his *Demonstration of the Apostolic Preaching*. In this work, Irenaeus summarizes the basic teaching of Scripture in terms of what he calls the "rule of truth": the revelation of the Father, Son, and Holy Spirit in the gospel of Jesus Christ. This revelation marks, not some advanced level of Christian maturity, but the very root and foundation of Christian experience solemnized in baptism.

> So, faith procures this for us, as the elders, the disciples of the apostles, have handed down to us; firstly it exhorts us to remember that we have received baptism for the remission of sins, in the name of God the Father, and in the name of Jesus Christ, the Son of God, [who was] incarnate, and died, and was raised, and in the Holy Spirit of God; and that this baptism is the seal of eternal life and rebirth unto God, that we may no longer be sons of mortal men, but of the eternal and everlasting God. (*Demonstration of the Apostolic Preaching* 1)

This rule of truth, or rule of faith (*regula fidei*), builds on the baptismal formula of Matt 28:18–20 and represents an early example of creedal formulations that were used in preparing Christian catechumens for baptism. Resonances with the Western Old Roman Creed, which was a precursor to the well-known Apostles' Creed, can be detected in this early summary of Irenaeus. Its soteriological and ecclesiological dimensions are most striking: salvation and incorporation into the church through baptism are rooted in faith in the Father, Son, and Holy Spirit.

Also during the second and third centuries, Tertullian (c. 155–c. 240) similarly was laying the groundwork for the doctrine of the Trinity in the Latin-speaking West. He is well-known for coining the term *Trinity* (Latin *Trinitas*) as well as the key Latin terms that would remain in use into the fourth century and beyond: God is one in substance (*substantia*) and three in persons (*personae*). In *Against Praxeas* (the target could be a pseudonym, since Praxeas translates to "busybody"), Tertullian confronted an early expression of the heresy that would later be known as modalistic Monarchianism and was associated with figures such as Sabellius, Noetius, and Callistus. This viewpoint was *Monarchian* in that it saw God the Father as the sole divine monarch, or ruler. It was *modalistic* in that it saw the Father, Son, and Holy Spirit as successive modes of divine revelation, not as really existing divine persons in relation to one another. Tertullian feared that this modalistic understanding of the divine "persons" would entail the heresy of patripassianism, the belief that the Father somehow suffered and died in the death of Christ. Against this view, Tertullian argued that there are indeed three distinct divine persons that can be detected in the biblical narrative: the persons are distinct but inseparable and inseverable. The Trinity does not destroy the unity. Rather, "the Unity [is distributed] into a Trinity, placing in their order the three Persons—the Father, the Son, and the Holy Ghost: three, however, not in condition, but in degree; not in substance, but in form; not in power, but in aspect; yet of one substance, and of one condition, and of one power, inasmuch as he is one God" (*Against Praxeas* 2). As with other second-century theologians, there are hints of subordinationism in Tertullian's trinitarianism, but his basic trinitarian grammar would remain influential in Western churches for centuries.

As we move deeper into the third century, perhaps the most prominent theologian to note in the church's developing trinitarian doctrine is Origen of Alexandria (c. 185–c. 255). Origen's thought has always experienced a kind of ambiguous reception among Christian theologians. His incorporation of middle Platonic thought into Christian doctrine and his controversial opinions on a number of topics make many suspicious of his work. But his prodigious intellectual output, his exegetical method, and his doctrinal developments exerted influence on virtually everyone involved in the fourth-century debates in one way or another. For Origen, there was never a time when the Son of God did not exist. The Father is never without his Word/Wisdom/Reason. Because of God's immutability, he cannot become something he was not. Being Father is not something God becomes by begetting the Son or creating the world; it is who he is in eternal relation to his Son. Perhaps the most important contribution of Origen on the Trinity is his understanding of the eternal generation of the Son. The Father and Son are distinct but inseparable. The Son is eternally coming forth from the Father, as understanding from the mind. One is never without the Other. Still, the three divine persons are genuinely distinct from one another (Origen even uses the language of three *hypostases*, though not in exactly the same way the term would be used in the fourth century). As with other second- and third-century fathers, Origen's trinitarianism has shades of subordination in that he sees the Son occupying a mediating position between the Father and the created world.

The Council of Nicaea

It is commonplace to view the Council of Nicaea (325) as the watershed moment in the doctrine of the Trinity, to view Arius (d. 336) as the sole figure around whom heretical opinions of the Trinity coalesced, and to view the main theological debate under consideration the deity of the Son of God. But each of these assumptions ignores certain complexities that attend what would only later become known as the First Ecumenical Council. The council, convened by the recently converted emperor Constantine, most certainly concerned the controversy sparked in Alexandria by the Egyptian presbyter Arius, who understood the Son of God as the first and greatest of God the Father's creations. Arius had taught that "there was once when he was not"—there was a time when the Son of God did not exist. The Father alone is the true God, with the Son as his highest creation, through whom he created everything else that exists. But in the Arian scheme, there is still a place to consider the Son in some sense "God." But several theological trajectories of the late third and early fourth centuries, including the one represented by Arius, were willing to admit certain gradations within the divine life.

There is a sense in which the council was narrowly focused on Arius himself. Alexander, the bishop of Alexandria (250–326), accompanied by his young secretary Athanasius (296–373), was concerned that any lessening of the Son's divinity would undermine Christian devotion to the Son and the Son's divine work as the redeemer of humanity. Alexander and his allies persuaded a majority of bishops present at the council that Christ is the "only-begotten" (*monogenes*) Son "of the nature" (*ousios*) of the Father and that the Son is indeed "of the same nature" (*homoousios*) as the Father. The council produced a creed that affirmed these points and thus excluded the teaching of Arius. Nevertheless, as would become evident in the succeeding decades, not all of the bishops who affirmed these points agreed on their precise meaning and implications. The council, in other words, did not settle all disputes. Other theological trajectories, especially those associated with the two Eusebians—Eusebius of Caesarea (263–339) and Eusebius of Nicomedia (d. 341)—exerted influence in ecclesiastical and imperial contexts. Within just a few years after the council, Arius was recalled from his enforced exile and readmitted to communion with the church. Athanasius, who succeeded Alexander as bishop of Alexandria, refused to acknowledge Arius's readmittance and found himself on the losing end of the emperor's dictates. For his defense of Nicaea's *homoousios* and his own strict interpretation of it (along with some other political accusations against him), Athanasius experienced exile five different times for a total of seventeen years over the course of the mid-fourth century. Athanasius produced some of the most important "anti-Arian" writings of the century, including his important *Defense against the Arians* (350). In the West, Hilary of Poitiers (d. 367) took up a similar cause of defending Nicaea, primarily through exegesis rather than any sophisticated philosophical reasoning. His ten-volume *De Trinitate*, written during his own exile, stands as his most lasting contribution to the defense of the Nicene settlement against Arian and semi-Arian opponents.

Pro-Nicene Theology

Throughout the middle of the fourth century, several alternatives to Nicaea's *homoousios* were entertained by various theological trajectories. The so-called *Homoians*, especially Acacius of Caesarea (d. 366) and Eudoxius of Antioch (d. 370), suggested that the Son was merely "like" the Father. The *Heteroousians* Eunomius (335–393) and Aetius (d. 367) doubled down on the "Arian" position and suggested that the Son is of a "different" nature than the Father. *Homoiousians* like Basil of Ancyra (d. 362) were willing to concede that the Son's relationship to the Father was "like according to essence," but stopped short of Nicaea's *homoousios*. The confusion and contestation continued until a more coherent "pro-Nicene" consensus emerged and was eventually canonized at the Council of Constantinople in 381.

After Athanasius and Hilary, the figures who played perhaps the most decisive role in the development of this pro-Nicene theology are the theologians collectively known as the Cappadocian Fathers: Basil of Caesarea (330–379); his brother, Gregory of Nyssa (335–394); and their friend, Gregory of Nazianzus (329–390). Basil's *On the Holy Spirit* and his writings against Eunomius were especially influential, as were Gregory of Nyssa's *On the Holy Spirit*, *Against Eunomius*, and *On Not Three Gods*. Gregory of Nazianzus delivered a series of sermons in Constantinople during the height of the controversy in 380 that have come to be known as his Five Theological Orations. The first is on theological method, the second on God the Father, the third and fourth on God the Son, and the fifth on God the Holy Spirit.

At the risk of oversimplification, the following summary of the Cappadocians' contribution may be offered. The Cappadocian Fathers emphasized the absolute simplicity of God—God is not composed of parts—and thus excluded any notion of a gradation in deity from the Father to the Son to the Spirit, which was implicit in the alternatives to Nicaea's *homoousios*. They affirmed that in all things essential (that is, as regards the divine essence), the three divine persons are identical. The Father, Son, and Holy Spirit each share equally in one divine nature, power, authority, and will. According to the Cappadocians, the only distinctions that can be drawn between the divine persons concern their relations, especially their eternal relations of origin. The Father is ingenerate, or unbegotten, and he eternally generates the Son, as light from the sun. But this eternal generation is unlike creaturely generation in two important ways. First, it is indeed *eternal*; it is the timeless coming forth of the Son from the Father's nature. So, contra Arius, there was *not* when he was not. But, second, the eternal generation of the Son is also *internal*, so to speak. It does not produce a second god or a second nature. Instead, the Son who is generated from the Father is identical to the Father as regards his essence or nature. Likewise, the Spirit eternally proceeds from the Father and thus also shares in the identically same divine essence. The language of procession is taken from John's Gospel, which speaks of the Spirit "who proceeds from the Father" (John 15:26). The revelation of the divine persons in the economy of redemption (*oikonomia*, administration or plan) unveils their eternal relations to one another. God is as he reveals himself to be. These eternal processions—the generation of the Son and the procession of the Spirit—remain a mystery to creaturely understanding. In a memorable line from his *Third Theological Oration*, Gregory of Nazianzus warns against seeking to comprehend the mystery:

> How was he begotten?—I repeat the question in indignation. The begetting of God must be honored by silence. It is a great thing for you to learn that he was begotten. But the manner of his generation we will not admit that even angels can conceive, much less you. Shall I tell you how it was? It was in a manner known to the Father who begot, and to the Son who was begotten. Anything

> more than this is hidden by a cloud, and escapes your dim sight. (*Third Theological Oration* 8)

But in any event, these eternal relations of origin remain the only distinctions permissible among the divine persons. The persons are not distinguished by nature, authority, or will, nor even by function (since God acts as one), but only by their relations of origin, which are then revealed and extended in the economy. In other words, they are essentially (that is, "essence-wise") identical.

Another important contribution of the Cappadocians concerns the grammar of the Trinity. The important terminology that emerged from Nicaea concerned the *ousios*, or nature of God. As we have seen, Nicaea affirmed that the Son is "from the Father's *ousios*" and is indeed of the same *ousios* as the Father (*homoousios*). But what term serves best to distinguish the three? In the West, the Latin *personae* (persons) was the common coinage since Tertullian. But what about in the Greek-speaking East? At the time of Nicaea, *hypostasis* (literally, "that which stands under") had a semantic domain that overlapped significantly with *ousios*. To admit three *hypostases*, then, would be to admit three divine natures, and thus three gods. The Greek *prosopon* was a serviceable term, and it mirrored the Latin use of *persona* that developed in the West, but it was easily misinterpreted in modalistic ways—as if the persons were simply the distinct modes of revelation of a unipersonal God. The Cappadocian Fathers chose instead to co-opt, as it were, the term *hypostasis* and to utilize it as a way of distinguishing the three. Its close relation to *ousia* left intact the emphasis on divine unity—there are not three gods—but it gave the church a way of distinguishing three real relations of origin within the divine life: the unbegotten Father, the eternally begotten Son, and the eternally proceeding Holy Spirit.

Another key contribution of the Cappadocian Fathers relates to their teaching on the Holy Spirit. Earlier in the fourth century, the heart of the debate concerned the Son's relation to the Father, but as the century wore on, disputes about the Spirit's status also emerged. The original creed of Nicaea simply affirmed belief in the Holy Spirit but left his relation to the other divine persons undefined. But the heretical group known alternatively as the *Tropici* (from the "tropes" they used attempting to demonstrate the subordination of the Spirit from Scripture), the Macedonians (after their founder, Macedonius [d. 360]), or *Pneumatichoi* ("fighters against the Spirit") forced the issue to the fore. Athanasius had already written in defense of the Spirit's deity in his *Letters to Serapion* (358–61), but the Cappadocian Fathers devoted several of their most important works in opposition to the *Tropici* and in defense of the coequal divinity of the Holy Spirit.

The pro-Nicene theology was eventually affirmed ecclesiastically at the Council of Constantinople (381), which is recognized as the Second Ecumenical Council. The creed that emerged from the council, building on the early creed of Nicaea, is worth quoting in its entirety.

> I believe in one God, the Father Almighty, Maker of heaven and earth, and of all things visible and invisible.
>
> And in one Lord Jesus Christ, the only-begotten Son of God, begotten of the Father before all worlds; God of God, Light of Light, very God of very God; begotten, not made, being of one substance with the Father, by whom all things were made. Who, for us men for our salvation, came down from heaven, and was incarnate by the Holy Spirit of the virgin Mary, and was made man; and was crucified also for us under Pontius Pilate; He suffered and was buried; and the third day He rose again, according to the Scriptures; and ascended into heaven, and sits on the right hand of the Father; and He shall come again, with glory, to judge the quick and the dead; whose kingdom shall have no end.
>
> And I believe in the Holy Ghost, the Lord and Giver of Life; who proceeds from the Father; who with the Father and the Son together is worshipped and glorified; who spoke by the prophets. And I believe one holy catholic and apostolic Church. I acknowledge one

baptism for the remission of sins; and I look for the resurrection of the dead, and the life of the world to come. Amen.

Christians know this confessional symbol as the Nicene Creed, but again, it is better termed the Niceno-Constantinopolitan Creed, given the developments that occurred between 325 and 381. It summarizes many of the Cappadocians' achievements: the essential identity of the divine persons, the eternal relations of origin as the only permissible personal distinctions, and a fuller teaching on the Holy Spirit as a distinct but coequal divine person.

Trinitarian Consolidation: The Contribution of Augustine

Unlike Nicaea, which settled only a few debates and sparked several more, Constantinople should be considered the true turning point in the development of trinitarian doctrine from the first four centuries. Orthodox reflection on the Trinity thereafter operated within the parameters of the Constantinopolitan settlement. Although many important theologians of the late-fourth and fifth centuries are worthy of consideration, including Ambrose (c. 340–397), Jerome (c. 347–420), and Cyril of Alexandria (378–444), no other theologian exerted the kind of influence that Augustine of Hippo (354–430) did on the church's trinitarian thought. His monumental *De Trinitate* is perhaps most well-known for the psychological analogies he employs as a way of understanding how three divine persons can be one God. But the work as a whole is much more concerned with the kind of biblical exegesis that undergirds the doctrine of the Trinity.

One of the orienting principles of Augustine's *De Trinitate* is the dynamic between the temporal missions of the Son and Spirit and the eternal processions that they reveal. According to Augustine, a trinitarian mission is a visible manifestation of either the Son or Spirit, sent from the Father (and from the Son, in the case of the mission of the Holy Spirit). In the earlier parts of the work, Augustine considers whether or not the theophanies of the Old Testament constitute missions of one or another divine person. For example, is the Angel of the Lord, the man who wrestled with Jacob, or the fourth man in Daniel's fiery furnace, a mission of the Son? After a careful consideration of several Old Testament texts, Augustine concludes that it is not always possible to decide whether any of the Old Testament theophanies should be associated with a particular divine person or whether it is the whole Godhead who is manifested in them. Instead, we are to look to the New Testament for the definitive divine missions: the Son is revealed in his being sent from the Father in the incarnation, and the Holy Spirit is revealed in his being sent from the Father as a dove at Jesus's baptism and as cloven tongues of fire on the day of Pentecost. These missions unveil the triune nature of the one true God. The missions, in turn, reveal the divine persons' eternal relations to one another. The Son is *sent from* the Father because he *is from* the Father in his eternal generation. The Spirit is *sent from* the Father and Son because he *is from* the Father and Son in his eternal procession. Thus, the temporal missions reveal and correspond to the eternal processions. Again we see the principle that God is as he reveals himself to be. To be clear, not everything that obtains in the temporal missions can be read back into the eternal processions, as it were. For example, the Son is subordinate to the Father in virtue of his taking the form of a servant in his humanity: "The Father is greater than I." But in virtue of his consubstantiality with the Father, the eternal generation of the Son does not imply any subordination in the being of God: "I and the Father are one" (John 10:30).

Another important insight that emerges from *De Trinitate* and Augustine's other writings on the Trinity is the emphasis on the Trinity's inseparable operations. Augustine did not invent this doctrine (it had been emphasized by the Cappadocians as well), but he provides one of the classic expressions of it:

> For according to the Catholic faith, the Trinity is proposed to our belief and believed—and even understood by a few saints and holy

> persons—as so inseparable that whatever action is performed by it must be thought to be performed at the same time by the Father and by the Son and by the Holy Spirit. (*Epistle* 11.2)

The doctrine is sometimes summarized in the Latin phrase *opera trinitatis ad extra indivisa sunt*: the external works of the Trinity are indivisible, or inseparable. All that God does outside of himself (*ad extra*) in creation, providence, redemption, and judgment, he performs as Father, Son, and Holy Spirit. Certain divine works may be appropriated (the language of appropriation would become important in medieval reflections on the Trinity) to certain divine persons. We may say that the Father creates, the Son redeems, and the Spirit sanctifies. But this manner of speaking should not be taken to imply that the works of the Trinity constitute a kind of division of labor in which one divine person carries out a particular act separate from the others. No, it is the triune God who creates, redeems, and sanctifies. Because God is one, he acts as one. Each of the divine persons is to be identified, essence-wise, with the one, simple divine being, and therefore all of the Trinity's external works are inseparable. Still, each divine person's involvement, so to speak, in the inseparable works of the Trinity is marked by his own distinct personal property. Gregory of Nyssa had already given expression to this same truth in his *On "Not Three Gods"*:

> If, then, every good thing and every good name, depending on that power and purpose which is without beginning, is brought to perfection in the power of the Spirit through the Only-begotten God, without mark of time or distinction (since there is no delay, existent or conceived, in the motion of the Divine will from the Father, through the Son, to the Spirit): and if Godhead also is one of the good names and concepts, it would not be proper to divide the name into a plurality, since the unity existing in the action prevents plural enumeration. (p. 335)

So, for Gregory and for Augustine after him, there is an inseparable unity in the divine operations. But there is also an order (Greek *taxis*) to the Trinity's work, marked here by Gregory's use of differing prepositions: the motion is from the Father, through the Son, and to the Spirit.

As mentioned earlier, Augustine's *De Trinitate* is often associated with his use of psychological analogies in book 9 of the work. Only after giving a lengthy exegetical defense of the orthodox doctrine of the Trinity does Augustine turn to reflections of a more speculative sort. Augustine suggests that the best candidate for an analogy of God lies in the creature who bears the image of God: humanity. Can we see a picture of the tripersonal God in a lover, a beloved, and the love between them? Is there an analogy of the Trinity in the mind, its understanding, and its will to love? Augustine believed that triads like these (mind-understanding-love or mind-memory-will) have the potential to cast light on the unity and the distinctions of the divine persons. These speculations, it should be noted, have their limitations, but they are not entirely without scriptural support. The New Testament does speak of the Son as the Logos (word, reason) of the Father. And the Holy Spirit is often associated with the themes of love and gift, and is said to be the Spirit of the Father and the Spirit of Christ—in other words, the shared Spirit of both. Later in the medieval era, these themes would be taken up by Thomas Aquinas (1225–1274) in his exposition of the Trinity.

One final note on Augustine is worth mentioning, namely, the relationship of his so-called Latin approach to the Trinity to the Greek-speaking Eastern approach of, say, the Cappadocians. It has sometimes been argued, going back to Theodore de Régnon (1831–1893) in the late nineteenth century, that Latin Trinitarianism "begins" from the unity of the divine persons and asks how they can be three, while Eastern Trinitarianism "begins" from the distinction of the divine persons and asks how they can be one. The assumption of the so-called de Régnon thesis is that there is a sharp wedge between the two traditions on the priority of unity versus distinction. But more recent scholarship has called into question this dichotomy and has demonstrated that the two theological traditions, while distinct in some ways, exhibit much more family resemblance than any fundamental difference in orientation. The quotations from Augustine and Gregory of Nyssa cited above show at least part of this convergence: Gregory is as eager to guard the unity and inseparability of the triune works as Augustine is. Likewise, Augustine is as concerned with affirming the real distinctions between the divine persons as Gregory is. The trinitarian missions reveal, not a unipersonal, modalistic God, but real relations of origin that distinguish the divine persons from all eternity.

CASE STUDIES

The historical overview above has covered some of the major theologians, controversies, and themes that shaped the church's trinitarian thought in the earliest centuries. The case studies below focus more attention on two important exegetical practices that lie underneath this doctrinal consensus.

Case Study 1: Prosopological Exegesis

Historians of early Christianity have noted a particular reading strategy, employed by both the New Testament authors and the Fathers of the early centuries, known as prosopological, or prosopographic, exegesis. (Note especially the work by Matthew Bates, listed under "For Further Reading" at the end of this chapter). The focus of prosopological exegesis is on the particular person or character (Greek *prosopon*) who is speaking or being spoken of in Old Testament texts. For example, in one of the most frequently cited Old Testament passages in the New Testament, Psalm 110, we read about two central characters: "The LORD [Yahweh] said to my lord [Adonai], 'Sit at my right hand until I make your enemies your footstool'" (v. 1 NRSV). Jesus himself pressed the question about the identity of the second of these two "Lords" to the Pharisees in his own day: "If David calls him 'Lord,' how, then, can he be his son?" (Matt 22:45). The assumption is that Psalm 110 is a messianic prophecy about the son of David, and yet, as Jesus points out, David refers to him as "Lord" (LXX, *kurios*). So, here we have two figures who are identified as "Lord" in the psalm, who share the same authority to rule, reign, and execute judgment. Many other Old Testament passages (e.g., Psalms 2, 16, 40, 45; Isaiah 53) receive a similar treatment by the New Testament authors: although placed on the lips of human authors, these passages are ultimately seen as the utterances of divine persons.

The important point for our purposes is to note that this same reading strategy was employed by many of the church fathers after the New Testament. Justin Martyr, for example, writes:

> But when you hear the utterances of the prophets spoken as it were personally, you must not suppose that they are spoken by the inspired themselves, but by the Divine Word who moves them. For sometimes He declares things that are to come to pass, in the manner of one who foretells the future; sometimes He speaks as from the person of God the Lord and Father of all; sometimes as from the person of Christ; sometimes as from the person of the people answering the Lord or His Father, just as you can see even in your own writers, one man being the writer of the whole, but introducing the persons who converse. And this the Jews who possessed the books of the prophets did not understand, and therefore did not recognize Christ even when He came, but even hate us who say that He has come, and who prove that, as was predicted, He was crucified by them. (*First Apology* 36)

So, the person of the Father or the person of the Son can speak, as it were, through the voice of the human authors of the Old Testament. The truest and most ultimate meaning of the texts in question can only be understood when they are understood as utterances of the divine persons.

Tertullian also discerned the voice of the divine persons speaking through the human voices of the Old Testament. In his *Against Praxeas*, he notes that "almost all the Psalms which prophesy of the person of Christ, represent the Son as conversing with the Father—that is, represent Christ (as speaking) to God. Observe also the Spirit speaking of the Father and the Son, in the character of a third Person: The Lord said to my Lord, 'Sit on my right hand, until I make Your enemies Your footstool'" (11). Note that in the case of Ps 110:1, Tertullian sees all three divine persons: the first Lord is the Father, the second Lord is the Son, and the one who inspired these words about them is the Holy Spirit.

For a couple of reasons, prosopological exegesis was significant for the church's developing Trinitarian doctrine. First, it gave the earliest Christian interpreters a way of demonstrating how the Old Testament bore witness to the coming revelation of the Trinity in the New Testament. Though in a veiled way, the Hebrew Scriptures were already preparing the way for the manifestation of God's triune nature in the saving missions of the Son and Spirit. Second, prosopological exegesis also established, especially in the Western tradition following Tertullian, the language of person as the preferred term for the Father, Son, and Holy Spirit. As we have seen, Tertullian is especially noted for developing the key trinitarian grammar for the Latin-speaking Western church, with *personae* the chosen term for the three divine persons.

Case Study 2: Partitive Exegesis

Another important interpretive strategy employed by the pro-Nicene theologians and their heirs is a practice known as partitive exegesis. In short, this method of exegesis asks the following question about passages that refer to Jesus Christ: Is this passage speaking of the Son of God as such, or is it speaking of the Son of God in his incarnate state? Carefully discerning whether or not a given biblical text is speaking of the Son *qua* divine (as God) or *qua* human (as a human) enabled the pro-Nicene theologians to account for passages that seem to subordinate the Son to the Father, without diminishing the Son's status as "true God." Augustine spells out this reading strategy in terms of a "canonical rule":

> To resume, then, we find scattered through the scriptures, and marked out by learned Catholic expositors of them, a kind of canonical rule, which we hold onto most firmly, about how our Lord Jesus Christ is to be understood to be God's Son, both equal to the Father by the form of God in which he is, and less than the Father by the form of a servant which he took. In this form indeed he is seen to be not only less than the Father, but also less than the Holy Spirit, less what is more, than himself—and not a self that he was but a self that he is. For when he took the form of a servant he did not lose the form of God, as we learn from the evidences of scripture examined in the previous book. (*De Trinitate* 2.2)

Augustine was echoing the language of Philippians 2: the Son is in the "form of God" (*forma Dei*) but takes on additionally the "form of a servant" (*forma servi*). Passages that subordinate the Son to the Father are to be interpreted in terms of Christ's humanity; passages that assert his equality with the Father, in terms of his deity. The two-natures Christology that was developing in the fifth century gave further support to this particular reading strategy, but it was already present in the fourth-century Fathers as well. For example, Gregory of Nazianzus writes, "What is lofty you are to apply to the Godhead, and to that Nature in Him which is superior to sufferings and incorporeal; but all that is lowly to the composite condition of Him who for your sakes made Himself of no reputation and was Incarnate" (*Third Theological Oration* 29.18).

So, passages that speak of God being the head of Christ (1 Cor 11:3) or of the Son being subject to God (1 Cor 15:28) should not be taken to introduce some kind of hierarchy of authority between the divine persons. Instead, they speak of the Son with reference to his having taken on the form of servant in his incarnate mission. To be sure, it is the one person of the Son who is the subject of both kinds of attribution. Partitive exegesis was never intended to sever Christ into two persons. But it gave the church a way of discerning the precise sense in which Christ is spoken of in all of Scripture. It preserved the Trinity without diminishing the incarnation.

FOR THE CHURCH

Several important lessons emerge from the development of the doctrine of the Trinity in the first five centuries.

The Trinity is for Christian biblical interpretation. Scriptural exegesis led the early church fathers to faith in the Trinity. Theologians such as Origen and Augustine were first and foremost biblical exegetes. Before and underneath their theological speculations stood a serious engagement with the biblical text. On the other hand, the doctrine of the Trinity, emerging as it does from a close reading of Scripture, in turn guides faithful interpretation of Scripture. The Trinity is, as Irenaeus argued, a significant part of the rule of truth, or the rule of faith. It regulates how we read and understand texts that might be difficult to understand. The practice of partitive exegesis—carefully discerning whether a particular text is speaking about the Son of God as such or about the Son of God in his incarnate mission—helps us to see how "the Father is greater than I" and "I and the Father are one" do not constitute a contradiction but a coherent vision of the Son's divine and human natures. Similarly, a robust understanding of the *homoousios* will keep us from misunderstanding texts that seem to subordinate the Son to the Father. The doctrine of the Trinity (paired with the doctrine of the incarnation) helps us to guard the Son's divine status as one in "the form of God" without diminishing his condescension in taking on "the form of a servant."

The Trinity is for the Christian life. As Irenaeus reminds us, the Trinity is not some abstract datum of theological speculation, reserved only for advanced Christians, but constitutes the very beginning of Christian experience. Believers are baptized into the triune name. We are immersed into the divine life as our initiation into the faith. To put it colloquially, the Trinity is not graduate-level Christianity but Christianity 101. Of course, there are always new depths to be plumbed and new heights to attain in our ongoing reflections on the Trinity. Nonetheless, whatever advanced learning we might acquire in the doctrine of the Trinity does not present to us some God other than the One we already know in our baptism, in our prayers, in our experience of redemption, and in our worship of the God who is Father, Son, and Holy Spirit. Deepened knowledge of God's triune life simply undergirds and strengthens our experience of the love of the Father, through the redemptive mission of the Son and the sanctifying mission of the Holy Spirit.

The Trinity is for Christian preaching. It might seem unfathomable to modern Christians, but the theologically dense orations of Gregory of Nazianzus were not academic tomes written for experts but sermons addressed to the faithful. Certainly, we should be sensitive to cultural differences between, say, fourth-century Constantinople and twenty-first-century Chicago, but contemporary Christian ministers should not be timid in proclaiming the doctrine of the Trinity in our preaching, teaching, and catechesis. The fourth-century theologians who developed the doctrine expressed in the Nicene Creed were all pastors and preachers. They worked diligently to apprehend and defend the doctrine of the Trinity because they knew that the faith and life of the church was at stake. The gospel we proclaim is not just a matter of personal fulfillment or self-betterment, but it is the saving life, death, and resurrection of the incarnate Son of God who reveals the Father by the inner working of the Holy Spirit. Christian preaching should be firmly anchored in the being and work of the triune God as the beginning, middle, and end of Christian faith.

For Further Reading

Anatolios, Khaled. *Retrieving Nicaea: The Development and Meaning of Trinitarian Doctrine.* Grand Rapids: Baker Academic, 2011.

Augustine. *The Trinity (De Trinitate).* Translated by Edmund Hill. Hyde Park, NY: New City, 1991.

Ayres, Lewis. *Nicaea and Its Legacy: An Approach to Fourth-Century Trinitarian Theology.* Oxford: Oxford University Press, 2006.

Basil of Caesarea. *On the Holy Spirit.* Translated by Stephen M. Hildebrand. Crestwood, NY: St. Vladimir's Seminary Press, 2011.

Bates, Matthew W. *The Birth of the Trinity: Jesus, God, and Spirit in New Testament and Early Christian Interpretations of the Old Testament.* Oxford: Oxford University Press, 2015.

Behr, John. *The Way to Nicaea.* The Formation of Christian Theology 1. Crestwood, NY: St. Vladimir's Seminary Press, 2001.

———. *The Nicene Faith.* The Formation of Christian Theology 2. Crestwood, NY: St. Vladimir's Seminary Press, 2004.

Gregory of Nyssa. *On "Not Three Gods."* Translated by H. A. Wilson. From Nicene and Post-Nicene Fathers. Second Series. Vol. 5. Edited by Philip Schaff and Henry Wace. Buffalo, NY: Christian Literature Publishing, 1893.

Hardy, Edward R., ed. *Christology of the Later Fathers.* Louisville: Westminster John Knox, 1954.

Holmes, Stephen R. *The Quest for the Trinity: The Doctrine of God in Scripture, History and Modernity.* Downers Grove, IL: IVP Academic, 2012.

Irenaeus. *On the Apostolic Preaching.* Translated by John Behr. Crestwood, NY: St. Vladimir's Seminary Press, 1997.

Origen. *On First Principles.* 2 vols. Translated by John Behr. Oxford Early Christian Texts. Oxford: Oxford University Press, 2018.

Rusch, William G., ed. and trans. *The Trinitarian Controversy.* Sources of Early Christian Thought. Minneapolis: Fortress, 2009.

Tertullian. *Against Praxeas.* In *Latin Christianity: Its Founder, Tertullian. Ante-Nicene Fathers* 3. Edited by Alexander Roberts and James Donaldson. Revised by A. Cleveland Coxe. Peabody, MA: Hendrickson, 1994.

Questions for Study or Discussion

1. What is the relationship between the biblical teaching on the Trinity and the later development of the doctrine of the Trinity in the first several centuries?
2. What were the major contributions of the second- and third-century Fathers? What were their strengths and potential weaknesses?
3. What were the major heretical positions on the Trinity in the fourth century? Why were they biblically and theologically deficient? How did the pro-Nicene fathers respond to them?
4. Is it legitimate to use extrabiblical terminology to define and defend the doctrine of the Trinity? Is it sufficient just to stick to the language of Scripture? What if heretical positions also cite scriptural support? How does the church determine which interpretation is correct?
5. What are the practical implications of the doctrine of the Trinity? How does the Trinity give shape to Christian spirituality, proclamation, and worship?

3

SCRIPTURE AND TRADITION

By Stephen O. Presley

Introduction

One of the most fundamental questions in the history of Christian thought concerns the proper interpretation and ordering of authoritative sources. In various areas of life, we all follow authorities that help guide and shape the patterns of our daily routines: children obey their parents, employees fulfill the requests of their employers, and students follow the directions of their teachers. In a similar way, theological reflection is dependent on various sources that guide and shape the church's faith, and from the earliest days, theologians have naturally appealed to two main sources: Scripture and tradition. Unlike later periods of Christian history, these two sources in the early church were intertwined and converged like two streams flowing together through the river of theological discourse.

This is not to say that everyone interpreted these sources correctly or even understood Scripture and tradition to mean the same things. Certainly, discussion about these sources involves debates about the inspiration of Scripture and the development of the canon, as well as the oral transmission of the Lord's teaching that was received by the apostles and proclaimed to the church. Many of these debates were sparked by heretical figures such as Marcion and other Gnostic teachers who exploited Scriptures and interpreted them in ways that supported their peculiar theological systems. In this context, these figures undermined the "tradition" of the church; the Christian community responded by continuing to show the continuity between the apostolic teaching and the Scriptures. Of course, the Reformation and post-Reformation context is radically different. In those settings the church had to address the imposition of certain forms of tradition that distorted the proper interpretation of the Scriptures. But the faithful in the early Christian community were still in the process of gathering their sacred texts and carefully articulating and passing on the basic teaching of the apostles. The historical overview below traces the development of these two sources in the early church, and the case studies that follow isolate a few key examples of canonical and confessional development.

Historical Overview

In the years following the apostles, the church continued to thrive despite living as a marginalized community and suffering through many internal and external pressures. The prevailing philosophical and theological assumptions of Greco-Roman culture competed with Christianity. What the early church demanded above all was an entire revision of the first principles that challenged the foundations of classical culture. Amid their Greco-Roman world, the early church claimed to possess a new identity in Christ superior to any religious ideology or spirituality the culture had to offer. It was on this basis that they worshipped and served, worked and played, lived and died. Greco-Roman culture did not, at first, warm to the teachings of the church. Christian communities also suffered sporadic episodes of persecution that escalated, leading up to the great persecutions of Diocletian and Galerius (303–311). There is no shortage of accounts of persecution or martyrdom stories, such as the *Martyrdom of Polycarp* (c. 155) or the accounts in the *Letter of the Churches of Vienne and Lyons* (177), that shape the church's interaction with the culture. These conditions motivated Christians to think carefully about which texts were worthy of preservation and how to articulate the gospel in convincing ways so that their teaching might influence the culture.

The church also struggled to maintain its theological convictions among other competing religious communities. On one hand, Jews challenged the church's reception and interpretation of the Hebrew Bible just as they had done in the apostolic period. The early church made a record of Jewish-Christian interactions, such as Justin Martyr's *Dialogue with Trypho the Jew* (c. 150), that involve debates about the proper interpretation of the Old Testament. Since the church confessed that Christ was the key that unlocked the Scriptures (Luke 24:13–27), they needed to distinguish their reading (derived from the apostolic teaching) from Jewish interpreters who rejected Christ as the Messiah. On the other hand, there were many heretical teachers, especially various Gnostic figures, who filtered in and out of the church, drafting converts away from the Christian community. These figures composed heretical texts, such as the *Gospel of Thomas* and the *Gospel of Truth*, which redeployed the Christian Scriptures and apostolic tradition to support their own theological systems.

Nestled between the various cultural and theological pressures, early Christian thought was shaped by the intermingling of Scripture and tradition. First, these pressures required that the church begin recognizing which Scriptures were inspired and useful for the worship and ministry of the church. Second, alongside Scripture, Christian thinkers began developing or clarifying the essential teachings of the church handed down from the apostles. These teachings were often drafted in the form of creeds and linked with discipleship (or catechesis) and baptism. The church also required ministers to oversee the reception and preservation of both Scripture and tradition and faithfully pass on what they had received. Through this intermingling of canon, creed, and clergy, the church clarified and proclaimed the teachings of Christ and the message of the gospel.

Recognizing Scripture

First, when the Fathers speak of "Scripture," they typically have in mind the general contours of the canon that is recognized today, though there is significant debate surrounding the process of transmission and extent of the canon. There is a close connection between the church as a worshipping community and the canon, because as they gathered, they made conscious decisions about which texts were appropriate for Christian worship. This does not mean, however, that these decisions transformed a text into Scripture. The canon was neither determined by the community nor a natural consequence of historical development. Instead, the church began asking the basic theological question: "Which books are inspired?" In this sense, the early church did not *decide* what was or was not Scripture; instead, they *recognized* which books were inspired. In other words, the church did not envision that they were imposing the status of Scripture on texts, but simply recognizing which texts God had already inspired through the Spirit for the life and ministry of the church.

To help organize which books were recognized as sacred Scripture, the church began distinguishing between the threefold classification of accepted, questioned, and rejected books. Books that were accepted were considered inspired by all churches and used regularly in Christian worship. Books that were questioned were recognized as inspired by some but not all, and their status remained uncertain. The rejected books were not considered inspired. In some cases, they might be useful and edifying even though they were not Scripture; in other cases, they were deemed heretical and not to be read at all. For example, the church father Eusebius (c. 260–340) distinguished between books that "are true, genuine, and accepted in the tradition of the church"; "disputed books" that are "not canonical yet familiar to most church writers"; and "spurious books" that are "discarded as impious and absurd" (*Church History* 3.25).

Based on texts such as 2 Tim 3:16 and 2 Pet 1:20–21, the church already assumed that the writings of the Old Testament were inspired, but the New Testament canon was a serious point of debate. To help recognize which of these books were inspired, they pointed to several criteria, including a text's apostolicity, catholicity, and orthodoxy. Again, these criteria were not imposed on texts but rather used to identify the features of an inspired text. When a child is born into a family, the child's physical features generally reflect those of the parents. As the child grows, the family will notice things such as facial features or personality traits that they identify with one or more of their relatives. In a similar way, the discussion of apostolicity, catholicity, and orthodoxy are the features of a text that help point to its identity as inspired Scripture. By apostolicity, the early church believed that only texts composed by an apostle, or someone close to an apostle, should be considered Scripture. The apostles were eyewitnesses of the Lord's teaching and ministry, and they received instructions they passed on in writings. Texts considered "catholic" (meaning "universal") were affirmed and used widely in Christian worship. No individual church determined the canon, but a book had to enjoy broad acceptance for it to be recognized as Scripture. Finally, books that were considered Scripture were theologically consonant with the other Scripture texts. In other words, even if a book was claimed to be written by an apostle and used widely, it was rejected if it did not reflect the teaching resident in the other recognized books.

In the centuries following the apostolic period, it is not unusual to find lists of books that were considered Scripture. A few important early canon lists include the Muratorian Fragment, which has been dated to the late second century and Eusebius's account mentioned earlier, which distinguished between accepted and rejected books (*Church History* 3.25.1–7; 6.25). The earliest list containing all sixty-six books that are today recognized as Scripture is Athanasius's famous *Letter 39* (367). There were also several councils that recognized canon lists, including the Council of Hippo (393) and the third and fourth Councils of Carthage (397 and 419), though these councils also recognized the Old Testament Apocrypha alongside the rest of the canonical books. In general, the consistency among these theologians and councils demonstrates that the church recognized the sixty-six books of the canon, even if the later tradition would eventually reject the Apocrypha.

Developing Tradition

Although the Scriptures served as one source of authority, tradition also contributed to the church's theological formation. The word *tradition* for some might conjure up negative connotations involving elaborate liturgical forms of worship. But in the early church, the language of tradition simply refers to the doctrine given to the church by Jesus or the apostles, or a summation of biblical doctrine. The New Testament uses this language of tradition to emphasize the transmission of the teaching of the apostles (1 Cor 11:2; 2 Thess 2:15; 3:6); several other passages offer summaries of basic confessions of faith that resemble the outline of later creeds (1 Cor 8:6; 15:3–5). The most important text is Matt 28:19, which encouraged Jesus's followers to go into all the world, make disciples, and baptize them in the name of the Father, Son, and Spirit. This triadic formula reflected the basic summary of essential points of early Christian conceptions of tradition.

Initially, in the second century, the Fathers used the language of "rule (or canon) of faith" to describe a summary of the church's teaching and how it was used as a standard for orthodoxy. The term *rule* is the same term used to describe the *canon* of scripture, which simply means a standard or measuring line. There is no single, static articulation of the rule of faith that is formally and universally accepted. Nevertheless, all the expressions of the rule of faith bear a family resemblance. Just as the members of a family share similar traits, so also do the articulations of the rule of faith. These resemblances and similarities include a triadic structure organized around the persons of Father, Son, and Spirit. They also have common theological descriptors that are often derived from Scripture and explain the nature of God and the economic functions of each divine person, with the person of Christ receiving the most attention. The rule of faith did not cover every theological issue, but instead it provided a framework that expressed the church's faith and unified the church against heretical deviation.

One important distinction between tradition, or the rule of faith, and the Scriptures is the notion of doctrinal development. Although the written revelation was in a fixed form, the tradition of the church was developing as the church faced new challenges and contexts. In terms of doctrinal development, a major turning point was the great Constantinian shift beginning in the fourth century. Constantine called the first ecumenical council, the Council of Nicaea (325), to try to bring unity to a fractured church. This was the first of a series of ecumenical councils, including the Council of Constantinople (381), Council of Ephesus (431), and Council of Chalcedon (451). These councils often produced written statements called creeds that express the common faith affirmed by the universal church and serve as the principal example of the expression of the tradition. Each creedal statement brought greater clarity and understanding of the nature of God, the relationship of the divine persons, and the two natures of Christ. This kind of activity always involves making theological judgments and using the grammar, language, and concepts of the Scriptures. Any normative theological statement in the early church, therefore, is always closely associated with Scripture. In this way, these two sources of authority flow together in the early church, intermingling and mutually supporting each other.

The church also relied on pastors to ensure the proper dedication, preservation, and interpretation of the inspired books of Scripture. These clergy were responsible for providing regular instruction on the church's teachings, as well as evangelizing and catechizing new converts to the faith. The decisions about preaching and worship, as well as discipleship or catechetical curriculum, necessitated that pastors play an active role in transmission of Scripture and development of doctrine. Early catechetical manuals, such as the *Didache*, Irenaeus's *On Apostolic Preaching*, and Augustine's *On Catechizing the Uninstructed*, show that new converts to the faith were thoroughly immersed in the Scriptures. Together these texts and figures show how Scripture and tradition work in harmony to prepare the church to face the challenges of every new generation.

CASE STUDIES

Case Study 1: The *Muratorian Fragment*

One of the earliest and most important canon lists is the *Muratorian Fragment*. The manuscript was discovered in 1700 in a library in Milan and dates to around 180. The text contains only eighty-five lines but still mentions twenty-two of the twenty-seven books that currently make up the New Testament. Hebrews, James, and 1–2 Peter are the only books not mentioned. This list is conclusive evidence that there was a set of core canonical books that were used early and quickly recognized as Scripture. But just as fascinating as the list of books is the discussion surrounding them and the defense of their canonical status. As mentioned earlier, this text provides a window into the ways that the early church recognized Scripture based on the appeals to the apostolicity, catholicity, and orthodoxy of texts. The author's discussion of this criteria is more implicit and assumed than explicitly imposed on the canonical process. Nor does the author discuss all criteria with every book. Instead, he mentions the criteria at specific points in the canon list to address questions about the status of different books. Clearly no text was recognized as canonical based on any one of these criteria alone, but they worked together to help the church recognize what texts were already inspired.

First, the fragment appeals to a text's apostolicity at several points. For example, in the discussion of Luke's Gospel, the author defends the text's apostolicity by observing the close association between Luke and Paul. Even though Luke had not seen the Lord in the flesh, he was "zealous for the Law" and joined Paul on his missionary journeys. Thus, his Gospel relates the events accurately and authoritatively (*Muratorian Canon* 3–8). He also mentions the travel narratives in Acts and remarks that "Luke compiled the individual events that took place in his presence" (*Muratorian Canon* 35–36). In another place, the fragment emphasizes the fact that John was an eyewitness to the events of the Lord by alluding to John's comments in 1 John 1:1–4, where he "professes [himself] to be not only an eye-witness and hearer, but also a writer of all the marvelous deeds of the Lord, in their order" (*Muratorian Canon* 27–33). The appeals to apostolicity assured a standard that any text that was admitted was the product of someone who had direct conversation with the Lord or a close relationship with one who did. Still other texts, such as the *Shepherd of Hermas*, "ought indeed to be read; but it cannot be read publicly to the people in church either among the prophets, whose number is complete, or among the apostles, for it is after [their] time" (*Muratorian Canon* 77–80). This book is considered part of a collection of texts known as "the Apostolic Fathers," which comprise Christian writings composed by church leaders during the generation after the apostles. Although these texts might be helpful for the church's ministry, they are not apostolic and therefore not included in the canon.

Second, the *Muratorian Fragment* also points to the orthodoxy of texts as a basic criterion for including in the canon. In other words, even if a text was ascribed to an apostle or one of their close associates, it was rejected if the contents did not reflect a theological continuity with the other inspired texts. This became particularly important in the *Fragment*'s discussion of the differences between the four Gospel accounts. Although the *Fragment* assumes an awareness of other false gospels, the author points to the theological unity of the fourfold Gospels to defend their inspiration. The author argues that "though various elements may be taught in the individual books of the Gospels, nevertheless this makes no difference to the faith of believers, since by the one sovereign Spirit all things have been declared in all [the Gospels]" (*Muratorian Canon* 16–20). The passage emphasizes the unity of "the faith" that transcends the texts and the inspiration of all four Gospels by "one sovereign Spirit." Though the Gospels may differ in "various elements," they are unified in their basic confession of Jesus Christ as Lord and the organized commentary on every major segment of Christ's life and ministry including his birth, life, death, resurrection, and second coming (*Muratorian Canon* 20–26). The content and arrangement point to a unified witness of one gospel in four inspired, coordinating forms.

Finally, the *Fragment* also uses the category of catholicity, or universality, to point to the texts that are recognized as inspired throughout the church. For example, the author describes how Paul wrote a letter to Philemon and Titus and two letters to Timothy that "are all held sacred in the esteem of the church catholic for the regulation of ecclesiastical discipline" (*Muratorian Canon* 59–63). In other words, these particular books are used widely in the church to help shape the church's practice. The *Fragment* also mentions several forgeries and heretical texts that "cannot be received into the catholic [i.e. universal] Church—for it is not fitting that gall be mixed with honey" (*Muratorian Canon* 66–67). Other texts the author mentions include the *Apocalypse of John* and the *Apocalypse of Peter*. He considers both of them inspired, though he recognizes that some "are not willing that the latter [*Apocalypse of Peter*] be read in church" (*Muratorian Canon* 71–72). This shows that a text such as the *Apocalypse of Peter* was accepted as inspired by some but not universally, and eventually it was rejected from the canon. The *Muratorian Fragment* demonstrates that even at an early date, assembling the canon was not a spontaneous or haphazard development but the intentional work of the Christian community to recognize which books were inspired by God and useful for the life and ministry of the church. Together these instances reveal the theology of canon at work in the life of the church and a canon core that has already taken shape well before the end of the second century.

Case Study 2: Athanasius *Letter 39* (c. 367)

Athanasius (c. 295–373) was the bishop of Alexandria during the tumultuous years of the fourth century. Though the church enjoyed a newfound measure of religious freedom in the years following Constantine, internal disputes between Nicene Christians and Arians threatened the unity of the church. Athanasius was the ardent defender of Nicene orthodoxy, and he was often persecuted and exiled by Arian leaders. By the late fourth century, many canon lists had circulated, and the canonical books had already been in use in the churches for some time. But Athanasius's *Letter 39* composed in 367 is the first extant list of all sixty-six books that comprise what we recognize as the Old and New Testaments. Athanasius, however, did not create this list *ad hoc*. He probably inherited his list from his teachers in Alexandria and composed it to help solidify the books that teach Christian orthodoxy.

Before listing the books, Athanasius remarked that there had been many conversations about the extent and number of the canonical texts. There were also some who mixed apocryphal books, such as the *Book of Enoch* or the *Ascension of Isaiah*, with the inspired writings and, as a result, were led astray. Instead, Athanasius composed his list "to set forth in order the books that are canonized, transmitted, and believed to be divine, so that those who have been deceived might condemn the persons who led them astray, and those who have remained pure might rejoice to be reminded (of these things)" (*Letter 39*, 16). These books, Athanasius went on to write, "are the springs of salvation, so that someone who thirsts may be satisfied by the words they contain" and in "these books alone the teaching of piety is proclaimed" (*Letter 39*, 19). He exhorted the faithful, echoing the words of Rev 22:18–19, to neither add nor subtract from these books. Although Athanasius rejected the apocryphal texts, he found some of them helpful for edification. Like Eusebius, he mentioned a third category of books that were neither canonical nor apocryphal, but ought to be read by new converts to the faith who "want to be instructed in the word of piety" (*Letter 39*, 20). This includes such books as the Wisdom of Solomon, Judith, the

Didache, and the *Shepherd of Hermas*. But while these books may be helpful, they are not to be read in worship or included among the inspired books of Scripture.

Case Study 3: Irenaeus on the *Rule of Faith*

Alongside the canonical development, early Christian thinkers also fashioned doctrines that formed the church's "tradition" and expressed its basic theological convictions. Early on, the language of "tradition" was often called the church's "rule of faith." One of the earliest church fathers to use this language was Irenaeus (c. 130–202), the bishop of Lyons. Irenaeus was from Smyrna, where he encountered the teaching of Polycarp (c. 69–155), but eventually he settled in Lyons in the second century. Irenaeus is known widely as the champion of Christian orthodoxy against the Gnostics in the second century, and he used the rule of faith to differentiate basic Christian convictions from the Gnostic worldview. Irenaeus provides several summaries of the rule of faith throughout his writings, and though they are not identical, the general structure is triadic and follows the basic points of the baptismal confession of Father, Son, and Spirit (Matt 28:19) (*Against Heresies* 1.10.1; 22.1). These points are then elaborated with the language and concepts of Scripture as Irenaeus explains the nature of God and what God has accomplished through the Son and the Spirit. For Irenaeus, the rule of faith is the epitome of Scripture, or what he calls Scripture's *hypothesis*, that summarizes the overarching argument or plot of Scripture (*Against Heresies* 1.8.1–10.3). In the early church, the rule of faith is also closely associated with baptism. It forms the content of discipleship instruction before baptism and the basis for the Christian's confession during baptism.

In his short catechetical manual, *On Apostolic Preaching* (c. 190), Irenaeus provides a summary of the rule of faith that states:

> This is the order of the rule of our faith, and the foundation of [the] edifice, and support of [our] conduct: God, the Father,

> uncreated, uncontainable, invisible, one God, the Creator of all: this is the first article of our faith. The second article: the Word of God, the Son of God, Christ Jesus our Lord, who was revealed by the prophets according to the character of their prophecy and according to the nature of the economies of the Father, by whom all things were made, and who, in the last times, to recapitulate all things, became man amongst men, visible and palpable, in order to abolish death, to demonstrate life, and to effect communion between God and man. And the third article: The Holy Spirit, through whom the prophets prophesied and the patriarchs learnt the things of God and the righteous were led in the path of righteousness, and who, in the last times, was poured out in a new fashion upon the human race renewing man, throughout the world, to God. (*On Apostolic Preaching* 6)

Irenaeus assumes that the revelation given in the Scripture is inspired and therefore entirely consistent. The Scriptures teach that there is only one God who is revealed as Father, Son, and Holy Spirit. As the rule unfolds, each person is characterized with scriptural language depicting their economic activity within the narrative structure of salvation history. Irenaeus assumes that when the Scriptures are read as a whole, they align with these three points of doctrine and this theological standard becomes the basic confession and tradition of the church derived from Scripture.

Like Irenaeus, others, such as Tertullian (c. 155–240), Origen (c. 184–253), and Augustine (354–430), also articulate versions of the rule of faith. Together these Fathers show the breadth and commonality of the rule throughout the ancient Christian world. Eventually, the summaries of the rule of faith give way to the fullest expression of "tradition" in creedal statements such as the Nicene Creed (325 and 381) and the Definition of Chalcedon (451). More than any other confession, the Nicene Creed unifies the Christian tradition. Therefore, what began in the second century as a summary of the church's faith eventually blossomed into these formalized statements of the church's faith articulated at Nicaea and reaffirmed in all the ecumenical councils.

Case Study 4: Hippolytus, *On the Apostolic Tradition*

As a final case study on "tradition," it is worth examining how the church's faith was passed on through the process of discipleship, or what is known as catechesis. Hippolytus (c. 170–235) was the bishop of Rome in the third century and composed an important manual of church order titled *On the Apostolic Tradition*. This text is one of the earliest and most important witnesses to the life and practices of the early church. The text discusses how the church ought to appoint church leaders, administer the process of Christian initiation, perform baptisms, and administer the Eucharist, as well as the procedures for the church's worship and devotional life. The section on catechesis and baptism walks through the whole process of Christian initiation that takes a person from the first contact with the church to their baptism (*On the Apostolic Tradition* 15–21). Those who are interested in joining the church are examined for up to three years, and once they are ready for baptism, they enter a time of fasting and prayer (*On the Apostolic Tradition* 17).

In Hippolytus's manual, the act of baptism involves a triple immersion with questions and confessional statements preceding each one. These questions and answers demonstrate the personal commitment of the one receiving baptism and his or her dedication to the basic confessions of the church. The text describes how the one who is being baptized enters the water and is asked, "Do you believe in God the Father Almighty?" The one receiving baptism then replies, "I believe," and on his or her confession, they are baptized the first time. Then they are asked a second question: "Do you believe in Christ Jesus, the Son of God, who was born of the Holy Spirit and Mary the virgin and was crucified under Pontius Pilate and was dead [and buried] and rose on the third day alive from the dead and ascended into the heavens and sits at the right hand of the Father and will come to judge the living and the dead?" Again, the person receiving baptism professes, "I believe," and is immersed a second time. Finally, a third question is asked: "Do you believe in the Holy Spirit and the holy church and the resurrection of the flesh?" The one who receives baptism responds a third time, "I believe," and is baptized again. After they are baptized, they are welcomed into the course, where they join the whole community in taking the Eucharist for the first time.

This account of baptism seams together the church's rule of faith or confessional standards with the ordinance of baptism and the believer's entrance into the church. Baptism in the early church was not just about conversion but also confession. Baptism was not just a time to talk about an experience or conversation that happened in the past but a time to join with the community and publicly confess the faith. Before the new convert received baptism, they were instructed in the teachings of the Scripture, and then at baptism they made a public profession of each point of the rule of faith at baptism. The threefold confession and immersion also shows the close association between Scripture and tradition in the liturgical patterns of the early church.

For the Church

From the earliest days of the church, Scripture and tradition are the two sources that inform Christian faith and practice. Although the rest of the tradition would continue to debate the relationship of these sources, they were closely intertwined in the early church. It seems clear that Scripture holds the primary place of authority, but the Fathers would not think that tradition is entirely separate and distinct. As the church gathered the inspired Scriptures, they also studied them regularly and continued to clarify the basic apostolic teaching expressed in them. Due to their proximity to the apostolic period and the way heretical communities challenged the interpretation of the Scriptures, they saw a need for both Scripture and tradition to inform their faith and practice. Following are a few points of summary and reflection for the church today on the importance of Scripture and tradition in the early church.

The early church assumed the inspiration of Scripture. There is no doubt that the early fathers of the church believed that God had spoken through Christ and that Christ delivered his teaching to the apostles. From the earliest writings of the church, the church began gathering the apostolic writings and using them in Christian worship. When the Baptist Faith and Message (2000) states that the "Holy Bible was written by men divinely inspired" and that it "has God for its author, salvation for its end, and truth, without any mixture of error, for its matter," the early church would undoubtedly agree. This assumption reminds us that the inspiration of Scripture has been the normative testimony of the church from the earliest days.

The proper ordering of Scripture and tradition. Given that Scripture is inspired, the early church also assumed a close relationship between Scripture and tradition. This emphasis on both Scripture and tradition reminds pastors that any good theological method is always biblically grounded, historically informed, and oriented toward the clear presentation of the gospel. Since the Scriptures are inspired, they are the supreme written norm and standard for all matters of Christian faith and practice. They are also authoritative over any expression of tradition, including all creeds, councils, churches, and any other human institution or opinion. The Baptist Faith and Message (2000) affirms that Scripture is "the true center of Christian union, and the supreme standard by which all human conduct, creeds, and religious opinions should be tried." It is imperative that, like the early church, those who teach in the church ought to return again and again to the Scriptures as the source and norm for all matters of faith and practice.

The church should not neglect tradition. Although all Christian faith and practice is rooted in the Scriptures, the church must recognize the abiding value of the history of creeds and confessions. These theological expressions of tradition formulate the ways the church has expressed the faith once for all delivered to the saints (Jude 3). Good confessional statements arise out of a good reading of Scripture, and these expressions of tradition help guide the teaching and instruction in the Scriptures. The statements address the important theological issues and heresies that the church has faced and will face again. This is also why a statement of faith such as the Baptist Faith and Message (2000) is so important for presenting a unified confessional statement that can help guide the church's faith and practice.

The discussion of Scripture and tradition in the early church situates a conversation that will continue throughout the church history. Though there will be times that tradition attempts to subvert Scripture, in the early church the sources are much more intertwined. The Scriptures are given for the life and ministry of the church, and the faithful will dedicate themselves to the study of those inspired texts within the context of the apostolic tradition.

For Further Reading

Fairbairn, Donald, and Ryan Reeves. *The Story of Creeds and Confessions: Tracing the Development of the Christian Faith*. Grand Rapids: Baker Academic, 2019.

Ferguson, Everett. *Baptism in the Early Church: History, Theology, and Liturgy in the First Five Centuries of the Church*. Grand Rapids: Eerdmans, 2009.

Gallagher, Edmond L., and John D. Meade. *The Biblical Canon Lists from Early Christianity: Texts and Analysis*. Oxford: Oxford University Press, 2018.

Haykin, Michael A. G. *Rediscovering the Church Fathers: Who They Were and How They Shaped the Church*. Wheaton, IL: Crossway, 2011.

Heine, Ronald E. *Classical Christian Doctrine: Introducing the Essentials of the Ancient Faith*. Grand Rapids: Baker Academic, 2013.

———. *Reading the Old Testament with the Ancient Church: Exploring the Formation of Early Christian Thought*. Grand Rapids: Baker Academic, 2007.

Kelly, J. N. D. *Early Christian Creeds*. New York: Continuum, 1972.

———. *Early Christian Doctrines*. New York: HarperCollins, 1978.

Kruger, Michael J. *Canon Revisited: Establishing the Origins and Authority of the New Testament Books*. Wheaton, IL: Crossway, 2012.

———. *The Question of Canon: Challenging the Status Quo in the New Testament Debate*. Downers Grove, IL: IVP Academic, 2013.

Wegner, Paul D. *The Journey from Texts to Translations: The Origin and Development of the Bible*. Grand Rapids: Baker Academic, 1999.

Williams, Daniel H. *Evangelicals and Tradition: The Formative Influence of the Early Church*. Grand Rapids: Baker, 2005.

———. *Retrieving the Tradition and Renewing Evangelicalism: A Primer for Suspicious Protestants*. Grand Rapids: Eerdmans, 1999.

———. *Tradition, Scripture, and Interpretation: A Sourcebook of the Ancient Church*. Grand Rapids: Baker, 2006.

Yeago, David S. "The New Testament and the Nicene Dogma: A Contribution to the Recovery of Theological Exegesis," *Pro Ecclesia* 3, 1994, 152–64.

QUESTIONS FOR STUDY OR DISCUSSION

1. Explain the various internal and external pressures that shaped Christian discussions about Scripture and tradition.
2. How did the church recognize which texts were inspired and considered Scripture?
3. What is the "rule of faith," and how was this statement of tradition composed?
4. Describe how the *Muratorian Fragment* and Athanasius's *Letter 39* frame the discussion of canon in the early church.
5. Explain the relationship between baptism and confession in the early church.

4

SALVATION

By Coleman M. Ford

Introduction

In the early centuries of the church, the unique message of Jesus's person and work continued to spread through the known world around the Mediterranean, North Africa, and Asia. Whether in persecution or in triumph, the Christian declaration "Jesus is Lord" reached the ears of both the common and the elite. Throughout the period, early Christian writers dedicated much time and energy to explicating the good news through treatises, letters, sermons, and songs. Indeed, many early Christian thinkers were pastors who preached and taught with the purpose of encouraging the faithful and helping them understand and live in light of the salvation that Jesus Christ had accomplished.

The doctrine of salvation in the early church was forged in the fires of controversy and molded on the anvil of Scripture. Christians from the beginning declared the message of salvation found in Christ alone, yet errant views forced early theologians to clarify the unique nature and role of

Jesus Christ in salvation. In fact, the driving force of Christian responses to heretical teaching was maintaining the biblical message of salvation found in Christ alone. To misunderstand the person and work of Christ was to miss the richness of salvation promised in him. Error had eternal consequences. This chapter will focus on developments related to the doctrine of salvation, specifically the understanding of the person and work of Jesus Christ in the first centuries of the church.

Historical Overview

Christological Controversies

Christological error is as old as the New Testament. Paul warned the church in Galatia not to accept another gospel even if it were proclaimed by an angel (Gal 1:6–9). The apostle John charged the church not to accept those who deny that Christ has appeared in the flesh (1 John 4:1–3; 2 John 7). Just a few decades later, at the turn of the second century, Ignatius of Antioch (c. 39–c. 110) warned the church of similar errors. Writing seven letters to different churches on his way to his martyrdom in Rome, Ignatius exhorted his readers to accept only those who confessed that Jesus Christ is both God and from the line of David (*Ignatius to the Ephesians* 18.1–2). Jesus is God and man, born of a virgin yet also of God (*Ignatius to the Ephesians* 7.1–2). Furthermore, it was the work of the cross that secured salvation and eternal life for all those who believe in Christ (*Ignatius to the Ephesians* 18.1). The person and work of Jesus Christ and his relationship to salvation would be the crux of Christological conversation for the next four centuries.

The second century would also see the rise of Gnostic teachers within the church. Gnosticism is a term that encompasses a wide range of religious thought. Though diverse, the key characteristics of Gnostic thought included a radical duality between the spiritual and physical realms, a cosmology of numerous spiritual beings or "aeons" with different roles and attributes, and a spiritual-only (i.e., nonbodily) salvation secured through secret knowledge (Greek *Gnosis*—"knowledge"). Numerous teachers arose within the second century and infiltrated the church, including Marcion of Sinope (c. 85–c. 160) and Valentinus of Rome (c. 100–c. 160). Marcion constructed his own Bible that rejected the Old Testament, which was associated with a lower being responsible for creation, and presented a severely truncated New Testament free from any Jewish elements. Marcion's canon was comprised of portions of Luke and many Pauline epistles, yet these, too, were edited to fit his Gnostic presuppositions. Valentinus likely had a position of authority within the Roman church yet was excommunicated and began a rival church. Though it used quasi-biblical language and categories, Gnostic soteriology viewed Jesus as a bringer of knowledge, denying his status as God in the flesh and the efficacy of the cross. Indeed, in some Gnostic renderings, the Spirit of Christ departed from the man Jesus at the crucifixion or was replaced by another person altogether.

Irenaeus of Lyons (c. 130–c. 202) and Tertullian of Carthage (c. 155–c. 240) addressed these Gnostic errors in their various writings. Their main concern was not necessarily to correct false teaching (though they certainly had that in mind) but to present the biblical portrait of Jesus Christ and the redemptive work of the triune God. In his *Against Heresies*, Irenaeus catalogued various Gnostic teachings and presented Jesus Christ as the recapitulation of creation and the new Adam in which all of cosmic reality was being renewed. Irenaeus envisioned the triune God as the Creator who at all times had his Word and Wisdom (Son and Spirit) as the hands which created the world and enacted and secured salvation. Tertullian addressed the errors of Marcion in his *Against Marcion*, demonstrating how Marcion destroys the unity of God's being and adulterates the goodness of God as creator and sustainer of all things. There is no salvific power in Marcion's Jesus because Marcionite salvation is incomplete in that it excludes the creation and the body. Thus, salvation is forfeited because Marcion's god is impotent and ineffective. Tertullian and Irenaeus asserted the need to maintain the "rule of faith" (*regula fidei*), which was a summary of the apostolic testimony and served as a guidepost for understanding the redemptive story of the Bible and the profound work of salvation in Christ.

Another Christological error to arise at this time was Monarchianism, which took two different forms. Monarchianism (Greek *Monarchia*—"rule of one") prioritized the unity of God's being to the detriment of his personhood. Dynamic Monarchianism was the belief that Jesus Christ was adopted at his baptism and was assigned a special place of honor yet was not the preexistent Son who took on flesh. Modalistic Monarchianism asserted that Father, Son, and Spirit were merely different manifestations of the one being of God. Hence, there was no separate personhood of Father, Son, or Spirit. Tertullian addressed these views in his anti-heretical writings, as did Hippolytus of Rome (c. 170–c. 235), among others. These thinkers made the case that such views provided no assurance of salvation and disrupted the clear biblical picture of God's triune work of redemption. Not only did they distort God's being and deny his personhood, but they jeopardized the gospel message altogether. Salvation is not possible apart from the biblical portrait of God and the person and work of Jesus Christ.

Arianism and its theological offspring arose in the early fourth century and defined much of the Christological conversation for the period. Arius, a presbyter from Alexandria, proposed a way of understanding Christ as unique yet not eternal. Christ was begotten at some point in time, thus separating him in essence from the Father. The Council of Nicaea (325), called by Emperor Constantine, attempted to address and correct this error. Although there were numerous opponents to Arius, Athanasius of Alexandria (c. 296–373) is counted as the most ardent defender of Nicene theology. His mission was to explicate Arius's false biblical reasoning and uphold the necessity of Christ's humanity and divinity for man's salvation. With Arian teaching falling in and out of favor over the period of his life, Athanasius was exiled a total of five times for championing Nicene orthodoxy. Later fourth-century orthodox theologians would carry on Athanasius's legacy of defending Nicaea. The later errors of Apollonarianism, Nestorianism, and Eutcyhianism were variations on the same theme, seeking to uphold either the divinity or humanity of Christ to the detriment of the other. These errors would be addressed by various thinkers in the late fourth and early fifth century, resulting in the Councils of Constantinople (381), Ephesus (431), and Chalcedon (451).

For early Christian thinkers, controversy arose out of conviction. The Christological battles of the early centuries demonstrated that the church was serious about maintaining the biblical account of Jesus's person and work. Truly no salvation is possible if Jesus is not both God and man. Such false renderings also disrupted the triune nature of God and the harmonious activity of redemption within the Godhead. Church fathers recognized these errors and reasoned from Scripture, affirmed doctrine through conciliar gatherings, and faithfully preached orthodox theology to "contend for the faith that was delivered to the saints once for all" (Jude 3). Another important facet of soteriology in early Christianity was the place of the atonement and the remarkable work of Jesus Christ on the cross.

The Atonement

The atonement should not be minimized, yet it is a part of the larger fabric of salvation represented in patristic thinking. There was no singular way of understanding what took place on the cross. According to patristic thinkers, the atonement of Christ on the cross rendered a myriad of cosmological effects as part of the history of redemption.

The view that has come to be called *Christus victor* interprets the atonement as a cosmic victory over sin, death, and Satan. It depicts God triumphing over the enslavement of mankind to spiritual forces, and it was a dominant view in the church for the first 1,000 years. In one version of this view, Christ paid a ransom, following Mark 10:45, to the devil. At the cross, God delivered Christ over to Satan in exchange for the souls the evil one held captive. Satan could not, however, hold Christ permanently as he rose from the grave. Another version of this theory looks at Col 2:15 and God battling Satan. God triumphs over death and the devil once and for all, rescuing those held captive by the power of darkness. Cosmological transformation was a major facet of the atonement according to patristic thinkers. This cosmological component was related to the victory of Christ over sin. This is seen clearly in Irenaeus and his view of Christ's work and recapitulation, where the entire created order is transformed and renewed in the work of Christ. Maximus the Confessor (c. 580–662) spent considerable time reflecting on cosmological transformation represented by the atonement. Athanasius likewise recognized that the cross brought about the "healing of creation" (*Against the Heathen* 1.4).

Origen of Alexandria (d. 254) believed that as a consequence of sin, humanity was bound by Satan and captive to hell. In exchange for the souls in his captivity, Satan demanded the blood of Christ. God handed over Christ, and thus Satan released the imprisoned souls. Though Satan was deceived by Christ's humanity that veiled his deity, Satan took the bait, so to speak, of his humanity and was caught on the hook of his deity. Also, Satan discovered that Christ could not be held in hell, rising on the third day victorious over the grave. Though Origen exposited this peculiar ransom theory, it was suffused in biblical language and sought to explicate believers' new position in the kingdom of Christ based on Christ's work of redemption. Gregory of Nyssa (d. 394) used the same bait-and-hook image in describing the ransom of Christ. He envisioned sinners as bound in the prison of death by Satan. Like a ravenous fish, Satan gobbled up the hook of Christ's deity along with the bait of the flesh (*Great Catechism* 24). John of Damascus (d. 749) used the same imagery but asserted that it was not Satan but death itself. Death is destroyed, and captive sinners are liberated to life (*Orthodox Faith* 3.27).

Alongside the idea of ransom, writers in this era also demonstrated an understanding of the atonement that would later become known as the penal substitutionary view. *The Epistle to Diognetus*, written in the mid- to late second century, clearly espouses this view when he says, "He gave his own son as a ransom for us—the Holy for the wicked, the Sinless for sinners, the Just for the unjust, the Incorruptible for the corruptible, the Immortal for the mortal. For was there, indeed, anything except his righteousness that could have availed to cover our sins? In whom could we, in our lawlessness and ungodliness, have been made holy, but in the Son of God alone? O sweet exchange!" (*Epistle to Diognetus* 9.2–5). Similarly, Irenaeus speaks of Christ's propitiatory work and his victory over death on the cross. He states, "He propitiated the Father against whom we had sinned for us and cancel[ed] our disobedience by his own obedience" (*Against Heresies* 5.17.1). Regarding the victory of Christ, he also states, "In his work of recapitulation, Christ has summed up all things, waging war against our enemy and crushing him who at the beginning led us away captive in Adam, and trampling on his head" (*Against Heresies* 5.20.2).

Differences between East and West

Though Christian writers in the early centuries remained consistent on core doctrines of orthodoxy, there arose different ways of understanding salvation and how it is applied to mankind and the created order. The person and work of Jesus Christ was central to salvation in Eastern and Western theologies, but there were key differences in the way salvation was expressed and how the person and work of Jesus Christ should be applied. In the East, salvation was often expressed in terms of deification, while Western theology tended to emphasize the atonement and forgiveness of sin as the central aspect of salvation.

Deification (Greek *theosis*) increasingly dominated discussions of salvation among Eastern thinkers, though aspects of deification were present in many thinkers, both Greek and Latin. Eastern thought, particularly from the fourth century onward, tended to emphasize this more due to its tendency to view corruption and death as the main consequences of the fall. Additionally, Alexandrian theologians such as Origen, Clement, and Athanasius emphasized the participatory nature of salvation. Athanasius asserted, in fighting against Arian Christology, that Christ became like us so that we would become like him. Put in other words, he participated in our humanity so that we might participate in his divinity. This was the benefit of salvation. Based on their reading of Origen and their desire to promote the thought of Athanasius, the Cappadocians also drew attention to *theosis* in their writings.

Another Eastern notion relating to salvation was a tendency to affirm some facet of universal salvation. Origen seems to be the first to introduce the idea of *apokatastasis* ("restitution, restoration"), or that all would be saved in the end. This was never a strong emphasis in his theology, and he felt that there were practical reasons for not promoting it among believers, especially new converts, lest they fall into moral laxity. The notion of universal salvation also found its way into Gregory Nyssa's thoughts, thanks largely to his close reading of Origen. Though Origen's writings would later be condemned on these points, Gregory's would not. Other thinkers, such as Maximus the Confessor, also seemed to leave open the possibility that all would be saved in the end.

In the Latin West, aspects of substitutionary sacrifice and suffering were more prevalent within soteriology. In his combat against the Gnostic teacher Marcion, Tertullian focused on the suffering of Christ for our salvation: "[According to Marcion] Christ suffered nothing who did not truly suffer; and a phantom could not truly suffer. God's entire work, therefore, is subverted. Christ's death . . . is denied although [Paul] asserts it so expressly as . . . the very foundation of the gospel . . . [saying] that Christ died for our sins" (*Against Marcion* 3.8; cf. 1 Cor 15:4). Hilary of Poitiers (c. 310–367) emphasized the redeeming work of Christ as a victory and a substitution for us: "While God, according to the Scriptures, is to die, he would triumph with the confidence in himself of a conqueror. While he, the immortal One, would not be overcome by death, he would die for the eternal life of us mortals" (*On the Trinity* 1.13).

Ambrose of Milan (c. 337–397) similarly noted the sacrifice of Christ, focusing on his death as the price of redemption: "Can he damn you, whom he has redeemed from death for whom he offered himself, whose life he knows is the reward of his own death?" (*Jacob and the Blessed Life* 1.6.26).

Augustine tied many of these thoughts together in his theology, focusing on certain facets of Christ's person and work. Christ served as a mediator between God and man to bring peace by his sacrifice. The mediator must be both God and man, "[for] we would not be freed even by the one mediator between God and man himself, the man Christ Jesus, if he were not also God" (*Enchiridion* 28.108). Augustine also focused on the substitutionary work of Christ to appease the wrath of God and reconcile mankind back to him. Augustine asserted, "For our sakes the Lord paid this one death which he did not owe in order that the death we do owe might do us no harm" (*On the Trinity* 4.13, 17).

Spirituality

The ways salvation was understood by early thinkers was deeply spiritual and experiential. The early church focused on baptism and the Eucharist (the Lord's Supper) as the means of entrance to the faith and spiritual growth. Baptism identified one with the salvation of Christ, while the Eucharist was part of the ongoing participation and remembrance of the work of Christ for our salvation. Although debates remain as to how and to what degree early Christians perceived the presence of Christ within the Eucharist, nevertheless a sacramental spirituality can be discerned in much of early Christian thinking. Ignatius of Antioch encouraged his readers to take the "medicine of immortality," that is the Lord's Supper, as a sign of unity around the confession of Christ. The mutual confession of Christ and his salvific work unified believers for the purpose of enduring persecution and false teachers. Just a few years after Ignatius, Justin Martyr recalled details on the Lord's Supper in his first apologetic treatise:

> For not as common bread and common drink do we receive these; but in like manner as Jesus Christ our Saviour, having been made flesh by the Word of God, had both flesh and blood for our salvation, so likewise have we been taught that the food which is blessed

> by the prayer of His word, and from which our blood and flesh by transmutation are nourished, is the flesh and blood of that Jesus who was made flesh. (*First Apology* 66)

Sometime later in the fourth century, in his *Catechetical Lectures*, Cyril of Jerusalem (c. 313–386) encouraged the newly baptized to consider all the senses when partaking of the eucharistic meal: "And while the moisture is still upon your lips, touch it with your hands, and hallow your eyes and brow and the other organs of sense. Then wait for the prayer, and give thanks unto God, who has accounted you worthy of so great mysteries" (*Catechetical Lectures* 23.22).

Imitation of Christ and his passion became a major spiritual theme from the earliest years of the Christian faith. This was especially true in seasons of persecution. Ignatius of Antioch consciously inhabited the sacrificial characteristics of Christ as he wrote his epistle to the Romans on his way to be martyred there. Ignatius was likely being sent to Rome for the gladiatorial "warm-up" events where Christians and other social outcasts were often executed. He saw it as God's sovereign plan to have him identify with his Savior: "Neither the ends of the earth nor the kingdoms of this age will be of benefit to me. It is better for me to die in Christ Jesus than to reign over the ends of the earth. I seek that one who died on my behalf. I desire that one who rose up on our account" (*Ignatius to the Romans* 6.1). A similar theme is found in the *Passion of Perpetua and Felicitas*, written in the early third century. This narrative recounts the martyrdoms of a noblewoman named Perpetua and a pregnant servant named Felicitas in Carthage. These women displayed enormous courage in the face of death as witnesses for Christ because of their assurance of what Christ did on their behalf. Imitation of Christ remained a theme in early Christianity even after waves of persecution subsided. Such imitation calls were connected to the salvation secured by Christ, and thus seen as a way to identify more closely with Christ and his passion.

Preaching in the early church reinforced the person and work of Christ and called hearers to faithfulness and action. Melito of Sardis (d. c. 180) vividly portrayed the work of Christ on the cross in a homily titled *Peri Pascha* ("On the Passover"). Expounding Exodus 12, Christ is typologically figured as the Passover lamb, and Melito extols hearers to hear Christ telling them, "I am the lamb slaughtered for you, I am your ransom, I am your life, I am your light, I am your salvation, I am your resurrection, I am your King. I shall raise you up by my right hand, I will lead you to the heights of heaven, there shall I show you the everlasting father" (*Peri Pascha* §103). This rhetorical move sought to connect the realities of Christ and his atoning work to the hearts of his hearers and stir them toward worship. Recalling to mind the work of Christ was a central theme in homiletic literature throughout the early centuries of the church. Fathers such as John Chrysostom, Basil of Caesarea, and Augustine of Hippo were known for their preaching and drawing the attention of their hearers to the person and work of Christ. Both in reminding hearers of Christ's atoning work and calling them to imitate Christ, early Christian preaching fortified the spiritual life of believers.

Case Studies

Case Study 1: Irenaeus and Gnosticism

Irenaeus of Lyons addressed numerous areas of Gnostic thought, including the Gnostics' erroneous view of salvation in light of biblical truth. Because Gnosticism was a tendency more than an organized movement, it is difficult to pinpoint exact Gnostic "doctrine." Overall, there was a bent toward elevating the spiritual over the material in that material represented evil and spiritual represented the good. This Gnostic tendency, especially as it was mixed with Christianity, produced a belief in two separate gods of the Bible. The Old Testament god was a corrupt being who tyrannized humanity. The god of the New Testament was a loving father who sent his son to save mankind from the evil, Old Testament god, often called the *demiurge*. The Gnostic tendency also elevated esoteric knowledge of salvation delivered to a few rather than a clear message of salvation delivered to all. Because of this, there was a tendency to elevate select New Testament writings over those of the Old Testament, as evidenced by Marcion and his canon of scriptures. In his *Against Heresies*, Irenaeus provided not only a thorough defense against Gnosticism, but a winsome defense of the Christian message of salvation.

Irenaeus's defense against Gnostic soteriology was twofold. First, Irenaeus sought to debunk the authority of Gnostic teaching and Gnostic texts. Gnostic texts were a hodgepodge of spiritualistic sayings, with some Christian bits mixed in. Gnostics provided a web of supposed proof texts from Scripture to back up their assertions, yet such an exercise destroyed the "beautiful image of the king" and produced a distorted image of "a dog or of a fox" (*Against Heresies* 1.8.1). Their cosmology was nonsensical and could not be substantiated by the biblical text, however much they tried. That said, Gnostic teaching was attractive because it provided a simplistic explanation for the existence of evil. Additionally, it gave adherents a plausible way out of suffering, since it proposed Christ himself (as a noncorporeal spiritual being) did not suffer on the cross. Such teachings attracted many, especially in times of uncertainty and persecution. Nevertheless, Gnostics could not provide a logical defense for their beliefs, nor could their beliefs hold up under the weight of a full reading of Scripture. Irenaeus was prolific in his use of Scripture in his *Against Heresies*, providing 629 citations from the Old Testament and 1,065 from the New Testament. His biblical defense was buttressed by his insistence on the *regula fidei*, which was a summary of the apostolic message of salvation in Christ alone. This summary of the gospel message was the key that unlocked the vault containing all the treasures of the Bible, and it was a key the Gnostics did not possess, due to their flawed and self-serving reading of Scripture.

Second, Irenaeus demonstrated how Gnostic modes of salvation did not comport with the clear gospel message presented in Scripture. Gnostics asserted that secret knowledge, given to a select few, was the means of salvation. The gospel, in contrast, was an unambiguous message of salvation for all. Additionally, this message of salvation included an incarnated Savior (contrary to Gnostic anticorporeal assertions) who, as the second Adam, came to redeem fallen humanity under the first Adam. At the center of this redemptive plan was the triune God who is perfect, eternal, and all-powerful, and who created all things. Thus, salvation was centered on a Person and not on esoteric knowledge. By denying Jesus's incarnation, Gnostics denied the very essence of salvation. The Bible tells one story of salvation, and the main character is Jesus. By distorting that story and importing nonbiblical gibberish, Gnostics provided no hope of true salvation.

Irenaeus wrote *Against Heresies* not only to defend against the faulty claims of Gnosticism but to provide a robust biblical theology of redemption. Gaining extensive firsthand knowledge of Gnostic teaching, likely while visiting Rome, allowed him to speak authoritatively and respond accurately. His defense of the unity of Scripture was also a defense for the redemptive message of the gospel. According to Irenaeus, God is a coherent unity and, out of love and mercy, sought to rescue humanity from the grips of sin and death by sending his Son in the flesh as the new Adam to accomplish what the first Adam could not. Though there is debate as to whether or not Irenaeus was martyred at the turn of the third century, the legacy he left the church in defending the message of salvation in Christ alone against pernicious nonbiblical teaching is undeniable.

Case Study 2: Athanasius and Arianism

In the early fourth century, a presbyter from Egypt named Arius began teaching that Jesus was a created being rather than the coeternal Son of God. A controversy ensued, culminating in the first ecumenical council at Nicaea in 325, convened by Emperor Constantine. Arius's theology was condemned and a creed was issued asserting the Son's full divinity and eternal unity and equality with the Father. Present at the council was the deacon Athanasius from Alexandria, the same region where Arius resided. Some years after Nicaea, Athanasius wrote against Arian theology and its followers. "Now He is Son from the Father; therefore He will not become other than is proper to the Father's essence" (*Against the Arians* 1.6.22). The life of Athanasius was filled with seasons of exile based on the pervasiveness of Arian thought within the Roman Empire, including various Roman emperors. Athanasius demonstrated tenacious pastoral leadership against all odds. Thus, he was given the Latin surname *contra mundum* ("against the world").

Athanasius's main argument against Arianism was their forfeit of salvation based on a faulty Christology. Athanasius was primarily concerned with the message of the gospel: if the Son was merely a creature, how could he have accomplished everything necessary for salvation? He asserted: "If the Word were a creature, how could he have power to undo God's judgment and to forgive sin, since . . . this is God's prerogative only?" (*Against the Arians* 2.67). Defending Nicaea, he vigorously affirmed that the Son is of the same essence (Greek *homoousias*) yet distinct in personhood. He emphasized that the unity of nature did not make the Father and Son the same, thus avoiding modalism. Athanasius also affirmed the substitutionary work of Christ: "The sacrifice on behalf of all, surrendering his own body to death in place of all, to settle man's account with death and free him from the primal transgression" (*On the Incarnation* 20.3). Only a Savior who was both God and man could make such a reckoning possible. In fact, the incarnation is proof of mankind's need for, and God's ability to provide, salvation.

In his perennial classic, *On the Incarnation*, Athanasius focused on the gracious intent of God to save mankind through the incarnation of the Son. Salvation was an initiation of love according to Athanasius: "[For] by the love for mankind and goodness of his own Father he appeared to us in a human body for our salvation" (*On the Incarnation* 1). To demonstrate the profundity of the incarnation, Athanasius coined a now familiar phrase: "He became human that we might become divine" (*On the Incarnation* 54). It was not merely Christ's incarnation that made salvation possible, but the entire incarnated life of Christ, culminating in the cross and resurrection.

Though the title of this work might lead some to think Athanasius was concerned only about one facet of Christ's work, Athanasius was concerned with integrating all facets of Christ's life and work into his theology.

Athanasius was exiled five times throughout his life for his ongoing defense of Nicene orthodoxy. The view that he defended, summarized in the Nicene Creed, represented the full biblical deposit of truth regarding the person and work of Jesus Christ. Though Arius and his followers claimed to read Scripture correctly, they missed the simple mystery of Christ and his gospel and all its theological implications. If Jesus is not fully God and fully man, then he cannot fully redeem mankind. Defending the message of salvation was an exercise in whole-Bible reading, with the priority of the apostolic gospel message as its foundation. Hence, Athanasius has long been recognized as one of the greatest Christian thinkers of the early church. His doctrinal influence was evidenced by those who came after him to uphold and defend Nicene orthodoxy. He focused his theological writings on the salvific significance of Jesus Christ's person and work. Dying in 373, Athanasius left a theological legacy that continued into the work of later fourth- and early fifth-century theologians and church councils.

Case Study 3: Augustine and Pelagianism

Around the year 380, the British-born Pelagius arrived at Rome, likely to study law. Toward the end of the century, he had dedicated himself as a monk and was writing numerous theological treatises and letters. While in Rome, Pelagius found himself distraught by the moral laxity of Christians he encountered there. Soon after, he entered the theological picture by questioning Augustine's doctrine of the universality of sin, the bondage of the will, and predestination, as presented in Augustine's work *Ad Simplicianum.* For Pelagius, God could not intervene on human freedom, nor could he command what is impossible or condemn the unavoidable. Upon reading the *Confessions* in the early 400s, Pelagius strongly objected to Augustine's description of man's need for grace, specifically upset by the line "Give what you command, and command what you will" (*Confessions* 10.31.45). He would go on to provide his rendering of man's condition in his treatise *On Nature*, written in 406. Pelagius and Augustine affirmed human freedom and grace, yet they differed on the meaning of these terms. Grace for Pelagius related to God granting the proper conditions for right action. These included natural freedom, the law, the example of Christ, enlightenment through baptism, and the gifts of the Holy Spirit to those who earnestly pursue purity. For Pelagius, human nature retained a permanent capacity for sinlessness, which in turn influenced will and action. He conceded that voluntary action might not match human nature, attributing sinful behavior to forgetfulness or some sort of personal bondage to carnal living inflicted on oneself.

Augustine asserted that Pelagius's theology jeopardized the entire Christian message of salvation. Through his reading of Paul, Augustine reasoned that all have been born in sin because all have been born in Adam; thus all are culpable apart from rebirth in Christ. Grace was not merely an aid to choosing what was good, but essential for being brought to life. He produced numerous other treatises, letters, and sermons dealing with Pelagian teachings and those who acted as "the enemies of the grace of God" (*On the Predestination of the Saints* 2.2.4). Augustine implored the Pelagians to see that Christ came as a physician, as savior, and as the redeemer of mankind. Christ's death was more than an example; it was a necessary sacrifice for our sin and our salvation. Augustine compiled a string of biblical texts on Jesus Christ as redeemer and our subsequent participation through baptism in the salvation and redemption he accomplished.

Augustine affirmed man's free will as a gift of God, but this side of the fall it was a will that was in bondage to sin. Among other texts, he leaned on Ps 143:2 and 1 John 1:8 in this regard. Augustine asserted that our renewal in the Spirit is gradual, beginning at our baptism, but grows each day until we attain complete redemption at the resurrection of our bodies. It is the Spirit for Augustine, reflecting on Rom 5:5, which demonstrates that we have the love of God that was secured by Christ on our behalf. Pelagian theology asserted that man's salvation lay ultimately within his own grasp. According to Augustine, specifically laid out in his *On the Spirit and the Letter*, God's grace grants the will and the power to do God's will. In the same treatise, Augustine appealed to Rom 6:3–11 that salvation and healing was revealed in the suffering and resurrection of Christ: "Now it is plain enough that here by the mystery of the Lord's death and resurrection is figured the death of our old sinful life, and the rising of the new; and that here is shown forth the abolition of iniquity and the renewal of righteousness. Whence then arises this vast benefit to man through the letter of the law, except it be through the faith of Jesus Christ?" (*On the Spirit and the Letter* 6.10). For Augustine, salvation was found by faith in the person and work of Jesus, not in following the law.

Case Study 4: Cyril and Nestorianism

Cyril of Alexandria (c. 376–444) was a significant theological voice in the fifth century, specifically regarding the Christological error of Nestorianism. Appointed bishop of Alexandria in 412, he impacted not only the theological conclusions at the Council of Ephesus (431), at which he was present, but also the statements rendered at the Council of Chalcedon (451). His consistent theological reasoning on the two natures of Christ would solidify the biblically orthodox teaching on the person and work of Jesus Christ. Responding to the views of Nestorius, who was bishop of Constantinople from 428–431, Cyril insisted on the theological accuracy of the title *Theotokos* ("Mother of God") assigned to Mary, the mother of Jesus. Nestorius had supposedly refused to affirm this title because of its implications that the divine nature had a point of origin rather than an eternal existence. Cyril's insistence on the use of *Theotokos*, which had been in use since the third century, was linked to the affirmation of the human and divine natures of Christ. Mary did not birth God in the sense that he came into being, but she is *Theotokos* because she was the mother of God incarnated for our salvation.

Cyril emphasized the true union of human and divine in the person of Jesus Christ. He was truly God and truly man. Both natures were present, not mixed together as to become indistinguishable, nor was one nature overtaken by another. Cyril's thought on the matter is found in his *Letter 17*, wherein he condemned various points related to faulty Christology put forward by Nestorius. This letter included several anathemas, or negative statements, that did not coincide with the orthodox understanding of Christ as both God and man. To affirm these would put someone outside the biblical understanding of the person and work of Christ. The following statements shed light on the crux of the argument according to Cyril:

1. If anyone does not confess that the Emmanuel is very God, and that therefore the Holy Virgin is the Mother of God, inasmuch as in the flesh she bore the Word of God made flesh: let him be anathema.
2. If anyone shall not confess that the Word of God the Father is united hypostatically to flesh, and that with that flesh of his own, he is one only Christ both God and man at the same time: let him be anathema.
3. If anyone shall say that Jesus as man is only energized by the Word of God, and that the glory of the only-begotten is attributed to him as something not properly his: let him be anathema.
4. Whosoever shall not recognize that the Word of God suffered in the flesh, that he was crucified in the flesh, and that likewise in that same flesh he tasted death and that he is become the first-begotten of the dead, for, as he is God, he is the life, and it is he that giveth life: let him be anathema.

At the heart of these anathemas was the confession that Jesus Christ is truly God and truly man and, as such, is the only one capable to ensure the salvation of mankind. For Cyril, there are significant consequences for affirming anything except the two natures of Christ. If Christ is not divine, he is unable to secure salvation in any real sense. If Christ is not human, humanity is unable to attain the redemption it needs.

Cyril's thought took center stage at the Council of Ephesus, and it would have a significant impact at the Council of Chalcedon, less than a decade after his death. Many scholars have noted the ferocity with which Cyril engaged his theological opponents. He worked to garner allies in his cause and was seemingly merciless in his attacks against error. Though there might be cause to assess his methods critically, his certainty in affirming the biblical portrait of Christ's person and work was unwavering. Indeed, Cyril had inherited the Christological convictions of his predecessor Athanasius in asserting that salvation is possible only because the eternal Son accommodated himself to human life.

For the Church

The centrality of Jesus Christ in salvation. The person and work of Jesus Christ is the key to unlocking the treasures of salvation. The early church defended the doctrine of Christ so vigorously because the gospel and salvation itself was at stake. Only a Savior who is truly God and truly man can secure man's salvation. From the earliest post–New Testament writers, the centrality of Jesus as both God and man was nonnegotiable.

In its statement on "God the Son," The Baptist Faith and Message (2000) faithfully transmits what early Christian thinkers concluded regarding the person and work of Christ:

> Christ is the eternal Son of God. In His incarnation as Jesus Christ He was conceived of the Holy Spirit and born of the virgin Mary. Jesus perfectly revealed and did the will of God, taking upon Himself human nature with its demands and necessities and identifying Himself completely with mankind yet without sin. He honored the divine law by His personal obedience, and in

> His substitutionary death on the cross He made provision for the redemption of men from sin.

According to the early church, there is no salvation apart from Christ taking on human nature. As the eternal Son of God, he redeemed and sanctified our human nature so that we might participate in the divine nature (cf. 2 Pet 1:4). The incarnation included the totality of Jesus's life, substitutionary death, and resurrection. The "Word became flesh" on our behalf to rescue and redeem us from sin and death (cf. John 1:14). All throughout Scripture, early Christian thinkers saw the centrality of Christ and his work. The only true biblical portrayal of salvation is man's spiritual inability to bring about salvation and our utter dependence on Jesus and his faithful obedience in becoming man for our sake.

The necessity for clear doctrinal formulation. This chapter has included numerous thinkers and their doctrinal positions, as well as discussions on councils that met to solidify orthodox doctrine. The pursuit of clear doctrinal formulation is necessary not only to combat error but to bolster our faith. Ambiguity disrupts faith; clarity fortifies it. This does not mean we fully understand God's nature and every detail of his redemptive work, but for the sake of the church, it matters greatly that we provide clear and meaningful language. This affects everything from teaching to worship to evangelism to one-on-one discipleship. Though salvation is secured by Christ and applied by the Spirit, the church has a responsibility to communicate clear and compelling doctrine about salvation and the person and work of Jesus. Again, The Baptist Faith and Message (2000) provides a helpful example of a clear doctrinal statement on salvation found in Christ alone:

> Salvation involves the redemption of the whole man, and is offered freely to all who accept Jesus Christ as Lord and Saviour, who by His own blood obtained eternal redemption for the believer. In its broadest sense salvation includes regeneration, justification, sanctification, and glorification. There is no salvation apart from personal faith in Jesus Christ as Lord.

When the church neglects its responsibility to communicate clearly and with conviction, the people of God inevitably suffer. Without consistent doctrinal guidance, in accordance with the orthodox commitment to the person and work of Jesus Christ, the church will eventually succumb to cultural whims and non-Christian philosophies. This has surely happened within mainline denominations, yet evangelical churches are not immune. In a relativistic and consumeristic culture, the need for certainty and clarity has never been more urgent. This does not require innovation in doctrinal formulation—for that is exactly what early Christians combated—but adherence to time-tested and biblically faithful confessions of faith applied to the needs and questions of our day.

The mystery of salvation leading to worship. Leo the Great (c. 400–461), bishop of Rome in the fifth century, declared that Christianity is "a religion founded on the mystery of the cross of Christ" (*Sermon* 82.6). Though the person and work of Jesus Christ was the crux of salvation, it remained a mysterious event. The only proper response to mystery is awe and worship. Theology is not a dry activity but a vibrant and transformative pursuit leading to true worship of the triune God. Thus, while salvation has numerous objective biblical components, its end result is humility and worship from the believer. The salvation secured by Jesus Christ is an extraordinary and awesome event, in the fullest meaning of those terms. How can we who have been saved by grace through faith not marvel in wonder at our Savior and the redemptive plan of God? Reflection on our salvation should always lead to worship. On considering the grace of God in salvation, The Baptist Faith and Message (2000) provides helpful clarity on this point:

> Election is the gracious purpose of God, according to which He regenerates, justifies, sanctifies, and glorifies sinners. It is consistent with the free agency of man, and comprehends all the means in connection with the end. It is the glorious display of God's sovereign goodness, and is infinitely wise, holy, and unchangeable. It excludes boasting and promotes humility.

Everything about salvation is meant to focus our attention and hearts on the triune God. Any boasting, as Paul reminds us, is antithetical to a proper understanding of salvation (cf. Gal 6:14; Eph 2:9–10). Humility can be our only response. Early Christian writers who defended the person and work of Christ held this as a central tenet: any notion of salvation that terminates on man's ability ultimately leads to pride. Church fathers such as Basil of Caesarea and Augustine of Hippo, among others, noted how humility was the chief virtue among Christians. Humility was the proper response to seeing the beauty of Christ and experiencing the redeeming love of God. True worship arises only when one recognizes just how lost they are apart from the grace of God in Christ.

For Further Reading

Athanasius of Alexandria. *On the Incarnation*. Yonkers, NY: St. Vladimir's Seminary Press, 2012.

Augustine of Hippo. *Answer to the Pelagians* I–IV. Hyde Park, NY: New City Press, 1998.

———. *Confessions*. Translated by Henry Chadwick. Oxford: Oxford University Press, 2009.

Aulén, Gustaf. *Christus Victor: An Historical Study of the Three Main Types of the Idea of Atonement*. Translated by A. G. Herbert. London: SPCK, 1931.

Christensen, Michael J., and Jeffery A. Wittung, eds. *Partakers of the Divine Nature: The History and Development of Deification in the Christian Traditions*. Grand Rapids: Baker Academic, 2008.

Cyril of Alexandria. *On the Unity of Christ*. Edited by John Anthony McGuckin. Crestwood, NY: St. Vladimir's Seminary Press, 2015.

Fairbairn, Donald. *Life in the Trinity: An Introduction to Theology with the Help of the Church Fathers*. Downers Grove, IL: IVP Academic, 2009.

Hall, Christopher A. *Learning Theology with the Church Fathers*. Downers Grove, IL: IVP Academic, 2002.

Kelly, J. N. D. *Early Christian Doctrines*, rev. ed. New York: HarperCollins, 1978.

Melito of Sardis. *On Pascha: With the Fragments of Melito and Other Material Related to the Quartodecimans*. Translated by Alistair C. Stewart. 2nd ed. Yonkers, NY: St. Vladimir's Seminary Press, 2017.

Norris, Richard A., ed. *The Christological Controversy, Sources of Early Christian Thought*. Minneapolis: Fortress, 1980.

Payton, James R., Jr. *Irenaeus on the Christian Faith: A Condensation of Against Heresies*. Eugene, OR: Wipf and Stock, 2011.

Pelikan, Jaroslav. *The Christian Tradition: A History of the Development of Doctrine, Vol. 1: The Emergence of the Catholic Tradition* (100–600). Chicago: University of Chicago Press, 1975.

Wilken, Robert Louis. *The Spirit of Early Christian Thought: Seeking the Face of God*. New Haven, CT: Yale University Press, 2005.

Questions for Study or Discussion

1. How did the various Christological controversies relate to salvation? What were the key issues at stake?
2. What are the main facets of the atonement according to early Christian thinkers? Who are some of the main voices?
3. How did Athanasius conceive of the incarnation? Why was the incarnation necessary for salvation?
4. What areas concerned Augustine most about Pelagius's thinking? In what ways does Pelagian theology persist today?
5. How can evangelicals continue to honor what early Christian thinkers achieved in regard to understanding salvation?

UNIT TWO

THEOLOGY IN THE MEDIEVAL ERA, AD 500–1500

5

THE CHURCH

By Zachary M. Bowden

Introduction

The church was a pervasive presence in the world of the Middle Ages, expansive in its reach. Today when we think of the doctrine of the church, we tend to focus on her people and practices: preaching, the sacraments, as well as her officers and members. To be sure, the church of the Middle Ages saw robust development in each of those areas. Nevertheless, it never saw itself as restricted to the walls of a given cathedral, nor even one's respective city. The church itself was a political and culture-shaping enterprise. Failing to see how entangled the church was throughout society is a failure to understand the church during the Middle Ages.

As many historians have lamented, dating the Middle Ages is an arbitrary affair. Even so, this chapter will follow the well-worn path of breaking down this remarkable era into three parts: early (500–1000), high (1000–1300), and late (1300–1500). Each period has its own unique aspects, due in part to the political context of the church during that time, theological controversy or schism, or the development of that most important of medieval institutions, the papacy. Arguably what unites the Middle Ages is the church. In a very true sense, one could summarize this time between the times as a striving to answer the question again and again, "What is the church?"

Historical Overview

The Early Middle Ages (500–1000)

Going into the Middle Ages, the church knew who she was. "One holy, catholic, apostolic church" had been the creedal mantra of Christians as they prepared for the baptismal waters for some time. Enduring persecution at the hands of Nero, Decius, and Diocletian, the church grew. Under Constantine, her fortunes changed dramatically. Now with imperial support, the church was lavished with beautiful buildings. Her bishops were elevated to positions of civic authority. And the emperor himself had a vested interest in ecclesiastical affairs. After Constantine, the church and the empire would be wed. One could not think of one without the other.

Growing up in the Roman Empire, church structure adapted to its context. Congregations formed around cities. According to Ignatius of Antioch (d. 108), church leadership was threefold: bishop, presbyter, and deacon. Although not consistent throughout the empire, this was the model for the time, with the bishop simply being one among equals. Eventually, by the end of the second century, the bishop rose to prominence as the leader of a city's congregation. And the more historic the city, the more powerful the bishop. The five most powerful were Alexandria, Antioch, Constantinople, Jerusalem, and Rome.

Inheriting the rule of faith (*regula fidei*) and the Scriptures, the church knew what she believed. Throughout the fourth and fifth centuries, that belief would be tested as the church strained to articulate the person of God and, in particular, the relationship between the Father and Son. Her worship indicated the Son's eternality. After all, candidates for baptism, or catechumens, were likely trained in the *Apostle's Creed* or rule of faith, ensuring they understood the name into which they were being baptized: Father, Son, and Holy Spirit.

The language of "person," "same substance," "nature," "three in one," and "one in three" came from the church coming together in ecclesiastical and political affairs known as "church councils." Called by the emperor himself, these gatherings served as deliberative bodies providing what became recognized as authoritative pronouncements on the doctrine of the church. Thus, the church not only had bishops, presbyters, and deacons to look to for guidance, but also creedal statements approved by councils, which were gatherings of bishops from across the empire, sanctioned by the emperor, with the aim of fostering ecclesial and political unity.

During the fourth and fifth centuries, the church's understanding of her nature and mission continued to develop. Much of that is due to the work of the bishop of Hippo, Augustine (354–430). Indeed, much of the Middle Ages, at least for the West, is a reckoning with his legacy, much of which was formed through controversy. One momentous dispute was with a group known as the Donatists, a dominant force in North Africa during Augustine's ministry. Fundamentally, the controversy concerned the nature of the church—particularly her purity. This was not a new concern for the church. From the pages of the New Testament, she was always concerned about her holiness. Yet new questions arose, especially during times of imperial persecution.

Some pastors, under the pain of persecution, gave up the Scriptures and other churchly books to the empire. They were thus marked as *traditores*—as "those who handed over," or traitors. It was found out that one of these traitors was involved in the ordination of another pastor, Caecilian, in 311. Was that act valid given the ordaining bishop's traitorous actions? No, answered the Donatists. As far as they were concerned, the efficacy of the church's sacraments, baptism, and the Eucharist depended on the moral standing of the one performing the work.

Augustine disagreed. The sacraments' efficacy was not based on the moral standing of the minister, precisely because the sacraments did not belong to him. They belonged to Christ. Because of that, the sacraments' efficacy was based on the work itself, not the worker. Behind this dispute on the validity of the sacraments stood two different conceptions of the church. For the Donatists, their communion was the true church, for it was the *pure* church. To maintain that purity, they separated from the Catholic Church that Augustine represented.

For Augustine, following the thought of Cyprian, such an act was unthinkable. The church was for the sick, not the healthy, after all. Arguing from Jesus's parable of the wheat and the tares in Matthew 13, Augustine contended that the church was a "mixed body," made up of saints and sinners. Moreover, as the Scriptures and the creed attested, the church was one. Schism was unacceptable. Preaching through 1 John, Augustine believed the Donatists' actions were tantamount to actions of the Antichrist. Thus, winning the day, both through argument and force, mixed bodies made up the majority of churches in the Middle Ages.

The Donatist controversy was so fierce precisely because it was understood that salvation was found only within the church. Yet what was the nature of that salvation? Such was the question that animated yet another controversy for the bishop of Hippo, this time with a moralist from Britain named Pelagius (c. 354–418). For his part, Pelagius's concern was that Augustine's understanding of the will as ruined by the fall of man in Genesis 3 would inevitably give way to licentiousness. Additionally, he thought it was absurd for God to knowingly command of his creatures what he knew they could not do. Augustine, however, believed that this was precisely the purpose of grace. Because the will has been ruined by sin, only grace can redeem man. Ultimately, the echoes of this controversy persisted, leading to the Council of Orange in 529, which condemned the teachings of Pelagius. In so doing, it clearly connected baptism as the sole means by which the will was to be repaired, with infant baptism already having been an established practice in the church, even though adult baptism had been the predominant form in the early church.

Yet Augustine's battle with Pelagius also helps make sense of Innocent I (c. 401–417), the bishop of Rome, and his self-perceived growth of authority. Augustine sent a copy of one of Pelagius's works to Innocent, simply looking for comment. Innocent, however, interpreted the act as a request for an official pronouncement from the apostle Peter's successor. Such a reaction from Rome illustrates how the Roman bishop's strength grew over time. The great city always had some measure of preeminence because it was the site of Peter's and Paul's deaths. Thus, early in the second century, one finds deferential questions being asked of Rome's bishop. For instance, Irenaeus consulted with Victor (c. 189–c. 199) over the controversy of what day Easter should be celebrated, otherwise known as the Quartodeciman Controversy.

Over time, Rome's claim to a unique authority grew, culminating in the work of Leo the Great (440–461), whose *Tome* not only served the church as a Christological masterpiece, but also laid the theological foundation for the papacy. Rooting his argument in Matt 16:19, he argued that the bishop of Rome was the one true successor of Peter, the "prince of the apostles" and the "rock" on which Christ promised to build his church. This exegetical argument, combined with this being the site of two apostles' deaths, and then taking into account Rome's historic influence within the Roman Empire, gave Rome its case for dignity above other churches. Yet beyond these aspects, the pope's rise to power resulted from a continuing succession of precedent-setting acts along with brute political necessity.

It must not be missed that the early Middle Ages were a time of survival, especially for the church. The sacking of Rome was a cataclysmic event, moving the balance of political power to the East to Constantinople. Military threats constantly surrounded the church, whether it was from the Germanic people who "invaded" Rome to the ever-growing threat of Islam, which would ultimately overtake much of the ancient Christian world.

Gregory the Great (590–604), sometimes noted as "the first medieval pope," was born into this situation. With the emperor tied up with his own military troubles in the East, Gregory was left not simply as the de facto leader of the church in Rome, but as the de facto leader of Rome itself. It was up to the pope to provide military direction, to feed the inhabitants of Rome, and to preserve the realm. This reality into which Gregory was flung would establish the precedent for future popes, who brought together spiritual and secular responsibilities within their purview.

Gregory was also the first monk to become pope. Monasticism itself was another key facet of the church in the Middle Ages. Once Christianity was legitimized under the reign of Constantine, many Christians became concerned over the church's growing laxness. The church was no longer a beleaguered, persecuted minority. It was now being doted on by the emperor himself. Thus, men and women took to the desert, not only as a means of tending to their own salvation, but also serving as a witness to the larger church and the "saltiness" Christ had called her to maintain (Matt 5:13–16). Typically, monks took on the mantles of either solitary or communal lifestyles. The latter, being the most prominent, was established by manuals for monastic life known as *rules*, as provided by the Cappadocian Basil of Caesarea (c. 329–379) and most famously, Benedict of Nursia (c. 480–c. 547). As time went on, monks were seen as the best spiritual advisers, and as spiritual heroes to everyday churchgoers. As such, they provided an aspirational ideal for the church and her members.

Eventually, then, the desert made its way to the city, with monks becoming bishops, as was the case with Gregory. In many ways, monasticism came to take up the center of medieval life, with various noblemen supporting monasteries with the hope of benefiting from the monks' prayers. Monks were also key to the spread of Christianity, as seen by Gregory's papacy. As historians have recognized, Gregory was the first bishop of Rome to intentionally evangelize a pagan people: the tribes in England. Not only would this be a means of spreading the gospel, but also of spreading Rome's particular understanding of her unique authority over other church locales.

The most famous of Gregory's missionaries was a monk named Augustine, who, through his evangelizing efforts, would go on to become Augustine of Canterbury (d. 604). And as the West's missionary efforts were successful, those converts all the more looked to the bishop of Rome for legitimization of their power.

When considering everyday efforts in the parish, the picture is harder to ascertain. Sources are scant on the normal activities of local churches. Even so, what is known is that the early Middle Ages were not a time of robust theological education. Given that the services were conducted in Latin, many priests, due to lack of training, were unable to understand what they were saying, much less the largely illiterate people to whom they were saying it. In large part, this resulted because the church did not have an educational plan to offer (at least not one that was required). This was also partly due to the ecclesiastical variety that existed. More often than not, local churches were founded by local lords, not bishops, making it difficult to sustain consistent church practice across the empire.

Consequently, sermons in normal local church life were not just short; they often did not exist. Again this was due to the priest's inability to prepare them and their parishioners' likely inability to understand them. As such, church life was highly ritualistic. Indeed, life itself was ritualistic. It centered on the sacraments, on these "sacred signs," as the priests did their best to bring God to the people, to bring heaven to earth. Relics were also in high regard as a means of bringing the power of the martyrs and the saints of old to bear on the lives of common folk.

Above all stood the Eucharist. During the Carolingian reign, with Charles the Great (748–814), or Charlemagne, crowned by the pope, questions arose concerning the presence of Christ in the Eucharist. Throughout the early church, it was largely assumed that Christ was present in the bread and wine of the sacrament. The mystery was preserved. Some theologians, like Augustine, emphasized the symbolic nature of the Eucharist, while still affirming the mysterious presence of Christ. Others, like Ambrose (c. 340–397), used concepts such as "conversion," which seemed to emphasize a change in the elements themselves to accommodate Christ's presence. Even so, this difference should not be read as a disagreement. Both Augustine and Ambrose, along with the early church, took seriously the mysterious presence of Christ in the Lord's Supper.

So did Carolingian theologians, who now had a patristic inheritance that included the likes of Ambrose and Augustine. With that, the discussion of Christ's presence in the Eucharist was furthered by two monks, Paschius Radbertus (785–865) and Ratramnus of Corbie (d. 868). In his work *Concerning the Body and Blood of the Lord*, Radbertus followed Ambrose, concluding that the bread and wine present in the Eucharist were actually converted into the body and blood of Christ. The bread was no longer bread, and the wine no longer wine, even though they appeared the same. A miraculous transformation had occurred. The eating that was done, however, was done spiritually, and only among those who were true followers of Christ. Ratramnus disagreed. Writing against his old master in *Concerning Christ's Body and Blood*, he followed Augustine, contending that while Christ's flesh and blood were mysteriously present in the bread and the wine, the elements remained precisely what they were, bread and wine.

Radbertus's viewpoint would grow in popularity going forward—so much so that those who argued against him risked condemnation by the pope. Such was the case for Berengar of Tours (1000–1088). In supporting Ratramnus's more symbolic understanding of the elements, Berengar was paraded through a series of condemnations and forced recantations, all over his position on Christ's presence in the Eucharist. These flashpoints, from Radbertus and Ratramnus, to those wrestling with their legacies, illustrate how seriously the church of the Middle Ages took the Eucharist, and how it still had much work to do in understanding this remarkable mystery that was at the heart of the church's worship.

The High Middle Ages (1000–1300)

Turning to the eleventh century, one turns to a time of reckoning. In prior centuries, the church experienced no shortage of struggle. Out of that struggle, the church made concessions to surrounding conquerors to ensure they had military protection from impending foes. To some degree, the concessions were a type of *quid pro quo*. Military aid would be provided in exchange for papal legitimization for the emperor's rule. Although this arrangement ensured the church's survival, it also resulted in unintended consequences, not least of which was the blurring of the lines between the authority of emperors, kings, and the pope.

One line that was not blurred was the division between the Western and Eastern church. Whatever the intent, the advancement of the pope's powers also furthered this ecclesiastical fissure. Within the great ecumenical councils, there was a constant tug and pull over the right relationship between Rome and Constantinople. Naturally, being the city of Peter and Paul, along with the original seat of the empire, Rome came to see itself as invested with unique dignity and authority. The East, however, while appreciating the historical backdrop to Rome, nonetheless understood itself to have its own authority.

In many ways, this struggle over authority was at the heart of what came to be called the "Filioque controversy." At some point during the early Middle Ages, the phrase *filioque*, or "and the Son," in relationship to the procession of the Holy Spirit, was added to the Nicene Creed, thus changing the creed. Although the West endorsed this theological shift, the East was not pleased. The Eastern church claimed that no ecclesiastical body had the right to change unilaterally an "ecumenical" creed, even the Western church. Worse, in the eyes of the East, such a shift threatened the Father's uniqueness as the "fount of divinity."

This controversy contributed to the Great Schism in 1054. Two years prior, Pope Leo IX (1049–1054), in the midst of reforming the churches under his care, sought to institute conformity by unifying the language of the Mass. As such, he required Latin for churches in Italy that had routinely used Greek. Of course, Greek was the language of the East, whereas Latin was the language of the West—another strain on their tenuous relationship. The bishop of Constantinople, Michael Cerularius (1043–1058), responded in kind, demanding that Latin-speaking churches change to Greek. This tit-for-tat resulted in a failed negotiation, in which the pope's emissary excommunicated Cerularius. Not surprisingly, Cerularius condemned Rome and the West in return.

With that, the West continued in its work of making itself distinct, especially as a church conformed to the standards of Rome. Such reform started with the clergy itself. Many of the existing congregations were founded by local lords who installed their own priests. Some would do this without regard for their capacities as a spiritual leader, seeing their local church as a monetary investment more than anything else. The priest was not merely concerned with the sacraments, but rather with blessing crops, with bringing the power of God to bear on the needs of their local patrons. Moreover, given that these churches were functionally outside of the Roman church's control, many would try to buy their way into the priestly office—a practice known as simony. Coupled with that, clerical celibacy was a fantasy. Many priests were married. Many priests had concubines. It was simply the way things were.

Even so, there were those in the church who were not content to rest with the status quo. One such reformer was a monk named Hildebrand, who would go on to be Pope Gregory VII (1073–1085). His vision of reform was one of centralization, believing the church to be at her best when she was under clerical control. He and his curia took measures to end the practice of lords appointing their own bishops, of enforcing celibacy, and altogether restoring what they believed to be the New Testament ideal. Consequently, in Gregory VII, the powers of the bishop of Rome would reach new heights, with the birth of the idea of the papacy itself. Yet Gregory was not content with restoring ecclesiastical control alone. Whereas in the past, popes contended that two powers existed between the spiritual and political realms, Gregory saw all power ultimately subordinate to the throne of Peter. Summarily, Gregory saw himself as freeing or "liberating" the church from the rule of the people.

The church's leadership was not the only thing that needed liberation. So did its land. With the Islamic kingdom overtaking key Christian locales, Jerusalem above all, the pope saw it as his holy obligation to restore that land to the church. It was "holy land" because it was the "Church's land." Thus, the pope and the church militant, in every sense of the word, took to the Crusades. To recruit soldiers for God's army, Pope Urban II used the best tool at his disposal, the keys of the kingdom, which allowed him to offer the remission of sins to any brave man willing to fight to regain Jerusalem. Combined with a desire to fight for pope and church, this was a compelling offer, so compelling that more than 60,000 men took up the call, stunningly toppling the Islamic Empire and retaking Jerusalem. For the West, what seemed a clear testament to divine favor ended up being nothing more than a flash of weakness for the Islamic Empire. With new leadership and a reinvigorated sense of purpose, they would regain much of what was lost from the Crusades, including Jerusalem itself.

Land was not the only thing the church gained and lost. This was also a time for significant theological advancement, especially in the church's most important possession, the sacraments. Perhaps none was more important in this work than Peter Lombard (d. 1160). Not to be confused with Peter Abelard (1079–1141), he was nonetheless likely a student of Abelard's. He learned his teacher's method of comparing authoritative sources, such as the Scriptures, the Fathers, and others. With that, he compiled the church's most precious pronouncements for future generations. Out of that work arose the *Four Books of Sentences* (1151), which became the theology textbook of the Middle Ages for the West. If anyone sought to be a theologian, they had to reckon with Lombard's *Sentences*, so much so that commentaries on the *Sentences* became a genre of literature unto themselves.

In the *Sentences*, Lombard aided in the development of the church's sacramental practices. Before Lombard, the church had a variety of sacramental lists. Baptism and the Eucharist were the constants, with the Eucharist taking center stage. To those, Lombard added confirmation, penance, extreme unction, ordination, and marriage (*Sentences* 4.2.1). Altogether this resulted in seven sacraments. As seven is the number of perfection, Lombard's list was adopted by the church later at the Council of Florence (1439), then officially codified at the Council of Trent (1545–1563).

One sacrament out of this seven that the church further developed was the Eucharist. The church's perennial question on the sacred meal was again the presence of Christ in the elements of the Eucharist. The Fourth Lateran Council in 1215 sought to bring all of the church's opinions together to clarify her understanding of this question. Called by Pope Innocent III (1198–1216), the council defined Christ's presence in the Eucharist through the concept of "transubstantiation." In short, the council contended that the body of Christ was truly present in the elements of the Eucharist. Additionally, the council reemphasized the unity and authority of the church, ruling that only a properly invested priest could oversee the sacrament—a reality that testified to the work of reform in establishing a stark divide between the clergy and the laity.

Thomas Aquinas (1225–1274) later clarified what is meant by the term *transubstantiation*. The "greatest of the schoolmen," Aquinas represented the flourishing of the medieval church's intellectual achievement. With the establishment of new religious orders like the Franciscans and Dominicans, along with the rise of universities, the church's intellectual tradition flourished, moving from the corridors of the monastery to the halls of the university. A monk who was by no means a "dumb ox" (his nickname), Aquinas exemplified what came to be known as the scholastic tradition. Scholasticism offered a clear, precise method for doing theology, in which questions were asked and answered from both sides of the question, using Scripture, the Fathers, and other authorities. Employing this method, along with insights from the "philosopher," Aristotle, whose works were translated in the thirteenth century, Aquinas helped the church to better understand the mystery of Christ's presence in the bread and the wine.

The Late Middle Ages (1300-1500)

If the high Middle Ages were a period of reform and theological development, so were the next 200 years. Yet reform is in the eye of the reformer. The prior age was one of freeing the church from the "captivity" of lay leaders and reinvesting power in the church, supremely in the pope. Nevertheless, what was freedom from the pope was bondage to others, at least when the pope was not living in a manner consistent with his high calling.

The late Middle Ages gave birth to some of the most creative thinkers in church history in Franciscan theologians such as John Duns Scotus (1265–1308) and William of Ockham (c. 1287–1347). Ockham stimulated the debate over the relationship between reason and theology, and the capabilities of each. More dangerously, he challenged the authority of the pope. Ockham, as someone who had been excommunicated by the pope, stood as a representative of "conciliarism," contending that the authority of a church council exceeded the authority of the pope. The pope was not perfect, Ockham argued. He could be wrong. Nevertheless, what was not wrong was the Bible, along with the rulings of the Catholic Church. In making this argument, Ockham sought to shift the balance of power, decentralizing the authority of the pope, even when it came to his relationship to the emperor. For Ockham, it was not within the pope's purview to depose an emperor. Shockingly, though, Ockham believed the emperor did have the power to remove a pope.

Ockham would not be the last to challenge the authority of a pope. An Oxford theologian, John Wycliffe (1330–1384), sometimes referred to as "the morning star of the Reformation," joined in Ockham's chorus, albeit with different theological motivations. Like Ockham, Wycliffe saw supreme authority emanating from the Scriptures alone, not the pope. More radical, Wycliffe believed that because the Scriptures are supremely authoritative, everyday people should have access to the Bible in their vernacular language. Additionally, when it came to spiritual leadership, Wycliffe believed that morality mattered. To be a leader in the church, whether it be as a priest, or even the pope, one had to lead a holy lifestyle. For the pope in particular, Wycliffe contended that his power was restricted to the spiritual realm. Yet that power was contingent, not on the pope's succession from the apostle Peter, but rather in his living in a manner emblematic of the great apostle. Ultimately and astonishingly, Wycliffe would eventually come to ascribe the title of Antichrist to the pope—at least to any pope who did not imitate the life of Christ.

Wycliffe's ideas on the role of Scripture and church authority were significant. His followers, known as the Lollards, did the work of preaching the gospel to the lost and spreading the ideas of their teacher along with them. Those who came to England might very well leave with the echo of the Oxford don in their ears. Such an echo eventually made its way to Bohemia, to the ears of a reformer named Jan Hus (c. 1372–1415). Hus prized the work of Wycliffe. What he valued most was Wycliffe's critique of papal authority and ecclesiastical corruption. Like Wycliffe, Hus would have none of it, and he was strategically placed within Bohemia to bellow forth his call for reform.

The papacy itself had been in disrepair. The fourteenth century brought momentous changes, such as growth in national allegiances across Europe, which competed against the universal claim of authority by the pope. Christendom was fracturing, and Rome was doing all it could to hold it together. Ultimately, it was not to be. Kings and emperors had significant levers of power to pull now, such as trade. They no longer needed to be legitimized by the pope. With that, the only powers of persuasion the pope had were spiritual. Thus, in his papal decree, *Unam Sanctum* (1302), Pope Boniface VIII (1294–1303) declared that salvation was not on offer, not just outside the church, but outside of the pope. Boniface's bull (papal letter) had the opposite effect he was hoping for, resulting in his being attacked and dying not long thereafter.

Following Boniface, the papacy would go into a time of further strife, known as the Avignon papacy or, more pejoratively, "the Babylonian captivity of the church." This period of time, which lasted most of the fourteenth century (1309–1378), stemmed from the pope's no longer residing in Rome but in France in the city of Avignon. Although in France, the papacy's popularity continued to wane, largely because of its perpetual need for money and the lavish lifestyle of many popes. One would think that once the papacy was able to return home to Rome in 1378, all would be well. Not so. Rather, the papacy entered into an era of controversy known as the Great Schism, in which multiple popes would be elected, fracturing the church as well as the Western world.

All of this was ultimately a struggle over the nature of the church, and in particular, church authority. Where does ultimate ecclesiastical authority lie? Wycliffe and Hus had their opinions, as did the leadership in Rome. Thus, in the midst of papal disarray, the Council of Constance was called in 1414 with the hope of reuniting the Roman church. Through a bizarre set of circumstances, including a runaway pope who called for the council, Constance determined that a council, when properly convened, represents the church in its entirety, and thus is authoritative over all others in spiritual affairs, including the pope. Not surprisingly, this decree did not last. Eventually Pope Pius II (1405–1464) would dismiss it entirely, reasserting papal power above all others.

Even so, Constance had more to deal with than rival popes. It also had to contend with the memory of Wycliffe, especially in the person of Hus. Ultimately, Constance found Hus guilty of heresy, particularly in his challenge to church authority. For this, he met a fiery death. For good measure, the council also condemned many of the teachings of Wycliffe, who died in 1384. Such a decision testifies to his lasting influence. Additionally, just as the Roman church burned Hus, so they later dug up Wycliffe's corpse and burned his bones as one final act of purification. Even so, the impulse for reform could not be burned away. Whether it be from the likes of the Lollards or from the fury of Savonarola (1452–1498), the times were changing. More reform was yet to come.

CASE STUDIES

Case Study 1: A Tale of Two Gregorys

Gregory the Great was born into a family of great expectations. His grandfather was Pope Felix III (483–492). Born in Rome, the great city would be at the heart of his life's work. At a young age, Gregory was given the position of prefect of the city. This pattern would reoccur throughout Gregory's life: constantly being placed into leadership positions he was not seeking. Yet Gregory was a particularly gifted theologian and administrator. Adding to that potent combination, Gregory was taken with the monastic lifestyle. He founded several monasteries and became abbot of one himself. Yet the quiet life of the monk was not to be. Upon the pope's death in 590, Gregory was chosen to take his place.

It seemed as if his entire life up to this point had prepared him to be the bishop of Rome. Having been sent to Constantinople as his predecessor's emissary, Gregory was well aware of the needed distinctness of the church at Rome from its counterpart in the East. Knowing that the emperor was too engaged in political and military affairs of his own, Gregory served as the *de facto* leader of Rome. With that, he expanded the powers of the pope to acquire land, to administer basic social services for the people, and perhaps most important, to engage in missionary endeavors unlike any bishop before him. Yet, in the main, the expansion of papal power was due in large part to the circumstance in which he found himself. The emperor was not in Rome. Leadership was needed, and Gregory, as the most recognizable figure in the great city, was necessarily flung into the task.

Even with all of his expansive administrative endeavors, Gregory never forgot his fundamental role as a spiritual shepherd. Of all of his writings, his *Pastoral Rule* stands as a model of what he expected not only of himself but of all those who would take on the mantle of church leadership. Above all, Gregory expected those who assumed the mantle of spiritual authority to live in a manner worthy of their calling. Gregory's *Rule*, harkening to his monastic background, is one filled with sobriety about the pastor's calling and responsibility. Understanding the pastor as the one who dispenses the holy things of God, how could he strive for anything else but holiness?

Humility is a key theme that animates his *Pastoral Rule*. And for his part, Gregory displayed marks of humility throughout his time as pope. Perhaps this is most clearly seen in his refusal to see the bishop of Rome as one to rule over other church locales. For all the advancements Gregory accomplished for the papacy, he was careful not to overreach.

Not so for his later successor, Pope Gregory VII. Like his namesake, Gregory VII, formerly known as Hildebrand, was also a monk. Unlike Gregory the Great, however, this monk was not known for his humility. Quite the contrary, he was known for his passionate outbursts and lack of moderation. Whereas Gregory the Great was a bishop who ensured the church at Rome's survival and expansion, Gregory VII was a reforming pope.

In a sense, it fell to Gregory VII to undo some of the unintended consequences of Gregory the Great's work, particularly the deals he had to make with neighboring tribes to provide needed military aid to Rome. This led to increased power for the emperor and local lords, which blended over into the church—a power that Gregory VII was adamant to curtail. Thus, when one compares the Gregorys, one finds two very different understandings of papal power. Gregory the Great understood himself as the "servant of the servants of God." Moreover, he found it reprehensible to be called the "universal priest." Conversely, Gregory VII decreed in *The Dictates of the Pope* that "the Roman pontiff alone can with right be called universal."

Furthermore, Gregory VII believed that as pope he had the right to depose emperors, a significant development beyond Pope Gelasius's (492–496) understanding of the two powers—spiritual and political—wielded by the bishop and emperor, respectively. Gregory VII memorably wielded this power over Henry IV—one too many times, in fact. Because of Gregory VII's overreach in his use of his deposing powers, he was left in ruin. It would not be until Pope Innocent III (1198–1216) that the Middle Ages would see the apogee of papal power that Gregory VII initiated. Even so, Gregory VII made great strides in centralizing the power of the church in the pope, and in so doing, "freeing" the church from the perceived captivity of the laity.

Altogether the tale of the two Gregorys displays the development of the papacy throughout the centuries. Both made significant advancements, especially as it regarded the administrative powers of the pope. Yet this tale also reveals two fundamentally different viewpoints on the role of ecclesiastical authority. For Gregory the Great, as outlined in his *Pastoral Rule*, authority was a stewardship, a holy service that demanded a lifestyle of holiness. For Gregory VII, his emphasis was less on humility, on the role of pope as servant, than as the pope as the ultimate authority of the earthly and spiritual realms, established to maintain uniformity in Christ's church, above all other bishops and councils.

Case Study 2: Transubstantiation

So Jesus said to them, "Truly I tell you, unless you eat the flesh of the Son of Man and drink his blood, you do not have life in yourselves. The one who eats my flesh and drinks my blood has eternal life, and I will raise him up on the last day" (John 6:53–54). These were some of the most difficult words Jesus ever uttered. And the church of the Middle Ages took them seriously.

Yet the difficulty remained. How is one to eat the flesh and drink the blood of Christ? Does such a command mean that he, the Son of God, is somehow present in the elements of the Eucharist? In a sense, much of the Middle Ages was a search for the answer. From the work of Radbertus and Ratramnus wrestling with the legacies of Ambrose and Augustine, to Berengar of Tours appearing to reduce the Eucharist to mere symbolism, the church struggled to articulate its position.

Such a concern is seen in the actual practice of the Eucharist. For the most part, the laity simply observed the priests' partaking of the sacred meal.

If they were to have anything, it was the bread, and even then, that was rare. The reason, of course, stemmed from the question of Christ's presence in the bread and wine. If he was in fact mysteriously present, was it not far too great a risk to hand out the elements to everyone? What if a bread crumb fell on the floor? Worse, what if someone spilled a bit of wine? Understanding the presence of Christ is why the church eventually went to using a wafer instead of bread. Since that was the element most laity were able to take part in, it reduced the risk of the mishandling of Christ's body.

Clearly the Eucharist mattered to Jesus. He said as much in the Gospel narratives, which was later reinforced by the apostle Paul. Peter Lombard helpfully listed the Eucharist as one of the seven sacraments of the church and also clarified its purpose. According to the master of the *Sentences*, the sacrament is given for "humility, instruction, and activity." Considering the Eucharist, it is a humbling sacrament since its elements are beneath man. In placing himself in submission to the bread and wine, he is rightfully humbling himself before the command of God. Second, he is instructed through what the Eucharist visibly portrays—the sacrifice of Christ. Third and finally, the Eucharist is a catalyst for work, particularly the work of partaking of the Eucharist.

The Fourth Lateran Council (1215) clarified this work and Christ's presence in it by using the word *transubstantiation*. As the first canon of the council states:

> There is one universal church of the faithful, outside of which there is absolutely no salvation. In this church the priest and the sacrifice are both the same Jesus Christ. His body and blood are truly contained in the sacrament of the altar under the forms of bread and wine. The bread is transubstantiated into his body and the wine into his blood, by God's power. This is so that we may receive of him what he has received of us in order to realize the mystery of unity. No one can affect this sacrament except a duly ordained priest.

Transubstantiation was the church's answer to the question of Christ's presence in the Eucharist. Nevertheless, the word itself did not completely explain how Christ was present in the elements. Yet clarity was still to come. One of the most momentous happenings in history, much less the history of the Middle Ages, was the translation of Aristotle. Now at the fingertips of schoolmen like Thomas Aquinas, they had "new" philosophical categories and tools for doing the work of theology. Thomas excelled at this type of work. And one of the Aristotelian tools he found quite useful was the distinction between "substance" and "accidents." According to Aquinas, after the priest provided the words of consecration, the elements are mysteriously transubstantiated, or transformed, into the body and blood of Christ. Observing the bread and wine with one's senses, they still look, feel, smell, and taste like bread and wine. In other words, their accidents, or what can be ascertained through one's senses, have not changed. Nevertheless, the substance of the elements—what makes them what they are, and which can only be perceived by the mind—has changed to the body and blood of Christ in the bread and wine. It is this substantial change that can only be seen through the eyes of belief, not one's physical senses.

To be sure, Aquinas did not understand Christ's presence in the Eucharist to mean he was in the particular locale where the elements were. Presence, for Aquinas, was not brute physicality. Christ's presence was no less real because it was a *substantial* presence. Additionally, Aquinas's use of Aristotle shielded the Eucharist from charges of cannibalism. What was being eaten were not the accidents of Christ, actual flesh and blood, but rather his substance.

Altogether the theological development of the Eucharist speaks to the development of the church as a whole throughout the Middle Ages. Ecclesiology was intimately wed to Christology, as seen here in the sacraments. At stake in the bread and the wine was nothing less than the presence and thus the power of Christ, which, as Christ said, all must partake of for life eternal.

For the Church

The great medievalist C. S. Lewis (1898–1963) once warned against "chronological snobbery," or the tendency to look down on the past in favor of the apparent progress of the present. Along with that warning, when thinking about the Middle Ages, especially as a Protestant, one must also beware the danger of ecclesiastical tribalism. Imagining the history of the church as a school playground, it is all too easy to approach it like picking a team for a game of pickup basketball. Surveying the players available, Luther, of course, is picked first. Calvin, possibly second. But Gregory, Lombard, or Aquinas? They are left to the last few, anxiously looking around, hoping they are not picked last. After all, who wants a papist on their team?

Even though Protestants have significant disagreements with the Roman Catholic Church, especially on the point of the papacy, Protestants can still learn from popes—both popes striving to be faithful to their stewardship as they understood it, and those who simply seem to be making a power grab. Consider again the tale of the two Gregorys. *The Book of Pastoral Rule* remains a book that all pastors, regardless of their particular tradition, should avail themselves of, if for nothing else than its clarion call to live in a manner worthy of one's calling—that true doctrine is lived, not merely taught. This is why Gregory the Great preferred his title to be "the servant of the servants of God." As for Gregory VII, he stands as a warning to all in leadership of the dangers of unchecked power, of viewing leadership without the lens of Christlike service. As church history shows up to the modern day, abuses of ecclesiastical power have never been limited to Rome.

Or consider Lombard's *Sentences*. Even for those who only understand the Lord's Supper and baptism as ordinances, not sacraments, Lombard's threefold purpose for the sacraments remains instructive. Humility, instruction, and a call to ecclesiastical activism are good concepts for us to consider as we practice the Supper. Certainly, we should approach it with humility, recognizing it as a celebration and remembrance of a reality done *for* us, not *by* us. Moreover, the Supper is instructive in that it pictures the work of Christ, in all of its biblical-theological fullness. Finally, it spurs us to remember what Christ has done for us, because the great besetting sin of God's people has been and continues to be forgetfulness. The Supper also spurs us to proclaim the gospel, with our partaking of it being an act of gospel proclamation itself.

Altogether then, it is imperative to approach the church of the Middle Ages not as a blight on the church's story. Rather, simply, it is our story. Are there significant, serious points of disagreement? Absolutely. But that by no means discounts the reality that men and women of this time between the times are as much a part of the church's story as the Reformation is. In fact, as the next portion of this book will show, the Reformation cannot be understood apart from the Middle Ages. Nor, for that matter, can the church or the world today.

For Further Reading

Brown, Peter. *The Rise of Western Christendom*, 2nd ed. Malden, MA: Blackwell, 2003.

Evans, G. R., ed. *The Medieval Theologians*. Malden, MA: Blackwell, 2001.

Gregory the Great. *The Book of Pastoral Rule*. New York: St. Vladimir's Seminary Press, 2007.

Holcomb, Justin S. *Know the Creeds and Councils*. Grand Rapids: Zondervan, 2014.

Lane, Tony. *A Concise History of Christian Thought*. New York: T&T Clark, 2006.

Madigan, Kevin. *Medieval Christianity: A New History*. New Haven, CT: Yale University Press, 2015.

Ortlund, Gavin. *Theological Retrieval for Evangelicals: Why We Need Our Past to Have a Future*. Wheaton, IL: Crossway, 2019.

Ozment, Steven. *The Age of Reform 1250–1550: An Intellectual and Religious History of Late Medieval and Reformation Europe*. New Haven, CT: Yale University Press, 1980.

Pelikan, Jaroslav. *The Growth of Medieval Theology (600–1300)*. The Christian Tradition: A History of the Development of Doctrine. Vol. 3. Chicago: University of Chicago Press, 1978.

Southern, R. W. *Western Society and the Church in the Middle Ages*. New York: Penguin, 1970.

Wilken, Robert Louis. *The First Thousand Years: A Global History of Christianity*. New Haven, CT: Yale University Press, 2012.

Questions for Study or Discussion

1. When you approach the Middle Ages, what images come to mind? Do you have a generally negative viewpoint? Why do you think that is?
2. How did the legalization of Christianity in the Roman Empire affect the makeup and practice of the church?
3. What were the key factors in the development of the papacy?
4. What are the various answers the church provided in response to the question of Christ's presence in the Eucharist?
5. Should present-day evangelicals look to the Middle Ages as a resource to mine for theological reflection? Why or why not?

6

SALVATION

By W. Madison Grace II

Introduction

As a Protestant I am used to engaging works on the Reformation and the modern period, and I have been encouraged by the recent renaissance of patristic historical theology. All of these periods provide a great deal of insight and thought into theology and, especially, salvation. Nevertheless, for many Protestants, the medieval period is often untouched or dealt with only as a foil against what should not be. The medieval era becomes either a place of darkness (e.g., the Dark Ages) or it becomes the locus of evil that has infiltrated the church that Martin Luther and company rightly rectified. This is not only a deficient approach to medieval historical theology but also one that is quite wrong.

Though there is some debate about when the patristic era ends and the medieval era begins, we can loosely see this period ranging from the fifth century to the sixteenth century. To think that there is not much of value for historical theology in this 1,000-year period is, at best, too simplistic.

Further, to focus only on the negative aspects of this period of time is unfair because the so-called evils in the medieval era are also found in other times of Christian history—patristic, Reformation, and modern thought are fraught with the same problems. An investigation into medieval thought in church history will help bring greater understanding in theology and soteriology. It will also provide a retrieval that helps Protestants and all Christians progress in theology.

In what follows, we investigate the period and especially look at the development and contributions to the doctrine of salvation. We will look solely at the European medieval tradition and will not take up the developments elsewhere, such as Byzantine Christianity. Particularly, we will present a brief engagement, with a variety of soteriological thoughts in the era ranging from predestination to the Christian life with a special emphasis on the doctrine of the atonement.

Historical Overview

As the patristic era ends in the fifth century, the medieval era begins. It is in this century that Rome falls, the fourth ecumenical council at Chalcedon is held (451), and Augustine of Hippo dies. It is this latter theologian who helps bridge the gap in the West from the patristic era into the medieval period. The fall of Rome led to political instability in the West for hundreds of years. That consequently aided in the development of theologians and movements, especially Gregory the Great (540–604) in Rome and the growth of monastic orders. The Council of Chalcedon solidified Christological orthodoxy (though not stopping heterodoxy) on the person of Christ, which led to other developments on the nature of Christ's work. But it is the work of Augustine that will have some of the most lasting impact on medieval theology. Some have even called the medieval period a footnote on Augustine. His influence is still felt today, and his work is widely used throughout the entire period even if tweaked or rejected at times.

With these changes we should not think of the shift to the medieval period as a paradigmatic change, but one of subtle development over time. As it is built on the work of Augustine, so, too, is it built on the work of the entirety of the patristic era.

Semi-Pelagianism

One of the first major developments in medieval salvation occurred in the time of Augustine and continued for the next 100 years. It was concerned with the debate about free will and grace. On the heels of the Pelagian controversy, another position arose that also would prove to be heretical, called semi-Pelagianism. This view was a middle ground between Pelagius's position and Augustine's. It taught that humans and God cooperate in salvation such that the will of humanity is free to initiate the salvation process and then God completes the work through his gracious activity. This synergistic view of salvation was initially taught by John Cassian and later propagated by Faustus of Riez. Semi-Pelagianism was condemned in 529 at the Second Council of Orange, as was a denial of double predestination (or reprobation). This condemnation did not eradicate the thought but only nuanced it, leading to more questions and positions to be developed later.

Gregory the Great

Gregory the Great, a bishop of Rome in the sixth century, was second in importance to Augustine during the early medieval period. Gregory the Great is known for his writings, but it was his role as bishop of Rome that led not only to reforms for the city but also for the church as a whole. We will look to his specific work regarding purgatory, mission work, and monasteries in relation to his connection to medieval salvation.

The doctrine of purgatory did not have its origins with Gregory, nor would it find its final form with him, but the doctrine grew under his leadership. The doctrine is concerned with the state of a believer who dies without adequately finding forgiveness for all of their sins and is not, therefore, ready to enter into the beatific vision. The believer is saved in the sense that they are not condemned to hell, but they have not quite received enough grace to merit full salvation. Gregory understood the doctrine to be important for the assurance that all sins are forgiven. He stated, "Yet, there must be a cleansing fire before judgment, because of some minor faults that may remain to be purged away." He based this belief in part on his reading of Matt 12:32 and declared, "From this statement we learn that some sins can be forgiven in this world and some in the world to come" (*Dialogue* 4:41). It is with Gregory that the sacrifice of the Mass is connected with purgatory. We can see this most clearly in his relation to the monk Justus, who died in shame for breaking the communal code. After his death, Gregory called for a particular sacrifice of Mass to be offered for thirty days so that Justus could be released from purgatory (*Dialogue* 4:57). This event led to the practice of the Gregorian Mass today.

Gregory is also connected to the missionary work in the medieval period. Missions as practiced in the twenty-first century might have a particular genesis in the modern period, but missionary endeavors have occurred throughout history since the early church. This is due in large part to the belief that all people need to hear the message of the gospel to be able to find salvation in Christ. Though missionaries such as Saint Patrick already had been on the scene in the fifth century, it was Gregory who would send missionaries to England to convert King Ethelbert (560–616). There is great debate about why Gregory was motivated to engage in missions to England. A tradition repeated by the Venerable Bede (672–735), an English monk from the Northumbria monastery of Wearmouth-Jarrow, stated that he saw an English slave in Rome and inquired about him. He was told he was an *angle*, and he responded, "No, an angel," and thus desired to convert those in England. Though the validity of this story is questionable, we do see a desire to engage in missions with the sending of Augustine of Canterbury (d. 604) to lead missions efforts in Britain for the conversion of those people, which had a lasting effect in Britain and beyond.

A final lasting work of Gregory was the growth of monasteries during his time. Monastic movements were not new, and they were built on the work of Anthony, Basil, Jerome, Rufinius, and John Cassian. In the medieval era, European monastic work grew out of the work of Benedict, whose *Rule* would be the base for many of the developing orders. Benedict was born in Nursia in 480 in Italy, where he would react against the immorality he witnessed there. He was initially driven to a solitary ascetic life, but he found that a monastic life in community had great value. He began developing monastic communities and soon had a few. By 520 Monte Cassino was established as the center of Benedictine monastic life.

The Benedictine model was based on a certain rule that established the particular ascetic life of the community. This *Rule* covered the government and daily life of those in the community. The major purpose was for members to grow closer to the love of God. These monasteries became centers in the medieval period of Christianity alongside church life. In them one finds the preservation, transition, and development of Christian art, thought, and theology, as well as a means to grow in faith and grace.

By the time of Gregory, this system was well in place. Gregory himself had helped establish a few monasteries and had been a monk until he was called out to help with ecclesiastical affairs. Nevertheless, even though he left the monasteries, he did not cease to aide in the development and growth of monastic communal life. In fact, as pope, he continued to try to follow the monastic rule as closely as possible and constantly lamented the fact that he was no longer a monk. Part of his legacy is connected to the attention he gave to monasteries, many of which he oversaw. Even his famous work on pastoral theology, *The Book of Pastoral Rule*, has a monastic title and feel. This way of life is connected to the ways Gregory and many after him would understand salvation as a means of receiving merit and grace through the spiritual works accomplished in this life and in the life to come.

John Scottus Eriugena

Though the issue of semi-Pelagianism seemed to be settled in the sixth century, questions about the will and predestination were still raised. This was especially so in the ninth-century debate, in the midst of the Carolingian renaissance, between John Scottus Eriugena (815–877) and Gottschalk of Orbais (808–867). Though the Council of Orange condemned the doctrine of double predestination, Gottschalk was teaching it and insisting that this was the position of Augustine. To settle this issue, the bishop Hincmar of Rheims asked Eriugena to address predestination and refute Gottschalk. In his work *De Divina Praedestinatione*, Eriugena answered the question, but not in the way the bishop desired, which was to advocate for a single predestination position. Though he did advocate against a double predestination position, he also took the conversation into the question of theology proper. Here he argued for God's simplicity. In so doing he denied any real sense of predestination or foreknowledge, since anything that was good was found in God and anything that was evil was not in God. In concluding his work, he stated, "The one eternal predestination of God is God, and exists only in those things that are, but has no bearing at all on those that are not" (*De Divina Praedestinatione*). Eriugena's work was controversial not only because it circumvented the question but also because it entertained the method of philosophy, which he would equate with theology. This movement to philosophical concerns in theology gradually grew into medieval scholasticism beginning with Anselm.

Anselm of Canterbury

Many of those who study medieval theology focus on its history from the eleventh century on, due in part to their interest in the work of Anselm of Canterbury (1033–1109). Born in Aosta in Italy, Anselm eventually left Italy, searching for a school in which to learn, and ended up at the monastery at Bec, studying with Lanfranc, who would convince him to take vows as a monk. Eventually, Anselm would succeed Lanfranc as prior. During this time Anselm wrote some of his famous philosophical works, *Monologion* and *Proslogion*, and that's when he developed his ontological argument for the existence of God. Eventually, Anselm would become the abbot at Bec before going to England to take up the position as archbishop of Canterbury after the late Lanfranc.

For many, the work of Anselm was the beginning of medieval scholasticism that would also include the works of others, such as Abelard, Bonaventure, Thomas Aquinas, Duns Scotus, and Occam. This was a particular method of philosophy and theology that depended on logic and reason. It took various forms and eventually grew from the cathedral schools to universities. Anselm's method in his theology was *faith seeking understanding*, which was his way of growing one's faith by seeking deeper thoughts of God.

In the doctrine of salvation, Anselm shifted the thought of the atonement for the church from the ransom view, which had been held since the patristic era. This theory of the atonement is called the satisfaction theory and has a few varieties. Anselm's presentation is considered in our first case study below.

Peter Abelard

With the rise of scholasticism, the twelfth century saw a growth in theology in a variety of places, with Peter Abelard (1079–1142) perhaps the most famous among those drawn to scholasticism, due in part to his own biography. Abelard was born in Brittany and sought to become a scholar. Early on he was involved in theological controversies while being trained by Roscelin, who would be tried for the heresy of tritheism. Abelard rejected this teaching and sought education elsewhere, to include a brief time with Anselm of Laon. He moved to Paris, where he became the master at Notre Dame. This is where the best-known part of Abelard's life unfolded, that being his love affair with Héloïse. Abelard paid the consequence for what others perceived as his indiscretion. This turn of events pushed him into the monastery, where he would pour himself into teaching and writing about theology. We will look more closely in our second case study at Abelard's particular understanding of the atonement, which is in distinction to the satisfaction theory that Anselm presents.

Bernard of Clairvaux

As stated with Gregory, the growth and diversity of monasteries is a hallmark of the medieval period and is often thought to be the only light that was part of this 1,000-year dark period. Though there were communities that existed in solitude and preserved the faith, there were many other orders in development at the time that greatly influenced the life and theology of medieval Christianity. By period's end these included—besides the Benedictines—the Carthusians, Franciscans, Dominicans, Augustinians, and Cistercians. All of these groups had a different order, or rule, to live by. They had different theological emphases as well, but they did have in common a belief that their existence was to help the spiritual life. A close connection here between salvation and the Christian life would raise the issue of justification, which would have a role in a sixteenth-century controversy involving Protestantism.

Meanwhile, to return to our discussion of the medieval period, one major theologian in the twelfth century was Bernard of Clairvaux (1090–1153), also known as the Theologian of Love. Bernard was a Cistercian—a monastic order known for seeking to follow Benedict's *Rule* strictly and for communing in remote places. Bernard became an abbot at the monastery at Clairvaux, although his work would not be limited to the quiet life. That's because he helped found other monasteries (more than 360), engaged in ecclesiastical affairs, and was involved with the Second Crusade. His theology differed from that espoused by Anselm and Abelard (whom he helped condemn in 1141), and his beliefs in that regard could be seen as more spiritual than the scholasticism that was growing around him.

In his doctrine of salvation, Bernard incorporated his thoughts on spirituality as well as his system of love. At a time when Anselm and Abelard were discussing the atonement and why God became man, Bernard held to a type of Christus Victor model, which saw that Christ's work is one of victory over Satan and sin. The victory is attained through Christ's descending and becoming human so that humanity, in turn, can unite to him and ascend to the spiritual. This view of salvation comes through a transformation over time as a person contemplates Christ's love through his works from birth to ascension. The believer grows in salvation communally as he or she engages in the practices of the church.

Peter Lombard

Scholastic Peter Lombard (1096–1160) was second only to Thomas Aquinas in the late medieval period. His theological work the *Four Books of Sentences* was the theological text for schools and universities until Aquinas's *Summa Theologica* replaced it. Lombard met Bernard of Clairvaux in the 1130s and was encouraged to study theology in a variety of places, to possibly include Hugh of St. Victor. Soon his teaching became well-known, and he was invited to join Notre Dame in Paris, where he would become a master. Here he would spend the rest of his life advancing to the bishopric of Paris before his death in 1160.

Lombard's lasting theological work was his *Sentences*. He wrote it as the completion of decades of teaching systematic theology in Paris and after reading the works of John of Damascus. The books are arranged by topic and cover God, creation, Christology, and sacraments. Lombard's method was to provide theological propositions, or sentences, followed by commentary utilizing logic, reason, and tradition—especially Augustine. This methodology was not unique, but his approach had a lasting effect due to the comprehensive nature of his work.

When we come to Lombard's doctrine of salvation, we find a theologian writing at a time after Anselm, Abelard, and Bernard, and as such, we find a type of hybrid in his understanding of the atonement, meaning that he had both objective and subjective ideas of the atonement. Objectively, he saw that Christ's work was making a payment to free humanity from bondage to Satan and sin, but subjectively, he believed that Jesus's work justifies a person by instilling a love within him or her that then enables that individual to overcome sin. Christ is able to do this for us because his life is of such a virtuous character that it has obtained the merit necessary for salvation. Particularly, Christ's humanity had to have the true character of humility so that it could counter the core of sin, which is pride.

Lombard also answered the question of why there was a need for a God-man, and he emphasized Christ's true humanity as a necessary and active part of his work for the sake of all of humanity that would engage his love. Christ had to be fully human so that humans would have the ability to commune in his love. This raises the question of how Lombard could still be said to hold onto an objective sense of the atonement. Though he does see that believers must come to and engage the love of Christ individually, he also sees that Christ's work actually frees humans of their sin, not just creates a possibility that is self-actualized in the believer. Christ has attained redemption and has freed us from the bondage of sin, but this freedom is worked into man in connection to Christ's love particularly found in the sacraments. Because of this theology, we find in Lombard the beginnings of the sacramental system that would grow in the medieval era.

Thomas Aquinas

When one thinks of medieval theology, one theologian stands out above the rest—the angelic doctor of the church, Thomas Aquinas (1225–1274). Born in Italy, Aquinas would eventually join the Dominican order and complete his studies in Naples and Paris, where he would spend many years teaching. He is best known for his writings found in *Summa Theologica*, which demonstrated his appropriation of Aristotle's thought, which was reintroduced into Europe. Thomas had much to say regarding the doctrine of salvation, but we will briefly look at his thoughts on predestination and consider his understanding of the atonement in our third case study.

As we saw earlier, the doctrine of predestination was not merely engaged by Augustine and then left dormant until the Reformation. The question of predestination and the concept of grace and free will were often discussed during the medieval period. Aquinas also engaged the question in *Summa Theologica* by looking at predestination in question 23 and election in question 24, separating the two. He began his discussion with an appeal based on Rom 8:30 and posited that God does predestine on the basis of his providence. All of creation is dependent on God's work and provision, which includes the ability to be saved. This necessitated the predestination of humanity, which was an active work of God in which humans remained passive. To be consistent, Aquinas also claimed a doctrine of reprobation, wherein God allows some to turn away from him. His providence must allow for punishment of sin. The work of predestination also cannot be understood as predicated on some merit or grace in the believer either previously or foreseen; rather, it must depend on the divine work alone. This work is, again, based on providence and therefore has the end in mind so that predestination ultimately is about bestowing God's goodness on people. How salvation is applied to individuals is a different matter that will be taken up below.

Conclusion

This brief overview of the concepts of salvation in the medieval era is only an introduction to the variety of thoughts that existed on the doctrine of salvation. Whereas the patristic era was concerned with the nature of Christ, the theologians in the medieval era asked how God through the God-man brought about salvation to his people. Central to many medieval minds was the providence of God over creation and his work in determining for whom and how salvation would be enacted. The concepts of grace and merit were greatly important as well, especially when seen through the doctrine of purgatory as well as later developments of the means through which grace and forgiveness can be given to believers, initially through the sacraments as well as in special times and ways, such as in the Crusades and indulgences. The most enduring aspect of the doctrine of salvation is the development of the atonement and willingness to critique traditional understandings of what was actually accomplished in Christ's passion. These beliefs in salvation set the stage for the debate over justification that would ensue in the Reformation era.

Case Studies

As we have seen in our brief overview of medieval salvation, quite a few people and concerns were addressed, but the most important development was in the doctrine of the atonement. Though there are indeed nuances in atonement theologies throughout church history, many ascribed to the ransom view, or classic view, of the atonement. This view taught that Christ's work was a ransom paid to Satan to redeem and release humanity from its bondage. This classic view would be challenged in the medieval era but bring great development to understanding Christ's work. We will now look at three approaches to understanding the atonement and salvation in the work of Anselm, Peter Abelard, and Thomas Aquinas.

Case Study 1: Anselm's Satisfaction Theory

When it comes to the atonement, Anselm takes up the question of the necessity of the Son becoming incarnate for the salvation of humanity in his work *Cur Deus Homo* ("Why the God-man?"). It is in this book, which is a two-part dialogue with a pupil of Anselm's named Boso, that he challenges the classic theory of the atonement and offers what will be called the satisfaction theory.

Initially, Anselm seeks to answer a question that unbelievers and believers alike are asking: "By what logic or necessity did God become man, and by his death, as we believe and profess, restore life to the world, when he could have done this through the agency of some other person, angelic or human, or simply by willing it?" (*Cur Deus Homo* 1.1). Anselm here challenges the position that payment was made to the devil for humanity. In Anselm's mind whatever ransom was made through Christ cannot be to the devil since humanity belongs only to God and is only within God's power. Moreover, there is nothing inherent in the devil that would obligate God to make payment to him. So, if it is not a ransom paid to the devil, to whom is this payment made? The answer to this question is bound up in understanding the nature of sin and its offense, the type of payment or reparation needed to ransom humanity, and the type of person who could offer this payment.

First, the effects of the sin committed by Adam and Eve were so egregious that they ruined all of humanity. This ruining needed to be rectified, but it was not a simple forgiveness offered by God. The saving of mankind needed to occur in a particular way to restore the right order of creation. For humanity to achieve eternal "blessed happiness," which is the purpose for humanity's existence, it is necessary to be without sin, and thus, there must be a remission of sins to obtain God's purposed blessedness.

It is given, then, that for sins to be forgiven, one must understand the nature of sin. Anselm defines sin simply as "not to give God what is owed to him" (*Cur Deus Homo* 1.11). When one gives God what is his due, one finds righteousness and honors God. When one does not give God what is due him, not only is one robbing from God what is rightly his, but he or she is also not rendering the honor due to God. Anselm states the sinful situation thusly:

> And it is not sufficient merely to repay what has been taken away: rather, he ought to pay back more than he took, in proportion to the insult which he has inflicted. . . . Therefore, everyone who sins is under obligation to repay God the honour which he has violently taken from him, and this is the satisfaction which every sinner is obliged to give to God. (*Cur Deus Homo* 1.11)

If a sinner does not pay back the honor that is due to God, punishment will surely follow. This is the state of humanity for ruined sinners. All are in need of paying back to God the honor that is stolen from him by their sin. But could God not simply offer mercy and forgive these sinners? To this question Anselm appeals to the fittingness of God to be able to offer that type of mercy. He claims, "If it is not fitting for God to do anything in an unjust and unregulated manner, it does not belong to his freedom or benevolence or will to release unpunished a sinner who has not repaid to God what he has taken away from him" (*Cur Deus Homo* 1.12).

If humanity has sinned but is unable to make a reparation of sin to God's satisfaction, and if it is not fitting or right for God to offer mercy and simply forgive humankind, who then can offer satisfaction so that payment can be made to God to remit these sins? This line of reasoning creates the need for a particular person to offer payment. Only the one who has committed the sin is fit to offer satisfaction for that sin. Nevertheless, there is no human able to make such a satisfaction for their sin since "a man who is a sinner is in no way capable of doing this, for one sinner cannot make another sinner righteous" (*Cur Deus Homo* 1.23). So, who can make this payment if there is no one who is righteous? Anslem believes that whoever this person is that will make payment must be able to make a payment that is "greater than everything that exists apart from God." This person also must "be superior to everything that exists apart from God." Therefore, only God is able to offer the satisfaction that is required for the remittance of the sin of humanity, or as Anselm says of this payment for sin, "No one can pay except God, and no one ought to pay except man: it is necessary that a God-Man should pay it" (*Cur Deus Homo* 2.6).

This God-man able to make payment for the sin of humanity must exist in such a way that he is perfectly God and perfectly human. The humanity of this person has to be of the exact same type as Adam's race, since it is Adam's race that owes the payment. This person also would be fully God in every way such that "he will never be without God's power and fortitude and wisdom" (*Cur Deus Homo* 2.13). In making this voluntary sacrifice of his life, the God-man is able to make satisfaction for sins and make humanity righteous so that blessedness can be achieved.

Case Study 2: Peter Abelard's Moral Influence Theory

The objective work of Anselm's atonement was not accepted by all. Peter Abelard entered the discussion on the work of Christ in the twelfth century by not looking to Christ as a ransom to Satan or a satisfaction to God, but as an example of love that we are to emulate.

Abelard's treatment of the atonement is found in his *Exposition of the Epistle of Romans* (Library of Christian Classics, hereinafter LCC), in which he intended to take up the same question that Anselm queried: Why did God become man?

> A most pressing problem obtrudes itself at this point, as to what that redemption of ours through the death of Christ may be, and in what way the apostle declares that we are justified by his blood. . . . And so it seems that we must first investigate why it was necessary for God to take human nature on him so that he might redeem us by dying in the flesh; and from what person holding us captive, either justly or by fraud, he has redeemed us; and by what standard of justice he has liberated us from the dominion of that person who has given commands to which he willingly submitted in order to set us free. (*Exposition*, LCC 10:280)

From this introduction to the question of the atonement in Abelard, we see that he was not only engaging with Anselm's specific question but was also questioning the classic view of the atonement. What did Christ do on the cross that liberated us? He begins answering this question by addressing the ability the devil has to actually hold anything over us. Abelard surmises that if a slave is to leave his lord and go to another, it is still the prerogative of the lord to take back his slave. This is especially the case if the other master has seduced the slave into his bondage. Abelard sees that this seductive master has no right over the slave and finds it unjust for the righteous lord to have to pay anything. "And how unjust it would be that he who seduced the other should deserve, as a result to have any special right or authority over him!" (*Exposition*, LCC 10:281). Thus, he finds that there is no payment that needs to be made to the devil for humanity's salvation, except only what the Lord himself would permit.

For Abelard, like Anselm, the recipient of the payment of sin is important. It is not the devil who receives that payment but the Lord himself. "And to whom was the price of blood paid for our redemption but to him in whose power we were—that is, to God himself, who (as we have said) handed us over to his torturer?" (*Exposition*, LCC 10:283). Nevertheless, he finds the sin that led humanity to the torturer to be far less than the sin of crucifying Christ, and he sees an injustice in offering Christ as a blood sacrifice for anything. He states:

> Indeed, how cruel and wicked it seems that anyone should demand the blood of an innocent person as the price for anything, or that it should in any way please him that an innocent man should be slain—still less that God should consider the death of his Son so agreeable that by it he should be reconciled to the whole world! (*Exposition*, LCC 10:283)

So, unlike Anselm, even though Abelard sees that any ransom paid should be paid to God and not the devil, the sacrifice of Jesus is not something that God should demand at all. This type of sacrifice would be "cruel and wicked." What is the solution to the problem of why God became man? In answering this, Abelard finds that the life and work of Christ provide justification and reconciliation, but in what way if the cross is cruel and wicked? His answer is found in the example of love that Jesus presents to us that we have redemption:

> Through this unique act of grace manifested to us—in that his Son has taken upon himself our nature and preserved therein teaching us

> by word and example even unto death—he has more fully bound us to himself by love; with the result that our hearts should be enkindled by such a gift of divine grace, and true charity should not now shrink from enduring anything for him. (*Exposition*, LCC 10:283)

Abelard's position is that redemption comes upon a person when that person is bound to the love of Christ. It is not the blood that has brought justification but the love that is shown in the sacrifice. He appeals to John 15:13 for this in that "no one has greater love than this: to lay down his life for his friends." The redemption that humanity achieves is found in this love that Christ has given to us:

> Wherefore our redemption through Christ's suffering is that *deeper affection* in us, which not only frees us from slavery to sin, but also wins for us the true liberty of sons of God, so that we do all things out of love rather than fear—love to him who has shown us such grace that no greater can be found. (*Exposition*, LCC 10:284)

Abelard's short excursus on the question of why God became man in his exposition of Romans does not give the robust answer that one would find in Anselm or Aquinas, but it does present a position that rejects not only the classic view but also any objective view of the atonement. Reconciliation and justification are obtained for the sinner, not by a blood sacrifice, but through the act of love of Christ on the cross, and it is subjectively applied to those who love him.

Case Study 3: Thomas Aquinas and Salvation

When Thomas Aquinas approaches the question of the atonement in his *Summa Theologiciae* (hereinafter *ST* in this chapter), he keeps the medieval tradition of following Anselm. There is a satisfaction theme that comes out in his work; however, he is not merely appropriating an Anselmian position but is also critiquing and progressing from Anselm. Aquinas affirms that it is necessary for someone to make satisfaction for sin and that someone would need to be a sinless person. This necessitates the God-man, for it would not be fitting for God to forgive in another way. What distinguishes Aquinas from Anselm is the subjectivist way in which he argues that satisfaction is made. For Anselm, the God-man made satisfaction to God for sin objectively; for Aquinas, there is a necessitated participation of humans and humanity with God in order for this salvation to be obtained. Something must be changed in humanity for satisfaction to be obtained. This satisfaction occurs through the works of grace available to believers and, in particular, to penance, confession, and contrition:

> As soon as a man falls into sin, charity, faith, and mercy do not deliver him from sin, without Penance. Because charity demands that a man should grieve for the offense committed against his friend, and that he should be anxious to make satisfaction to his friend; faith requires that he should seek to be justified from his sins through the power of Christ's Passion which operates in the sacraments of the Church; and well-ordered pity necessitates that man should succor himself by repenting of the pitiful condition into which sin has brought him. (*ST* III 84.5 ad.2)

Aquinas describes the work in medicinal metaphors so that, for instance, penance is a medicine for sin that the divine doctor Jesus will use to heal.

Another aspect of Aquinas's doctrine of salvation is the way it relates to the church. The passion of Christ objectively "merited salvation" for all in the body. So whatever satisfaction Christ obtained through his work is given to those who comprise his mystical body in the church. We see this clearly where Aquinas explains how we have received forgiveness of sin through Christ's passion by love, redemption, and the power of God. He draws the church into it thusly:

> For since He is our head, then, by the Passion which He endured from love and obedience, He delivered us as His members from our

> sins, as by the price of His Passion: in the same way as if a man by the good industry of his hands were to redeem himself from a sin committed with his feet. For, just as the natural body is one though made up of diverse members, so the whole Church, Christ's mystic body, is reckoned as one person with its head, which is Christ. (*ST* III.49.1)

This participation with the head is intended to be a complete participation. It is not simply that one is now in Christ and receives all the benefits there. Rather, the believer's own life and sufferings are participatory in meriting grace, bringing salvation, and growing in Christlikeness.

Therefore, in Aquinas's theology, salvation comes to believers to the extent that they are participating in God and receiving the grace of Christ that merits salvation for them. This grace is not simply imparted to them; rather, it is gradually infused into them as they participate in the acts of grace in the church, namely, the sacraments. Aquinas understands that the sacraments are necessary for salvation, so that "through the institution of the sacraments man, consistently with his nature, is instructed through sensible things; he is humbled, through confessing that he is subject to corporeal things, seeing that he receives assistance through them: and he is even preserved from bodily hurt, by the healthy exercise of the sacraments" (*ST* III.61.1). In short, God has decided to provide grace to humanity by means of the sacraments in the church such that there is no way to receive saving grace apart from them.

For the Church

It is intriguing to think of the medieval period as a footnote on the work of Augustine, for many Protestants conceive of the period as more of a period to leap over, to learn what not to do, or the foil the great saviors of the Reformation have to confront. There is no doubt that the theological development we have seen has gone in a direction away from what Protestants see in the Bible. Nevertheless, as we have also seen, this period is rich with a diversity of thought and is in need of a retrieval, especially for evangelicals today. Let me conclude by pointing to a few areas that we can ponder from medieval soteriology that can be beneficial for our work today.

First, the doctrine of predestination is not merely a Reformation construct. Evangelicals typically think about the tension that exists between Calvinistic and Arminian understandings of salvation. However, as we have seen, the questions on the ability and the freedom of an individual person in salvation are greatly debated in all periods of church history. We have especially seen this in the works of Augustine, John Scottus Eriugena, Gottschalk, and Thomas Aquinas, to name a few. We have seen positions presented, such as Augustiniansim, Pelagianism, single predestination, and double predestination, and in looking at these we should notice the particular nuances that arise in every conversation. The medieval theologians were greatly interested in the mechanics of salvation and especially of predestination, and we should be as well. We also should note that this conversation is complex and entails more than proof-texting the Bible or Augustine. Exegesis and reason are important tools to utilize in trying to answer this age-old question of to what extent our salvation is dependent on the freedom that is in our personhood.

Second, when we think about salvation and the work of Christ, we need to see that Christ actually accomplished salvation for us through that work. The multiple theories of the atonement that we have presented show that the medieval theologians were greatly interested not just in supporting orthodox Christology of the God-man, but also in answering the question of why God became man. In fact, the many systems of the church developing during the medieval period were intended to aid in the obtaining and retention of salvation for people. Even Abelard's conception of Jesus as a moral influence believed that his work actually obtained justification and reconciliation for those who are united to him. The Thomistic turn to an infused righteousness through the works of the church in the life of a believer was motivated by a desire to bring the effects of Christ's work to individual believers. Even when we do not agree with some of the positions in the medieval period, we can join them in their tireless work to ponder the mechanics of the atonement and aid individuals in receiving that atonement. We should continue to ponder these questions and develop our belief in the atonement as we stand on the shoulders of Irenaeus, Athanasius, Anselm, Calvin, and others.

Finally, we should see the medieval period not as a time of divergence from the truth but as an important period of theological development. Admittedly, we as Protestants will find teachings in this era with which we greatly disagree, but we do not let that keep us from engaging this period, for if we did we would be missing out on the works of theological grace given. In short, we as evangelicals need to have a retrieval of medieval theology for the betterment and progress of our own.

For Further Reading

Anselm. *Anselm of Canterbury: The Major Works*. Oxford World's Classics, edited by G. R. Evans and Brian Davies. Oxford: Oxford University Press, 1998.

Evans, G. R., ed. *The Medieval Theologians: An Introduction to Theology in the Medieval Period*. Malden, MA: Blackwell, 2001.

Fairweather, Eugene Rathbone, ed. *A Scholastic Miscellany: Anselm to Ockham*. Library of Christian Classics. Vol. 10. Philadelphia: Westminster, 1956.

Madigan, Kevin. *Medieval Christianity: A New History*. New Haven, CT: Yale University Press, 2015.

Thomas Aquinas. *The Summa Theologiæ*.

van Nieuwenhove, Rik. *An Introduction to Medieval Theology*. Cambridge: Cambridge University Press, 2012.

QUESTIONS FOR STUDY OR DISCUSSION

1. Who are the major figures who developed medieval salvation doctrines, and when and where did they live?
2. How is the medieval era's consideration of salvation more than just a commentary on the teaching of Augustine?
3. What areas in the medieval era require further study for retrieval to help evangelicals in the twenty-first century?

7

SCRIPTURE AND TRADITION

By William M. Marsh

Introduction

In his 1520 treatise, *To the Christian Nobility of the German Nation Concerning the Reform of the Christian Estate*, the sixteenth-century German reformer Martin Luther (1483–1546) famously sought to tear down three "paper walls" he believed the Roman Catholic Church had erected during the Middle Ages to enshrine its own ecclesiastical authority. These were the superiority of the spiritual estate over the temporal (first wall); the supremacy of papal authority in the interpretation of Holy Scripture (second wall); and the claim that only the pope could call and confirm a council (third wall). Typically, Protestants look to this treatise as a foundational source for the Reformation doctrine of the priesthood of all believers, yet one must not overlook the root of Luther's concern: the proper relationship between Scripture and tradition. All three walls are interrelated, but the second and third walls particularly testify to the problematic state of the church's grasp and practice of the dynamic between Scripture and tradition by the end of the late Middle Ages that became Luther's inheritance.

Even if the later medieval period gave occasion for the Reformers to recapture what has come to be regarded as Protestantism's Scripture principle (i.e., *sola Scriptura*), the 1,000-year span that constitutes the Middle Ages should not be superficially reduced to a monolithic position on the relationship between biblical and ecclesiastical authority. The medieval period's significant contribution to fields such as the history of the Bible, the doctrine of Scripture, biblical interpretation, and the role of tradition within the church witnesses to its lasting value and contemporary relevance while also offering a cautionary tale not to be quickly forgotten. This chapter will draw attention to the major developments representative of the three divisions of the medieval period (early, high, and late Middle Ages) pertinent to the church's understanding of Scripture and tradition.

Historical Overview

Early Middle Ages (500–1000)

In the years that passed from the end of the patristic age to the eleventh century, Christianity grew to become the dominant cultural influence within Europe and the Western world as the Roman Empire faded. The Bible itself played a critical role in spreading Christianity's pervasive impact on European identity and society, largely due to the lasting legacy of the early church fathers. The transition from the patristic period to the early Middle Ages exhibited general agreement on Scripture and tradition and their interrelationship, even as immediate medieval beneficiaries of the Fathers' legacy built on the massive body of literature left behind for them. The two major figures from the Latin tradition, whose influence greatly shaped the early medieval period, were Jerome (347–420) and Augustine (354–430).

Jerome's translation of the Bible, known as the *Vulgate,* became the established biblical text for much of the medieval West. This was particularly true as it grew in use from the fifth century up to Charlemagne's demand in the eighth century for better practices in Bible transmission for the sake of a noncorrupted text that he perceived as integral for uniting the kingdom in Christian worship. Under Jerome's impact from his commitment to the biblical languages, especially Hebrew, and his exegetical commentaries, early monastic communities shifted in their vision as places of ascetic "wilderness" refuge to centers for intensive Bible reading and study as well as the preservation and reproduction of the scriptural text.

Jerome's contemporary, Augustine of Hippo, likewise exerted tremendous influence that reached all the way from the end of the patristic era to the late Middle Ages and the sixteenth-century Reformation. The principal contribution from Augustine that shaped so much of the medieval period's view of and approach to Scripture was his classic work on scriptural interpretation, *De doctrina Christiana* ("On Christian Teaching"). In this book, Augustine advances his theory of signification (i.e., the Bible as a text of "signs" [*signa*] pointing to "things" [*res*]) and puts forward the seven "mystical rules" for discerning the "hidden" meaning in Scripture from the fourth-century Donatist, Tyconius. These two primary points in *On Christian Teaching* set in place the well-known medieval commitments to the division of Scripture into "the letter and the Spirit" and the multiple senses of scriptural meaning. This "multiple sense" approach received further establishment as the prime practice of reading Scripture during the Middle Ages by the fifth-century monk John Cassian (360–435), who similarly separated theoretical knowledge of Scripture into historical and spiritual understandings. This division took shape into what often is recognized as the *Quadriga*, the fourfold method of literal (historical), allegorical (spiritual, theological), tropological (moral), and anagogical (eschatological, hoped for) senses.

The move from the age of the Fathers to the early Middle Ages cannot be determined by a clear break, but instead was gradual. Nevertheless, the Venerable Bede (672–735), an English monk from the Northumbria monastery of Wearmouth-Jarrow, could be seen as one who stands as a link between the two periods in the early eighth century. He also represents the expansion of the patristic legacy beyond the world of the Roman Empire further into western and northern Europe. Famous for his *Ecclesiastical History*, Bede produced much more with works in biblical chronology, biblical commentaries, and homilies. Although he sought to live underneath the tutelage of the Fathers, especially Augustine, desirous for their work to be handed down, Bede aimed to make his own contributions. He wrote commentaries on books of the Bible without patristic precedent, like Ezra–Nehemiah, and his approach to scriptural interpretation continued the fourfold method while exhibiting freedom from it as he sought to guide laymen into a clear understanding and application of the biblical text. Even though Bede maintained a high view of the place of "teachers" within God's plan, this "tradition" remained distinct for him from his confidence in the supreme authority of Holy Scripture over all of life and truth, whether Christian or secular.

The next major period within the early Middle Ages came with the Carolingian era shortly after Bede's death, stretching from the late eighth to the ninth century. Known also as the "Carolingian Renaissance," Charlemagne (Charles the Great) built an empire that covered and shaped continental Europe like never before, initiating educational reforms with the Bible at their center. In 789, Charlemagne issued his *Admonitio generalis*, which led to the creation of new monastic and cathedral schools, where preservation, production, and study of sacred literature, foremost among them the Holy Scriptures, could flourish. As aforementioned, the Carolingian age standardized Jerome's Vulgate for the remainder of the medieval period through its efforts to establish a corrected text with notable achievements from Theodulf of Orleans (760–821), a bishop of Orleans in France who labored to arrive at a Bible that contained the *Hebraica Veritas* (Jerome's notion of the "Hebrew truth"), and Alcuin of York (735–804), abbot of the Tours monastery. York's "Touronian Bible" underwent such careful scholarship and quality production in mass copies that some scholars have supposed it to be the official Bible of the Carolingian empire.

Besides critical work on the biblical text, the Carolingian age witnessed substantial commentarial contributions. Still, these biblical commentators aimed to make the patristic legacy accessible for other teachers and students of the Scriptures. Their labors resulted in the compilation and organization of the Fathers' comments into a running biblical commentary in cases like Alcuin's commentary on the Gospel of John, Haimo of Auxere (840–870) on the Song of Songs, and Hrabanus Maurus (780–856) on the books of Samuel and Kings. The efforts of the latter two, in particular, to generate biblical commentaries by collecting the comments of the early church Fathers, set the stage for the formation of the *Glossa ordinaria* ("Ordinary Gloss") in the twelfth century.

In sum, the Carolingian renaissance could be recognized as the program of Augustine's *On Christian Teaching*. Reforms in education were motivated by the notion that learning was for the study of the Holy Scriptures. Yet reading and interpreting the Bible did not happen apart from the study of the Fathers. Nevertheless, the early medievals' high view of the patristic tradition ought not to be mistaken for a denial of the material sufficiency of Scripture. The Fathers provided an interpretive service to the church that was perceived to support the preservation and grasp of the divinely authoritative revelation of God from the prophets and the apostles disclosed in Holy Scripture. The elevation of "tradition" to a source on equal footing with the material authority of the Bible would not strongly develop until the fourteenth century.

High Middle Ages (1000–1300)

From the eleventh to the thirteenth century, the Middle Ages matured into a period of many significant developments that are a testimony to the richness of this moment in Christian history for Scripture and tradition. This time witnessed heavy output from monastic and cathedral schools. At the

Norman abbey of Bec, Lefranc of Pavia (1005–1089) devoted considerable attention to the Pauline corpus, employing a form of "rhetorical" analysis on the apostles' letters to discern their "argument." Similarly, Bruno of Cologne (1035–1101) (or Bruno the Carthusian) at the cathedral school of Reims authored commentaries on the Psalter and Paul's epistles, including Hebrews, applying the tools of the liberal arts for close grammatical, literary, and rhetorical interpretation of the Scriptures. Both Lefranc and Bruno engaged the biblical text to discern authorial intention. In Liège, the Benedictine monk, Rupert of Duetz (1075–1129), wrote a commentary on the whole Bible titled *On the Trinity and His Works*. Rupert sought to understand God's nature as triune through examination of his creative and redemptive acts in Scripture, with special focus on God the Son and "the mystery of Christ" in the Old Testament. Additionally, his work on the Song of Songs introduced an original, spiritual reading of it as a hymn to the virgin Mary.

Perhaps one of the most influential places during this period of the Middle Ages for the study of the Bible was the School of St. Victor. Founded in 1110 by William of Champeaux, the abbey of St. Victor became a well-known center for biblical history and studies, which manifested strong embrace of an Augustinian vision as set forth in *On Christian Teaching*. Hugh of St. Victor (1096–1140) based his *Didascalicon* on Augustine's "signification theory," allowing for multiple senses in Scripture; however, he gave priority to the literal, historical meaning as the ground for and from which all other senses were understood. Hugh's student, Andrew of St. Victor (d. 1175), continued to privilege the Bible's literal sense in his exegetical work, drawing from Jewish sources for his approach to the Old Testament. In contrast to Andrew, Richard of St. Victor (d. 1173), another of Hugh's students, practiced a more experiential reading of Scripture with preference for the allegorical and tropological senses. His *Book of Notes* sought to complete the introduction to the Victorine approach to biblical interpretation started by Hugh in the *Didascalicon*, which Richard believed his commentary on Revelation exemplified.

The eleventh and twelfth centuries were also a period of major literary contributions on Holy Scripture. The first notable achievement is the *Glossa ordinaria*. "Glosses" were explanations of a biblical passage added into the margins or in between the lines of the text (i.e., interlinear). By the end of the twelfth century, the cathedral schools had compiled the patristic and Carolingian exegetical comments into glosses on the whole Bible. At this point, only "glossed" biblical books came off of the printing press. Not until 1485 in Strasburg was the *Glossa ordinaria* printed as one book, though in four volumes. Often Anselm of Laon (1050–1117) is attributed as the source and director of the *Glossa*. For some scholars, Anselm's precise involvement in the *Glossa* project remains obscure; nevertheless, it is likely that his brother Ralph of Laon and a colleague, Gilbert the Universal (d. 1134), labored extensively to complete the work of glossing the entire Bible. The *Glossa* would become the standard commentarial work on Scripture throughout the Middle Ages.

The second notable accomplishment during this period is Peter Comestor's (1100–1178) *Historia scholastica*, written near the end of the twelfth century. Biblical chronology and history were of central importance in the proper reading and interpretation of Holy Scripture in the high Middle Ages. Hugh of St. Victor had already submitted his own attempt at utilizing world history as a frame for the right approach to the Bible and doctrine in his work *Chronicon*. This commitment flowed from his view of the foundational priority of Scripture's literal sense. Carrying this outlook forward, Peter Comestor, a "master" from the Paris cathedral, wrote the *Historia scholastica*, a running commentary on the chronological, historical sequence of Scripture, with the aim of explaining the Bible according to its literal sense. If the *Glossa* could obscure the story line of the Bible, due to the abundance of glosses from the other "senses" (e.g., allegorical, tropological, anagogical), then Comestor's *Historia scholastica* would narrow their attention directly to Scripture's literal meaning. Like the *Glossa*, on which he heavily relied, Peter's *Historia* soon became an established textbook for teaching Holy Scripture all the way through the late Middle Ages.

At the start of the thirteenth century, the mendicant orders of the Dominicans and the Franciscans were founded. Likewise, this same century saw the emergence of the "university" (e.g., Paris, Oxford, and Cambridge) that created "faculties of theology" shortly filled with secular clerics and mendicant friars, principally from the two orders aforementioned. The former received the title "Masters of the Sacred Page," which reflected their primary role as interpreters and preachers of the Word of God. Men such as Peter the Chanter (d. 1187) and Stephen Langton (1150–1228) desired to enact ecclesiastical reform among the practice of biblical exegesis and the training of clergy to prioritize the doctrinal and moral teaching of Holy Scripture over the monastic contemplative tradition for concrete application of the Bible to daily medieval life. In addition to highlighting the inseparability of biblical interpretation from practical holiness, this group—eventually recognized as the "Biblical-Moral School"—produced various aids for engaging Scripture, such as concordances, sermon collections, and further standardization of biblical chapter divisions.

Mendicant orders soon established a strong presence in the universities before the middle of the thirteenth century, exerting lasting influence on Scripture and tradition throughout the remainder of the Middle Ages. The Dominicans located at the convent in Paris, led by Hugh of St. Cher (1200–1263), provided an early accomplishment with the *Postilla*. The name derives from the Latin words *post illa*, which mean "after that" or "after these things." Cher's *Postilla* was another running commentary on Scripture originally intended to complement the *Glossa*, though it held a specific purpose for the preaching vision of the Dominican order. Hugh's "glossed Bible" would serve as a primary text for mendicant teaching of Holy Scripture until the fourteenth century.

In the second half of the thirteenth century, the Dominican Thomas Aquinas (1225–1274) left his indelible mark on Christian history and theology. Famous for his magisterial *Summa theologica*, Aquinas also penned biblical commentaries on books such as Job, the Psalter, and the Pauline epistles. Additionally, he prepared a gloss on the Gospels called the *Catena*

Aurea, introducing students to a wide array of exegetical sources from Athanasius to Hugh of St. Cher's *Postilla*. Besides literary contributions, Aquinas endeavored to make a methodological one. He engaged in focused reflection on the relationship between scriptural interpretation and theological argument, granting further authoritative priority to the literal sense of Scripture in the path of the Victorines. As heard in writings like his *Quodlibetal Questions*, all spiritual senses, allegorical or otherwise, should be authorized by the biblical text's literal sense so as to safeguard the univocal meaning of Scripture's unified message. In this way, the literal sense governs all matters of Christian faith propagated by a spiritual sense.

Aquinas's Franciscan contemporary Bonaventure (1221–1274) likewise devoted consideration to exegetical and theological method. He authored many works adding to the list of the biblical commentary tradition within the medieval period, including ones on Ecclesiastes and the Gospels of Luke and John, while also generating a compendium of theology with the *Breviloquium*. The latter showed movement in Bonaventure away from a view of theology primarily as *scientia* (i.e., science) toward theology as faith for *sapientia* (i.e., wisdom), or rather Scripture *as* theology. On the one hand, holy Scripture contains the definitive revelation of God, yet on the other hand, the Spirit continues to shed scriptural light on further elicited theories and divine truth through the world that accord with the Word. Both Aquinas and Bonaventure upheld the final authority of Scripture, but they also exhibit early signs of divergent ways of conceiving of how the Bible functions in relation to extrabiblical tradition and theological argument where Scripture is silent.

Late Middle Ages (1300–1500)

The fourteenth century marked a turning point in Scripture and tradition during the Middle Ages. Up to this juncture, medieval theologians and interpreters remained in basic harmony with their patristic forebears on the matter of Holy Scripture's supreme sufficiency and authority in relation to tradition. Yet, despite the continual affirmation of this view at the beginning of the fourteenth century, a dual understanding of Scripture and tradition as equally authoritative sources was undergoing construction. Some of this transition will be discussed shortly. Beforehand, attention needs to be drawn to other important figures and contributions for the study of the Bible in the late Middle Ages.

The biblical commentator who could be argued as, perhaps, the most influential for this medieval period is the Franciscan Nicholas of Lyra (1270–1349). As a member of the Franciscan mendicant order, Lyra also served as a "master" of theology at the University of Paris. His greatest achievement was his commentary on the entire Bible known as the *Postilla Litteralis*, which he likely composed while engaged in the "cursory" reading of the Bible, an approach established in the thirteenth century under the influence of Peter the Chanter's educational program, whereby lecturers and students would read the Bible from beginning to end according to its literal sense. To aid Lyra in his diligence to discern the literal sense resistant to the distraction of "spiritual" or "mystical" senses, he drew heavily from rabbinic exegesis, particularly from the work of Rashi (1040–1105; Rabbi Solomon). He was an eleventh-century French rabbi known for his preference for the *peshat* (i.e., the plain meaning of the text) approach to Hebrew exegesis. Eventually, Lyra's *Postilla* would be printed along with the *Glossa ordinaria*, surpassing Hugh of St. Cher's "postils" to become the primary resource for teaching Scripture in the schools into the sixteenth century.

Indebted to Lyra, the English theologian John Wyclif, also spelled Wycliffe (1328–1384), was next to produce a "whole Bible" commentary in the last quarter of the fourteenth century, once again giving primacy to the biblical text's literal meaning. Subsequent to his *Postilla super totam bibliam*, Wyclif penned a defense, *On the Truth of Holy Scripture*, to counter notions at the time of the illogical coherence of the Bible's literal sense. In this treatise Wyclif charges interpreters not to retreat to extrabiblical tradition or literature like the Fathers to clarify obscurities or uncertainties about the meaning of a biblical text, but rather, Scripture itself should be consulted so as to interpret itself, a principle that would later figure prominently in the

Reformation era. Alongside these writings, one other major contribution that appeared in the last decades of the fourteenth century for which Wyclif is known is the "Wycliffite Bible." Although bearing his name, Wyclif most likely merely inspired and oversaw this work while the translation efforts to render the Bible in its entirety into English were shared by a group of scholars working at the University of Oxford.

An opponent of the ecclesiastical reform that Wyclif and others (e.g., Jan Hus) launched, Jean Gerson (1363–1429), the chancellor of the University of Paris, shared similar commitments to the foundational importance of Scripture's literal sense in the early fifteenth century. Nevertheless, Gerson recognized that interpretations of the literal meaning of a biblical text in theological argumentation needed some of kind of authoritative means for determination of the truth. In a treatise titled *On the Literal Interpretation of Sacred Scripture and the Causes of Error*, Gerson advocated for a rhetorical approach in the way of Augustine's *On Christian Teaching*, where the literal sense is not equated with the "letter" of the scriptural text, since the *verba* ("words") could signify *res* ("things") beyond the mere "letter" of the human author as the true intention of the divine author, the Holy Spirit. To arrive at the proper literal meaning of Scripture, in contrast to Wyclif's exhortation to "let Scripture interpret Scripture," Gerson put forward the church's tradition as an interpretive norm to resolve disputes over variant renderings of a biblical text's literal sense. This methodological move served to raise tradition as a source inspired and preserved by the Holy Spirit at an authoritative level with Holy Scripture.

Case Studies

Case Study 1: The Literal Sense of Scripture, Authorial Intention, and Authority

As the medieval period progressed from the high to late Middle Ages, the question of method increasingly received treatment from interpreters and theologians to clarify questions about biblical and ecclesiastical authority. Early developments in this discussion can be traced back particularly to the School of St. Victor in the twelfth century. The impact of the Victorines on biblical interpretation should be observed in its proper context. The "spiritual," or even more precisely, the "allegorical and tropological" senses gained prominence in the early Middle Ages in part due to the influence of monastic reading and teaching of Holy Scripture. Although dating back to the sixth century, the practice of *lectio divina* experienced renewal in the early twelfth century through the commendation of the Cistercian monk Bernard of Clairvaux (1090–1153). *Lectio divina* was a prayerful, meditative exercise in Bible reading that one pursued for contemplation of the divine mysteries (i.e., mystical sense) contained in Scripture and to undergo proper Christian formation in communion with God in his Word. Bernard's sermon collection on the Song of Songs was meant to demonstrate and cultivate this endeavor. But with the emergence of the monastic and cathedral schools and the universities during the twelfth century, free contemplative meditation on Scripture lacked adequate authoritative determination to address the multiplicity of interpretations. The answer was a revived understanding of the literal sense of Scripture.

Hugh of St. Victor played a significant role in the reinvigoration of the literal sense. Instead of treating the "letter" of the biblical text as simply an entryway into a deeper, spiritual meaning, Hugh desired to ground allegorization in the historicity of Scripture's record. In his treatise *On Sacred Scripture and Its Authors*, Hugh submitted that one should not make claims to knowing Scripture if he does not know the "letter" (i.e., the literal sense).

Ultimately, for Hugh, the literal meaning was identified with biblical history, which was also the authoritative interpretation of world history. His efforts led to increased medieval interest in the place of history and chronology in biblical interpretation.

Andrew of St. Victor, a student of Hugh's, continued to promote the primacy of the literal, historical sense by attempting to learn from Jewish exegesis. The Jewish commentaries, he believed, ought to carry an authoritative weight for the right interpretation of Old Testament texts, even if their authors did not embrace Christian faith. This commitment often caused Andrew to locate the literal sense of an Old Testament passage with its immediate historical context, thereby precluding common Christian interpretations from assuming Christ as the direct referent of prophetic utterances. "The mystery of Christ" might remain present within a given Old Testament text, but this understanding would be grasped in its spiritual sense, not literal meaning. Andrew's fellow canon at the School of St. Victor, Richard of St. Victor, was unsettled by Andrew's preference for Jewish commentary over the tradition of the Christian reading of the Old Testament. In a notable instance, Richard responded to Andrew in a treatise titled *On Emmanuel*, concerning the latter's decision to regard the literal sense of Isa 7:14 as a historical reference to the son of the prophet Isaiah's wife rather than the birth of Jesus Christ, the Incarnate One, to the virgin Mary. Richard upheld that the literal sense of Isaiah's prophecy was, indeed, the sign of the virgin birth of Christ to Mary for the advent of the incarnation of God's Son. Once again, this literal meaning, for Richard, should not be mistaken for the biblical text's "spiritual sense." To ascribe to the literal sense the immediate historical context instead of widening the scope to consist of all of God's history of salvation exposed, according to Richard, the absence of the Spirit's illuminating work on Christian readers who approach the Holy Scriptures in faith.

Like Hugh and Andrew, Richard continued to stress the foundational importance of the literal sense for biblical interpretation that witnessed the movement of appeal made to it for authoritative determination of Scripture's truth. One result of these labors was an extended conception of the literal sense of Scripture that freed it from being too historically particularized, thus allowing for a "parabolic" or "prophetic" dimension. The Dominican scholastic theologian, Thomas Aquinas, further developed this approach in the thirteenth century with his own attempt to ground the spiritual sense of Scripture in its literal meaning. To do so, Aquinas taught that the verbal signification of the "letter" of the biblical text could be extended to consist of not only the historical referent, but also a "figurative" sense or biblical metaphor. The faith to be believed and matters of theological argument ought to rest on the revealed truth of God, and Aquinas considered the Scripture's *verba* ("words") themselves as that revelation, not the *res* ("things") they might signify; therefore, the Christian faith stands on the sufficiency and authority of Holy Scriptures according to their literal sense.

Central to Aquinas's position was authorial intention, an element of biblical interpretation that experienced significant theoretical construction during the thirteenth century and the late Middle Ages. Divine authorship of Scripture had always loomed large in the study of the Bible to this point in the history of interpretation, but with the literal sense undergoing renewal, focus began to be redirected to the human author's meaning as the locus of the biblical text's literal sense. The assumption that the literal meaning of a human author's intent could pertain to doctrinal content delivered through "figurative," or symbolic, expression caused the spiritual (or "theological") sense from the Divine Author to be conveyed verbally through grasp of the biblical author's meaning. Analysis of biblical discourse and genre became a means to arrive at the revealed knowledge of God. Additionally, over the course of the thirteenth century, medieval literary theory itself developed precise understandings for the terms *auctor* ("author") and *auctoritas* ("authority"). An *auctor* was more than a writer; it was someone to be trusted, worthy to be heard. *Auctoritas* communicated that something was regarded as authoritative and worth belief because of its truthfulness and sagacity. Applied to Scripture, the biblical authors were approached as those whose writings supremely held intrinsic *auctoritas,* conveyed at the level of their literal sense, namely, their authorial intention, wherein they disclosed divine speech from the inspiration of the divine author, God the Spirit, to be heard and confessed in their revelatory *verba*. The assignment of doctrinal authority to the literal sense of Scripture would become a key element in the battles over Scripture and tradition in the late Middle Ages leading up to the beginnings of the sixteenth-century Reformation.

Case Study 2: The Literal Sense and Papal Infallibility

For some observers of church history, it might come as a surprise to learn that the Roman Catholic doctrine of papal infallibility did not receive an official declaration until Vatican I in 1870. Movement in that direction certainly increased during disputes over the proper relationship between the authority of Scripture and the church's teaching on ecclesial matters. In such conflicts, tradition served a deliberative role in discernment of Christian truth and practice that coheres with biblical teaching. For most of the Middle Ages, tradition stood for the "deposit of faith," that is, the sacred literature that expounded what the church was to believe. Before the expansion of the literal sense, spiritual or allegorical exegesis of Scripture held primary responsibility for preserving and handing down this tradition to successive generations. With the advent of a revised conception of Scripture's literal sense, tradition entered into a more formal articulation rather than contemplative assent as it had in the early medieval period. Instead of faithfulness to tradition as the exercise of receptive learning from the patristic heritage, the late Middle Ages saw tradition change into the establishment of authoritative, doctrinal positions and ecclesial practices to the point that tradition no longer represented a person's disposition toward the patristic legacy, but, instead, tradition became what one accepts in submission to religious authority.

One such debate surrounded the question of papal infallibility; that is, could the pope err? By the fourteenth century, the literal sense had undergone complex development so that it might extend to spiritual or mystical senses intended by human authorship as the communication of divine meaning. To determine the God-revealed truth of Scripture, extrabiblical tradition provided numerous sources to enlist for theological determination from the writings of the Fathers to canon laws to papal decrees. For example, the Franciscan nominalist William of Ockham (1287–1347) rallied in support of the papacy by explicating a type of two-source theory of divine truth in his *Dialogus*. In reply to the rejection of papal use of Matt 16:18–19 to support its doctrine of Petrine primary as the origin of the pope's office and authority, Ockham conceded that the doctrine of the papacy was not intended by the evangelist's literal sense. The lack of witness, however, in the biblical text's literal meaning did not exhaust the possibility of doctrinal truth for Ockham. In the first place, discernment of universal, Christian truth could come in ultimately two modes: the revelation of God and/or as found in Holy Scripture. On the first mode, the true Christian church could receive a valid doctrine through extrabiblical revelation that was contained in nonscriptural, reliable sources passed down from the apostles to their disciples, and so on to the Fathers. This exegetical tradition carried with it divine authority in theological argument as a source next to the principal, divine authority of Holy Scripture.

The Franciscans remained at the center of debates concerning the papal office and its authority during the late Middle Ages, for they maintained that the papacy had sanctioned the rights and privileges of their mendicant order and life of Christian poverty in a papal bull decreed by Pope Nicholas III in 1279. In an attempt to protect against any retraction of their rule by a false pope, Peter John Olivi (1248–1298) became an early advocate for the doctrine of papal infallibility. Alongside Matt 16:18–19, Olivi placed Luke 22:32, which he understood as Christ's words addressed directly to Peter with the promise that his "faith would never fail." It was already established that the true church could not err in matters of truth essential for salvation. If error in this way were possible, the church would be emptied of its authority concerning the faith to be believed. Likewise, the papal office, in succession from Peter, holds the "office of the keys" over the universal church, and thus, Olivi concluded, God would never have given the fullness of power (*plenitudine potestatis*) to someone responsible for deciding on matters of Christian faith, truth, and divine law who could err. Here, one can see the walls slowly being erected that Martin Luther in the early sixteenth century would strive to tear down.

For the Church

It is the authors' hope that this introduction to Scripture and tradition in the Middle Ages will persuade you that the medieval period should not remain darkened in our evangelical mind. This survey has only scratched the surface of the rich soil during this 1,000-year stretch of Christian history, ready to be plowed and resourced for the church's ongoing faithful devotion to the Holy Scriptures. In light of the material covered in this chapter, four main considerations capture well some initial rationale for the church not to neglect the medieval period as it continues to pursue a right understanding of Scripture and tradition.

First, the Middle Ages can teach us how to appreciate and read the Bible as a book. The Bible underwent extensive development as a codex to a printed literary work during this period, witnessing the creation and addition of many paratextual aids, such as verses, chapter divisions, prologues, and concordances. The medievals exhibited keen awareness that the everyday Christian would require some assistance to read and study the Holy Scriptures, and they endeavored to provide ample resources for the church and the individual to hear the Holy Spirit speak clearly through the prophets and the apostles in the biblical canon. Especially from the twelfth century onward, increased attention to grammatical, philological, and literary analysis helped refresh the church's interpretive vision toward pursuit of authorial intention as a way for rightly prioritizing the "letter" of the written revelation of God's Word. Central figures of the Protestant Reformation, such as Martin Luther and John Calvin, continued this attentiveness to the *text* of

Scripture as foundational to their contributions to bibliology and biblical interpretation during the sixteenth century that have come to characterize evangelical commitments to the Bible. If Reformers like Luther and Calvin were not entirely novel in their view of and approach to Scripture, then gaining greater familiarity with the medieval period could only strengthen the church's present-day handling of the inspired and inerrant biblical *text*.

Second, current trends among evangelicals show renewed interest in the history of interpretation, theological interpretation of Scripture, and the use of tradition for theological retrieval. From the early to late Middle Ages, medieval scholars and theologians never ceased to read and interpret the Bible apart from tradition, whether patristic or even contributors from their own era. Overwhelmingly, this interpretative and theological approach was practiced underneath resolved confession of Holy Scripture's absolute sufficiency and authority. As the medieval period displays, the question of Scripture's relation to theology will remain a perennial one. Today's church will benefit from awareness of how the medievals wrestled with this issue from the development of sermons to the cultivation of biblical and theological wisdom for facing contemporary challenges. How to proceed in fields such as hermeneutical discussions about the proper way to read the Bible theologically, or what might constitute a theological commentary, or how to draw upon church tradition for doctrinal discernment would find in the Middle Ages many guides, examples, and fresh material ready to be retrieved.

Third, the medieval period saw the coexistence of the ecclesial, monastic, and university communities. Although these groups experienced significant division as the friction, in particular, between the schoolmen ("masters") and the mendicant orders during the late Middle Ages attest, a significant portion of the medieval period displayed impressive academic activity. Such activity was done precisely for the church, with the spiritual condition of the individual Christian in view across monastic and cathedral schools as well as theology faculty from the university. Present-day dichotomies between church and the academy could learn much from the positive demonstrations of the collaborative scholarly and ecclesial work done for the sake of the faithful ministry of the Word of God always for the people of God. Careful study of their interplay during the medieval period manifests that such a division is late, foreign, unnecessary, and unfortunate for the church.

Finally, the Middle Ages issue a warning to the contemporary church that should not go unheard. Precursors to the Reformation scripture principle *sola Scriptura* abound throughout the medieval period; however, the search for final authority on a given theological matter, especially one that is either implicit in Scripture or on which the Bible remains totally silent, will soon realize that competing interpretations or conclusions are made with both parties claiming their view as the "biblical" one. The later Middle Ages moved in the direction of resolving such situations with reenvisioned ideas about ecclesiastical authority and recourse to extrabiblical sources. For Protestants, these options would undo the achievements of the Reformation, yet these sorts of dilemmas will not cease this side of Christ's return and the Beatific Vision. In the meantime, evangelicals would do well to continue thinking carefully about how central commitments to scriptural sufficiency and authority properly relate to theological method, especially as it pertains to how one might answer the enduring question of what makes any given doctrine or position "biblical."

For Further Reading

Allison, Gregg R. *Historical Theology: An Introduction to Christian Doctrine.* Grand Rapids: Zondervan, 2011.

Bray, Gerald. *Biblical Interpretation: Past and Present.* Downers Grove, IL: IVP, 1996.

Froehlich, Karl. "'Always to Keep the Literal Sense in Holy Scripture Means to Kill One's Soul': The State of Biblical Hermeneutics at the Beginning of the Fifteenth Century." In *Literary Uses of Typology from the Late Middle Ages to the Present*, ed. Earl Miner, 20–48. Princeton, NJ: Princeton University Press, 1977.

Hagen, Kenneth, ed. *The Bible in the Churches: How Various Christians Interpret the Scriptures*. 3rd ed. Marquette Studies in Theology. Milwaukee, WI: Marquette University Press, 1998.

Harkins, Franklin T., and Frans van Liere, eds. *Interpretation of Scripture: Theory: A Selection of Hugh, Andrew, Richard and Godfrey of St. Victor, and of Robert of Melun*. Victorine Texts in Translation. Belgium: Brepols, 2012.

Levy, Ian Christopher. *Holy Scripture and the Quest for Authority at the End of the Middle Ages*. Notre Dame, IN: University of Notre Dame Press, 2012.

———. *Introducing Medieval Biblical Interpretation: The Senses of Scripture in Premodern Exegesis*. Grand Rapids: Baker Academic, 2018.

———. "The Literal Sense of Scripture and the Search for Truth in the Late Middle Ages." *Revue D'Histoire Ecclésiastique* 104 (2009): 783–827.

Levy, Ian Christopher, Philip D. W. Krey, and Thomas F. Ryan, eds. *The Letter to the Romans*. Translated by Ian Christopher Levy, Philip D. W. Krey, and Thomas F. Ryan. The Bible in the Medieval Tradition. Grand Rapids: Eerdmans, 2013.

Lubac, Henri de. *Medieval Exegesis: The Four Senses of Scripture*. Vol. 1. Translated by Mark Sebanc. Grand Rapids: Eerdmans, 1998.

Marsden, Richard, and E. Ann Matter, eds. *The Bible: Volume 2: From 600 to 1450,* The New Cambridge History of the Bible. Cambridge: Cambridge University Press, 2012.

Mathison, Keith A. *The Shape of Sola Scriptura*. Moscow, ID: Canon, 2001.

Minnis, Alastair. *Medieval Theory of Authorship: Scholastic Literary Attitudes in the Later Middle Ages*. 2nd ed. Philadelphia: University of Pennsylvania Press, 2010.

Oberman, Heiko A. *The Dawn of the Reformation: Essays in Late Medieval and Early Reformation Thought*. Grand Rapids: Eerdmans, 1986.

———. *Forerunners of the Reformation: The Shape of Late Medieval Thought*. Philadelphia: Fortress, 1981.

———. *The Harvest of Medieval Theology: Gabriel Biel and Late Medieval Nominalism*. 3rd ed. Grand Rapids: Baker Academic, 2000.

Ocker, Christopher. "Biblical Interpretation in the Middle Ages." In *Dictionary of Major Biblical Interpreters*, ed. Donald K. McKim, 2nd ed., 14–21. Downers Grove, IL: IVP, 2007.

Ozment, Steven. *The Age of Reform, 1250–1550: An Intellectual and Religious History of Late Medieval and Reformation Europe*. New Haven, CT: Yale University Press, 1980.

Preus, James S. *From Shadow to Promise: Old Testament Interpretation from Augustine to the Young Luther*. Cambridge, MA: Harvard University Press, 1969.

Smalley, Beryl. *The Study of the Bible in the Middle Ages*. 1952. Reprint, Notre Dame, IN: University of Notre Dame Press, 1964.

Thomas Aquinas. *Quodlibetal Questions*. Translated and introduced by Turner Nevitt and Brian Davies. Oxford: Oxford University Press, 2020.

Wyclif, John. *On the Truth of Holy Scripture*. Translated with an introduction and notes by Ian Christopher Levy. TEAMS Commentary. Kalamazoo, MI: Western Michigan Publications, 2001.

Questions for Study or Discussion

1. Describe the impact of the early church fathers Jerome and Augustine on the Middle Ages.
2. What was the Carolingian era known for in the early Middle Ages?
3. What was the School of St. Victor's lasting influence on medieval biblical interpretation?
4. How did Thomas Aquinas understand the relationship between the literal and spiritual senses of Scripture?
5. Explain the relationship between the literal sense of Scripture, authority, and tradition in the late Middle Ages.
6. How can one determine whether a doctrine is "biblical" that is not explicitly stated or affirmed in Scripture?

UNIT THREE

THEOLOGY IN THE REFORMATION ERA, AD 1500–1700

8

SCRIPTURE

By Matthew Barrett

Introduction

The sixteenth-century Reformation was a soteriological movement at its core. Martin Luther's (1483–1546) conflict with the Catholic Church over the indulgence system can be traced back to the existential crisis within his own soul. Young Martin, haunted by the sinfulness of sin, could not escape God *as judge.* Faithful as he was to follow the penance system, Martin found no relief. Grace seemed an impossibility when one's works, even works driven by faith, fell short. As a result, his conscience was plagued by the incessant insecurity of his salvation, incapable of achieving a peace that guaranteed God would acquit him on the last day.

But as this novice lecturer started wrestling with books of the Bible such as Psalms, Romans, and Hebrews, his entire paradigm began to shift. Righteousness was a gift from God, one to be received by faith. God was merciful, after all. Rather than depending on his works of merit, Martin threw himself at the mercy of the divine throne, clinging to nothing but grace and grace alone. In time, young Martin's eyes were also opened to what kind of gratuitous righteousness God extended to the ungodly. It is none other than the perfect righteousness of Christ Jesus, imputed to all who believe. No longer did Martin see Christ as his implacable judge, but as his sacrificial lamb, laying down his own life out of love for the ungodly.

Now that his theology of the cross had undergone a paradigm shift, Martin stood in the pulpit and the lectern alike as a new man, eyes wide open to the Savior he no longer hated but clung to for eternal life. The rest of Martin's reforming ministry can be summarized by the 1547 altarpiece by Lucas Cranach the Elder. In the middle hangs Christ crucified with Luther's family, congregation, and even the painter himself on the right. But on the left side of Christ and his cross stands Martin Luther himself. Elevated in the pulpit with the Scriptures open, Martin points with his finger to Christ, signaling his congregation to look to Christ alone for their justification. For Luther believed the Scriptures were the swaddling clothes in which Christ was born, delivering to the world a Savior through its inspired pages.

If the story of the Reformation ends with a concentration on the material principle alone, then the story is left unfinished. When Rome released its finest theologians on Luther—some seeking to silence him, others to debate him, and still others demanding a recantation—another issue bubbled to the surface: *Who has final authority to decide this debate over indulgences and justification?* Although soteriology might have been the spark that started the fire, authority was the gas that fueled that spark into a blazing flame. For when Luther was told to recant, he was faced with the ultimate decision: who should be obeyed, Scripture or Rome's popes and councils?

Historical Overview with Case Studies

Sola Scriptura *and the Reformation's Claim to Catholicity*

This question, Who has final authority to decide this debate? uprooted Germany and all of Europe as well when the Reformers answered with as much clarity as they did bravado: *Scripture alone*. Church councils and popes are to be followed and obeyed where they align with Scripture, but where they depart from Scripture, they can no longer be followed. For Scripture alone is inspired by God, and on that basis Scripture alone is impeccable, sufficient, and the church's final authority. The Reformers had a high place for tradition—many of them were experts in patristic and medieval exegesis and theology. They also held ecclesiastical authority in high esteem, as their own polity revealed in due time. Nevertheless, only Scripture is revelatory, breathed out by God himself. For that reason only, Scripture is the church's ultimate court of appeal, a court that can sit in judgment of the church itself when necessary.

It sometimes goes unnoticed by historians and theologians alike how persuaded the Reformers were that this formal principle—the very muscle of the Reformation cause—was *catholic* at its core. Rome put no little energy behind their well-organized broadcast of an unrelenting stereotype: *sola scriptura* is a novel belief, the banner of heretics alone. In response, the Reformers demonstrated that *sola scriptura* had roots, a heritage that could be traced back to some of the earliest and most important church fathers. The Reformers concluded that they were the true heirs of catholicity, not a novel movement of schismatics. This point deserves emphasis, since a common misreading of the Reformation persists today: *sola scriptura* was a debate between Scripture and tradition. To be precise, it was not. It was a debate between Scripture and a revisionist view of tradition, or what Protestants have called "traditionalism." To see why, the medieval context of this Reformation debate needs attention.

Tradition versus Tradition

Heiko Oberman, a medieval and Reformation historian, is acclaimed for introducing three historic views of tradition, differentiating between the otherwise clustered rivalries of the sixteenth century. Consider the first two (the third will come later):

First, take into consideration Tradition 1 (T1), the position of the church fathers and Reformers. T1 is the belief that tradition is a maidservant to Scripture, which alone is inspired by God and therefore the church's final authority in faith and practice. Scripture is not against tradition nor antithetical to tradition, as long as tradition is subservient to Scripture. For the Reformers, tradition carried an authority, one to be heeded; nevertheless, it is a ministerial authority. Scripture alone is the magisterial authority for the church. As mentioned, the Reformers were convinced they were not alone in their advocacy of T1, but a slew of patristic and medieval theologians likewise affirmed, or at least presupposed, the same position.

Second, over against the Reformers, many in Rome (though not all) insisted on Tradition 2 (T2). There is not just one source of inspired authority but two. Ecclesiastical tradition, consisting of Fathers, councils, the pope, and magisterium, is a conduit of inspired, divine revelation. It, too, is revelatory by nature. There are then not one but two conduits of revelation, which means Scripture cannot be sufficient, at least not in the way the Reformers implied. The voice of tradition must supplement Scripture, adding further clarity or even imperatives where the latter is either silent or ambiguous.

With Rome standing behind T2 and the Reformers behind T1, debates ensued as to which view of revelation and tradition was taught by the Roman Catholic Church. Rome believed T2 was the majority position of the church down through the ages. Whatever is made of that claim, T2 was present by the late medieval era. The years 1100–1400, for example, exhibited T2 in the endless disputes over ecclesiastical, papal, and conciliar power. As popes and councils vied for control, each became vocal that their authority was God-given, Spirit-inspired, and in some cases, on par with Scripture itself as a revelatory vehicle for infallible biblical interpretation, dogmatic formation, and ecclesiastical and (sometimes) even political declarations. One must not assume, however, that the wielding of tradition (in the spirit of T2) meant everyone agreed as to *who* that authority should be. The closer one approaches to the sixteenth century, the more defined the two schools become: (1) The *conciliarists* believed church councils were to be the voice of tradition, wielding authority even over the most prestigious of popes. (2) The *curialists* disagreed, believing the pope, the vicar of Christ on earth, was entrusted with the keys of the kingdom as Peter's proper heir. Therefore, he had final authority, even over the gathered consensus of councils.

The Rise of Curialism

By the end of the fifth century, there were signs of curialism, or at least the seeds had been planted for its future. The bishop of Rome took on a stance of political power, positioning him as head above other ecclesiastical authorities. For instance, Pope Gelasius I (d. 496) promulgated his own supremacy. As much as priests were to be obeyed, even priests were to bend the knee to Gelasius, a priest like no other, preeminent by nature of his office itself.

In the middle of the medieval era, Pope Gregory VII patterned himself on a similar mindset but perhaps one that went a step further. Not only was he preeminent but also infallible. As he announced in *Dictatus Papae* (1075), he was a bishop without error. So bold was Gregory VII that he also predicted he would never err. His decisions were as impeccable as Scripture.

A century later, other popes continued this upward trajectory, each intensifying and increasing their authority and its scope. Innocent III, whose reign extended from 1198 to 1216, not only was persuaded that priests were inferior to himself, the true mediator in the absence of Christ, but extended his authority to society as well. Even the emperor himself was to be subject to the vicar of Christ on earth. Boniface VIII extended papal authority to its logical end. In 1302 he issued a papal bull, *Unam Sanctam,* which declared subjection to the Roman pontiff a condition of salvation.

Such claims to papal power and infallibility gave birth to an era ripe for papal rivalry. At the start of the fifteenth century, not just one but three popes posed as the rightful heir to Peter's keys: Gregory XII, Benedict XIII, and John XXIII. They did so by means of a litany of ecclesiastical and political maneuvers in an effort to seize territories. This papal schism, better known as the "Great Western Schism" (1378–1417), resulted in each pope excommunicating the other popes. The irony of it all was not lost on the Reformers, who were quick to point out that the type of tradition certain Roman theologians claimed to be on par with Scripture had a history that proved its lack of uniformity and consensus.

The irony further thickened when a council, not a pope, met to settle the dispute. From 1414 to 1418 the Council of Constance gathered and appointed not one of the three but a fourth figure, Martin V, as pope. Conciliarism, so it would seem, had won. After all, *Sacrosancta* (1415) displayed a noted perspicuity concerning the preeminent authority a church council possessed from God. But Martin V turned right around and undermined *Sacrosancta,* positioning himself as the superior Godsend. So much for conciliarism.

Less than sixty years before the Reformation, curialism flexed its power with unprecedented finality. Pius II's papal bull *Execrabilis* (1460) announced that anyone who sidelined the pope for the sake of a council would be excommunicated. *Execrabilis* was aggressive, silencing *Sacrosancta* and, in no uncertain terms, establishing the pope as the divinely ordained and chosen authority, second to none. Then, with Martin Luther's personal crisis just underway, the Fifth Lateran Council (1512–1517) convened under Pope Julius II and, with no room for ambiguity, reiterated the pope's preeminent authority. There is reason to believe, however, that Julius was strategic, instilling curialists across the council to ensure this outcome. With papal power and supremacy at its height, who could have imagined that in just a few years the legitimacy of the papacy's authority would be called into question by an obscure German Augustinian whose conscience refused to be held captive by anything but the Word of God?

Captive to the Word: Luther versus Prierias, Cajetan, and Eck

A difference can be seen between Luther's writings before excommunication and his later writings as a hunted heretic. In his early writings, Luther appeals to the pope himself. Missing is the biting sarcasm and unwavering condemnation that colored Luther's more mature writings—writings that sometimes labeled the pope the Antichrist and without nuance. Early on, the inexperienced Luther might have been naive enough to think that the pope was unaware of abuses in the German indulgence system. *If only the system is exposed for what it is, then the pope will take action to reform the church from within.* But it was not long until Luther's eyes were opened and he saw just how informed the pope and his theologians were. That moment reached its pinnacle when Luther hung the papal bull threatening excommunication over the flames, and then let it burn along with volumes of canon law.

But years before the burning of the papal bull, Luther had to discover for himself what was at the center of his conflict with Rome. That discovery took form when Luther encountered the Dominican Sylvester Prierias (1456–1523), commissioned by Pope Leo X to refute Luther. Prierias's *Dialogue concerning the Power of the Pope* was lucid: even the Scriptures derived their authority from the pope and the Roman Catholic Church. Such a claim assumed a unified, divinely embedded, even revelatory authority, and Luther knew it. That was why he wasted no time stripping the papal history of its pristine façade. From Julius II to Boniface VIII, the papacy exhibited its impurity. By contrast, Luther appealed to the authority of councils—councils Prierias knew to be catholic (universal) in nature.

Yet Prierias upheld papal supremacy and, with it, papal infallibility. The latter was not grafted into Rome's official doctrines until 1870 at the First Vatican Council. Nevertheless, as historians of Rome have observed, the concept itself was present for centuries, sometimes beneath the surface but at other times conspicuous. This much is evident with the polemical agenda of Prierias, who brandished infallibility like a sword to pin Luther's heresy to the wall. For Luther not only appealed to councils instead of popes but also to the Scriptures as his infallible rule. Being the perceptive debater that Luther was—other Reformers paled in comparison (e.g., Andreas Karlstadt)—he resurrected Augustine's testimony that only the Bible was to be labeled God-breathed and insusceptible to error. Luther was implying that popes and councils were not, nor could they ever be, the final court of appeal in his debate with the Dominican.

Although many other debates with Rome might be explored, Luther's conflicts with Cajetan in Augsburg (1518) and Johann Eck in Leipzig (1519) stand out. When Cajetan appealed to bulls like Pope Clement VI's *Unigenitus* (1343), Luther responded that he could not side with an ambiguous decree by a pope over Scripture which has God's authorization. Cajetan's irritation blistered when Luther added that the average churchgoer with the Scriptures stood on a surer authority than any council or pope. But the Scriptures need the pope as their infallible interpreter, responded Cajetan. They do not, Luther retorted, for no one is above the Scriptures, not even His Holiness.

As tough an opponent as Cajetan proved to be, Eck (1486–1543) was tougher yet. Perhaps with even more of an agenda than Prierias and Cajetan, Eck capitalized on the issue of authority. By now, Luther was maturing in his gradual transition to biblical authority, and Eck could see this theological metamorphosis unfolding before him. Eck put forward his stance: Scripture derives its authority from the pope. The trap was set, and Luther walked right into it, responding that Eck was mistaken. It must be the other way around, and not just for popes, but for any church father or council. Then he reiterated with greater gusto his reply to Cajetan: a schoolboy with the Scriptures in hand had a foundation far superior than if the pope himself walked by his side. The reason was now plain to Luther: the Scriptures alone did not err. The same could not be said of the pope. In this statement, Luther had dug his own grave. Here was the point of no return, whether the reformer from Wittenberg knew it or not.

Eck knew it, that is for certain. With Luther's declarations now vocalized for all to hear, Eck and others claimed Luther was no different than John Wycliffe (1330–1384) and Jan Hus (c. 1372–1415). Such guilt by association surprised Luther. Everyone knew Hus's outcome: burned at the stake by the Council of Constance in 1415. During a brief deliberation, Luther took time to investigate Hus and the charges against him, but he returned and without equivocation aligned himself with Hus. The only matter left unclear was whether Luther would meet the same fate. Although Luther intended to reform the church from within, Luther left Leipzig with a disheartening epiphany: as long as Rome elevated the pope to the level of Scripture or, in some cases, even above Scripture, internal renewal was no longer feasible. Now Luther was faced with a dilemma: Would he stand his ground with the same unflinching resolution he exhibited under Eck's scrutiny?

The Diet of Worms gave the answer. Keep in mind, by the time Luther made his pilgrimage to Worms in the spring of 1521, preparing himself to stand before Emperor Charles V, Luther had already been excommunicated by Leo X at the start of the new year. He traveled to Worms a condemned man, exiled from the church, his soul to face eternal punishment. All that awaited him was the destruction of his body. Despite the pleas of some, Luther went to Worms ready to die if he must. Unlike previous encounters with Rome's theologians, Worms would not be a debate. Luther was told, plain and simple, to recant or suffer the consequences the emperor deemed fit for an insubordinate heretic. But Luther refused still. For unless they convinced him that his writings had contradicted the Scriptures, there was nothing about which to be sorry. His conscience was not only clear before God; it was captive to God and his Word. Not even the emperor himself could bind Luther's conscience. For all his power, he, too, was subservient to the divine authority resident in the Word.

Luther survived somehow, and death did not come for him at Worms. From that defining moment forward, Luther resolved to introduce the German people, and the whole of the Roman Empire if he could, to the same Scriptures that first made him a new man. Through his translation of the Bible into German, his exposition of the Bible from the pulpit, and his defense of the Scriptures from his pen and lectern, Luther remade the German people according to the Scriptures—Scriptures that so many of them knew so little about up to that point in time. Whether because of the inability to read Scripture in the vernacular or due to the misleading teaching on Scripture by

Rome, Luther was now on a path to retrieve the written Word as the final, sufficient, and perspicuous authority for the German church.

A New View of Scripture and Tradition: Radical Reformers

The sixteenth-century debate between the Reformers and Rome was not so much Scripture versus tradition, but tradition versus tradition, as Oberman suggests with his T1 and T2 categories. But some took this debate in a more radical direction: Scripture versus tradition. Or what Oberman labels Tradition 0 (T0). *Sola scriptura* was not a call to reject all tradition but to position tradition in its ministerial role, subservient to Scripture yet an essential servant to Scripture, nonetheless. That assumes tradition still had a critical role to play in the church, whether it be as a hermeneutical guide or by means of creedal accountability. But others had little or no role left for tradition. *Sola scriptura* evolved into *nuda scriptura,* and the evolution did not take long at all. For example, Sebastian Franck (1499–1542) quipped that no church father, not even Augustine, was a Christian, but all were apostles of the Antichrist. Not all were as radical as Franck: for instance, Balthasar Hubmaier was sometimes closer to the magisterial Reformers, appreciating, even quoting, the Fathers in his own writings to support his own views. Nevertheless, Franck's quip does deliver in stark terms the T0 viewpoint.

George Williams (1914–2000) has surveyed the variegated wings of these more radical Reformers and believes they fall into three categories: (1) Anabaptists, (2) spiritualists, and (3) rationalists. Although these categories might not be perfect—some figures overlapping categories or failing to fit into any one category in every locus—they do capture the essence of each group. The Anabaptists, for example, were determined to return the sixteenth-century church to the apostolic era, a golden era for Christianity, still unburdened by the weight of tradition's missteps. Many Anabaptists directed the church's attention to the New Testament in particular. The New Testament, in contrast to the Old Testament, was established by the apostles to instruct the church what to believe and how to live. Appeals to the Old Testament by Rome did not always sit well with an Anabaptist hermeneutic. Nor did appeals to the tradition of infant baptism by Reformers carry much weight when the Anabaptists believed a greater authority, Scripture itself, taught believer's baptism only.

The spiritualists, as their name indicates, drew attention to the Scriptures too, but with the priority of understanding what the Spirit might say to them afresh. The Reformers believed Word *and* Spirit were both crucial; without the Spirit the reader remained blind to the truth intrinsic to the Word. But the spiritualists so focused on the Spirit that the Word became secondary to what the Spirit might say or do in the present. Prioritizing the Spirit took on functional consequences in the way the spiritualists ordered their ministries, although it was explicit in their teaching as well. The traditions of the church, past or present, were dismissed as corrupt and antithetical to the Spirit. Not even the most historic sacraments escaped scrutiny. Caspar Schwenckfeld (1489–1561), for example, disregarded baptism and the Lord's Supper.

Or consider Thomas Müntzer (1490–1525), who claimed he received new revelations from the Spirit, revelations that went above and beyond the written Word. The Bible was a dead letter compared to the living voice of the Spirit. Like the prophets of old, Müntzer waited on the Spirit to speak with a new word or prophecy, instructing the church what action to take or what the future would bring. In time, Müntzer announced he was the Daniel of the last days, the eschatological prophet to usher in the final hour of the church. Claims like these were ironic in the eyes of the Reformers. Müntzer claimed to part with Rome, even judging the Reformers for a reformation left incomplete. But in the end Müntzer had reestablished a new papacy with himself as its pope. Luther called the pope the Antichrist, so it is little surprise he concluded Müntzer was the Satan of Allstedt. For all his commotion about the spirit, Müntzer's apocalyptic individualism demonstrated to Luther that the latter had swallowed the Spirit feathers and all. In Luther's estimation, Müntzer left no objective foundation or standard to stand on;

instead, the spiritualist's experience—cloaked as it was in the name of the Spirit—became the new normal for the church under his spell. Others were as radical as Müntzer. David Joris (1501–1556) is a case in point. Faith, he claimed, was not revealed through the Scriptures, the apostles, or Jesus himself. Faith was revealed in the Spirit's power. But who was to give God's church this revelatory Spirit? None other than Joris himself, the true David who ushered in the kingdom of God.

Not everyone turned as radical as Müntzer or David Joris. Menno Simons (1496–1561) is one example of a reformer who believed Luther and Melanchthon did not go far enough but nonetheless refused to exercise violence in the name of the Spirit or claim eschatological fulfillment. Simon's teachings and writings did not set the Spirit over the Word, but they did exhibit a biblicism that was strict, suspicious of creeds that confessed orthodoxy for more than a century. No creed but the Bible may be a contemporary slogan, but the seeds of that slogan were present in Simon's posture toward orthodox statements of faith. For Simon, creedal subscription was a step too far—beyond and above the Bible. If the Reformers were consistent advocates of the formal principle, they would have thrown off the yoke of creedalism rather than embrace it.

Simon's consistency with his own methodology had doctrinal consequences. He parted ways with the Reformers not only on doctrines such as predestination or baptism, but on orthodox Christology as well. By advocating a celestial humanity for the incarnate Christ, Simon could not affirm Jesus as true man, at least not consistently. But as Nicaea and Chalcedon clarified as far back as the fourth and fifth centuries, if the Son did not assume a human nature, then he cannot represent humanity to save our fallen flesh. But these creeds were dismissed by Simon as extrabiblical. Without creedal accountability, Simon led his followers into Christological confusion that made the Reformers cringe and only gave credence to Rome's accusations of novelty.

A third group is not to be forgotten: the evangelical rationalists. These individuals took radicalism into terrain that foreshadowed the most extreme voices of the Enlightenment yet to sweep across Europe. Neither the Spirit nor the Scriptures held final authority; reason itself was the ultimate decider in matters of faith and practice. That did not mean the Spirit and the Scriptures had no role. Evangelical rationalists consulted both and believed both should be an influence on the church. But their rationalism came through whenever a doctrine from the Spirit or the Scriptures appeared illogical. They claimed a Christian identity—atheism is a postmodern reality, not a Reformation one—but when confronted with the pillars of Christian belief, such as the Trinity, they concluded doctrines like these were unreasonable.

The Formal Principle in the Reformed Churches

Huldrych Zwingli versus Johannes Fabri

The Reformation had innumerable consequences for universities in Germany and across all of Europe. Luther's theses were posted for academic debate, his discovery of *sola gratia* was birthed out of lectures, and his professorate in Wittenberg proved just the protection he needed from Rome's political allies. But the Reformation was a reform of the church first and foremost, and, apart from its application in the church, the Reformation might never have taken flight. When Luther was called out of hiding, cloistered for months on end in the Wartburg Castle, it was, at least in part, because churchgoers were implementing reform but in all the wrong ways. Luther was needed; he had taken Rome apart with his stance on biblical authority, and now it was time to put the church back together according to the Word he claimed was sufficient.

The Reformation's ecclesiastical focus is notable across the continent, but the reformed churches stand out for their scrupulous dedication to implement *sola scriptura,* however difficult it proved to be. Consider Huldrych Zwingli (1484–1531), the reformer who changed the church in Zurich. Zwingli was a studious biblical scholar and theologian with obvious literary and linguistic talents. He mastered Paul's epistles in Greek, for example, learning each word for word until he dedicated them all to memory—a feat almost impossible without Erasmus's 1516 Greek New Testament. Yet Zwingli did not retreat to an ivory tower, as much as he admired the academic life Erasmus was content to live. Zwingli was a humanist—his writings have a humanist imprint throughout—but the church was a major priority for the Zurich reformer.

At the start of 1519, the Minster church in Zurich opened its pulpit to Zwingli, summoning him as their new priest and not many years later as their preacher. Zwingli decided *lectio continua* was the right way to preach from the pulpit. If the Scriptures were the authoritative voice of God, then each book of the Bible deserved attention; indeed, every verse. This method was not Zwingli's invention. The Fathers had modeled *lectio continua* long before the sixteenth century. John Chrysostom, sometimes labeled "the golden-mouthed preacher," walked through books of the Bible in a sequential manner. Fathers like these influenced Zwingli, who believed the church needed nothing more than to hear the Scriptures exposited without Rome's bias. The outcome was impressive: Zwingli exposited the New Testament and, when finished, told his people the Old Testament was next.

The road to reform was not easy, despite Zwingli's rigorous and persistent exposition of the Scriptures. Whether the entire city would follow Zwingli's model remained to be seen. In 1523, hundreds assembled in the town hall with the hope a decision could be made. The event called for a disputation, and Johannes Fabri (1504–1558) was determined to challenge Zwingli's reforming efforts. Many issues were contested, but one of them was authority. Fabri put forward Rome's theology, but Zwingli challenged Fabri's epistemological presuppositions, asking Fabri to demonstrate the validity of Rome's beliefs from the Scriptures. By the end of the disputation, the contrast between Fabri, who cited Rome's tradition as the church's authority, and Zwingli, who cited the Scriptures as the final arbiter, was obvious to the crowd. It was even more evident when Zwingli listed sixty-seven articles, each challenging Roman beliefs Zwingli believed were erroneous to one degree or another.

Zwingli's case against Rome was not, however, ahistorical in nature, empty of tradition. When asked if the Fathers should be discarded for the sake of scriptural authority, Zwingli replied they should not. Their voices were invaluable, even authoritative. Where would Zwingli's humanist training be if not for the Greek and Latin fathers? How could he interpret and preach the Scriptures with such faithfulness if not for patristic sermons? But, unlike Scripture, no voice in tradition, not even the collective voice of Rome's councils, was without error. Zwingli encouraged his audience to read the Fathers, to let the Fathers act as interpretive guides to Scripture, but never to elevate any human voice above the voice of God the Spirit who has spoken through the prophets and apostles. To elevate the Fathers above the Scriptures is to contradict the Fathers themselves, a point that insinuated Fabri's misinterpretation of the tradition from the start of the debate.

The verdict reached was in favor of Zwingli, and the Zurich reformer's *lectio continua* was not to be opposed. Furthermore, every preacher was to follow suit, turning to the Scriptures for his sermon because the Scriptures and the Scriptures alone can stand over the church as her superior authority. This was but the beginning of Zurich's break with Rome, a divide that in time led to bloodshed and Zwingli's own death on the battlefield. Nevertheless, Zwingli's scriptural commitment did not die with him but was implemented once again with Heinrich Bullinger, who not only preached on the basis of biblical authority but also developed a biblical theology covenantal to its core. Bullinger's covenantal theology taught his people the Bible's story and how that story should be recapitulated in the life of the church, from baptism to the Lord's Supper.

John Calvin versus Jacopo Sadoleto

If Luther defended biblical authority in his disputations and Zwingli reintegrated *sola scriptura* through the sermon, then John Calvin (1509–1564) was a master practitioner at both. Pressured by William Farel (1489–1565) to sideline academic plans and pastor the church in Geneva, Calvin became one of the most enduring voices of the Reformation, although he was a second-generation reformer indebted to the original contributions of those who came before him, such as Luther. But his late arrival on the Reformation scene by no means belittled his contribution to the Reformation's survival. There were many other reformed pastors besides Calvin, but without Calvin it is questionable whether Geneva would have survived Rome's efforts to subsume its churches. These churches were instrumental in commissioning legions of catechized pastors to return to France (and in some cases die) or even take the gospel to new territories. All of that was possible because of Calvin.

Calvin was no mere literary pen or pulpit preacher, but his presence resulted in the implementation of the Reformation among Geneva's company of pastors. Calvin, to the detriment of his own health, involved himself in the ecclesiastical affairs of the church. His presence was not always welcomed and at times situated Calvin in the heat of controversy. Historians often question the merits of Calvin's decisions to this day, but what remains unquestionable is the doctrinal presupposition that enabled Calvin to institute reform in the first place. Scripture's supremacy was the basis of every catechism, confession, commentary, sermon, and book in his *Institutes of the Christian Religion,* as well as every ecclesiastical contention or rivalry.

Each of these is worthy of attention, but few of them showcase *sola scriptura* in the flesh like Calvin's debate with Cardinal Jacopo Sadoleto (1477–1547). The bishop of Carpentras (southern France) wrote to the Genevans, urging them, even threatening them, to return home to mother Rome. Calvin had been banished from Geneva, but when the Genevans looked for a worthy responder, no one proved as capable and credible as Calvin. Their invitation landed in Strasbourg, where Calvin was flourishing writing books and observing the success of Martin Bucer's (1491–1551) reforming endeavors. Despite the bitter history between them, Calvin accepted, perhaps in part because the cause of the Reformation itself compelled him.

Sadoleto's letter intended to expose the Genevan's drift from the one true church. Parading Rome's catholicity, Sadoleto claimed Rome not only was without error but also was incapable of error. For the same Holy Spirit that breathed out Scripture and superintended the biblical authors had guided and authorized the church's decrees, whether they be conciliar or curial. Given the church's divine origin and infallible authority, the Genevans were risking their own salvation by positioning themselves outside Rome's ecclesiastical and spiritual care.

History was not on Geneva's side either. Rome could boast tradition's support for more than a century and a half, while Geneva could only claim the innovations of the past twenty-five years. Even her best Reformers were nothing in comparison to the Roman Catholic Church itself. But worst of all, the Genevans risked becoming schismatics. As long as they stayed under the wings of the Reformation, they tore the church apart. Rome stood for unity—it always had—but the Genevans had created division. If the church represented a marriage with Christ, the Genevans were issuing a divorce. Nevertheless, there was still hope. Now that they had banished Calvin, they could return to the one church that alone was infallible.

Sadoleto's argument was standard fare for Rome; it was the same argument Luther encountered. And just like Luther, Calvin parsed it one argument at a time until he believed Rome's claims had been stripped of biblical fidelity. First, Sadoleto's appeal to the Spirit was in vain. Yes, the Spirit was instrumental in the formation of the Scriptures as well as the church, but not in the same way. The church may experience the providential guidance of the Spirit, but only the biblical authors were under the Spirit's inspiration. For that reason, the church could err—and had erred—but Scripture could not. Scripture is the church's Lydian stone; all doctrines that shine like gold are brought to the Lydian stone, which can alone decipher between the authentic and the fallacious. By light of Scripture, the church is led by the Spirit, not vice versa.

At the root of Calvin's argument was a different view of the canon than Sadoleto's. For Calvin and all the Reformers, the church neither created the canon nor invested the canon with its authority. Rather, the canon created the church, and on its authority the church stands. Although the church carries an authority, it is always a derivative authority, dependent on the definitive authority of the Word.

As to catholicity and schism, Calvin turned the table on Sadoleto. Innovation was Rome's defining quality, not the Reformation's. A scan of its doctrines—from transubstantiation to purgatory to relics and indulgences—revealed just how inconsistent Rome was with the patristic heritage Calvin claimed to be his own. Calvin was in full support of unity but not at the expense of the gospel, which Calvin said Rome had corrupted or abandoned. Unity was achievable, yet such unity could not be reached through Rome's fallible declarations but only by placing itself under the pure teaching of Scripture. Calvin was not after a church emptied of tradition but one reformed by the right tradition.

The challenge Sadoleto posed was not the last one the Genevans encountered. The Council of Trent made similar claims at its Fourth Session (1546), which inspired Calvin's *Antidote*, a fuller treatise that elaborated his original argument but this time against official Catholic dogma. Calvin guided the Genevans once again, and this time instructed them not to be sold on the hype. Let the smoke clear, said Calvin, and you will remain standing, surefooted on the authority of God's Word. Citing Augustine in support, Calvin reassured the church that her faith came from the Scriptures, so it need not waver when threatened by the fallible declarations of Rome. In the end, the Genevans survived not only Sadoleto but also Trent, thanks to Calvin's theological polemics and especially his pastoral care. Calvin was a Reformation *theologian*, but also a *shepherd* who was convinced he could lead the church forward only with the sufficiency of Scripture as his guiding light.

For the Church

The Longevity of the Formal Principle

At the start of the Reformation, Rome predicted *sola scriptura* would result in chaos, in which every man was his own interpreter, and, for that reason, the Reformation would be short-lived. In some cases, this prediction proved true, but sometimes it was not *sola scriptura* that caused dissemination, but *nuda scriptura*, due to the latter's elevation of individual experience, the Spirit, or reason above the Scriptures. Historians have been slow to recognize that *sola scriptura* was not an Enlightenment call to the autonomous individual, a sixteenth-century precursor to Immanuel Kant or René Descartes. Such a reading falls prey to a Roman Catholic hermeneutic of the Reformation along with its aggressive propaganda, calling the match before it can begin.

By contrast, the Reformers submitted themselves to the Scriptures, exercising a hermeneutic of humility. If they were subversive, it was not because they desired to divide the church—an interpretation as misguided as it is common. The Reformation's subversive nature was due to the gospel Rome found offensive, and to the divinely authorized book that gave birth to that gospel. The Reformers elevated this book above all else, a maneuver Rome said was insubordinate to their infallible magisterium.

The scriptural posture of the Reformers proved anything but temporary—at least when interpreted as they intended. Although space precludes further investigation, any student of the Reformation eager to determine how the formal principle advanced would do well to consider Luther's right-hand scholar, Philip Melanchthon (1497–1560) and his *Loci Communes*; Zwingli's successor Heinrich Bullinger (1504–1575) and his *Decades*; the many catechisms and confessions that sprouted from Calvin's Geneva with his successor Theodore Beza (1519–1605); or the way *sola scriptura* rooted itself in English soil through the translation of the New Testament by William Tyndale (1494–1536) and the hypnotic liturgy of

Thomas Cranmer (1489–1556) in the *Book of Common Prayer*, the *Books of Homilies*, and the *Thirty-Nine Articles*.

These and many others were but the beginning. Century after century, *sola scriptura* has been the *idée fixe* of the Protestant mind, its foundational premise on which all its doctrines are built and established. Where it has not, Protestants have misaligned themselves with their own heritage, their own tradition. Where it has, the gospel can be heard with clarity and authority, with sufficiency and life-giving power.

For Further Reading

Primary Sources

Bray, Gerald, ed. *The Books of Homilies: A Critical Edition.* Cambridge: James Clarke, 2015.

Calvin, John. *Institutes of the Christian Religion.* 2 vols. Edited by John T. McNeill. Translated by Ford Lewis Battles. Philadelphia: Westminster, 1960.

———. *Tracts and Letters.* Edited and translated by Henry Beveridge. Edinburgh: Banner of Truth, 2009.

Cummings, Brian, ed. *The Book of Common Prayer: The Texts of 1549, 1559, and 1662.* Oxford: Oxford University Press, 2011.

Dennison, James T., Jr., ed. *Reformed Confessions of the 16th and 17th Centuries.* 4 vols. Grand Rapids: Reformation Heritage Books, 2008–2014.

Hillerbrand, Hans J., ed. *The Protestant Reformation.* Rev. ed. New York: Harper Perennial, 2009.

Luther, Martin. *Career of the Reformer I.* Vol. 31 of *Luther's Works.* Edited by Jaroslav Pelikan and Helmut T. Lehmann. 55 vols. Philadelphia: Fortress, 1958–1975.

Williams, George H., and Angel Mergal, eds. *Spiritual and Anabaptist Writers.* Philadelphia: Westminster, 1957.

Zwingli, Ulrich. *Ulrich Zwingli (1484–1531): Selected Works.* Translated by Lawrence A. McLouth. 1901. Reprint, Philadelphia: University of Pennsylvania Press, 1972.

Secondary Sources

Barrett, Matthew. *God's Word Alone: The Authority of Scripture. What the Reformers Taught . . . and Why It Still Matters.* Grand Rapids: Zondervan, 2016.

———, ed. *The Theology of the Reformers.* Wheaton, IL: Crossway, 2017.

George, Timothy. *Reading Scripture with the Reformers.* Downers Grove, IL: InterVarsity Press, 2011.

———. *The Theology of the Reformers.* Rev. ed. Nashville: B&H, 2013.

Gordon, Bruce. *Calvin.* Oxford: Oxford University Press, 2011.

———. *The Swiss Reformation.* New York: Manchester University Press, 2002.

Hendrix, Scott H. *Luther and the Papacy: Stages in a Reformation Conflict.* Philadelphia: Fortress, 1981.

Kolb, Robert. *Martin Luther and the Enduring Word of God: The Wittenberg School and Its Scripture-Centered Proclamation.* Grand Rapids: Baker Academic, 2016.

Oberman, Heiko A. *Forerunners of the Reformation: The Shape of Late Medieval Thought Illustrated by Key Documents*. Philadelphia: Fortress, 1981.

———. *The Harvest of Medieval Theology: Gabriel Biel and Late Medieval Nominalism*. Rev. ed. Cambridge, MA: Harvard University Press, 1963.

Pearce, Meic. *The Great Restoration: The Religious Radicals of the 16th and 17th Centuries.* Carlisle, UK: Paternoster, 1998.

Rupp, E. Gordon. *Luther's Progress to the Diet of Worms.* New York: Harper & Row, 1964.

Tierney, Brian. *The Crisis of Church and State, 1050–1300.* Englewood Cliffs, NJ: Prentice Hall, 1964.

Williams, George H. *The Radical Reformation.* Kirksville, MO: Sixteenth Century Journal, 1992.

Questions for Study or Discussion

1. What is the difference between Tradition 1 and Tradition 2?
2. Why did curialism and conciliarism conflict on the eve of the Reformation, and how did Luther encounter each in his debates with Rome?
3. What is Tradition 0, and how did it affect certain radical Reformers and their view of church history?
4. Why did the *lectio continua* methodology prove instrumental to Zwingli's recovery of *sola scriptura*?
5. How did Calvin and Sadoleto differ on the relationship between Word and Spirit?

9

SALVATION

By Stephen Brett Eccher

Introduction

In 1546, as a feeble Martin Luther lay dying in his birth town of Eisleben, a close friend named Justus Jonas questioned the German Reformer about his commitment to the Protestant cause. Luther famously replied, "We are beggars. This is true." Even in the waning moments of the Reformer's life, the transforming power of the gospel, as he understood it, shone through and overshadowed any vestige of fear that once consumed him. The hope that sustained Luther in that moment was not based on his work as a Reformer; it was rooted in the salvation that Christ had gifted to him.

The story of Luther's inner struggle to find a gracious God and assurance of his salvation charted a new course for Christianity. Luther's well-documented personal struggle situated him within a larger era of inquiry that not only included the Wittenberg Reformer but also found resonance among many other figures. As questions related to the nature of faith, Scripture, and church tradition stirred, a more foundational question regarding religious *veritas* rose to the fore: Who is the true church? Luther's rediscovery of the doctrine of justification by grace through faith alone stood at odds with the Roman Catholic Church's sacramentalism, thereby challenging Rome's authority. Yet this wasn't the only issue that Luther and other Protestant Reformers questioned about the Roman curia, or even each other. Different readings of the biblical text led to divergent views on issues such as the sacraments, church polity, and worship practices. As the dethroning of papal authority gave way to the doctrine of the priesthood of all believers, the Western church began to splinter. Ironically, the battle to define the nature of the true church defined the Reformation itself.

The Protestant Reformers generally agreed that the gospel had been veiled over the centuries and needed to be recovered if the church were to remain in the apostolic tradition. This recovery centered on two main ideas: (a) the proclamation of the gospel, especially articulated through the phrase "justification by grace through faith alone," and (b) a reinstitution of the two biblical sacraments of baptism and the Lord's Supper—tangible word pictures of the gospel. Although the Reformers were by no means in agreement on the precise definition or understanding of these ideas, they spoke with one unanimous voice corroborating the veracity of one confessional heritage: salvation was at stake.

Given that debates over the nature of faith served as the principle issue identifying who maintained a true, biblical church, the purpose of this chapter is to explore the doctrine of salvation during the Reformation. Special attention is given to the developmental nature of this doctrine among the Reformers, the divergent hermeneutical commitments that undergirded their soteriologies, and the unique historical contexts that shaped the differing understandings of salvation offered during the period.

Historical Overview

Martin Luther

Martin Luther (1483–1546) was born into a superstitious world consumed with death and riddled with guilt. Against this unique backdrop, the Roman Catholic Church posited that healing and salvation were realized through the church's sacramental system. Late-medieval sacramental theology argued that the church had been established by God as the sole dispenser of the salvific medicine of divine, saving grace. The clergy stood as heaven's gatekeepers, administering the sacramental medicine of immortality to humanity plagued by sin.

Luther languished in this sacramental system, especially during his time as an Augustinian monk. He was a man caught between God and the devil, a medieval viator moving from heaven to hell and back again with every sacramental act of righteousness, followed by more sinful deeds of his flesh. According to Luther's 1545 *Preface to the Latin Writings*, this changed once he began searching the Scriptures for answers to the questions that vexed him. He finally came to see salvation through the lens of the cross instead of the sacraments. Salvation was not something to be realized by human effort but a gift from God based on the work of the Son, Jesus Christ. Faith in the accomplished work of Jesus, itself a gift of God, became the means of finding a right standing before the Lord.

A reappropriation of an Augustinian understanding of the human will served as a theological presupposition that shaped Luther's emerging soteriology. As he argued in his 1525 treatise *The Bondage of the Will*, the fall left humanity powerless to overcome Adam's lingering sin problem. In fact, looking at the Scriptures through his hermeneutical law/gospel dialectic, Luther positioned the law (Old Testament) as the standard for holiness that reminded humanity of its inability to obey it. What the law condemns, Luther believed, the gospel (New Testament) brings to life through the atoning work of Jesus. Thus, the cross of Jesus, not the actions of humanity, are the means of redemption.

Luther's theology of the cross saw the work of God in salvation as primary. And while Luther jettisoned Augustine's (354–430) sacramental impartation and sanative language, he remained faithful to Augustine's predestinarianism, which had been forged in debate with the Pelagians. As Luther made clear during the Heidelberg Disputation in 1518, "Free will, after the fall, exists in name only, and as long as it does what it is able to do, it commits a mortal sin."[1] This led Luther to affirm double predestination; a doctrine that he admitted was "strong wine" for the more mature in the faith. In the end, Luther's corrective of the late medieval church's soteriology repositioned God as the author of salvation and oriented Jesus Christ, through his work on the cross, as the main character in the narrative of redemption.

The Swiss Magisterial Reformers

Although Luther helped reshape the church's soteriology, the Protestant Reformers' views on salvation were not monolithic. In the Swiss confederation, others offered their own unique arguments related to the true church's foundation. For instance, Huldrych Zwingli (1484–1531), the Reformer of Zürich, affirmed justification by grace through faith, but he cast that doctrine in a different light than Luther's. Zwingli viewed God as the initiator of justification, like Luther, but he framed justification through a moralistic ethos not found in the Wittenberg Reformer. Zwingli's commitment to Renaissance humanism compelled the Swiss Reformer to stress the external, life-changing reality of the gospel in the one justified. So, while Luther focused more on God's activity in justification, Zwingli shifted the

---

[1] Helmut T. Lehmann, ed., *Luther's Works* (Philadelphia: Fortress, 1957), 31:40.

attention toward humanity's moral responses to that divine activity. What Luther implied regarding justification became explicit in Zwingli. Zwingli's covenantal reading of Scripture also led him to focus more on the communal nature of God's act of justification rather than on the individual, as with Luther. The Swiss Reformer saw Zürich as analogous with ancient Israel, thereby setting a theocratic foundation undergirding his soteriology. Thus, personal justification was a smaller, less significant part of the larger whole of the Christian Zürich community.

Zwingli anchored his understanding of salvation to God's providence, or what he called "the mother of justification." God as the Creator oversaw and dictated the affairs of human history according to his providential hand. Zwingli's understanding of God's providence was forged at the crucible of dramatic life experiences and his humanist reading of historic texts. After a near-death experience in 1519, Zwingli recorded his commitment to this principle in a *Plague Song*:

> To you I cry: If it is your will, take out the dart that wounds me,
> nor lets me have an hour's rest or repose.
> Will you, however, that death take me in the midst of my days, so
> let it be.
> Do what you will, nothing shall be too much for me.
> Your vessel am I, to make or break altogether.[2]

Zwingli's engagement with ancient sources, especially the Bible, Augustine, and Seneca, left him repeatedly viewing humanity as a "vessel" in the Potter's hands.

Zwingli's view of election and his openness to philosophy were most evident in his later years of life. In his 1530 treatise *On the Providence of God*, he contended that God was the first moving cause behind salvation.

---

[2] Scott H. Hendrix, *Early Protestant Spirituality* (New York: Paulist, 2009), 183–84.

Election, therefore, was rooted in God's will and not based on divine foreknowledge. His vision of heaven that included non-Christians, such as Hercules and Theseus, presented in his 1531 *An Exposition of the Faith*, reinforced this strong view of election. This commitment also pushed back contextually against the Anabaptist's affirmation of a believers' church by deferring knowledge of one's election to God alone.

Similar to Zwingli, Martin Bucer (1491–1551), the Reformer of Strasbourg, labored to safeguard the importance of the fruits of faith following salvation. Thus, Bucer posited a doctrine of double justification, in which he bifurcated the foundational Protestant doctrine into two parts. He argued that the first justification, *iustitia imputata* ("imputed righteousness"), related to God's gracious activity in declaring the wayward sinner righteous. The second justification, *iustitia inhaerens* ("inherent righteousness"), was linked to the believer's obligation to obey the commands of God. The impartation of God's righteousness and human works of obedience were inseparable for Bucer, a point he illustrated by referencing the interconnected nature of fire and heat. Bucer spoke here of believers co-laboring with God by loving one's neighbor. The irenic Bucer crafted this double justification to promote unity among the Reformers as their differing readings of Scripture began to fracture Protestantism, especially in the 1530s. Yet this position did not gain traction among other Protestants, mostly because it too closely aligned God's determinative activity and humanity's posterior obedience. In the end, it looked too much like Roman Catholic soteriology.

Bucer also applied a pastoral lens to the doctrine of predestination, which would later be passed on to his son in the faith, John Calvin (1509–1564). Bucer stressed the importance of God's benevolence in the doctrine. He also exhorted others to consider predestination as a gift from God that strengthens one's faith. Bucer believed that God's sovereign declarations, which flow from his magnanimous nature, are infinitely more trustworthy than humanity's pursuit of righteousness. For Bucer, predestination was a comfort, not a consternation.

The Radicals and Evangelical Anabaptists

Although the division between the magisterial Reformers and the radicals that emerged during the 1520s and 1530s was most acute in the area of ecclesiology, stark contrasts in their respective soteriologies also served as a point of contention. Certain ecclesiological commitments, such as believer's baptism and regenerate church membership, were logical corollaries based on preceding soteriological affirmations. One of the earliest and most prominent deviations from the magisterial forms of Reformation came from Luther's colleague at Wittenberg, Andreas Bodenstein von Karlstadt (1486–1541).

Like most of the Swiss Reformers, Karlstadt affirmed in principle Luther's language of justification by grace through faith alone. Yet his departure from an Augustinian view of the human will left him with a radically different interpretation of what that phrase meant. Karlstadt eschewed Luther's explanation of the bondage of the will and understood God's grace through two interconnected ideas. Divine grace bestowed an awareness of the truth of the gospel on a person; it also freed humans to make conscious, volitional decisions regarding their salvation. This meant that God's grace was not based on an abstract, exterior declaration by God that was divinely applied to humanity. Grace was substantive and empowering to humanity's participation in the choice of regeneration. The shift away from Luther's forensic view of justification meant Karlstadt spoke more in terms of the believer being *simul bonus et malus* ("simultaneously good and bad"), rather than *simul iustus et peccator* ("simultaneously righteous and a sinner"). It also meant rejecting any form of an unconditional predestination.

In his 1520 *Tract on the Supreme Virtue of Gelassenheit*, Karlstadt stressed that human "yieldedness," or "submission," was requisite to true faith. Consequently, authentic faith was tethered to a willful submission of one's life to God's commands. Faith became more visible in Karlstadt's soteriology than in Luther's, hence his eventual suggestion of a believers' church. Citing Jesus's exhortation to "follow me" in Luke 9:23, Karlstadt argued, "If I must desire to suffer something or carry a cross for God's sake, I must first deny and forsake myself. I must totally submerge my will in God's will and drown self-will in all things. Hence, I must will as God wills."[3] Rebutting Luther's use of the marriage analogy in his 1523 work *The Meaning of the Term Gelassen*, Karlstadt contended that the spiritual marriage that takes place between Christ (the bridegroom) and the believer (the bride) is only realized as the individual yields or surrenders to Christ.

A synergistic soteriology similar to Karlstadt's also surfaced in some of the evangelical Anabaptists. The most nuanced example came from Balthasar Hubmaier (1480/1–1528), the Reformer of Waldshut and Nikolsburg. Hubmaier's anthropology, which was similar to and influenced by Erasmus's, affirmed a tripartite view of humanity in which the human will remains uncorrupted after the fall. This view of humanity charted a soteriological course away from Luther, whom Hubmaier perceived to hold an antinomian view of justification that overstressed *Sola fide*. As Hubmaier reasoned in his 1526 *A Christian Catechism*, Luther's rejection of free will failed to recognize that "God's image has never yet been completely obliterated in us," even after the fall in Genesis 3.

Yet Hubmaier's soteriology was not semi-Pelagian, for humanity's residual goodness was not able to secure salvation. Hubmaier believed God's divine grace mediated through the Word, and the Holy Spirit was what facilitated one's regeneration. His subsequent understanding of human freedom was largely an adaptation of a Thomistic way of thinking about justification, best embodied through the Latin phrase *facere quod in se est* ("Do that which lies within you"). The nominalist influence of Johann Eck (1486–1543) here is apparent and forced Hubmaier away from Luther's soteriology.

This human freedom had an important qualification for Hubmaier. Human freedom was situated after God's preceding act of regeneration, not before it. Thus, for Hubmaier, justification is realized through God's divine activity of regeneration. But his synergistic soteriology tethered this

[3] E. J. Furcha, ed., *The Essential Karlstadt: Fifteen Tracts by Andreas Bodenstein (Carlstadt) from Karlstadt* (Scottdale, PA: Herald, 1995), 38.

saving act of God with the believers' post-conversion response of obedience and Christian love. The changed inner heart of a person, made new by the grace of God, produces an authentic faith in the believer. Hubmaier stressed that one's confessional commitment to God must also coalesce with neighborly deeds of love. Such a response serves as a fruitful demonstration of the veracity of one's faith. Hubmaier's language of salvation stressed process more than Luther's, which focused attention on a static point of justification. Much like Karlstadt, his view also had stronger ethical moorings than Luther's. Thus, while Hubmaier was deemed a radical because of his commitment to a believers' church ecclesiology, he was far more traditional than other Reformers, such as Luther, on the nature of grace and election.

John Calvin

Despite the association of his name with predestination, John Calvin understood salvation through the lens of incarnation and the believer's mystical union with Christ. The person and work of Jesus were central to Calvin's doctrine of redemption. Highlighting the theme of God's glory, this Reformer argued that salvation was based on a deep, personal relationship with the one who was united to Christ by faith. Here Calvin employed terms such as *adoption*, *participation*, and *ingrafting* to stress the biblical nature of this Spirit-generated union and the soteriological import of this divine act in believers. Thus, while Luther and Zwingli placed a greater emphasis on what Jesus's work does for an individual and the Christian community externally, Calvin's theology focused on Christ's internal work on the believer via this mystical union.

Beginning in 1539, Calvin stressed that one's union with Christ expanded the focus of salvation beyond justification. Emphasizing the *duplex gratia* ("double grace") benefit of this union, Calvin contended, "By partaking of him, we principally receive a double grace: namely, that being reconciled to God through Christ's blamelessness, we may have in heaven instead of a Judge a gracious Father; and secondly, that sanctified by Christ's spirit we may cultivate blamelessness and purity of life."[4] Accordingly, justification and sanctification are the salvific fruits of the believer's union with Christ.

This union with Christ also denoted the eschatological trajectory of Calvin's soteriology. Salvation was not to be associated with residence at a place like heaven but was rooted in a consanguinity with the person, Jesus Christ. Moreover, union with Christ also set the believer on a pilgrimage, not just in a right standing before God, as Luther contended. Christians live as aliens and sojourners in a place not their home until Christ's return. That Calvin lived as a French exile at Geneva for most of his career undoubtedly informed his reading of Scripture on this point. Exile also shaped the motivation behind Calvin's work to make Geneva welcoming to refugees during an era of unprecedented religious displacement.

Calvin, of course, affirmed that believers were sovereignly dispatched on this journey at the Lord's behest. His views on predestination and election developed over time and were deeply contextual given his ministry at Geneva. Scriptural texts such as Romans 9–11 and Ephesians 1 embodied the biblical nature of this doctrine, while the Jacob and Esau narrative from Genesis rejected any notion of divine foreknowledge as the basis for election. Such examples led Calvin to characterize predestination in his final 1559 edition of the *Institutes* as a *decretum horribile* ("awful decree"). That God would condemn some like Esau to damnation was awful. Yet this judgment was tempered by the awe-inspiring grace of God seen in Jacob's predestination to salvation.

Additionally, the doctrine of election appears practical and pastoral for Calvin. His experiences, both during his time at Strasbourg and at Geneva, are informative here. In the original 1536 edition of the *Institutes*, Calvin offered only brief comments on election. By the 1539 edition, election covered four chapters and continued to grow in scope until the final 1559 edition. Why the change? In contexts where the gospel saturated the whole of society, Calvin was perplexed by the successes and failings of the

---

[4] Furcha, 725.

evangelical message among the people. Given that Geneva was awash with preaching services, access to the gospel didn't necessarily bear the fruit of regeneration for all. Thus, the doctrine of election was a practical explanation for the evangelistic successes and failings of the gospel in a thoroughly Christian context.

Jacob Arminius

In an ironic twist, Jacob Arminius (1560–1609), whose name is most often cast as the theological antithesis of Calvin, suffered from similar historical distortions and mischaracterizations of his soteriology. Arminius was steeped in the Reformed orthodoxy of the Dutch church, even studying under Theodore Beza (1519–1605) at the Genevan Academy. Yet, by the late 1580s, Arminius deviated from the Dutch Reformed tradition with his rejection of Beza's supralapsarian monergism. This theological pivot left him embroiled in controversy for the rest of his life.

Antagonists often mistakenly chide Arminius for grounding his soteriology on human freedom. In truth, Arminius's views were shaped by two different concerns: (1) the rise of Reformed orthodoxy, which correlated Christian orthodoxy exclusively with that tradition's narrow soteriological convictions, and (2) the biblical tension between divine sovereignty and human responsibility spurned by those more committed to a theological system than scriptural fidelity.

Driven by these apprehensions, Arminius used many of the categories, terms, and biblical passages of Reformed orthodoxy to set forth alternative soteriological beliefs that shaped the Arminian tradition. Election, for instance, was retained but cast in terms of groups rather than individuals. The mercy and compassion seen applied by God in Romans 9 shifted away from individuals in particular toward a more broadly defined group who responded to his indiscriminate offer of salvation through Jesus. Here, Arminius famously defined predestination as "the decree of the good pleasure of God in Christ, by which he resolved from all eternity, to justify, adopt, and endow with everlasting life . . . believers on whom he had decreed to bestow faith."[5] Such an offer naturally necessitated that Jesus's death be made on behalf of all humanity; otherwise, the Bible's repeated appeals for people to repent and believe ring hollow. For Arminius, this meant that faith preceded election, yet it still allowed him to understand God as the One who decreed the faith of the individual.

Arminius understood divine sovereignty to work symbiotically with divine foreknowledge. Romans 8:29 became an important text for Arminius, who contended that God's omniscience granted him a window into the decisions of all people regarding their individual responses to the general call of the gospel. This emphasis on divine foreknowledge under the sovereign rule of God in election allowed him to avoid the heresy of semi-Pelagianism, though such accusations dogged him throughout his life. His focus on foreknowledge also served Arminius's pastoral concerns by highlighting a twofold view of God's love—the love of humanity and the love of righteousness. Without the tempering balance of these two loves, one might mistakenly assume election without repentance or that one's inability to achieve sinless perfection left that person outside the saving reach of God. Both of these were the dangerous paths mistakenly offered by supralapsarianism and semi-Pelagianism.

Moïse Amyraut

In the years following the proceedings at Dort, a Frenchman named Moïse Amyraut (1596–1664) suggested a modification to the synod's declarations, especially on the extent of the atonement. Amyraut believed Dort was correct in most of its assertions, but he was concerned that limiting the scope of Jesus's work to the elect not only violated texts such as John 3:16 but bifurcated humanity into two kinds, thereby rejecting the biblical teaching

[5] John D. Wagner, ed., *Arminius Speaks: Essential Writings on Predestination, Free Will, and the Nature of God* (Eugene, OR: Wipf and Stock, 2011), 8.

of one race in Adam. Driven by such concerns, Amyraut pressed for a soteriological modification in his 1634 work *A Short Treatise on Predestination.* There he posited what came to be known as a hypothetical universalism, which stressed that God purposed a universal intention behind the work of Jesus on the cross. Thus, Jesus's sacrificial death was sufficient to atone for the sins of all humanity but efficient in its application to the elect—those who embraced the gospel by faith in Jesus. For Amyraut, faith served as a necessary precondition that made Jesus's gracious work of benefit to the individual.

By stressing the importance of faith in his formulations, Amyraut elevated the office of preaching. He believed that God ordained gospel proclamation as the principle means by which the Lord generates faith in the elect. Accordingly, the preacher's common plea for his audience to embrace Jesus by faith was pastoral and theological. Amyraut's belief in two salvific divine wills dominated his thinking at this point. The first of God's wills desires that all humanity might be redeemed. The second will generates the believer's faith, which is requisite for God's desired redemption. Without this distinction, Jesus's work was meaningless. Given these two interrelated wills, the call to believe must be indiscriminately offered to all. Accordingly, a person's response to the gospel served as an indication of God's divine intention to generate faith in that individual based on the universal atoning work of Jesus. Adherents to Amyraut's views came to be known as Amyraldian Calvinists, or those affirming the points of Dortian Calvinism *sans* limited atonement.

Case Studies

Case Study 1: Martin Luther and Justification

Justification became the pillar upholding Luther's view of salvation. For years Luther was vexed by one question: How does one find a right standing before God? Sacramental theology had left him devoid of the assurance of his salvation and on an endless pursuit to become righteous on his own.

Luther became captivated in his pursuit by Rom 1:17. He initially maintained a late-medieval reading of that passage, linking Paul's words regarding "the righteousness of God" with God's holiness. Thus, Luther formerly understood God's righteousness to be manifest when the Lord condemned sinners to death and damnation. The gospel was initially not a comfort for the Reformer but a crushing blow of divine judgment.

Luther's breakthrough on justification eventually came as he began reading Rom 1:17 in its original context and through the lens of other Pauline texts. For instance, in Rom 1:16, Paul had already placed the power of salvation in the Lord's hands. The apostle also stressed in verse 17 that the "righteousness of God" was linked in two different ways with faith. God's righteousness was revealed "from faith for faith" and "the righteous shall live by faith." The beauty of God's righteousness was that it became known through the gospel. Accordingly, Luther came to affirm that justification was by grace through faith.

For Luther, finding a right standing before God was not dependent on humanity's morality or actualized by participating in religious rites. Luther knew the futility of such paths. He ultimately affirmed that any right standing before God was realized only as God granted to an individual his righteousness, perfection, and holiness. The sinner, who shared in the nakedness of Adam, was covered only as he or she was clothed with Christ's righteousness, just as God promised in Ezek 16:8. To highlight humanity's passive, even impotent, role in this, Luther stressed the *iustitia aliena* ("alien righteousness") of God. Nothing in humanity could produce the holiness that was required to stand before the Lord. The hope for reconciliation with the Creator was external to humanity and only to be found through Jesus. Thus, as Paul contended in Rom 1:16, God's faith, the faith of Jesus, becomes the believer's according to God's grace.

Drawing from Ephesians 5, Luther believed that God's alien righteousness becomes the believer's in what he famously described as a "sweet exchange." Paul's marriage illustration described this transference, for what was previously the bridegroom's becomes the bride's and vice versa. As

Luther clarified in his famous 1520 treatise *Freedom of a Christian*, "Christ is full of grace, life, and salvation. The soul is full of sins, death, and damnation. Now let faith come between them and sins, death, and damnation will be Christ's, while grace, life, and salvation will be the soul's."[6] Thus, the imputed sin of the first Adam, which Paul referenced in Romans 5, is only to be overcome at God's initiative by means of the imputed righteousness of the second Adam, Jesus Christ.

As Luther pondered how Christ's righteousness was imputed to the believer, Philip Melanchthon (1497–1560), Luther's successor at Wittenberg, helped the Reformer articulate this salvific "sweet exchange" using legal language. One becomes justified, not when the individual becomes righteous, but when God declares that person righteous based on Jesus's work. Thus, the hospital imagery of sacramental theology was replaced by a courtroom analogy and a forensic view of justification. The residual presence of sin in those justified subsequently highlighted the already/not yet tension for the believer and imbedded in Luther's soteriology an eschatological perspective. Here, Luther postulated that the believer was *simul iustus et peccator* ("simultaneously righteous and a sinner"). This anthropological paradox not only allowed for the assurance of one's salvation, but it also addressed the practical reality of ongoing sin for the believer in a preglorified era.

Faith, of course, played a prominent role in justification for Luther. As Paul reminded the believers at Ephesus, faith was a gift from God. Given his deep concerns to see any human action as meritorious, Luther saw faith as the human self-realization of an already existing regeneration. Faith doesn't cause justification, but it points back toward God's earlier act of redemption. Still, Luther understood this gift of faith to be deeply personal and linked with God's Word. The theme of *promissio,* which was woven throughout the tapestry of Luther's theology, guided his thinking here. True faith trusts in the promise of salvation made in the written Word and in the sacrificial work of the incarnate Word, Jesus Christ. Authentic faith also extends

[6] Lehmann, *Luther's Works*, 351.

beyond affirming the historical veracity of Jesus's propitiatory work on the cross and recognizes that the Son's work at Calvary has been done for that individual manifesting faith. Moreover, authentic faith moves the believer toward action. To illustrate, Luther suggested that true faith does not merely affirm a boat's capacity to cross a sea. Rather, true faith is found when the believer boards the sea vessel. Faith begets action. This aspect of Luther's understanding of justification was often overlooked by his detractors, hence the frequent mistaken charge of antinomianism.

Case Study 2: From Calvin to Tulips

John Calvin warned about "excessive curiosity" when considering predestination. The failure of his future followers to heed that sapient advice set a divisive trajectory for Protestantism that still casts a long shadow of controversy today. Theodore Beza, Calvin's handpicked successor, helped mediate his mentor's theology to the next generation of Genevan ministers. Beza's decision to appropriate a more scholastic way of thinking modified the Calvinism that was handed down. For instance, while Calvin situated predestination under his doctrine of redemption, Beza moved it to the doctrine of God proper. This change shifted focus away from the benefits of a believer's union with Christ toward God's omnipotence manifested through divine determinative decree. Moreover, Beza pondered philosophically probing questions about the atonement, which would have been foreign to a humanist, like Calvin, committed to a theology of Christian living.

Beza's interpretation of Calvin birthed a decretal theology that moved well beyond Calvin's affirmation of God's divine decree regarding election by further pondering how that decree situated relationally with others. This resulted in supralapsarianism, a theological commitment that views God's decree of election as before both his declarations regarding creation and the fall. This soteriological permutation replaced Calvin's appeal to mystery in election with a speculative, deductive theology that saw the predestination of some to salvation (and others to damnation) as ontologically necessary. The impact of this shift on the character of God was striking.

The eventual wedding of Beza's deterministic soteriology with theological arrogance proved explosive, especially when some, like Arminius, dared to raise rebutting questions. This revision of Calvin's theology was important to what came to be known historically as "Calvinism" on two fronts. First, Beza's theology sparked a movement, known as Reformed orthodoxy, which overstressed God's sole decree for salvation at the expense of biblical texts that Jacob Arminius and others believed highlighted human responsibility. This theology also made the imperative command to go and make disciples in texts such as the Great Commission passage in Matthew 28 appear disingenuous at best. Second, as per the moniker Reformed orthodoxy, adherents were adamant that their specific, narrow soteriological position *was* orthodoxy, not just an orthodox position among others.

The soteriological convictions of Reformed orthodoxy were eventually codified into five basic points at the Synod of Dort in the early seventeenth century. The historical irony undergirding these five points, commonly identified by the *TULIP* acronym, is striking given the movement's history. The Calvinists at Dort established a theology based on reaction to the declaration of Arminius's followers, the remonstrants, rather than building their position directly from the Bible. Thus, the *TULIP* acronym finds its historical expression in relation to the taproot of Arminian theology. Perhaps more paradoxically, the canons of Dort crystalized a Calvinist theology that was distinct from Calvin's, while branding itself in direct relation to a Reformer who demanded he be buried in an unmarked grave to dissuade theological veneration.

Case Study 3: British Conviction and Confession

Although the genesis of the English Reformation was based mostly on political intrigue related to Henry VIII (1491–1547), divergent theological convictions, including soteriological ones, eventually embroiled the British

Isles in controversy. As evidenced by meetings at the White Horse Tavern Inn at Cambridge, Luther's soteriology influenced England as early as the 1520s. However, by the middle of the sixteenth century, a move away from Lutheranism was evident, though that move did not generate a soteriological consensus for the English. In fact, two contextual realities helped fragment the Anglican Church.

First, Elizabeth I's (1533–1603) commitment to a *via media* way of governance, alongside Martin Bucer's (1491–1551) conciliatory voice of influence, led Thomas Cranmer (1489–1556) to soften some of the Lutheran language undergirding the Anglican Church's theology. Although this change was most apparent on the divisive issue of the Lord's Supper, the eventual removal of double predestinarian language when Cranmer's *Forty-Two Articles* from 1553 was pared down to the *Thirty-Nine Articles* in 1563, was emblematic of the Anglican Church's desire to mediate a soteriology more amenable to a wider sector of England wearied by years of theological unrest. Second, soteriological influences from the Swiss confederation were contrasted against Elizabeth I's vision for England. Many of those exiled under the cruel reign of Mary Tudor (1516–1558) fled to places on the continent such as Zürich and Geneva. When these Marian exiles returned to Elizabeth's Britain, they arrived with covenantal soteriologies in tow. In the North, John Knox (1513–1572), who had been mesmerized by Calvin's Geneva during an extended stay in the late 1550s, imported Calvin's covenant theology into Scotland, the birthplace of Presbyterianism. In England these deep-seated soteriological commitments led to the eventual rise of Puritanism and Separatism.

Charles I's (1600–1649) eventual attempt to force the Anglican Church to appropriate an Arminian soteriology was but one of the factors that led the Puritans to a political-religious alliance with the Scots. Charles's failed strategy led to England's long parliament and its demand for religious reform. When the divines gathered as the subsequent Westminster Assembly, one of their tasks was to establish liturgical commitments replacing Cranmer's *Book of Common Prayer*. Given their Puritan heritage, theological connections with the continent were apparent and soteriological changes became inevitable. The resulting *Westminster Confession of Faith* (1646) rejected foreknowledge of faith, affirming instead God's exclusive activity in salvation. Westminster framed the concept of predestination via the language of effectual calling, which stressed God's divine act of justifying a believer through a decretal pardon, not an infusion of righteousness. This positional change in status subsequently led to the believer's adoption by God and his ongoing work via sanctification to allow for a greater degree of holy living. Double predestination was affirmed in this argumentation. Yet Dort's Calvinism was muted by Westminster's emphasis on the natural liberty of human freedom, a position driven by England's desire to facilitate personal, not state-coerced, obedience.

Arguably, the most important shift made by Westminster was its elevation of the concept of covenant to a confessional status. Having seen God's initial covenant of work thwarted by Adam's sin, the Westminster divines recognized God's establishment of a second covenant of grace. This positioned God as one who offers eternal life by means of Jesus Christ via faith, while also casting the Lord as the giver of life through the Holy Spirit who makes individuals to believe.

During the latter part of the sixteenth and early seventeenth century, some in England became convinced the Anglican Church was beyond repair. Amid oppressive persecution, the separatists, as they came to be known, followed figures such as Robert Browne (1550–1633), Francis Johnson (1563–1618), and John Smyth (1566–1612) to the more tolerant Netherlands. The Dutch church was embroiled in the Arminian controversy at the time, and Smyth and his fellow churchman Thomas Helwys (1550–1616) were persuaded by Arminius's theology. Helwys's eventual return to England led to the founding of the General Baptists, so named for their belief that Jesus died for all of humanity. The General Baptists' commitment to an election based on foreknowledge, a general atonement, and a resistible position on saving grace were subsequently established in Helwys's 1612 *Declaration of the Faith*.

Although ecclesiological concerns dominated the Particular Baptists' departure from the Anglican Church, their commitment to covenant theology, including a limited atonement and irresistible grace, surfaced in their confessions. This was true of the *First London Baptist Confession* (1644), which the Particular Baptist William Kiffin (1616–1701) heavily influenced. The *Second London Confession of Faith* from 1689 maintained Dortian Calvinism's soteriology in its synthesis of the ideas from the earlier *First London Baptist Confession*, *Westminster Confession*, and *Savoy Declaration* (1658). Thus, the unity once hoped for by figures such as Cranmer and Elizabeth remained elusive.

FOR THE CHURCH

One of the modern misnomers about the Reformation is that it caused the church's division. To be sure, the fracture with Rome and the subsequent splintering of Protestantism into a myriad of confessional heritages was a regrettable inheritance bequeathed to modernity. Nevertheless, the church was already divided before the sixteenth century, as evidenced by pre-Reformation figures John Wycliffe (1330–1384) and Jan Hus (1369–1415) or movements such as conciliarism. Given that divided past, what remains striking about the Reformation was the all-too-often-forgotten unity that was realized among most of the Reformers. Following a time when the gospel was either misunderstood or veiled by rampant moral abuses of the church and the sacramental theology of the late-medieval era, the Reformers came to a general accord regarding salvation. Gospel clarity came through an embrace of justification by grace through faith and a rejection of the Roman Mass.

Still, varying life experiences, different contextual influences, and contrasting hermeneutics led the Reformers to proclaim their understanding of salvation in unique and at times discordant ways. For similar reasons, the Reformers also maintained distinct views regarding their understanding of the word picture of the gospel, as embodied in the sacraments. Theological divisions on these matters were inevitable and should be expected. Yet most of the Protestant Reformers shared a basic commitment to the evangelical gospel, namely, that one finds a right standing before God by means of his grace through faith in the Son, Jesus Christ. This stood in contradiction to Rome, which doubled down on its appropriation of late-medieval sacramental theology as a part of the Catholic Reformation. The Council of Trent, for instance, used Zech 1:3 as evidence of human participation working symbiotically with God's divine grace through the seven Roman Catholic sacraments in salvation. Nevertheless, changes to Roman Catholicism's understanding of salvation in modernity, as evidenced by doctrinal amendments at Vatican II and in the Catechism of 1993, detoured from Tridentine theology and demonstrate a vindication for Luther and the other Reformers in their soteriological departure away from Rome's medieval sacramentalism. Thus, while the Protestant Reformers covered in this chapter held to differing soteriologies, each of their unique positions remained within the safe waters of orthodoxy.

Given this history, it is not surprising that the Reformers' doctrinal commitments set a trajectory for the ways modern Christians of various confessional backgrounds understand salvation, in terms of content and conversation. The Reformers framed much of the language employed today as Christians ponder the doctrine of salvation. Still, this is often done without recognition of the specific contexts in which these unique soteriologies were framed or the rich pastoral and theological meaning behind their language. This omission has sadly left figures such as Calvin and Arminius either vilified or lauded for beliefs that those historical figures never embraced. Such dissonance in remembrance should remind us of the need to read directly, widely, and carefully from the figures who have shaped our respective soteriological traditions, rather than exclusively through the lens of their historiographies.

Regrettably, the language of salvation wasn't the only inheritance passed on to us today. The Reformers' divisive rhetoric and penchant for theological hubris was passed down to us as well. However, a strong commitment to the Bible's authority, alongside some historical perspective and humility, should remind us that we hold more in common with other Christians than otherwise first thought. We would do well not to fall prey to the Reformers' repeated prideful mistakes and instead to focus attention on our shared creedal convictions regarding salvation. This emphasis on unity would allow us to celebrate soteriological diversity while maintaining our convictions, rather than looking down on others in a prideful attempt to make our own soteriologies normative. Healthy, robust conversations among brothers and sisters can prove profitable, but these must always be framed as a dialogue *of* orthodoxy and not *for* orthodoxy. To that end Martin Luther was correct: there is one unifying consensus cry from all of humanity: "We are *all* beggars." That is what we confess. That is what we proclaim.

For Further Reading

Asselt, Willem J. van, J. Martin Bac, and Roelf T. te Velde. *Reformed Thought on Freedom: The Concept of Free Choice in Early Modern Reformed Theology*. Grand Rapids: Baker Academic, 2010.

Bagchi, David, and David C. Seinmentz, ed. *The Cambridge Companion to Reformation Theology*. Cambridge: Cambridge University Press, 2004.

Barrett, Matthew. *Salvation by Grace: The Case for Effectual Calling and Regeneration*. Phillipsburg: P&R, 2013.

George, Timothy. *Theology of the Reformers*. Rev. ed. Nashville: B&H Academic, 2013.

Goertz, Hans-Jürgen. *The Anabaptists*. London: Routledge, 1996.

Graybill, Gregory B. *Evangelical Free Will: Philipp Melanchthon's Doctrinal Journey on the Origins of Faith*. Oxford: Oxford University Press, 2010.

Kim, Changkyu. *Balthasar Hubmaier's Doctrine of Salvation in Dynamic and Relational Perspective*. Eugene, OR: Pickwick, 2013.

McGrath, Alister E. *Reformation Thought*. 4th ed. Oxford: Wiley-Blackwell, 2012.

Muller, Richard A. *Calvin and the Reformed Tradition: On the Work of Christ and the Order of Salvation*. Grand Rapids: Baker Academic, 2012.

Olson, Roger E. *Arminian Theology: Myths and Realities*. Downers Grove, IL: IVP Academic, 2006.

Sider, Ronald J. *Andreas Bodenstein von Karlstadt: The Development of His Thought, 1517–1525*. Leiden, NL: Brill, 1974.

Stjerna, Kirsi. *Women of the Reformation*. Oxford: Blackwell, 2009.

Trueman, Carl. *Grace Alone: Salvation as a Gift of God*. Grand Rapids: Zondervan, 2017.

Questions for Study or Discussion

1. In what ways did Martin Luther and Andreas Karlstadt differ on their understandings of justification?
2. Despite their shared commitment to Renaissance humanism, how did Huldrych Zwingli and John Calvin differ in their views about salvation?
3. Contrast John Calvin's thought with Dortian Calvinism. In what ways were they similar? In what ways were they different?
4. How should one respond to a question about his or her soteriological position given the historical baggage related to terms such as *Calvinism* and/or *Arminianism*?

10

THE CHURCH

By Jason G. Duesing

Introduction

In the twentieth century, C. S. Lewis (1898–1963) advocated for a "mere" Christianity in the main, but the notion of mereness also washed upon the shores of his doctrine of the church. In his *Letters to Malcolm*, Lewis, an Anglican Protestant, followed the workings out of the English Reformation as he suggested a simplified liturgy, one in which the priest minimized the distractions, the pomp, and the obstacles for the people of God. The sentiment here of a mere ecclesiology captures well the initial spirit of the Reformers in the sixteenth century. Their reforms were driven by doctrinal change and motived by a simplicity that pulled back layers of Roman complexity, especially in terms of the definition and practice of the church. Yet, as the Reformers focused on establishing their core *solas* in the church, over the ensuing decades their reforms of the doctrine of the church would vary in emphasis and thoroughness and lead to increased variance among their movements. As all Protestant and Free Church traditions trace their origins to the Reformation, this era serves as ground zero for the historical formation of ecclesiology and thus serves as a helpful era of study.

Historical Overview

As previous chapters have presented, with the advent of the Reformation era, the *conciliarists* and *curialists* represented competing definitions for the doctrine of the church. From Constantine to the fifteenth century, the conciliarists sought authority for the church from Scripture and the church councils and held influence and power over the curialists. However, following the Great Schism of the fourteenth century, the curialists came to power with Pope Pius II (1405–1464) and viewed authority as emanating from the pope. Thus, when Martin Luther (1483–1546) arrived, even in his early Ninety-Five Theses (1517) he called for reform of doctrine in the understanding of how man relates to God, and the error of indulgences as "nets" with which one fishes for wealth (Thesis 66). Pope Leo X (1475–1521) permitted the sale of indulgences, which gave assurance to the masses that their purchase would aid their loved ones to see a quick release from purgatory. While at first Luther sought a reformation of the church's understanding of the doctrine of salvation, those in power interpreted Luther as calling for reform of church authority. Such notice came as the result of the translation into the common language of Luther's persuasive theses. To question doctrine is to question the church, and a call for a reformation of the doctrine of salvation is a call for a reformation of the doctrine of the church.

Thus, as Luther and the Reformers discovered the depths of theological corruption in the church when compared to Scripture, they expanded their aims to include a reformation of church authority, establishing Scripture as supreme and tradition a helpful servant, and they categorically rejected papal authority. With revisions to their doctrine of Scripture and doctrine of salvation, implications for the doctrine of the church followed. The Reformers returned to fundamental questions, asking the Scriptures, "What is the true church?" The result was a simplified and redefined ecclesiology that identified essential components of the church distinct from Roman Catholic sacramental constructions. By upholding *sola Scriptura* and *sola fidei*, the Reformers did not need to advocate for the *sola ecclesiae* of Rome, a "church alone" understanding of the relationship between the church and salvation. Instead, they developed their *notae ecclesiae*, or marks of the church.

Martin Luther

Martin Luther's initial questions of doctrinal reform prompted many critiques, and prominent among them were those of Johann Eck (1486–1543). In 1519, Luther engaged Eck in a public debate that proved pivotal for Luther's own understanding of church authority. Eck challenged him to define the origin of the papacy, and when Luther responded that the papacy was of human design, Eck attempted to label him a follower of the teachings of John Wycliffe and Jan Hus. These tactics allowed Luther to conclude that he had moved beyond the conciliarists and the curialists to assert that only Scripture can form articles of faith—the pope and councils should be rejected. Thus, Luther's doctrine of Scripture served as the foundation for his call for reform of the doctrine of the church.

The Reformers affirmed the Niceno-Constantinopolitan definition that the church is one, holy, catholic, and apostolic. However, given the irregularities they observed in Roman Catholic doctrine and practice when compared with the Scriptures, they asked how one is to know whether a congregational meeting is a true representation of the church. Martin Luther first classified these identifiable characteristics as signs of the church in his letter *On the Papacy* (1520), listing the preached Word of God, baptism, and the Lord's Supper. That year, Pope Leo X issued *Exsurge Domine*, which promised excommunication unless Luther recanted. Luther burned the document and wrote his three treatises, of which *On the Babylonian Captivity of the Church* (1520) also asserted that only the two sacraments of baptism and the Lord's Supper are biblical. Following the Diet of Augsburg

(1530), the resulting Confession affirmed these characteristics, and Philip Melanchthon's *Apology* (1531) employed the term *notae ecclesiae*, or notes or marks of the church, to describe them. Melanchthon (1497–1560) continued to use this term in his *Loci Communes* (1535), and it became the classification used in ongoing debates regarding the doctrine of the church. By 1539, Luther had written *On the Councils and the Church* and articulated seven total marks to give specific identification to the church he was defending, with the first three marks centering on the preaching and primacy of the Word of God with the people of God, and the practice of baptism and the Lord's Supper.

Luther's Word-centered ecclesiology developed around his concept of the church as a community of saints. For Luther, Christians serve as believer-priests, one to another, as they intercede and care for each other. Here he broke through the traditional separate classes of clergy and laity to emphasize that all believers share the responsibility of the work of the church. While Luther did maintain that the church has specific leadership offices and represents those who gather in local settings, much of his doctrine of the church also focused on a broader or invisible collection of saints that extend beyond territorial borders.

Swiss and South German Reformers

Huldrych Zwingli (1484–1531) studied at universities in Vienna and Basel and encountered humanism, the practice rediscovering classical texts and bringing them to bear on present society and culture. Thus, when he met Desiderius Erasmus (1466–1536), Zwingli prepared for further discipleship in humanist studies particularly as it relates to the New Testament. In the early 1520s, Zwingli left Roman Catholicism to advance the Reformation from Zurich. Zwingli's doctrine of the church, called the Zurich Disputations, developed as he called the town to gather for councils to discuss topics for reform. Following the Second Disputation (1523), several of his disciples grew weary with the slow rate of reform given the clarity they concluded the Scriptures gave for the errors of Rome. On the issue of baptism, these followers broke with Zwingli in 1525 to practice an illegal believer's baptism and to start a free church movement. Zwingli opposed the Anabaptists and defended infant baptism but distinguished his view from that of Roman Catholics. He believed that baptism could not remove original sin, and therefore, there was no need to practice the rituals associated with baptism that Roman Catholics employed to communicate sacramental action.

In 1529, Zwingli joined Lutheran and South German Reformation leaders at the request of Philip of Hesse (1504–1567) at what would be known as the Marburg Colloquy. Philip gathered all Reformation movements to unite them against Roman Catholic advance. Led by Luther and Zwingli, those gathered came to agreement on several core doctrinal positions but could not reconcile over their understanding of the Lord's Supper. At issue was a difference over belief in the presence of Christ in the elements. Luther asserted Christ was present and Zwingli argued such belief was illogical. The disagreement resulted in a schism between the two movements and a failure to unify as Protestants.

Zwingli's *An Exposition of the Faith* (1530) articulated his understanding that the church is both invisible and visible. The invisible church is composed of "all who believe the world over," known only to God. The visible church consists of those who make a profession of faith in Christ, not the established Roman Catholic Church. Thus, Zwingli believed that within the visible church, there are some who are not a part of the invisible church "who are called Christians falsely."

Heinrich Bullinger (1504–1575) followed Zwingli in Zurich and, as a contemporary of John Calvin, served to systematize the Swiss Reformed movement as Calvin and the Calvinists grew in influence within the Reformed tradition. In 1536, Bullinger coauthored the First Helvetic Confession, which, regarding the doctrine of the church, gave clarity to the Swiss Reformed view of the Lord's Supper. The Second Helvetic Confession (1566) ensured Bullinger's long-lasting influence on the Reformed movement. The Second Confession recognizes the preaching of the Word of God and participation in the sacraments instituted by Christ as the signs of the true church.

Martin Bucer (1491–1551) shaped the outworking of the early Reformed movement in Strasbourg and served as a historical and doctrinal bridge from Luther to Calvin, and even the Reformation in England. Present while studying in Heidelberg when Luther gave his first defense of his call to reform in 1518, Bucer's life and thought transformed after he heard Luther's argument. Likening him to the apostle Paul, Bucer followed Luther into the Reformation and landed in Strasbourg, where he served as a conduit between Luther and Zwingli. After the adoption of the Augsburg Confession (1530), Bucer and others adapted it to fit the Swiss Reformed tradition as the Strasbourg Confession. Therein, the church is "plainly known by its fruits," which include the pure administration of the gospel and sacraments, and Bucer, along with others in the Reformed tradition, included the practice of church discipline as a third ordinance to comprise the *notae ecclesiae*. Bucer also later coauthored the First Helvetic Confession with Bullinger.

John Calvin

John Calvin (1509–1564) discovered humanism while studying law to please his father. A gifted linguist, Calvin tested his skills in commitment to returning to the original sources through a published commentary on the work of Seneca (1532). Once he joined the Reformation soon thereafter, Calvin employed his humanism in the publication of commentaries on most books of the Bible and, of course, his timeless *Institutes of the Christian Religion*. As he led the second generation of the Reformation from Geneva, Calvin's ascendancy as a theologian of influence came when many of the other movements had lost their initial leaders and when Roman Catholicism had regrouped and mobilized. Calvin put into theological order a new, clear Reformation theology born from the fruit of his own study and the influence of Luther and the Reformed tradition.

Timothy George terms Calvin's doctrine of the church as "bipolar." By this he means that Calvin held in tension both the visible and invisible characteristics of the church. The invisible church consists of all the elect of God as a communion of saints, and as such, God will preserve his church. The visible church, or church external, is seen as true by its marks. Namely, "Wherever we see the Word of God purely preached and heard, and the sacraments administered according to Christ's institution, there, it is not to be doubted, a church of God exists" (*Institutes* 4.1.9). For Calvin, the visible church can be destroyed by Satan, and therefore the marks serve as a test of veracity for the church. If a church does not exhibit the *notae ecclesiae*, Calvin advised the believer to proceed with caution and to avoid the congregation. However, when the marks are present, Christians should acknowledge the visible church even if there are false Christians within the congregation. Where the marks of the church exist, the blessing of God will follow, and no visible church is pure in a sinful world.

Calvin's doctrine of baptism followed the Reformed tradition of extending infant baptism to all in the visible church. Baptism is a sign of initiation to the covenant community, like circumcision, as Calvin drew close connections between the New Testament church and Old Testament Israel. While in Strasbourg in the late 1530s, Calvin studied with Martin Bucer and followed his influence in the development of his understanding of the presence of Christ in the Lord's Supper that formed a mediating position between that of Luther and Zwingli.

The Radical Reformers

George Williams, acclaimed former professor of ecclesiastical history at Harvard University, labored throughout the twentieth century to assert that the Radical Reformation served as a significant movement that influenced modern Christianity more than often was acknowledged. The Radical Reformation was a broad movement consisting of many branches, and Williams pioneered a helpful classification system that allowed for the correction of much of historical interpretation. In the early twenty-first century, Carlos Eire, professor of history at Yale University, provided a helpful update and expansion to Williams's typology of the three primary groups of the Radical Reformation: the Anabaptists, the spiritualists, and the evangelical rationalists. Of the three, the Anabaptists stayed closely aligned to the core doctrines of the other Reformation movements, even as they questioned the role of tradition in a step further toward rejecting the use of tradition altogether (see Matthew Barrett's chapter).

That said, as Eire chronicled, the Swiss Brethren and later moderate Anabaptists, which Eire labeled Magisterial Anabaptists, found their motivation not in the rejection of the role that tradition might play as a servant to Scripture, but in the quest for a church separate from the influence of state authority. For example, two of the Magisterial Anabaptist theologians, Pilgram Marpeck (1495–1556) and Balthasar Hubmaier (1480/1–1528), used and referenced the Apostles' Creed and the Athanasian Creed in their works. Thus, their pursuit of *sola Scriptura* meant all that it meant for the Magisterial Reformers but sought to rid the Scriptures of the latent entanglements of the state that were still tied to the church. The doctrines they developed of believer's baptism and a believers' church were visible symbols of this free church quest. While they referred to themselves as the Brethren, their enemies labeled them ana-baptists for their visible practice of baptizing "again." The brief *Schleitheim Confession* (1527) articulated their simple ecclesiology of Christians separate from the world and identified by visible ordinances and gathering outside the institutional church. Zwingli, Luther, and Calvin all rejected these and subsequent Anabaptist arguments, though they also had in view the spiritualists and rationalists and their rejection or modification of the authority of Scripture.

Hubmaier trained as a theologian with zeal under Johann Eck before his conversion to the Reformation and then the Anabaptist movement. By 1525, Hubmaier had connected with the Swiss Brethren in Zurich and written *On the Christian Baptism of Believers* to lend a theological voice to the growing movement. Once carrying out his Anabaptist convictions in his parish church in the town of Waldshut, Hubmaier gained the attention of the Roman Catholic authorities and fled. During his exile he wrote *Concerning Heretics and Those Who Burn Them*, an influential tract that advocated religious freedom from state coercion. Captured by Zwingli in Zurich for a time, Hubmaier eventually was tried by Austrian authorities and executed in 1528.

Marpeck worked as a city engineer in Augsburg and yet wrote many influential Anabaptist tracts and pamphlets as a lay theologian. As he regularly engaged society and politics, Marpeck is distinct, yet his work paved the way for long-lasting influence. Marpeck's *Admonition of 1542* affirmed the *notae ecclesiae* of the broader Reformation movements that a true church consists of the proclamation of the gospel, correct baptism, and correct communion.

English Reformers

William Tyndale (1494–1536), translator of the New Testament in English, resisted the authority of Roman Catholicism. In his *Obedience of a Christian Man* (1528), Tyndale encouraged support of the magistrate while rejecting the authority of the established church. Yet, by 1530, he declared Henry VIII's desire for divorce unbiblical. Thomas More, a debater of Luther, directed his *A Dialogue Concerning Heresies* (1528) at Tyndale, questioning why Tyndale translated *ecclesiae* as "congregation" instead of "church." Tyndale defended his choice of words in *An Answer* (1531) as emphasizing the role of the gathered people in the church, not the clergy. This exacerbated More and Roman Catholic authorities and ended in Tyndale's execution in 1536. However, earlier in 1532, Henry VIII declared his intent to form a new church in order to secure his divorce, and by 1534 Parliament had passed the Supremacy Act, acknowledging the king as head of the Church of England.

Before Henry VIII's death, his third wife bore him a son, Edward VI, who assumed the throne in 1547 at age nine. Archbishop Thomas Cranmer

(1489–1556) led a theological reform of the new church through an initial collection of *The Forty-Two Articles* (1536–1553), the Book of Common Prayer (1549–1552), and *The Ordinal* (1550). In the *Articles* Cranmer established that the church visible "is a congregation of faithful men, in which the pure word of God is preached, and the sacraments are duly ministered according to Christ's ordinance." With the death of Edward VI, Mary I reigned from 1553 to 1558, and many English Protestants fled as she endeavored to return the church to Rome. While Cranmer and many others were executed for heresy, a group of English exiles led by John Knox (1514–1572) continued the reformation. Elizabeth I came to power in 1558, and her middle way of seeking appeasement between Protestants and Catholics restored the Book of Common Prayer and reduced the *Articles* to thirty-nine, while keeping most of Cranmer's reformation theology.

In the 1570s a new group of young enthusiasts attempted to reform further the Church of England from within. These Puritans aimed to change the hierarchical structure of the church from bishops to presbyteries to ensure the church remained separate from Rome. However, not all were so content, and some, like Robert Browne (1540–1633), called for full separation of congregations from the oversight of the monarchy. The spirit of separation persisted, and with the reign of James I (1566–1625) and increased toleration for Rome, several more Puritans followed the path to Separatism. These distinct congregations followed only Scripture for their further development of their ecclesiological practice, and some amended further their doctrine of baptism. Thomas Helwys (1575–1616) led the first congregation in England to institute baptism for believers while advocating also for religious freedom.

The reign of Charles I (1600–1649) was marked by increased persecution for those who did not conform to the strictures of the Church of England, and ended with the king's execution. Nevertheless, the 1640s and 1650s saw the advance of many nonconforming churches, including the new English Baptist congregations. By 1644, a group of Baptist churches were convinced that the New Testament practice of believer's baptism should follow full immersion to identify with the death, burial, and resurrection of Christ. These churches drafted the London Baptist Confession, which defined the church as a "company of visible saints" called to "the visible profession of the faith of the gospel . . . joined . . . by mutual agreement in the practical enjoyment of the ordinances."

Case Studies

As Matthew Barrett's chapter presented the Reformation doctrine of Scripture, and Stephen Eccher's chapter presented the Reformation doctrine of salvation, two doctrines that comprise what was preached as a part of Reformation ecclesiology, this chapter's case studies focus on the administration of the ordinances in Reformation ecclesiology.

The terms *sacrament* and *ordinance* are often interchanged by the Reformers and used to define the same things. Roman Catholics developed a sacramental theology around seven sacraments following the translation of the Greek word for *mystery* into the Latin *sacramentum*. The early church did this because they believed that baptism and the Lord's Supper conveyed a mystery of divine grace. The connection between grace and these sacraments evolved until Augustine (354–430) solidified the understanding that the sacraments worked for grace for the recipient. Thus, as a corrective, many Protestants employed the term *ordinance* to indicate that two, not seven, practices were given, or ordained, by Christ for the church's practice.

Case Study 1: Pilgram Marpeck's Correct Baptism

In Pilgram Marpeck's articulation of the *notae ecclesiae*, he denoted baptism as "correct baptism," implying that a true visible church must employ the right practice of baptism as a matter of ecclesiological integrity. He, therefore, identified infant baptism as false practice. This case study will present a summary of his argument.

Marpeck saw infant baptism as an unnecessary innovation. He stated, "If people would have stayed with Christ's one simple order or command it would not have been necessary to raise so many orders of baptism" (*Admonition of 1542*). Marpeck pointed to Christ's command in Matthew 28 to make disciples and baptize them, and insisted that this instruction applied not only to those who heard it, but to all future disciples and nations until the last day.

In addition, Marpeck advocated that Matthew 28 also gives a prescriptive order for who should receive baptism: "first teaching, then faith, and only then baptism" (*Confession of 1532*). Teaching comprises the meaning of "make disciples" as an unbeliever is taught the gospel (Matt 28:19). Faith follows teaching and precedes baptism, for baptism "springs from faith in Christ" (*Confession of 1532*). Marpeck cited Mark 16:16, "Whoever believes and is baptized will be saved," and the teaching of Philip to the eunuch in Acts, which concluded in baptism after a response to the gospel. Baptism, as a visible practice, follows the inward baptism of the Spirit at conversion and is a symbol or a witness of this inward work.

In 1542, Marpeck did not prescribe a clear practice for the mode of baptism and affirmed either immersion or sprinkling of water. The clear focus was on who was to be baptized, the believer. Marpeck explained further that the believer needs baptism only once, as "it is a portal of entrance into the . . . church of Christ" (*Admonition of 1542*). Here Marpeck agreed with those who advocated infant baptism, but he made his argument for believer's baptism, as well as the beginnings of an argument for a believers' church, with an emphasis on the confessional nature of baptism. Just as the Lord indicated he would build his church following Peter's confession of faith (see Matt 16:13–18), Marpeck said such a confession is needed to join Christ's church, and baptism is the entrance to the church that follows that confession.

Therefore, for Marpeck, correct baptism served as a necessary requirement for the *notae ecclesiae* due to the command and order he saw in Christ's teaching in Matthew 28. It was a visible expression that, for Anabaptists like Marpeck, served to represent not only right practice, but also a commitment to following the authority of Scripture and the establishment of a free church, separate from the state, composed of confessing believers.

Case Study 2: The Lord's Supper

The development of the theology and understanding of the extent of the presence of Christ at the Lord's Supper in the Reformation is first a reaction to the Roman Catholic articulation of transubstantiation. The belief that the bread and the wine were transformed into the body and blood of Christ by the power of God while still retaining the properties of bread and wine ensured a means by which grace was transmitted to participants (see Zachary Bowden's chapter). As the Reformers developed *sola fidei* and *solus Christus*, their doctrine of the church mandated a revision to their understanding of the Lord's Supper.

Consubstantiation

Advocated by Martin Luther, consubstantiation is the view that Christ is present within the substance of the elements of the Lord's Supper, but the bread and the wine are not changed. Luther rejected transubstantiation on biblical grounds, citing the error in Rome's reliance on irrational philosophical constructions as "a figment of the human mind" (*On the Babylonian Captivity of the Church*, 1520). Luther understood Jesus's words "this is my body," proclaimed on the night he was betrayed (Matt 26:26), to convey that Christ's body can be in multiple places at once, or everywhere. God literally puts Christ's presence in the elements during the administration of the Lord's Supper. The recipients put their faith alone in the promise or testament of Christ that forgiveness of sins is available by the body and blood of Christ but receive the presence of Christ through the sacrament of the bread and wine. The term *consubstantiation* represents this distinction, for Christ is present with, or *con*, the substance of the bread and wine, but does not transform into the substance.

Symbolic or Memorial View

Zwingli articulated an opposing view of the Lord's Supper that refuted transubstantiation and consubstantiation. He insisted that Jesus's proclamation in Matt 26:26, "this is my body," could not be literal, as such a reading is confusing and resists simple interpretation. If Jesus meant the bread is literally his body, then his body would be "torn about by teeth" *(On the Lord's Supper,* 1526). Further, there would be no reason to reject transubstantiation in favor of consubstantiation, for clear transformation of the bread had to occur. Further, Zwingli recognized a Christological problem with the notion that God the Son is present everywhere, for the body of Christ to be omnipresent is to "drag Christ down from heaven and from his Father's throne" (*An Exposition,* 1530). Instead, Zwingli understood the bread and wine to function as symbols to memorialize the death of Christ. Citing Luke 22:19 and 1 Cor 11:25, where Jesus instructed the disciples to practice the Lord's Supper "in remembrance" of him, Zwingli asserted that the point of the Lord's Supper is to memorialize the sacrifice of Christ by the symbols he instituted. Zwingli stated, "As Christ is broken, that is, put to death for us, so in remembrance of him we offer one another the bread and break it, each representing and communicating with each other, as Christ did for us all" (*On the Lord's Supper,* 1526).

Spiritual Presence

Following the influence of Martin Bucer, John Calvin developed his own understanding of the presence of Christ in the Lord's Supper that might have come closer to achieving unity at Marburg with the Lutherans than did Zwingli's view. Calvin did not advocate for a physical presence of Christ in the elements, but rather a spiritual presence brought about by God the Holy Spirit. Calvin reminded his readers that even though it seems impossible that Christ could be present in the Supper, it is foolish to measure the work of the Spirit, which is immeasurable. When the apostle Paul stated that in the bread and cup, we participate in the body and blood of Christ

(1 Cor 10:16–17), Calvin acknowledged that this is symbolic language. Yet "we shall nevertheless duly infer that by the showing of the symbol the thing itself is also shown" (*Institutes* 4.17.10). In the elements Christ is truly present by the power of the Spirit.

For the Church

The Reformers' pursuit of a simplified doctrine of the church followed their initial decisions to pursue a reform movement that returned to the sources of authoritative Scriptures for the establishment of a biblical understanding of the doctrine of salvation. This resulted in a mere ecclesiology centered on *notae ecclesiae* that affirmed the church as an invisible collection of all believers and a visible gathering that upheld the centrality of the preached Word of God and the gospel and the regular practice of baptism and the Lord's Supper as the ordinances instituted by Christ. Yet ecclesiological variances of practice and specific understanding of church doctrines abounded by geographic region, political influence from the state, and pressure from surrounding movements. With this variance, what is sometimes lost is the larger picture that the recovery of churches built around the gospel ensured that future generations received the same gospel. Had the Reformers not wrestled with the doctrine of the church, the recovery of the *solas* might not have lasted more than a generation. Therefore, in our own day, church reform needs to continue, not only for the quest of seeking to follow the Scriptures, but also to ensure there remain future visible communions of saints who will treasure and proclaim the gospel of Jesus Christ until he returns.

The Baptist tradition emerged from the English Reformation in history and continued, in tandem with other Protestant traditions, to advocate for the doctrine of the church. As one group that remained committed to *sola Scriptura*, the Baptists did not reject the councils and confessions of the church, but saw them as servants to Scripture and helpful tools to summarize and express what they concluded as biblical. The Baptists developed a church-focused confessional tradition of their own following the Reformation that underwent revision as Baptists moved throughout the globe and encountered different cultural experiences. Through the centuries, however, their convictions about the *notae ecclesiae* remained. Thus, this chapter concludes with the statements on the church, baptism, and Lord's Supper from the twenty-first-century Baptist Faith and Message (2000).

Article VI. The Church

A New Testament church of the Lord Jesus Christ is an autonomous local congregation of baptized believers, associated by covenant in the faith and fellowship of the gospel; observing the two ordinances of Christ, governed by His laws, exercising the gifts, rights, and privileges invested in them by His Word, and seeking to extend the gospel to the ends of the earth. Each congregation operates under the Lordship of Christ through democratic processes. In such a congregation each member is responsible and accountable to Christ as Lord. Its scriptural officers are pastors and deacons. While both men and women are gifted for service in the church, the office of pastor is limited to men as qualified by Scripture.

The New Testament speaks also of the church as the Body of Christ which includes all of the redeemed of all the ages, believers from every tribe, and tongue, and people, and nation.

Matthew 16:15–19; 18:15–20; Acts 2:41–42, 47; 5:11–14; 6:3–6; 13:1–3; 14:23, 27; 15:1–30; 16:5; 20:28; Romans 1:7; 1 Corinthians 1:2; 3:16; 5:4–5; 7:17; 9:13–14; 12; Ephesians 1:22–23; 2:19–22; 3:8–11, 21; 5:22–32; Philippians 1:1; Colossians 1:18; 1 Timothy 2:9–14; 3:1–15; 4:14; Hebrews 11:39–40; 1 Peter 5:1–4; Revelation 2–3; 21:2–3.

Article VII. Baptism and the Lord's Supper

Christian baptism is the immersion of a believer in water in the name of the Father, the Son, and the Holy Spirit. It is an act of obedience symbolizing the believer's faith in a crucified, buried, and risen Saviour, the believer's death to sin, the burial of the old life, and the resurrection to walk in newness of life in Christ Jesus. It is a testimony to his faith in the final resurrection of the dead. Being a church ordinance, it is prerequisite to the privileges of church membership and to the Lord's Supper.

The Lord's Supper is a symbolic act of obedience whereby members of the church, through partaking of the bread and the fruit of the vine, memorialize the death of the Redeemer and anticipate His second coming.

Matthew 3:13–17; 26:26–30; 28:19–20; Mark 1:9–11; 14:22–26; Luke 3:21–22; 22:19–20; John 3:23; Acts 2:41–42; 8:35–39; 16:30–33; 20:7; Romans 6:3–5; 1 Corinthians 10:16, 21; 11:23–29; Colossians 2:12.

For Further Reading

Allison, Gregg. *Historical Theology: An Introduction to Christian Doctrine.* Grand Rapids: Zondervan, 2011.

Bainton, Roland H. *Here I Stand: A Life of Martin Luther*. Peabody, MA: Hendrickson, 2011.

Barrett, Matthew, ed. *Reformation Theology: A Systematic Summary*. Wheaton, IL: Crossway, 2017.

Bromiley, G. W., ed. *Zwingli and Bullinger.* Philadelphia: Westminster, 1953.

Calvin, John. *Institutes of the Christian Religion.* 2 vols. Edited by John T. McNeill. Louisville: Westminster John Knox, 1960.

Dever, Mark. *The Church: The Gospel Made Visible*. Nashville: B&H Academic, 2012.

Eire, Carlos. *Reformations: The Early Modern World, 1450–1650.* New Haven, CT: Yale University Press, 2016.

Estep, William R. *The Anabaptist Story: An Introduction to Sixteenth-Century Anabaptism*. Grand Rapids: Eerdmans, 1996.

George, Timothy. *Theology of the Reformers*. Rev. ed. Nashville: B&H, 2013.

Gordon, Bruce. *Calvin*. New Haven, CT: Yale University Press, 2009.

Hendrix, Scott H. *Martin Luther: Visionary Reformer*. New Haven, CT: Yale University Press, 2015.

Klaassen, Walter, ed., *Anabaptism in Outline.* Edited by Walter Klaassen. Scottdale, PA: Herald, 1981.

Lathrop, Gordon W., and Timothy J. Wengert. *Christian Assembly: Marks of the Church in a Pluralistic Age*. Minneapolis: Augsburg, 2000.

Lull, Timothy, ed. *Martin Luther's Basic Theological Writings*. Minneapolis: Fortress, 1989.

Pipkin, H. Wayne, and John H. Yoder. *Balthasar Hubmaier: Theologian of Anabaptism*. Scottdale, PA: Herald, 1989.

Williams, George Hunston. *The Radical Reformation.* Ann Arbor, MI: Edwards Brothers, 2000.

QUESTIONS FOR STUDY OR DISCUSSION

1. How does the Reformers' search for a "mere" church inform our own church practice?
2. What role does tradition or culture play in our interpretation of Scripture, specifically as it relates to ecclesiology? In what ways do we allow tradition or culture to serve as a higher authority when it comes to the local church?
3. If you had lived in the Reformation era and could have joined any of the new church movements throughout Europe, which would you have chosen?
4. Based on the Reformers' understanding of the marks of a church, what is a false church?
5. Which practice of baptism and the Lord's Supper follows most closely to the biblical witness?

UNIT FOUR

THEOLOGY IN THE MODERN ERA, AD 1700–2000

11

SCRIPTURE AND AUTHORITY

By Nathan A. Finn

Introduction

The theological disruption of the Reformation extended into the modern era, the beginnings of which can be dated to around 1700. By this time, Western Europe had witnessed the advent of nation-states, many of which were characterized by the gradual waning of ecclesial influence over the state. Explorers had claimed lands in the Western Hemisphere for various European powers, normally staking claims for various Christian churches as well (especially the Roman Catholic Church). Protestants continued to subdivide into proto-denominational movements committed to various versions of Reformational theology and practice, sometimes including national loyalties. Meanwhile, Catholics tried to navigate a post-Reformation Europe marked by increasing pluralism among professed Christians. Eastern

Orthodoxy remained mostly confined to eastern Europe and northern Asia, largely isolated from these trends until the nineteenth century.

Arguably, no single doctrine was subject to greater revision during the modern era than bibliology (the doctrine of Scripture). At the very least, revisionist views of Scripture were uniquely important; one's view of the inspiration, authority, and interpretation of the Bible necessarily affects how one conceives every other doctrine. When it comes to Scripture (and many other topics), one could even interpret modernity as an ever-evolving crisis of authority and the various responses to that crisis. This chapter will focus on developments related to biblical inspiration, authority, and interpretation during the past three centuries.

Historical Overview

Enlightenment and Romanticism

The eighteenth century is often referred to as the Age of Reason, or the Enlightenment, because of the advent of new philosophical assumptions that dramatically influenced the transatlantic intellectual world. In reality, though the Enlightenment dates to the seventeenth century, there was no single Enlightenment—and scholars do not agree in their interpretations of various versions of the Enlightenment. Furthermore, contrary to popular understanding, not all theologians (even the more conservative) perceived the Enlightenment as a threat to the faith. Many Christian thinkers embraced certain Enlightenment emphases to help buttress their understandings of orthodoxy.

Despite these caveats, it is true that a number of Enlightenment currents did present challenges to traditional understandings of Christian thought, including the doctrine of Scripture. Many Enlightenment thinkers from René Descartes (1596–1650) forward sought rational certainty and championed the omnicompetence of autonomous human reason, setting reason in opposition to faith. This was a far cry from the Augustinian commitment to "faith seeking understanding," which animated theological inquiry for well over a millennium. Some thinkers, such as the English deist Matthew Tindal (1657–1733), went so far as to reject the very conception of special revelation, opting for natural revelation alone. Others such as Scottish philosopher David Hume (1711–1776) went further and endorsed religious skepticism, denying the reality of the supernatural. Revisionist views of Scripture coincided with, and reinforced, revisionist understandings of doctrines such as human sinfulness, miracles, the Trinity, and the person and work of Jesus Christ. These revisionist doctrines were in turn embraced by heretical forms of Christianity such as Deism, Unitarianism, and Universalism.

Although many Enlightenment thinkers still claimed the Christian faith as their own, their assumptions about the relationship between reason and faith fed the argument that the Bible is not the inspired written words of God but rather the words of pious men. The most famous was philosopher Immanuel Kant (1724–1804), who sought to rescue Christianity from skepticism, but at the expense of the inspiration of Scripture. By making a distinction between "pure" (rational) reason and "practical" (moral) reason, and relegating matters of religion to the latter, Kant contended the value of Scripture was limited to ethics and morality.

Enlightenment views of Scripture were widely held by leaders of the American and French Revolutions. American founding fathers such as Benjamin Franklin (1706–1790), John Adams (1735–1826), and Thomas Jefferson (1743–1826) were Protestant "theistic rationalists" who imbibed of Deist and sometimes Unitarian thought, while still deeply valuing the role of the Bible in forming personal and civic virtue. (Jefferson famously published an edited version of the New Testament in 1820 that excluded all the miracles and references to Jesus's divinity.) In France, leaders such as Voltaire (1694–1776) and Maximilien Robespierre (1758–1794) embraced a more radical skepticism, leading to an anti-Christian posture that revolted against the *Ancien Régime*'s commitment to Catholicism, replacing it with a state-sponsored atheism that prevailed until Napoleon Bonaparte (1769–1821) came to power and restored nominal relations with Rome.

Some thinkers reacted to the Enlightenment, most notably the proponents of Romanticism. As with the Enlightenment, *Romanticism* is a debated term that defies scholarly consensus. Nevertheless, by the end of the eighteenth century, a number of philosophers had grown unhappy with Enlightenment rationalism but also refused to embrace historic Christian orthodoxy. They valued human feelings and emotions over rational autonomy and emphasized the subjective elements of religion over objective truth claims. The upshot of Romanticism was a Bible that might well be inspirational but that should not be considered inspired in the sense that premodern theologians affirmed.

The Historical-Critical Method

During the premodern era, theologians practiced a variety of strategies of biblical interpretation, many of which you have read about in previous chapters. What these approaches had in common was a belief that the Bible is God's inspired written Word. As such, Scripture is authoritative and trustworthy, reflecting God's own character. This changed with the advent of modernity and its revisionist views of the Bible. Many theologians now believed the Bible to be a thoroughly human book, that it should be interpreted like any other book, and that its historical and scientific truthfulness should not be assumed.

Modern assumptions about the doctrine of Scripture gave rise to the historical-critical method of interpretation (also called higher criticism). The historical-critical method focused more on the historical circumstances that ostensibly gave rise to the biblical text rather than the content of the text itself. History (and later science), rather than the text of Scripture or church tradition, functioned as the determinative factor in biblical interpretation. This approach also meshed well with the Enlightenment emphasis on human autonomy, which championed individual conclusions over communal or churchly interpretations. For modern critical interpreters, the connection between biblical reflection and theology was severed, or at least stretched to the point of great tension.

One result was the so-called first quest for the historical Jesus, which began in the mid-eighteenth century. Scholars such as Hermann Reimarus (1694–1768), David Friedrich Strauss (1808–1874), and their successors embraced higher critical assumptions and attempted to reconstruct the life of Jesus without the supernaturalist worldview of the New Testament authors. For these scholars, the Bible contained many things about Jesus that were likely true, but biblical phenomena needed to be verified externally to validate its authenticity. The twentieth century witnessed two more quests for the historical Jesus, both of which included voices more and less sympathetic to inspired Scripture than the original questers.

A second result of the historical-critical method was the documentary hypothesis, identified especially with German scholar Julius Wellhausen (1844–1918). Proponents of this view rejected the primary Mosaic authorship and unified message of the Pentateuch, arguing instead that the canonical biblical material represented four different sources that were edited and combined over a period of about three centuries. Other Old Testament critical scholars argued that Daniel was authored in the second century BC rather than the more traditional fifth century, and contended that Isaiah was written by two or three authors, sympathetic to some of the same traditions that authored portions of the Pentateuch.

The evolutionary theory popularized by Charles Darwin (1809–1882) served to reinforce the historical-critical method in the mind of many scholars. With this theory in mind, critical scholars now had further reason to doubt supernaturalist biblical accounts of creation. Some traditionalist scholars attempted to synthesize aspects of evolution with Scripture, while others rejected evolution in principle as being incompatible with the Bible. Evolution proved to be more controversial than the historical-critical method itself, in part because the former was more widely known among everyday Christians, while the latter was mostly a debate confined to scholars and ministers.

Fundamentalist-Modernist Controversies

By the turn of the twentieth century, Protestant theologians were divided between traditionalists, progressives, and mediating theologians who tried to find a middle way. The traditionalists took on the name "fundamentalists" following the publication of a twelve-volume series of pamphlets titled *The Fundamentals: A Testimony to Truth* (1910–1915). Though they were divided by denominational differences and classical debates over matters such as election and baptism, fundamentalists saw themselves as a loose-knit movement that argued for traditional views on the very fundamental doctrines that had become contested in the modern era.

In their view of Scripture, most fundamentalists argued that every word of the original manuscripts was inspired by God (verbal-plenary inspiration) and that Scripture, when rightly interpreted, was fully trustworthy, even in matters of history and science (biblical inerrancy). In these views, they drew on the insights of post-Reformation theologians, as well as nineteenth-century theologians such as Charles Hodge (1797–1878) and Basil Manly Jr. (1825–1892). Although some fundamentalists such as John R. Rice (1895–1980) argued that God divinely dictated the words of Scripture to the biblical authors, most theological conservatives (and all the key theologians) argued that the Scriptures represented a concurrence of the Holy Spirit's divine inspiration and the words freely chosen by the original authors. This followed the trajectory established by Hodge at Princeton Theological Seminary. (See the case study that follows.)

Contra the fundamentalists, modernists embraced critical views of Scripture. In many cases, this led to a rejection of biblical miracles, a redefinition of human sin and the atonement, and a downplaying of salvation through Christ alone. The father of theological modernism was Friedrich Schleiermacher (1768–1834), who put forward a critical-romantic synthesis of the Christian faith that was intended to defend the validity of Christianity against modern skepticism. In his influential book *On Christian Faith*, Schleiermacher argued that reflection on the human experience of dependence on God, rather than appeal to God's revelation in Scripture, was the heart of theological inquiry. Roger Olson calls this a "Copernican revolution" in the history of doctrine. Scholars and pastors such as William Newton Clarke (1841–1912), Adolf von Harnack (1851–1930), Shailer Mathews (1863–1941), and Harry Emerson Fosdick (1878–1969) advanced the modernist cause into the twentieth century. By the postwar era, modernists were increasingly called liberals. Today the term *progressive* is another common label for this theological trajectory.

In the period between World War I and World War II, many of the major Protestant denominations split over debates between fundamentalists and modernists. In most cases, modernists and their mediating allies maintained control of the denominations. Fundamentalists either formed new denominations or (more often) cooperated through interdenominational networks of schools, mission boards, and publishing houses. Verbal-plenary inspiration and biblical inerrancy remained hallmarks of fundamentalism, especially among scholars and educated ministers. Postwar evangelicals (discussed below) also embraced this view of Scripture, even as they distanced themselves from fundamentalists for other reasons.

Neoorthodoxy

Modernists controlled what became known as mainline Protestantism in North America and most of the state churches in Europe. Many continued to advance liberal views of Scripture. For example, the influential biblical scholar Rudolf Bultmann (1884–1976) argued for the "demythologization" of the Bible in favor of a focus on an ethical gospel compatible with modern assumptions. Modernist views of the Bible also contributed to the ecumenical movement, which culminated in the World Council of Churches (1948). In general, the ecumenical movement tended to downplay doctrinal distinctiveness and the role of evangelism in the missionary task, which eventually led to the prevalence of religious pluralism among liberal theologians in the later decades of the twentieth century.

Not all mainline Protestants drifted so far leftward—some carved out doctrinal real estate in the middle. Following World War I, some theologians broke with modernism and advanced a mediating theology that came to be called "neoorthodoxy." Key neoorthodox theologians included Emil Brunner (1889–1966), Dietrich Bonhoeffer (1906–1945), and the brothers Reinhold (1892–1971) and H. Richard Niebuhr (1894–1962). Nevertheless, the most famous of the neoorthodox theologians was Karl Barth (1886–1968), arguably the most influential theologian of the twentieth century. (See the case study that follows.) Unlike modernists, the neoorthodox movement sought to synthesize elements of classical orthodoxy with modern critical scholarship.

Neoorthodoxy was never a unified movement, and few scholars used the term to describe themselves. Indeed, the key theologians disagreed on many issues, emphasized different themes, and varied in the stridency of their respective critiques of both modernism and more conservative views. However, despite embracing historical-critical methodology and a more cautious view toward the miraculous, neoorthodoxy took seriously the text of Scripture. Although not identifying Scripture as the written, inerrant words of God, most neoorthodox theologians believed that Scripture was inspired by God, and they valued the role of Scripture in preaching and theological inquiry.

Roman Catholic Responses

Catholics responded differently than Protestants to the modern challenges to authority. Though individual Catholic theologians could be found across the spectrum, the church itself offered more (officially) unified responses than was possible among Protestants. The first response was mostly reactionary. In 1869–1870, the First Vatican Council (Vatican I) condemned higher-critical views of the Bible and reaffirmed the canonical Scripture (including the Apocrypha) as divine revelation. In addition, the council expanded on the Catholic notion of supreme papal authority by adopting the doctrine of papal infallibility. According to this view, when the pope formally speaks to matters of faith and practice (*ex cathedra* = "from the chair"), his pronouncements are free from error. These were decidedly antimodern views of both biblical and papal authority.

Almost a century later, the Second Vatican Council (1962–1965) offered a more constructive engagement with modern culture. Many of the council's decisions touched on the doctrine of Scripture. For example, the council affirmed the validity of modern biblical criticism, provided that the conclusions did not contradict the received teaching of the church. Vatican II also encouraged greater engagement with patristic theologians, who themselves were premodern interpreters steeped in the biblical narrative. Finally, the council encouraged the personal study of Scripture by laypersons. Although this was not an affirmation of the modern notion of the private interpretation of Scripture, it did make important strides in putting the Bible into the hands of everyday Catholics.

Postwar Evangelicalism

In the early years of the twentieth century, the terms *evangelical* and *fundamentalist* communicated significant overlap of beliefs. In the years following World War II, conservative Protestants in American (and to a lesser extent the British Isles) divided into two trajectories, each identified with one of these labels. Those who continued to call themselves "fundamentalists" emphasized separation from sinful culture and often from other conservative Protestants with whom they shared disagreements over theology and practice. They also emphasized evangelism more than cultural engagement and tended to prefer Bible colleges to liberal arts colleges and seminaries. They continued to affirm verbal-plenary inspiration and biblical inerrancy. By the 1960s, most fundamentalists believed that the *Textus Receptus*, which was first published by Erasmus, was the most faithful collection of biblical manuscripts. Some even claimed that the King James Version of the Bible was the only appropriate English translation, while others simply preferred it to the growing number of modern translations that relied on more recent biblical manuscripts.

Other conservative Protestants rejected the fundamentalist label, calling themselves new evangelicals (later the "new" was dropped). Evangelicals were more open to cultural engagement than most fundamentalists, seeing it as complementary to, rather than in competition with, evangelism, and tended to prefer liberal arts colleges and seminaries to Bible colleges. Postwar evangelicals agreed with fundamentalists concerning the inspiration and truthfulness of Scripture, but they were far more open to critical editions of the biblical manuscripts and the modern Bible translations based on them.

Both evangelicals and fundamentalists made frequent use of confessional statements for their various ministries. These statements always included an article on Scripture, often at the beginning of the statement. This evidenced the central role that the Bible continued to play in conservative Protestant theology. In 1949, evangelical scholars formed the Evangelical Theological Society (ETS), which required affirmation of biblical inerrancy for membership. ETS became the most prominent venue where evangelical scholarship was advanced, including scholarship related to bibliology. Evangelical theologians such E. J. Young (1907–1968), Carl F. H. Henry (1913–2003), Robert Preus (1924–1995), and J. I. Packer (1926–2020), among others, authored important books putting forward traditional evangelical views of Scripture.

By the 1960s, evangelicals began to increasingly debate the doctrine of Scripture. Some evangelical theologians adopted a dynamic view of inspiration, wherein God inspired biblical themes but not necessarily the words of Scripture themselves. A growing number of evangelicals also rejected biblical inerrancy, preferring the term *infallibility*, which they applied more narrowly to salvation, morality, and ministry rather than historical and scientific matters. Evangelical theologians such as G. K. Berkouwer (1903–1996), Bernard Ramm (1916–1992), Donald Bloesch (1928–2010), and Clark Pinnock (1937–2010) published works advocating for the more progressive evangelical understanding of Scripture (in some cases after previously writing in favor of more conservative views). Although nearly all evangelicals had a high view of Scripture in comparison to theological liberals, debates continued between inerrantists and infallibilists for the remainder of the century. (See the case study that follows.)

Biblical Interpretation

The twentieth century also witnessed ongoing debates about biblical hermeneutics: the science of biblical interpretation. Based on their belief in verbal-plenary inspiration and biblical inerrancy, most conservative Protestants championed the grammatical-historical method—which focused on detailed study of the biblical text—to the historical-critical method preferred by modernists and later liberals. Resonating with the insights of secular literary critic E. D. Hirsch (1967–), evangelical scholars emphasized the authority of authorial intent, though evangelicals expanded this concept to account for the dual divine-human authorship of biblical texts. Even those conservatives who used higher critical methods such as form criticism and redaction criticism did so within the framework of their traditionalist bibliology, normally seeing critical tools as supplemental to the grammatical-historical method.

By the latter years of the twentieth century, scholars across the theological spectrum evidenced renewed interest in premodern approaches to biblical interpretation that were overtly theological in their orientation. In particular, scholars gave renewed emphasis to the genre of biblical narrative, the presumed thought world of the biblical authors, the unity of the final form of the canon, exegetical strategies such as allegory and typology, and the conviction that the Bible animates the life of the church. The "Theological Interpretation of Scripture" proved to be a truly ecumenical movement, resonating with both conservatives and liberals, and systematic theologians and biblical scholars, among Protestants, Catholics, and Eastern Orthodox. Nevertheless, critics across the theological spectrum raised questions about its methodology and boundaries.

Conservative scholars had always been more open to premodern approaches than liberals, in part because of their suspicion of higher biblical criticism. However, evangelicals tended to emphasize canonical unity or practice typology or allegory from within the context of their particular theological traditions. For example, dispensationalists and Reformed theologians emphasized the importance of biblical covenants in unifying the biblical canon, though they interpreted covenants differently. Many conservatives embraced typological interpretations of Old Testament texts, such as the construction of the tabernacle (Exod 25–40) and the Song of Solomon, though this tended to be more common in preaching than scholarly writings.

As progressive scholars warmed over to premodern hermeneutics, they did so from a perspective that synthesized postmodern thought, higher criticism, a neoorthodox view of Scripture, and appreciation for historical theology (especially patristic and medieval thought). Many of these scholars were connected to Yale Divinity School and referred to themselves as "postliberal." They offered a center-left mediating position between evangelicals and liberals that influenced theological method and biblical hermeneutics. The key theologians who shaped the postliberal approach to theological interpretation included Yale Divinity School scholars Hans Frei (1922–1988), Brevard Childs (1923–2007), and George Lindbeck (1923–2018).

Case Studies

Case Study 1: The Princeton Tradition

Princeton Theological Seminary was founded in 1812 by Archibald Alexander (1772–1851), who might be considered the father of the Princeton tradition. For more than a century, Princeton represented a bastion of conservative Calvinist orthodoxy whose influence extended well beyond the confines of Presbyterianism. Alexander defended a traditionalist Protestant understanding of biblical inspiration and authority. His protégé Charles Hodge (1797–1878) further promulgated this conservative view of Scripture in his influential three-volume *Systematic Theology* and his writings against Darwinism. Hodge's son, Archibald Alexander Hodge (1823–1886), also wrote numerous volumes on the doctrine of Scripture. Through their writings, Princeton became identified with verbal-plenary inspiration and the inerrancy of Scripture.

Benjamin Breckenridge Warfield (1851–1921) and J. Gresham Machen (1881–1937) extended the Princeton tradition into the early twentieth century. The former published numerous essays on biblical inspiration and authority, while the latter proved to be the most erudite scholar among the fundamentalists. Machen's best-known book, *Christianity and Liberalism* (1923), suggested that the modernist view of Scripture had led liberals away from historic Christianity. By the time of the fundamentalist-modernist controversies, conservatives with few ties to Princeton, such as dispensationalists, many Baptists, and Holiness and Wesleyan believers, had been influenced by the Princeton tradition's commitment to verbal-plenary inspiration and inerrancy.

In 1929, Princeton Seminary was reorganized. By this time, the faculty was theologically diverse, and Machen and other conservatives were on the outs with an administration that was sympathetic to the liberal Auburn Affirmation, which denied biblical inerrancy. That same year, Machen and his fellow conservatives left Princeton and founded Westminster Theological Seminary. The new institution perpetuated the Calvinist orthodoxy of the Princeton tradition, including its conservative bibliology. Though they did not always use the same terminology as the Princeton theologians, the Dutch Reformed theologians Abraham Kuyper (1837–1920) and Herman Bavinck (1854–1921) advocated similarly conservative views of the Bible that proved influential among Reformed Christians in Europe and North America.

Case Study 2: Karl Barth and Barthianism

As mentioned earlier, Karl Barth (1886–1968) is widely considered the most influential theologian of the twentieth century. Though he was educated in the context of German liberalism, an early pastorate led him to be skeptical of the modernist view. In 1919, he published a commentary on Romans that one fellow theologian claimed fell "like a bombshell on the theologians' playground." In contrast to his professors and many contemporaries, Barth affirmed the divine inspiration of Scripture and offered robust theological reflections on the biblical text. Barth continued to distance himself from his liberal roots, inspiring other European theologians to do the same. By the 1930s, his works were being translated into English and influencing theologians in the English-speaking world.

At a time when most modernist theologians were endorsing the Nazi Party's syncretistic revision to the German state church, Barth was involved in resisting the abhorrent claims of Nazism. He was the primary author of the Barmen Declaration (1934), an anti-Nazi confession. He remained a prolific writer, and from 1932 until his death, he worked on an unfinished dogmatics series that stands at fourteen volumes in English translation.

Barth closely identified the Word of God with the eternal Son, who himself was the focus of God's divine revelation. Scripture is not itself a revelation but is a written witness to the revelation: Jesus Christ. Although Barth rejected the idea that the Bible should be considered the Word of God, he did believe Scripture becomes God's Word when the Holy Spirit reveals God to its readers and hearers through human witnesses, including the biblical authors and preachers. Biblical authority is not inherent but is existential, as God revealed himself in Jesus Christ through one's engagement with Scripture. When God works in this way, the Bible becomes an infallible witness to the Word of God.

This Barthian view of Scripture proved influential, especially in the English-speaking world. Many mainline theologians who were disillusioned with liberalism found in Barth the path to a postliberal view of Scripture and theology that allowed for orthodox affirmation of doctrines such as the Trinity, the deity and humanity of Christ, his bodily resurrection, and human beings as the image of God. (See the earlier discussion.) Nevertheless, many liberal theologians rejected Barth's view of Scripture as being too focused on divine inspiration.

Among evangelicals, progressives who had reservations about the Princetonian view of Scripture believed the Barthian position offered a better account of how the Bible is both a divine and human book. It also reverenced the role of the Bible in theological inquiry and the life of the church. Many conservative evangelical theologians who continued to affirm verbal-plenary inspiration and inerrancy appreciated Barth's Christ-centered view of Scripture and his elevated view of the reading and preaching of the Bible. However, Barth's refusal to identify Scripture with God's Word and his rejection of biblical inerrancy left most evangelicals understandably concerned about Barth's views and their implications. Though Barthianism represented an improvement over modernism in many respects, it nevertheless fell short of classical orthodoxy.

Case Study 3: The Chicago Statement on Biblical Inerrancy

As mentioned earlier, by the 1960s a growing number of evangelical theologians were rejecting the Princeton consensus on biblical inspiration and authority. Many were embracing the Barthian view and/or accommodating their bibliology to theistic evolution, higher criticism, or the growing embrace of gender egalitarianism among Protestants. Fuller Theological Seminary, long the flagship evangelical seminary, revised its statement of faith in 1970 to remove the claim that Scripture is "free from error in the whole and in the part."

The move away from inerrancy on the part of some evangelicals led to a steady stream of books related to the trustworthiness of Scripture. Two examples: in 1976, *Christianity Today* editor and former Fuller faculty member Harold Lindsell (1913–1998) wrote an exposé titled *The Battle for the Bible*. In his book, Lindsell criticized Fuller's rejection of inerrancy, but he also named numerous other scholars and denominations that had departed from the Princetonian view of Scripture. Jack Rogers (1934–2016) and Donald McKim (1950–) responded with *The Authority and Inspiration of the Bible: An Historical Approach* (1979). In their work, the authors contended that the historic Christian position was that the Bible's message was infallible, and that verbal inerrancy was an overly scholastic minority view that had been popularized by the Princeton theologians. Some evangelicals believed the Rogers-McKim proposal settled the matter, while others wrote rebuttals.

The most noteworthy response to the evangelical drift from inerrancy was the formation of the International Council on Biblical Inerrancy (1977). The following year, 200 evangelical scholars from dozens of denominations adopted the Chicago Statement on Biblical Inerrancy. The Chicago Statement reaffirmed the classical evangelical commitment to verbal-plenary inspiration and biblical inerrancy. The thirteenth article claimed, "We further deny that inerrancy is negated by biblical phenomena such as a lack of modern technical precision, irregularities of grammar or spelling, observational descriptions of nature, the reporting of falsehoods, the use of hyperbole and round numbers, the topical arrangement of material, variant selections of material in parallel accounts, or the use of free citations." This clarification suggested that the Bible is without error, but it must be rightly interpreted according to the context of the original authors and the various genres contained in Scripture.

Among conservative evangelicals, the Chicago Statement became the preferred way to frame the doctrine of inerrancy. Progressive evangelicals continued to reject verbal inerrancy, though many were comfortable with the idea that the Bible's teaching on salvation and ethics is inerrant (or, more commonly, infallible). This debate persists to the present day, especially among American evangelicals, and whether or not one uses the word *inerrancy* to describe Scripture often indicates beliefs about a host of other debated doctrines.

Case Study 4: The Southern Baptist Inerrancy Controversy

Evangelical debates about inerrancy also played out within particular denominations. Unlike in the 1920s and 1930s, when conservatives lost and subsequently retreated from their denominations, the results were mixed in the final quarter of the twentieth century. In the mid-1970s the Lutheran Church–Missouri Synod endured a controversy that led to the departure of the denomination's progressives, most of whom later became part of the mainline Evangelical Lutheran Church in America. During the same period, conservatives exited the southern Presbyterian Church in the U.S. (which later became part of the mainline Presbyterian Church in the USA) and founded what became the Presbyterian Church in America (PCA). Both the Lutheran Church–Missouri Synod and the PCA affirm biblical inerrancy.

Nevertheless, by far the most significant denominational controversy took place in the Southern Baptist Convention (SBC) between 1979 and 2000. The SBC had long been a conservative denomination, and since 1925 its confessional statement, The Baptist Faith and Message, had claimed that the Bible "has God for its author, salvation for its end, and truth, without any mixture of error, for its matter." Nevertheless, in decades after World War II, a growing number of Baptist scholars and ministers rejected biblical inerrancy, often opting for a version of the Barthian view. The 1963 revision to the Baptist Faith and Message, drafted in response to a controversy over the interpretation of Genesis 1–11 that was provoked by a seminary professor's commentary, even tried to synthesize inerrancy with Barthianism. By the late 1970s, the denomination was divided between conservatives (who were in the majority) and progressives (who dominated the convention's leadership). Though the two groups disagreed on many issues, the conservatives believed the most important was their differing perspectives on biblical inerrancy.

Beginning in 1979, Southern Baptist inerrantists, who called themselves "conservatives" and their opponents "liberals," launched a plan to change the convention's leadership, and ultimately remake its institutions, via the annual elections of the SBC president and his subsequent leadership in the trustee-appointment process. SBC noninerrantists and their allies, who called themselves "moderates" and their opponents "fundamentalists," proved unsuccessful in preventing a conservative takeover of the convention. Throughout the 1980s and 1990s, conservative and moderate theologians made the case for their respective views in print, most notably in the compilation volume *The Proceedings of the Conference on Biblical Inerrancy, 1987*. By the early 1990s, the SBC was firmly controlled by conservatives, who revised the Baptist Faith and Message a third time in 2000. The revised edition retained the inerrantist language but replaced Barthian concepts of Christ's relationship to the Word with more classically evangelical language.

As Americans have continued to divide over the doctrine of inerrancy (see the previous case study), Southern Baptists have proven to be a key part of the conservative wing of evangelicalism. Southern Baptist seminaries, colleges, and universities employ hundreds of professors, nearly all of whom affirm verbal-plenary inspiration and biblical inerrancy. SBC scholars make up the largest denominational contingent within the Evangelical Theological Society, and these scholars have authored a growing number of essays and books that affirm a conservative view of Scripture (including this textbook).

FOR THE CHURCH

Scripture offers a trustworthy word. Though the modern era raised doubts in the minds of many, the consensus of the church for two millennia has been that the Bible represents God's trustworthy written words to humanity. This is because Scripture attests to its own truthfulness (2 Tim 3:14–17; 2 Pet 1:19–21) and the trustworthiness of the God who inspired it (2 Sam

7:28; Ps 33:4; 111:7; John 17:17). The health of the church is intricately connected to the soundness of her doctrine—and sound doctrine depends on a trustworthy Scripture. The closely related doctrines of verbal-plenary inspiration and biblical inerrancy are key bulwarks against the shifting sands of false doctrine, aberrant practice, and cultural accommodation.

The Baptist Faith and Message (2000) offers a helpful summary statement about the doctrine of Scripture, including its trustworthy character:

> The Holy Bible was written by men divinely inspired and is God's revelation of Himself to man. It is a perfect treasure of divine instruction. It has God for its author, salvation for its end, and truth, without any mixture of error, for its matter. Therefore, all Scripture is totally true and trustworthy. It reveals the principles by which God judges us, and therefore is, and will remain to the end of the world, the true center of Christian union, and the supreme standard by which all human conduct, creeds, and religious opinions should be tried. All Scripture is a testimony to Christ, who is Himself the focus of divine revelation.

Because Scripture is God's Word, and because God's Word is true, Scripture should ever remain the church's ultimate authority for faith and practice. Every aspect of the church's life together—her worship, witness, service, fellowship, nurture, and so on—should be rooted in Scripture. Churches, families, and individuals must never outgrow the Bible, which is God's Word for our flourishing.

The battle for the Bible is perennial. This chapter has recounted some modern battles over the Bible, in particular its divine inspiration and truthfulness. But this is not a modern phenomenon. In fact, the battle for the Bible is an ancient war that began in the garden of Eden when the diabolical serpent first raised doubts about the trustworthiness of God's words: "Did God really say?" (Gen 3:1). It all went downhill from there.

The debates of the modern era—which remain with us today—serve to remind us that Christians in every generation must be vigilant to guard against distorted views of Scripture and their implications. The enemy has many tactics, including the frontal assault of liberalism, the deceptive flank of neoorthodoxy, and the subtle infiltration of atheological neglect, among others. Each leads to the same place: spiritual defeat.

When challenges to the doctrine of Scripture arise, whether from inside or outside the visible church, pastors and other leaders must be ready to defend sound doctrine and equip others to do the same (1 Tim 3:1–2; Titus 1:9). To let down our guard is to invite the disaster of doctrinal and eventually moral drift. And to be clear, we only drift in one direction: away from biblical faithfulness.

For Further Reading

Carson, D. A., ed. *The Enduring Authority of the Christian Scriptures*. Grand Rapids: Eerdmans, 2016.

Dorrien, Gary. *The Making of American Liberal Theology*. 3 vols. Louisville, KY: Westminster John Knox, 2001–2006.

———. *The Remaking of Evangelical Theology*. Louisville, KY: Westminster John Knox, 1998.

Frei, Hans W. *The Eclipse of Biblical Narrative: A Study in Eighteenth and Nineteenth Century Hermeneutics*. Rev. ed. New York: Cambridge University Press, 1980.

Geisler, Norman L., ed. *Inerrancy*. Grand Rapids: Zondervan, 1980.

Legapsi, Michael C. *The Death of Scripture and the Rise of Biblical Studies*. Oxford Studies in Historical Theology. New York: Oxford University Press, 2011.

Olson, Roger E. *The Journey of Modern Theology: From Reconstruction to Deconstruction*. Downers Grove, IL: IVP Academic, 2013.

Packer, J. I. *"Fundamentalism" and the Word of God*. Grand Rapids: Eerdmans, 1958.

Simpson, Christopher Ben. *Modern Christian Theology*. London: T&T Clark, 2016.

Treier, Daniel J. *Introducing Theological Interpretation of Scripture: Recovering a Christian Practice*. Grand Rapids: Baker Academic, 2008.

Treier, Daniel J. "Scripture and Hermeneutics." In *Mapping Modern Theology: A Thematic and Historical Introduction*, edited by Kelly M. Kapic and Bruce L. McCormack, 67–96. Grand Rapids: Baker Academic, 2012.

Warfield, B. B. *Inspiration and Authority of the Bible*. 2nd ed. Phillipsburg, NJ: P&R, 1980.

Questions for Study or Discussion

1. In what ways did modernist and neoorthodox theologians revise the classical view of Scripture during the modern era?
2. Who were the key theologians in the Princeton tradition, and what did they contribute to the modern evangelical doctrine of Scripture?
3. What was up for debate in evangelical controversies over Scripture in the latter half of the twentieth century? What was at stake in those debates?
4. What modern threats to Scripture remain in the early twenty-first century, and who are some of the key contemporary defenders of a classically orthodox view of Scripture?
5. Should evangelical theologians continue to use the word *inerrancy*? If not, what is a better term to communicate the full truthfulness of God's written words?

12

CREATION AND HUMANITY

By John Mark Yeats

Introduction

"In the beginning God created . . ." (Gen 1:1).

Never has there been a line that confronts the human desire for autonomy and control quite like the opening of the book of Genesis. Yet that is the very line that shapes and forms the understanding on which Christian theology builds its understanding of humanity and creation. In short, if God is the God who spoke all of creation into existence and uniquely formed humanity from the dust of the earth, then God's revelation about humanity and his creation is of infinite worth. His divine act imbues humanity with a sense of value as a unique part of the special creation of the universe.

Although there have always been attacks on the claims of Scripture about human dignity, worth, and value, the modern era experienced a greater, more pointed attack than in any period prior. The parallels with the denigration of the authority of Scripture cannot be avoided. As critics, theologians, and cultures moved away from embracing the authority of Scripture, a corollary demise of the literal understanding of Scripture related to creation and humanity during the same period naturally followed. Additionally, a robust theological anthropology touches nearly every loci of systematic theology.

This chapter provides a historical overview of the changes relating to the broad topics of anthropology and the doctrine of creation that become increasingly intertwined in our period. By looking at the broad contours of the Enlightenment and modern era, we will see an overemphasis on the autonomy of humanity derived from an increasingly mechanistic view of the universe.

Historical Overview

A Humanity Independent from God

"Then God said, 'Let us make man in our image.'" Genesis 1:26 introduces the concept of the *imago Dei*—the image of God—into the vernacular of the people of God. This descriptor sets humanity apart from the rest of the creation of the animals. Humans are a special work of God, bearing his image and expressing that image through exercising dominion over creation (Gen 1:26, 29–30; 2:19–20). Humanity's sin in the garden destroyed the ability to display the image of God in full and highlighted our need for redemption. Although not fully displayed, the introduction of sin doesn't remove the image of God in humanity, as evidenced in the genealogy of Gen 5:1–3. In Gen 9:6, the condemnation of murder in God's covenant with Noah hinges on humanity being made in God's image.

In the New Testament, Jesus fulfills the Old Testament prophecies and provides salvation for a humanity separated from God. Jesus is the greatest expression of humanity, and every person who trusts Christ as his or her personal Savior is redeemed and, through the work of the Holy Spirit, is conformed to his image. Our humanity is restored through the death, burial, and resurrection of Christ. This redemption also heightens awareness on the part of Christians of the inherent worth and value of all people—believers or not. James 3:9 condemns the cursing of fellow humans due to their being image bearers. Jesus, in making the point to care for "the least of these" in Matt 25:40, builds on this scriptural ideal. The teleological aim of the anthropology of the *imago Dei* teaching finds its fullest conclusion as evidenced in Revelation 7 as the hosts of the redeemed of humanity praise their Creator.

Established in creation, codified in biblical narrative, ethics, and theology, the *imago Dei* is a foundational understanding of humanity's essence. It is essential in understanding the incarnation and the redeeming work of Christ. It undergirds our moral and ethical approaches to life that advocate for a high value of every human. Consequently, during the modern era, questions surrounding the image of God in humanity came under intense scrutiny.

Beginning with René Descartes (1596–1650), philosophers and thinkers of the early modern era attempted to posit new understandings of human nature, epistemology, and how humans reflect the divine image. Descartes himself argued that just as God drew on innate ideas when he created, so also can humans without any external referent. This connection of the *imago Dei* with rationality became a standard interpretation into the nineteenth century.

John Locke (1632–1704), drawing from the Aristotelian tradition, argued that humans were not born a *tabula rasa*—a blank slate that takes in sensory experiences to build a system of knowledge. This epistemological framing set the stage for separating humanity from a clear connection with the image of God in humanity. For many philosophers during the eighteenth century, knowledge came not from a connection to the divine but could be obtained independently, thereby reducing the reliance on the divine.

Enlightenment thinkers such as Denis Diderot (1713–1784), Voltaire (1694–1178), and Montesquieu (1689–1755) continued to press on the idea of an image of God that could be known in humanity at all. Humanity for these *philosophes* was increasingly individualistic, with desires bridled only by self-interest. David Hume (1711–1776) concurred and argued that humans derive our morality and sense of self-worth completely independent of a divine being and religion. Our ultimate happiness is instead found in the pursuit of our liberties. Immanuel Kant (1724–1804) would argue that those same liberties find their ultimate expression when hemmed in by our duty to society and others.

Friedrich Schleiermacher (1768–1834) reacted to the strain of philosophers arguing for separation between humanity and God by articulating that the *imago Dei* is located in the human self-consciousness. Consequently, any ability to think independently or to rationally engage in thought is evidence of God's image as revealed in the self. Albrecht Ritschl (1822–1899) argued that Jesus is the only true image of God. This is what enables Christ to show humanity the way to reconciliation with God.

Disciplines such as psychology and sociology matured during the nineteenth century, assuming a materialistic or naturalistic foundation for all of life. Sigmund Freud (1856–1939) took these and dismissed God and any need of humanity for God as simple wish fulfillment. William Newton Clarke (1841–1912) advocated for a sharp separation between theology and psychology. With advances in science, there was no need to define a God-concept, and humanity could finally be free from adhering to oppressive systems of religion.

In an attempt to center the *imago Dei* in trinitarian terms, Karl Barth (1886–1968) advocated for understanding the image of God as relational instead of something inherently possessed by a person. Barth argued, "The analogy between God and man is simply the existence of the *I* and the *Thou* in confrontation. This is first constitutive for God, and then for man created by God" (*Church Dogmatics*, 3/1, 185). This basic approach reflects Martin Buber's (1878–1965) "I-Thou" understanding of relationship between the divine and humanity. Reinhold Niebuhr (1892–1971) embraced the idea of the image of God as relational but saw it as a more holistic framing and rejected prior generations' claims of a dualism of body and soul.

Emil Brunner (1889–1966) argued that the image was intrinsic to human nature and is found in our pursuit of freedom and reason. Although Brunner still connected the *imago Dei* with a knowledge of God, Wolfhart Pannenberg (1928–2014) articulated an understanding of the image of God being located in our external relationship to the world. Humans would then, through the experiences of the finite world, intuit the infinite.

Liberation theology in the twentieth century asserted the inherent value of all humans, but it changed the loci of the theological construct toward the collective struggle against oppression. James Cone (1938–2018) argued that the *imago Dei* is found as humans identify with the oppressed and participate in human liberation. This connects humanity to Jesus, the "Oppressed One whose earthly existence was bound up with the oppressed of the land."[1] Feminist theologies also developed along the same lines, with the oppression being drawn between the sexes. Rosemary Radford Ruether (1936–) advocated for the reworking of theology due to the patriarchal oppression of the system, which does not reflect women as truly equal image bearers or equal recipients of redemption.

Carl F. H. Henry (1913–2003) responded by pointing back to classic orthodoxy and asserting that every person has some innate knowledge of God, some sense of rationality, and an understanding of our ethical responsibility. This understanding of the *imago Dei* is what Scripture contained and was the universal understanding of the image before the modern age's assertion of the self as central. Anthony Hoekema (1913–1988) put the emphasis on God instead of the human self. For Hoekema, the image is found as we reflect or "mirror" God and, in turn, represent him to the broader world. For evangelicals, the redemption or restoration of the image of God in the redeemed person becomes a foundation for biblical, cultural change and part of the motivation for evangelism and missions.

---

[1] James Cone, *Black Theology of Liberation* (Philadelphia: Lippincott, 1970), 202.

A Universe Independent from God

Seventeenth-century philosophy drew on ancient sources when talking about the nature of creation and the universe. Increasingly, instead of following a scriptural understanding of a divine act as the basis for all of creation, philosophers such as Thomas Hobbes (1588–1679) and René Descartes (1596–1650) drew on concepts of mechanistic philosophy to describe the world and the nature of humanity. Observed natural law was reflective of the mechanical and autonomous universe. So-called miracles or phenomena could be reduced to mechanistic, base principles and explained without appealing to a divine being. Isaac Newton (1643–1727) constructed a rational universe with natural laws discoverable by humanity. Although Newton had interest in sustaining Christianity, academics in subsequent generations used his philosophical and scientific discoveries to substantiate a universe independent from God.

Philosopher and Christian apologist William Paley (1743–1805) presented the perspective that scientific discoveries of his day led to an increasing certainty that nature's ordered and consistent components were evidence there had to be a designer. In his book *Natural Theology*, Paley argued that if someone discovered a watch on the beach, they would assume there was a watchmaker. Since the universe is ordered and remarkably consistent, Paley argued that there is evidence of a "Divine Watchmaker"'; therefore, the universe is, in fact, dependent on a creator.

Charles Darwin (1809–1882) read Paley as a young man but found his argument to be inconsistent. In his own observations about nature, Darwin found more variety and adaptation than Paley allowed for in his research. Instead, Darwin authored *On the Origin of the Species* (1859), arguing for a process of natural selection whereby the strongest and most adept are able to survive in any given generation. Darwin was hardly the first to articulate a framework for evolutionary development. His uncle, Erasmus Darwin, had postulated in his book *Zoonomia* (1796) that all of nature had originated from a single "filament" or substance and continued to improve with each successive generation. In 1809, Frenchman Jean-Baptiste Lamarck (1744–1829) authored his *Philosophie Zoologique*, which argued for the movement of creatures from simple toward increasing complexity. The complexifying force provided order in nature as creatures developed and adapted in their immediate environment.

Evolutionary theory advanced by Lamarck, Darwin, and others, when applied to the cultural progress of humanity, began to shape the social sciences as well. If humans were simple descendants of lesser beings moving toward more complex beings, arguments formed leading to the abuses of eugenics and the shaping of humanity through selective pairing of "ideal" humans and the elimination of "lesser" persons—frequently the infirm or minorities. In the early twentieth century, the Nazi Party used this thinking in an overt way by creating a eugenics movement that advocated for the extinguishing of "lesser" races. People groups such as Jews, Gypsies, the mentally challenged, or the handicapped were systematically eradicated in an attempt to create a purer "race"—a human escalation of evolutionary process.

The ideas surrounding evolution took hold in the realm of science as a means of explaining the universe in a materialistic fashion. Theologians pressed back against these ideas by asserting the authority of the biblical narrative relating to divine creation. In Britain, scientists working with the clergy formed the Victoria Institute (1865), with the expressed idea to defend the Scriptures. Key academics such as Charles Hodge (1797–1878), Herman Bavinck (1854–1921), Abraham Kuyper (1837–1920), and B. B. Warfield (1851–1921) began to weigh in on the destructive philosophy behind Darwinian evolution, while yet allowing science its place. To this end, Warfield and Bavinck argued over the nature of "days" and elongated dating structures, referring to the days in Genesis 1 as "God's working days" and not normative or consistent with what is observed. This view would allow Warfield to claim that even John Calvin thought along the lines of theistic evolution. Regardless, the Rubicon never crossed was the unique creation of humanity that did not evolve from some lower form of animal.

In the twentieth century, the tensions surrounding the question of creation remained unresolved and, due to the promotion of William Jennings Bryan (1860–1925), some fifteen states in America began considering anti-evolution laws in 1925. The famous Scopes Monkey Trial of 1925 put many of these laws to the test. Although this particular case was a legal loss for those pressing for the teaching of evolution in schools, it left a black eye on fundamentalists who were portrayed in the media as antiscience and anti-reason.

In the mid-twentieth century, other groups began to form to promote the literal view of creation as articulated in Scripture. Conservative groups such as the Southern Baptists and branches of the Presbyterian and Lutheran churches sought to provide balanced teaching relating to creation. Henry Morris (1918–2006) published *The Genesis Flood: The Biblical Record and Its Scientific Implications* (1961), arguing that the creation of the world occurred in a literal six days, but that the global flood of Genesis 7 created the expansive fossil record and a geological record that has the appearance of age. Morris went on to create the Institute for Creation Research in 1970 to continue his work. The Discovery Institute founded in 1990 aimed to move the conversation beyond the flood geology to advocate for intelligent design in creation based on newer research in DNA and other scientific discoveries.

CASE STUDIES

Case Study 1: Slavery in the United States

Nothing quite defined the cultural conversations of the nineteenth century like the issue of slavery in the West. Chattel slavery practiced in Europe, South America, the Caribbean, and the United States built its structures on the refusal to acknowledge a portion of humanity as image bearers, thereby embedding a concept of slavery based on the race of the enslaved.

Defenders of slavery argued that enslaving of fellow humans had been a practice held in perpetuity. In the United States, the argument attempted to co-opt biblical justification for the continuation of slavery by pointing out that Abraham and other Old Testament luminaries held slaves. Furthermore, the New Testament contained argumentation about how believing slaves and masters should interact. James Henley Thornwell (1812–1862), a fiery preacher from South Carolina, popularized this line of reason. Others like James Hunt (1833–1869) argued that slavery of those of African descent was due to mental and physical inferiority, claiming that they were somehow less than human or not as advanced on the evolutionary scale.

Jonathan Blanchard (1811–1892), Presbyterian minister turned Congregationalist, argued in a public forum in Cincinnati in 1845 for the immorality of the American framing of the slavery question. If slavery revolved around the question of race, it was fundamentally in error. Echoing abolitionists such as William Wilberforce (1759–1833), Blanchard argued for the common blood bond of all humanity regardless of race. Baptist James M. Pendleton (1811–1891) pressed further, claiming the systematic enslavement of a particular race not only violated Scripture but was fundamentally illogical.

Following the American Civil War, Jim Crow laws took root across the South, creating a "separate but equal" dogma that allowed for the continued suppression of African Americans across the South. Martin Luther King Jr. and other black leaders argued from a robust understanding of the *imago Dei* that all people had inherent dignity and worth and were therefore due equal treatment. When applied consistently, Dr. King's anthropology also extended into his ecclesiology, which argued for the church to be the redeemed, "beloved community" that showed true equality within and without her walls.

Although issues of racial strife and conflict continue in broader cultural contexts, denominations such as the Southern Baptist Convention (a fellowship forged on the anvil of slavery) have not only apologized for their involvement in the sin of slavery but continue to pursue racial reconciliation fully. In 1995, Southern Baptists formally resolved "to eradicate racism in all its forms from Southern Baptist life and ministry" and to pursue "racial reconciliation in all our relationships."[2]

Case Study 2: Missions and Evangelism Movement

> It was an amazing season of power among them, and seemed as if God had bowed the heavens and come down . . . and that God was about to convert the whole world.
>
> —DAVID BRAINERD, DECEMBER 29, 1745

A clear application of the theology of humanity, the missions movement sought to bring the only solution to humanity's separation from God to the entire world. By proclaiming Christ to the farthest corners of the globe, missionaries introduced people to hope for their fallen condition. With a scale unparalleled by any prior generation, the gospel was advanced during the modern era to every continent.

Puritan missionary John Eliot (c. 1604–1690) arrived on the shores of New England in 1644 with a burden to preach the gospel to Native Americans. He worked with the Massachusett and Algonquian tribes and translated the Bible into the Massachusett language in 1663, and that became the first complete Bible published in the Western Hemisphere. Other missionaries, such as Lutheran John Campanius (1601–1683) and Dutch Reformer Johannes Megapolensis (1603–1670), worked with other tribes for the same purpose. After experiencing the frontier of missions, Anglican Thomas Bray (1658–1730) helped create two essential organizations that worked to shape missions and evangelism in the eighteenth century—the Society for Promoting Christian Knowledge (1696) and the

[2] "Resolution on Racial Reconciliation on the 150th Anniversary of the Southern Baptist Convention," 1995, http://www.sbc.net/resolutions/899/resolution-on-racial-reconciliation-on-the-150th-anniversary-of-the-southern-baptist-convention.

Society for the Propagation of the Gospel in Foreign Parts (1701). Count Ludwig von Zinzendorf (1700–1760) abandoned his wealth and ignited a global missions enterprise in the Moravian movement that sent 226 missionaries to ten countries before his death.

William Carey (1761–1834), often called "the Father of Modern Missions," joined the ranks of those concerned with the souls of humanity. Combining gospel communication with robust Bible translation, Carey worked tirelessly to transform culture. He laid the foundation for ending harmful religious practices, better treatment of women, educational reforms, and civic change. Before Carey ever set sail for Calcutta, freed slave George Liele (c. 1750–1820) was leaving the shores of Georgia to minister to slaves held in Jamaica. His work laid the foundation for the conversion of many slaves as well as church-planting efforts in the Caribbean and South America.

A hallmark of the nineteenth century was the rapid expansion of evangelical engagement in missions on a global scale. From the founding of the Baptist Mission Society (1792) or the London Missionary Society (1795) to the Student Volunteer Movement (1886), evangelicals blanketed the globe with the gospel. Nearly every Western country had specific organizations targeting a people group, a country, or a continent to reach people in need of the gospel. John Mott (1865–1955), who chaired the famous Edinburgh Missionary Conference of 1910, captured the heart of this movement with the rallying cry "The evangelization of the world in this generation." Denominations such as the Southern Baptist Convention (founded 1845) pursued missions as the central issue to bring unity to a broad spectrum of local churches.

The missions movement continued to expand in the twentieth century despite the disruption of the world wars. New work gained footholds in Southeast Asia, Africa, and South America. Work by Baptists, Methodists, and Presbyterians in Brazil created new evangelistic movements that expanded beyond the cities into rural environments and continue to grow. A revival in Korea in 1907 catapulted evangelicalism into a period of growth that now encompasses more than 23 percent of the populace, and South Korea now sends the second-largest missionary force globally.

In 1974, evangelist Billy Graham (1918–2018) worked with other evangelicals in Lausanne, Switzerland. John Stott (1921–2011) chaired the committee that drafted the Lausanne Covenant, outlining the goals and necessity of evangelism in the modern period. Ralph Winter's (1924–2009) address at the same conference defined the challenge of unreached people groups—those without any witness of Jesus or available copy of God's Word in their language. This hallmark event created a broader network of evangelical organizations sharing the same hope and desire—that every individual life could be changed by the power of the gospel.

Case Study 3: Abortion

Abortion continues to be a politically and morally controversial issue for the present day. A subsequent demand to the free-love movement, the pro-choice movement claimed to give women autonomy over their bodies, freeing them from unwanted children. As pro-choice arguments were put forward by Margaret Sanger (1879–1966) in the early twentieth century, the emphasis was on human autonomy of choice without referent to any given authority. Sanger's work with birth control, eugenics, and abortion became foundational for the founding of Planned Parenthood, an organization she served as president from 1952 to 1959. Denominations such as the Southern Baptist Convention did not carefully consider the ideas undergirding the concepts of abortion, leading to a 1971 resolution at the annual meeting stating that abortion should be allowed in cases of "rape, incest, clear evidence of severe fetal deformity, and carefully ascertained evidence of the likelihood of damage to the emotional, mental, and physical health of the mother."[3] This motion, put together by the head of the Christian Life

---

[3] Southern Baptist Convention, "Resolution on Abortion," 1971, http://www.sbc.net/resolutions/13/resolution-on-abortion.

Commission, Foy Valentine (1923–2006), in part paved the way for the landmark 1973 *Roe v. Wade* case legalizing abortion in the United States.

By the late 1970s, the Southern Baptist Convention reversed their stance, leading to a commitment that "all human life, both born and preborn, is sacred, bearing the image of God, and is not subject to personal judgments as to 'quality of life' based on such subjective criteria as stage of development, abnormality, intelligence level, degree of dependency, cost of medical treatment, or inconvenience to parents."[4] This same commitment to the *imago Dei* in every life—including the unborn—remains a hallmark of conservative evangelical social engagement.

With the advent of the Moral Majority movement (1979), evangelicals joined with Catholics and other traditional religious expressions to fight in the political sphere for the issue of life. The loosely connected evangelical vote made the sanctity of life a lynchpin issue in local and national elections beginning in the 1980s. At the turn of the millennium, evangelicals made significant headway in state-level restrictions on abortion while at the same time increasing their work in the sphere of adoption and orphan care, thereby demonstrating the value of life.

For the Church

Humanity for the Church

The conversation relating to the fundamental nature of humanity cannot be held without the corollary discussion relating to creation. As the Creator, God wove into the fabric of the universe the design equations that result in human flourishing. These design equations lead to conclusions about the authority of biblical morals and what is best personally, culturally, and

---

[4] Southern Baptist Convention, "Resolution on Abortion and Infanticide," 1982, http://www.sbc.net/resolutions/20/resolution-on-abortion-and-infanticide.

structurally for all people. Those same principles also imbue humanity with purpose and value as beings made in the image of God himself. Biblical ideas about creation and humanity in Scripture may run counter to philosophies and ideas put forward by individuals in any given era, but since God's Word is his revelation to humanity as our Creator, we are always at our cultural best when we adhere to his design. "In the beginning God created . . ." (Gen 1:1).

The Baptist Faith and Message (2000) helps provide some general guidelines for thinking about the doctrines of humanity and creation in article III:

> Man is the special creation of God, made in His own image. He created them male and female as the crowning work of His creation. The gift of gender is thus part of the goodness of God's creation. In the beginning man was innocent of sin and was endowed by his Creator with freedom of choice. By his free choice man sinned against God and brought sin into the human race. Through the temptation of Satan, man transgressed the command of God, and fell from his original innocence whereby his posterity inherit a nature and an environment inclined toward sin. Therefore, as soon as they are capable of moral action, they become transgressors and are under condemnation. Only the grace of God can bring man into His holy fellowship and enable man to fulfill the creative purpose of God. The sacredness of human personality is evident in that God created man in His own image, and in that Christ died for man; therefore, every person of every race possesses full dignity and is worthy of respect and Christian love.

As the people of God known as *the church*, our understanding of humanity shapes our engagement with the world around us. In the twenty-first century, the claims are no different on the church than in the first century. The same God who sent his Son to be the Savior of the world is the same God who saves lives today. Consequently, every person matters to God.

As image bearers of the Creator, we should treat every person with dignity reflecting that same honor. The very nature of the incarnation undergirds and heightens the biblical concept of the *imago Dei*. Every person on the planet should be treated as a unique creation of God who is also loved by God. Those same people all share one essential need—to be reconciled to God (2 Cor 5:20) through Jesus Christ. This leads to three implications for the church:

1. If every person matters, every person needs the gospel. Missions and evangelism are *the* priority for believers in Jesus Christ, as evidenced by our commission in Matt 28:16–20 and exampled for us in the book of Acts and through the lives of the early church. Since the gospel is for individual persons, while we may work to change cultures and societal norms or engage in the political sphere, the ultimate aim for the church is to create a context whereby individual persons experience the life change available in Christ alone.
2. If every person matters, we should seek to eradicate racism and systemic injustice that leads to the ending of a life or the unscriptural subjugation of others. Such work should seek to ensure widescale freedoms, allowing the gospel to advance unhindered. The church should work when and where it is able to change political, economic, or cultural systems that devalue human life or provide roadblocks to the advancement of the gospel.
3. If every person matters, we should fight for human life from conception to natural death. Whether a person is uniquely gifted or needs extraordinary care due to disabilities, the church should seek to provide for appropriate gospel care. Scripture is explicit about the worth of every life *in utero* or in the twilight of life; whether sick or handicapped in some manner. Over and again, the church has confronted the injustices derived from the devaluing of life and, as a result, every generation of Christians that stands and

values the lives of people as made in God's image have seen the gospel advance.

In the twenty-first century, the ascendency of self is being revealed like never before. The ultimate claims placed by culture over sexuality and even self-directed understandings of gender confront the biblical understanding of God as Creator. The church's claim of submission to God in the areas of sexuality, God's gift of gender, and God's design of the universe continue to stand in opposition to cultural forces that demand subservience to their claims. The church will need to be attentive to its anthropology to avoid theological drift while lovingly introducing people to a loving God who made a way of redemption available through Jesus Christ.

For Further Reading

Allison, Gregg R. *Historical Theology: An Introduction to Christian Doctrine.* Grand Rapids: Zondervan, 2011.

Burns, J. Patout. *Theological Anthropology.* Philadelphia: Fortress, 1981.

Davis, David Brion. *In the Image of God: Religion, Moral Values, and Our Heritage of Slavery.* New Haven, CT: Yale University Press, 2001.

Emerson, Michael O., and Christian Smith. *Divided by Faith: Evangelical Religion and the Problem of Race in America.* Oxford: Oxford University Press, 2001.

Grenz, Stanley J. *The Social God and the Relational Self: A Trinitarian Theology of the Imago Dei.* Louisville: Westminster John Knox, 2001.

Jones, Kevin, and Jarvis J. Williams. *Removing the Stain of Racism from the Southern Baptist Convention: Diverse African American and White Perspectives.* Nashville: B&H Academic, 2017.

Strachan, Owen. *Reenchanting Humanity*, Ross-shire, UK: Mentor, 2019.

Tisby, Jemar. *The Color of Compromise: The Truth about the American Church's Complicity in Racism.* Grand Rapids: Zondervan, 2019.

Wills, Richard W. *Martin Luther King, Jr. and the Image of God.* Oxford: Oxford University Press, 2011.

Questions for Study or Discussion

1. How should our understanding of the *imago Dei* change our cultural engagement in the realms of politics, economics, and society?
2. What changes in the nineteenth-century view of creation corresponded to changes in theological anthropology?
3. How did the American slavery system undermine the biblical presentation of the *imago Dei*?
4. Why do missions and evangelism reveal our view of humanity?
5. Why should evangelicals continue to engage in the political discussions relating to abortion and euthanasia?

13

THE TRINITY AND JESUS CHRIST

By Matthew J. Hall

Introduction

On the other side of the Enlightenment, trinitarian orthodoxy in general, and Chalcedonian formulations about the person and work of Christ in particular, came under intense fire.

As already noted in the previous chapter covering the modern era, these challenges were rooted in a preceding epistemological crisis. If human beings have limited access to the supernatural or, as Immanuel Kant put it, the noumenal, how can we really make theological propositions about the nature of Jesus Christ?

Over the course of several centuries, this Kantian question was answered in a variety of ways, resulting in a myriad of deviations from classical Christological formulations. But at the center of these debates, the question remained for the church in every age, just as it does today: Does sinful humanity stand in need of a Redeemer? And if so, how does Jesus Christ function as that Redeemer?

Historical Overview

Rationalism and the Unitarian Age

At the Enlightenment's peak, many observers assumed that the future of Christianity would entail a rejection of trinitarian orthodoxy, presuming the latter had been rendered inherently irrational. Thomas Jefferson (1743–1826) captured this sentiment in his own prediction in 1822: "I rejoice that in this blessed country of free enquiry and belief, which has surrendered it's [*sic*] creed and conscience to neither kings nor priests, the genuine doctrine of one only God is reviving, and I trust that there is not a young man now living in the US who will not die a Unitarian."[1]

Jefferson's analysis was not without backing. Within the gaze of the transatlantic world, it certainly seemed as if this would be the case.

Rejections of classical Trinitarianism were not without precedent, of course. But the stark rationalism of the eighteenth century brought a new wave of this skepticism, concluding that the idea of a triune Godhead who is both one in substance and three in persons was inherently irrational.

By the 1770s, a number of churches in England had begun to turn in Unitarian directions, and, in the following decade, a number of prominent churches in the young United States followed suit, especially concentrated in Boston. By 1805, Harvard College had even appointed an avowed Unitarian, Henry Ware, to its famed Hollis Chair of Divinity. Perhaps no one would come to represent the Unitarian advance in North America more than William Ellery Channing (1780–1842), the pastor of Boston's Federal Street Church.

[1] "From Thomas Jefferson to Benjamin Waterhouse, 26 June 1822," Founders Online, National Archives, accessed September 29, 2019, https://founders.archives.gov/documents/Jefferson/98-01-02–2905.

Ultimately, Jefferson's prediction proved to be far from true. Although Unitarianism would retain some prominence among corners of elite American culture in the nineteenth century, and is still present in the contemporary Unitarian Universalist Association, it is particularly small. What Jefferson, along with many others, seemingly never anticipated was the resurgence of evangelical Christianity in North America that would soon come in the form of a series of nineteenth-century awakenings.

Nineteenth-Century Idealism

Unitarianism represented just one response to the epistemological crisis of the Enlightenment. A number of others emanated out of the Kantian revolution, all loosely held together by their response to the rationalism of the eighteenth century and by a shared commitment to philosophical idealism.

The Kantian synthesis, an attempt to mediate between empiricism and rationalism, has already been noted in this book. His distinction between the noumenal and phenomenological, along with the limitation of human knowledge to the latter, brought with it massive implications for theological method, particularly regarding the doctrine of the Trinity and Christology. If our knowledge of God is limited to how we experience him, what knowledge can we actually have of him as he exists independent of us ontologically? None, it would seem.

It seems virtually impossible to overestimate Kant's influence on Protestant theology. Moving forward, the significance of Jesus Christ seemed to be more ethical than redemptive. Rather than God incarnate who breaks into history to save sinners, Jesus emerges as a moral example, a demonstration of divine love, or some other historic phenomenon. This was premised on an "extratextual" theological methodology that could no longer rely on the biblical worldview, as previous generations of Christians had done. Instead, they birthed a series of "quests for the historical Jesus." The first of these (1778–1906) came to represent much of the essence of mainline Protestant theological liberalism and is considered more fully below.

In the first half of the twentieth century (1906–1953), the emphasis seemed to be on repositioning Christian faith as something that did not need historic claims or truths. Among the most influential of these was Rudolf Bultmann (1884–1976), whose entire "demythologization" project attempted to preserve some kind of Christian identity by relocating the very center of Christianity away from historic truth claims and prioritizing existential questions about humanity's relationship with the divine.

It could be argued that since 1953 there has been a new quest, one that retains the post-Enlightenment rejection of implicit historic plausibility in the New Testament accounts. Embedded within those accounts, especially the Gospels, are elements of historic truth.

Immanuel Kant's transcendental absolutism had already raised questions about human access to "pure reason," but subsequent philosophers moved into a variety of directions, birthing diverse streams of idealism. But what all would have to wrestle with was the epistemological chasm that Kant had introduced between subjects and the objects of their knowledge. In the nineteenth century, perhaps no one of these had a greater influence than G. W. F. Hegel (1770–1831), for whom Christology was largely a symbolic way of articulating the ways in which Jesus incarnated the presence of divine essence in human beings. But this is no mystery of the hypostatic union. Rather, it's a dynamic that is universal in all of humanity, not merely in the person of Jesus. Although historic Christianity had spoken of the eternal generation of the Son, Hegel spoke of God positing himself over against himself, in the world. God's own self-consciousness necessitated that he know himself in a finite self-conscious being.

Hegel similarly interpreted the doctrine of the Trinity as a representation of ultimate spiritual reality, of the universal. He had little interest in Christian theologians' previous questions, or in Chalcedonian formulas—even referring to the Chalcedonian two natures as a "monstrous compound"—but he seemed to aim to retain the metaphysical implications of trinitarian categories.

Hegel and his heirs exerted a jarring impact on Christian theology. It now seemed that the person of the historical Jesus was now something of an inconsequential thing. Seeking to understand the more philosophical dimensions of the relation of divine being to humanity seemed far more significant. Similarly, trinitarian theology could relocate away from focus on the ontological confessional questions that had preoccupied so much of the church's history.

The Quest for the Historical Jesus

Ever since the Enlightenment, a growing bifurcation between the Jesus of history and the Christ of faith remained remarkably conspicuous. Different theologians and different traditions might use their own terminology, but underlying all of these was the fundamental epistemological doubt that modern people could trust the portrayals of Jesus of Nazareth in the New Testament Gospels as historically reliable and accurate. Although evangelical scholars have defended a confessional Christology that presumes the verbal plenary inspiration of the Scripture, and therefore the reliability of the Gospels, they have had to do so amid hostile intellectual headwinds.

Theological liberalism generally presents itself as necessary intellectual accommodations to preserve some transcendent essence of the Christian faith in the face of new challenges. It presents itself as a rescuer of Christianity rather than a destroyer. And this is certainly true of its Christological articulations.

The ascendancy of Protestant liberalism in the eighteenth and nineteenth centuries largely brought with it a deemphasis on trinitarian doctrine, even as it gave significant attention to Christology, albeit largely heterodox.

In the modern age, Friedrich Schleiermacher (1768–1834) was among the most significant of these. A colleague of Hegel's at the University of Berlin, Schleiermacher attempted to inoculate some semblance of Christianity from its "cultured despisers" in Europe by relocating the center of Christian theology, and Christology, along the lines of Romanticism. If the essence of Christianity was no longer an abstract idea or set of theological and confessional formulations, but rather *gefuhl*—a feeling of "absolute dependence"—then Jesus was no longer a Redeemer who was the perfect God-man and substitutionary sacrifice for the atonement of divine wrath. Rather, Schleiermacher concluded that Jesus is best understood as the perfect embodiment and example of this God dependence. Along these lines, he saw the existence of God in Christ as "the innermost fundamental power within him, from which every activity proceeds and which holds every element together; everything human (in him) forms only the organism for this fundamental power."[2] Readers will note that this has echoes of Apollinarianism. But Schleiermacher's understanding of the incarnation was even more eccentric, positing the union of divine essence with human nature in Jesus to have been gradual rather than complete at his conception by the Holy Spirit.

For his part, Schleiermacher seemed to see the doctrine of the Trinity as generally inconsequential to this supreme concern with religious experience and dependence. His outlook would continue to shape his theological heirs.

Albrecht Ritschl (1822–1889) pushed this even further. Deeply shaped by Hegelian thought and formed by German higher criticism, Ritschl saw the essence of Christian theology in the experience of faith and necessary moral action within the Christian community. For him, questions about the ontological nature of Christ and his dual nature were unnecessary, having no bearing on the essence of faith. Rather, he advanced what may be thought of as a functional Christology, in which Jesus exemplifies the divine moral perfection in the world, spreading the kingdom of God. To speak of Jesus's "divinity," then, was to speak of how his will was united perfectly with the Father's will. In general, Ritschl's influence resulted in a far greater emphasis on Jesus's humanity at the expense of his deity.

---

[2] Friedrich Schleiermacher, *The Christian Faith*, trans. H. R. Mackintosh and J. S. Stewart (Philadelphia: Fortress, 1976), 397.

Among those shaped by this emphasis was Adolf von Harnack (1851–1930), who focused particular attention on the Jesus of history. For him, the core of Christian faith was the twin realities of the fatherhood of God and the nobility of the human soul. And so, the Jesus of history, removed from later theological speculation or additions, was a moral teacher of righteousness. Harnack saw the idea of the hypostatic union of Christ's dual natures as a hellenistic imposition on early dogma that could rightly be removed to retain essential ethical dimensions of Jesus's identity and mission.

Harnack's appropriation of functional Christology went even further than Ritschl had. In his model, Jesus was merely the human being who had a knowledge of God greater than any other person. Because of that, Jesus could now be said to offer something to humanity: "The Gospel nowhere says that God's mercy is limited to Jesus's mission. But history shows us that he is the one who brings the weary and heavy laden to God, and again, that it is he who raised mankind to the new level, and his teaching is still the touchstone, in that it brings men to bliss and brings them to judgment."[3] Harnack's Christology was unmoored from any prior commitment to biblical revelation or historic truth claims. Thus, Jesus was the only one whose teachings enabled humanity to understand the fatherhood of God and the nobility of the human soul.

This functional Christology exerted broad influence beyond Germany, shaping a whole generation of American Protestant theologians. Among these was Walter Rauschenbusch (1861–1918), whose book *A Theology for the Social Gospel* effectively redefined Christian theology and the nature of the kingdom of God along Ritschlian lines. Rauschenbusch said, "So we have in Jesus a perfect religious personality, a spiritual life completely filled by the realization of a God who is love."[4]

---

[3] Adolf Harnack, *What Is Christianity?*, trans. Thomas Bailey Saunders (London: Putnam, 1908), 156.

[4] Walter Rauschenbusch, *A Theology for the Social Gospel* (New York: Macmillan, 1917), 154.

Liberal theology thus presumed a bifurcation between the Jesus of history and the Christ of faith. The former was a real historical person about whom we have little to no reliable historical evidence. But the latter was the result of the formation of Christian dogma, having had a shaping influence on Christian faith and history. What matters, then, is this functional Christianity, an attempt to form a religious-ethical model of Jesus's person and ministry, rather than one grounded in his pre-eternal ontological identity as the second person of the Trinity.

In general, liberal Protestantism remained increasingly uninterested in the doctrine of the Trinity and effectively redefined Christology in ethical or functional terms.

Crisis Theology and Neoorthodoxy

European continental theology would witness a surprising corrective to classical Protestant liberalism in the first half of the twentieth century. Eventually known as "crisis theology" or neoorthodoxy, its proponents claimed to recover classical Christianity from the strangling grip of Ritschlian liberal theology.

On Christology, theologians such as Karl Barth (1886–1968), Emil Brunner (1889–1966), and Rudolf Bultmann issued a number of correctives to classical liberalism. The movement was hardly monolithic, including in its Christology. Bultmann's demythologization project, for example, led him to conclude that the New Testament is not primarily about history but about the formation of faith. Accounts of supernatural miracles or claims about Jesus's deity were later impositions, demanding that theologians recover the *kerygma* of Christian faith. What mattered most about Jesus, he claimed, was the subjective proclamation of the cross, which elicits an experience of faith.

In contrast, Barth spoke of human sin and the transcendent otherness of God, which was pierced by the person of Jesus Christ. Barth attempted to move closer to classical Protestant theology, in stark contrast to liberal theologies, by reframing Jesus Christ as the self-revelation of the divine Word who can be known only by faith and with the help of the Holy Spirit. Although not an evangelical, Barth's Christology is remarkably trinitarian and stands as a surprisingly contrarian voice against the corrosiveness of subjective liberal theological method. In contrast to Protestant liberalism's fascination with quests for the historical Jesus, Barth had serious doubts about their efforts. His reticence was not necessarily shaped by historic confessional delineations, but rather by a more existential animus. He saw the significance of Jesus as inseparable from his resurrection and present glory, and thus beyond historical definition.

Barth's effort to reconstruct a "theology from above" that relocated the transcendence of God to a central place in Christian theology accounts for his emphasis on the Word of God. As already noted, this shaped his doctrine of revelation and Scripture. But it also was formative of his Christology. The one eternal Word is revealed in an absolute way in Jesus Christ, the One in whom the God who is "wholly other" has made himself known.

Of particular significance was Barth's recovery of the centrality of trinitarian theology to Christianity. Rather than a dogmatic appendage that could be conveniently severed if the cultural or intellectual pressures demanded it, Barth understood that the doctrine of the Trinity was an essential component of historic Christianity. His magisterial *Church Dogmatics* gave it priority in the very first volume and identified it as the doctrine that "fundamentally distinguishes the Christian doctrine of God as Christian" (*Church Dogmatics*, 1/1, 346). For Barth, this connection was vital: the God who reveals himself to humanity is the God who is revealed as triune. In contrast with other monotheistic religions, Christianity was distinguished by its trinitarian doctrine. This put Barth directly at odds with Schleiermacher's emphasis and legacy, who had relegated the Trinity to the back of Christian theology. Rather, Barth saw clear trinitarian implications in the Bible, but saw Jesus as the One who most fully reveals to humanity the triune Godhead.

One of Barth's enduring contributions to trinitarian theology was his reflection on the ways in which the three persons of the Godhead eternally exist in perfect relationship—what theologians would later speak of as the "social Trinity." And within that, Barth emphasized the person of the Son as the center of trinitarian theology, the One by whom we come to fully know the other persons, or as he preferred to speak of them, "modes of being."

Barth's work has shaped a broad range of theologians in the twentieth and twenty-first centuries. Paul Tillich (1886–1965) was one of these. Tillich's vision of Christianity was largely existential and individual, locating Christian faith as "ultimate concern." Eventually, Tillich's theology led him not only to reject the idea of a personal God, but even to redefine Jesus as the One who had such a God-consciousness that he was able to live life in complete existential harmony with God and his fellow man. What mattered most, though, was how Christ now makes himself known to us in our own situations in a variety of forms. Although Tillich's influence in his own time was significant, his theology ultimately led to an endpoint that had evacuated virtually all essentially Christian truth claims.

For example, Jürgen Moltmann's *The Crucified God* (1973) identified Jesus as the God-forsaken One, who shows humanity how God enters into the sufferings of the world in solidarity. For Moltmann (1926–), the cross is not only the center of Christology, but also of the meaning of the Trinity itself. In a sense, he concluded, the intra-trinitarian suffering of God at the cross now meant that he was able to restore the suffering and fissures of human community in the world. Moltmann's work had vestiges of Hegel throughout as well. Largely rejecting historic Christian notions of God's impassibility, he claimed that in the incarnation God the Son was not only participating in human suffering, but actively experiencing it as "the pathos of God." For Moltmann, this experience of divine suffering is at the core of trinitarian theology and Christology: "God suffers with us—God suffers from us—God suffers for us." Along with this, Moltmann described God's unity as a perichoretic unity of the three divine persons within salvation history. In other words, God's triune unity is not primarily an ontological reality that comes from eternity past, but rather a reality that is played out within history as God relates to the world.

Similarly, Wolfhart Pannenberg (1928–2014) situated his doctrine of the Trinity within world history, claiming that the consummation of the work of the Son and Spirit in the world are essential to the eschatological fullness of the triune God.

Barth's work also prompted renewed interest in trinitarian theology among English-speaking scholars. Along with preceding figures such as T. F. Torrance (1913–2007), two of the most prominent of these in the past three decades were Colin Gunton (1941–2003) and John Webster (1955–2016). Both called for a renewed attention to the ontological realities of the Trinity, forming a needed corrective to the broad influence of liberal Protestantism's emphasis on the functional or ethical dimensions of trinitarian dogma. Nevertheless, Gunton's work faulted Augustine and the Augustinian tradition as the culprit for trinitarian confusion—a claim that is problematic at best. Webster would go so far as to claim that the doctrine of the Trinity is the necessarily prior doctrine to all other Christian theology: "The doctrine of the Trinity is not one doctrine among others; it is foundational and pervasive. To expound any Christian doctrine is to expound with varying degrees of directness the doctrine of the Trinity; to expound the doctrine of the Trinity in its full scope is to expound the entirety of Christian dogmatics."[5]

Evangelical Formulations

Thankfully, the onslaught of theological revisions to historic Christology and trinitarian orthodoxy did not go without evangelical responses. Not only did evangelical scholars offer rigorous defenses of historic doctrine, but they often also worked to further clarify what those classical formulations meant. At the close of the nineteenth century and the dawn of the twentieth, this vision was perhaps nowhere more evident than at Princeton Theological Seminary. More detailed attention will be given to some of those voices

---

[5] John Webster, *God without Measure: Working Papers in Christian Theology*, vol. 1 (London: T&T Clark, 2016), 159.

below. But in the years immediately after much of the fundamentalist-modernist controversy, a whole movement of evangelical scholars emerged, confident that historic orthodoxy could indeed stand up to the challenges of modernity, including its assaults on the Trinity.

Whereas liberal Protestantism had discounted any inherent self-conscious trinitarian theology within the Bible, Bernard Ramm (1916–1992) countered the opposite.

> The revelation of God eventually unfolds the doctrine of the Trinity, and conversely, the Trinity unfolds itself in revelation. . . . The doctrine of the Trinity comes to us enmeshed in the dynamics of redemption and in the successive inbreaking of revelation. It is the underlying presupposition of every page of Sacred Scripture.[6]

Similarly, Carl F. H. Henry (1913–2003) pushed back on the drift in contemporary theology away from the immanent ontological Trinity. "The basic issue is not whether theologians confine themselves to the vocabulary of Scripture, but whether the biblical revelation of God logically involves the doctrine of the ontological Trinity" (*God, Revelation, and Authority*, 5:184).

For Henry, the Trinity was at the very heart of Christian monotheism: "That the living God is triune—that three eternal persons coexist within the one divine essence—is the distinctive Christian affirmation about deity. . . . The doctrine of the Trinity is Christianity's unique declaration concerning the divine being and is definitive for Christian theism" (*God, Revelation, and Authority*, 5:191). Henry rejected the Ritschlian argument that the early ecumenical creeds were the fusion of Christianity with Greek philosophy. "What decided the formulation of the ecumenical creeds was not Greek philosophy or Christian consciousness but rather and only the biblical data" (5:202).

---

[6] Bernard Ramm, *The Witness of the Spirit: An Essay on the Contemporary Relevance of the Internal Witness of the Holy Spirit* (Grand Rapids: Eerdmans, 1959), 28.

A new generation of evangelical scholars would follow their lead in the second half of the twentieth century, reaffirming the historic biblical trinitarian formulations and mounting a strong response to the post-Enlightenment attacks on the doctrine.

Challenges in the Twenty-First Century

In more recent decades, orthodox Christology has continued to weather attacks. Perhaps most notable of these has been the Jesus Seminar.

A collective of liberal scholars, the Jesus Seminar attempted to identify which of Jesus's sayings in the New Testament Gospels could actually be verified as his own historic words. With a suspect methodology, to put it mildly, they concluded that 82 percent of the words attributed to Jesus in the Gospels were actually not his own. The Jesus Seminar was convened from 1985–1991, gathering nearly 200 mainline Protestant scholars twice a year.

Another of the more radical contemporary attacks on historic Christology came from philosopher John Hick (1922–2012), who concluded that the historic Jesus of Nazareth never claimed to be, nor understood himself to be, God or any incarnate person of the Trinity. This meant, Hick claimed, that the doctrine of the incarnation was misunderstood to be a literal reality, but rather that the doctrine of the incarnation is best understood metaphorically, referring to God's ability to act on earth in and through Jesus because of his openness and obedience to the divine will.

Hick's arguments were not alone. Overt rejections of anything resembling orthodoxy could be seen in the works of Marcus Borg (1942–2015), who saw Jesus as a Spirit-filled countercultural reformer, and of John Dominic Crossan (1934–), who presented Jesus as a "peasant Jewish cynic."[7]

---

[7] Marcus J. Borg, *Jesus: A New Vision: Spirit, Culture, and the Life of Discipleship* (New York: HarperOne, 1987); John Dominic Crossan, *The Historical Jesus: The Life of a Mediterranean Jewish Peasant* (New York: HarperCollins, 1991).

Their work had limited appeal within academic circles but did manage to capture popular attention in the media, who rightly saw it as an overt repudiation of two millennia of general Christian consensus.

But liberation and feminist theologies have also challenged historic Christology. Liberation theologies have generally contended for a Jesus who is the supreme deliverer of the oppressed. Largely emanating out of postcolonial context in Latin America, liberation theologies were deeply shaped by Marxist thought and concluded that the essence of Christianity was about God's identification with the poor, redefining salvation as liberation from present economic oppression. Ontological questions about the triune Godhead, the incarnation of the Son, or the dual nature of Christ were largely inconsequential. Rather, Jesus emerges in liberation theology as a prototype for class-conscious liberation for the victimized poor and oppressed, proclaiming a vision of the kingdom of God that demands present political action, often revolutionary.

These same trends were apparent in many streams of black liberation theology. For example, James Cone's (1938–2018) work appropriated Barthian Christological categories but fused them with an indictment of white supremacy and the oppression of black peoples. Thus, Jesus emerges in Cone's thought as a "black Messiah" who demonstrates God's solidarity with and redemptive work on behalf of those oppressed by white supremacy and racial injustice.

Among feminist theologians, perhaps none has had more impact on trinitarian dogmatic theology than Catherine Mowry LaCugna (1952–1997), a Catholic scholar. In her estimation, the development of Christian theology on the Trinity was one that had, over two millennia, gradually veered further and further from the original soteriological and doxological essence of the doctrine. To put it in other words, Christian theology had so emphasized the immanent Trinity that it had obscured, perhaps even lost, the priority of the economic Trinity. In fact, LaCugna proposed a model that would erase distinctions between the economic and immanent Trinity:

"There is only the *oikonomia* that is the concrete realization of the mystery of *theologia* in time, space, history, and personality."[8]

LaCugna's work, along with Elizabeth Johnson's (1941–), marked something of a turn in feminist theology. Previous theologians such as Mary Daly (1928–2010) and Rosemary Radford Ruether (1936–) had generally expressed disdain for the gendered-terminology of Father and Son. But what all of these have had in common is the centrality of experience to theological method, an assumption that is as old as Schleiermacher. For example, in Johnson's *She Who Is* (1992), she renamed the triune persons to incorporate feminine imagery: Mother-Sophia, Jesus-Sophia, and Spirit-Sophia.

Case Studies

Case Study 1: Kenotic Christology

Centered at the University of Erlangen in Germany, a group of Lutheran theologians in the 1840s articulated a Christology that they hoped would preserve what they saw as the essential core of Lutheran Christology. Largely responding to the emphasis on the humanity of the Jesus of history, they recognized that highlighting his divine attributes, such as omnipotence, omniscience, and omnipresence, was increasingly difficult. The most prominent of these theologians was Gottfried Thomasius (1802–1875), who posited that the hypostatic union was preceded by the Son divesting himself of all divine attributes not innate to natural human thought or volition. He tried to take exegetical grounding for this claim from Phil 2:5–7, claiming that Paul's use of "emptying" language there referred to this same kenosis.

[8] Catherine Mowry LaCugna, *God for Us: The Trinity and Christian Life* (New York: Harper, 1991), 223.

Thomasius went even further, concluding that the Son also must have surrendered his own divine "self-consciousness" at the incarnation. Thomasius conceded that this phenomenon was a temporary one. The resurrected and ascended Christ had taken back his divine attributes.

Of course, kenotic Christology had a poison pill within it. If all of the divine attributes are inseparable from the divine essence, any such divestment or emptying would represent a change in that essence, compromising divine immutability and corrupting the essential unity of all three persons of the Godhead.

Case Study 2: Ritschl and Christology

German theologian Albrecht Ritschl recognized that the claim that Jesus only saw himself as a moral teacher or an apocalyptic visionary was clearly historically untrue. In his estimation, "For beyond all doubt Jesus was conscious of a new and hitherto unknown relation to God, and said so to his disciples; and his aim was to bring his disciples into the same attitude toward the world as his own, and to the same estimate of themselves, that under these conditions he might enlist them in the worldwide mission of the Kingdom of God, which he knew to be not only his own business, but theirs."[9]

Nevertheless, Ritschl's formulation was anything but a reaffirmation of classical trinitarian Christology. In his model, understanding Jesus demanded locating the kingdom of God as the central dynamic in Jesus's own self-consciousness. For Ritschl, then, the essence of Christianity took on a religious-ethical emphasis that prioritized the ethical nature of relationships within the community of God now.

Ritschl's own epistemology was deeply shaped by the Kantian revolution, as he distinguished between the types of knowledge offered by science

[9] Albrecht Ritschl, *The Christian Doctrine of Justification and Reconciliation* (London: T&T Clark, 1900), 386.

and religion. The former, he argued, was premised on "judgment of facts." But the latter, including Christianity and Christian theology, was formed around "judgment of value." So theological fascination with any supposed ontological realities about God were a waste of time, since human reason had no real access to those dimensions. Far more urgent, he claimed, was for Christian theology to develop the ethical and social implications of the inbreaking of the kingdom of God.

For Ritschl and his liberal heirs, this largely redefined the very nature of trinitarian theology in general, and of Christology in particular. If we are to claim that Jesus is God, it is not because of any true knowledge of his preincarnate nature or ontological reality. It is, rather, because we know him as the perfect actualization of the divine will for humanity. Thus, Ritschl's model has often been referred to as a "functional Christology."

Ritschl attempted to invoke Martin Luther's writings as precursors to his own. His reading of Luther was eccentric and untenable, but telling: "According to Luther, the Godhead of Christ is not exhausted by maintaining the existence in Christ of the divine nature; the chief point is that in his exertion as man his Godhead is manifest and savingly effective."[10]

Ritschl had effectively dislodged any ontological divinity in the person of Jesus, claiming instead that we can speak of Jesus as divine insofar as he was "the first to realize in his own personal life the final purpose of the kingdom of God." Along with Ritschl's attempted demolition of historic Christology came the abandonment of a myriad of historic Christian doctrines, including anything resembling salvation.

Case Study 3: Princeton Theology

This chapter has outlined a series of ways in which modern theology reflected waves of deviations from historic trinitarian theology and Christology. But readers should not take that to mean that there was a complete absence of

[10] Ritschl, 393.

orthodox confessional witness during the period. Although modern theology was dominated, especially within elite culture and academic institutions, by these trends, there were voices who defended orthodoxy.

Among the most prominent of these were a series of theologians connected to Princeton Theological Seminary in the nineteenth century. For his part, Charles Hodge (1797–1878) insisted on the absolute truthfulness of historic Chalcedonian Trinitarianism. But he also was clear to point out that divine truth was never a merely abstract proposition, but that divine revelation always has a practical purpose in the life of the people of God: "Truth is in order to holiness. God does not make known his being and attributes to teach men science, but to bring them to saving knowledge of himself. . . . This is specially true of the doctrine of the Trinity" (*Systematic Theology* 1:443).

Hodge classified trinitarian theology along three aspects: biblical, ecclesiastical, and philosophical. And yet, as a theologian deeply committed to the Reformation principle of *sola scriptura*, Hodge acknowledged that "it is only the doctrine as presented in the Bible which binds the faith and conscience of the people of God" (*Systematic Theology* 1:444).

But Hodge saw ample biblical grounds for historic Trinitarian orthodoxy. Although he was not unaware of the epistemological challenges posed by the Enlightenment, his theological method evidences a Protestant theologian marked by an unflinching commitment to the verbal plenary inspiration of Scripture and therefore its historical reliability. He acknowledged that these biblical grounds were not isolated in a handful of passages that explicitly outline the ontological realities of the Trinity. Rather, he articulated a historical understanding of progressive revelation within biblical theology. Like other key doctrines, the Trinity is made increasingly clear with the unfolding of God's revelation in Scripture. But Hodge concluded that Scripture is indeed sufficient on its own to provide all of the contours of our necessary knowledge of the God who is one in essence and three in persons.

Because of this, Hodge concluded that most of the theological discourse of the post-Enlightenment period was what he called "pantheistic Trinitarianism."

> There are, however, many modern systems which profess to be Trinitarian, which are in fact mere substitutions of the formulas of speculation for the doctrine of the Bible. Men speak of the Trinity, of the Father, Son, and Spirit, when they mean by those terms something which has not the least analogy with the doctrine of the Christian Church. Many by the Trinity do not mean a Trinity of persons in the Godhead, but either three radical forces, as it were, in the divine nature, which manifest themselves in different ways; or three different relations of the same subject; or three different states or stages of existence. (*Systematic Theology* 1:481)

Hodge was not the only one of the old Princeton theologians to stand out against the modernist impulses in Protestant theology. B. B. Warfield (1851–1921) would do much of the same, responding to the Ritschlian turn. Like Hodge, he demonstrated the biblical foundations for the Trinity. However, it is also apparent that Warfield seemed less interested in defending historic personal properties, particularly the eternal generation of the Son and the eternal procession of the Spirit.

But what Warfield did insist on was that the doctrine of the Trinity was profoundly biblical. In contrast with liberal Protestant theologians who claimed it was the product of religious development, Warfield held firmly to the conviction that the Trinity was revealed in the Old Testament:

> The Old Testament may be likened to a chamber richly furnished but dimly lighted; the introduction of light brings into it nothing which was not in it before; but it brings out into clearer view much of what is in it but was only dimly or even not at all perceived before.

> The mystery of the Trinity is not revealed in the Old Testament; but the mystery of the Trinity underlies the Old Testament revelation, and here and there almost comes into view.
>
> Thus the Old Testament revelation of God is not corrected by the fuller revelation that follows it, but only perfected, extended and enlarged.[11]

The Princeton theologians played a crucial role in preserving a commitment to Trinitarian orthodoxy during some of modernism's most constant attacks.

FOR THE CHURCH

The Connection between Biblical Authority and Knowledge of the Triune God

If creatures are to know anything of their Creator, it is only by means of his condescension to reveal himself. And if those creatures are fallen in sin, as we most clearly are, divine self-revelation is all the more astonishing, gracious, and vital. Without God's special revelation in the form of his inspired, infallible, and inerrant Word, there can be no hope of knowledge of God. And this certainly applies to knowledge of the ontological realities of the triune Godhead.

Yes, there is mystery when we think and speak of what it means for the one God to exist eternally as three persons. But Christian theology and devotion begins and ends on the foundation of biblical authority. If that foundation is eroded, our very knowledge of God is at stake. And the bitter fruit of that compromise is on display in the history of modern theological development. With the erosion of confidence in the absolute truthfulness of

[11] Benjamin B. Warfield, "The Biblical Doctrine of the Trinity" in *Biblical Doctrines*, vol. 2 (New York: Oxford University Press, 1932), 141–42.

the Bible after the Enlightenment and the ascendancy of higher criticism, the very notion that we can know anything about God with confidence was shaken to the core.

In our time, as it will be until Christ returns, the call must be for churches to proclaim the whole counsel of God and to do so with absolute confidence that the Bible is without error, that the truths that it proclaims to the world are absolutely essential to any real knowledge of the triune God who made us and who calls us to repent and believe in Jesus's atoning work for sinners and promises the gift of the Spirit to all who are united to the Son by faith.

The Connection between Classical Christology and the Exclusivity of the Gospel

It is no coincidence that the trends noted in this chapter developed in parallel with growing skepticism about Christianity's central message: that salvation is found in Christ alone. In the modern world, such a claim is regarded not only as antiquated but as intolerant and even immoral.

Bluntly, if Jesus Christ really is the incarnate Son, then every human being must submit to his authority. If the testimony provided us in the New Testament is indeed accurate and reliable, if he truly was crucified and raised for our sins, then there can be no dodging him. Christianity cannot be lumped in as just another of the world's "great religions." It is premised upon, and ceases to exist apart from, the assurance that the triune God has indeed redeemed a people for himself through the redemptive work of Jesus Christ. Lose that and you lose Christianity. Lose that and you lose the urgency of the Great Commission. Lose that and you lose any basis for eschatalogical hope.

The Mystery of God and Theological Speculation

One of the by-products of the Enlightenment was an unwillingness to leave much of anything to mystery. True, there was that Kantian epistemological knowledge. But that had a very different quality to it than the epistemological humility that had marked the Protestant Reformers. For example, Martin Luther and John Calvin both warned of the dangers of theological speculation, especially when it came to questions of the Trinity and Christology. Largely reacting against medieval scholasticism, Luther seemed quite comfortable with Chalcedonian formulas, but anchored all of it in taking the Bible at its word, but not pressing further into that which God has not revealed.

For Further Reading

Holmes, Stephen R. *The Quest for the Trinity: The Doctrine of God in Scripture, History, and Modernity*. Downers Grove, IL: InterVarsity Press, 2012.

Horton, Michael. *Lord and Servant: A Covenant Christology.* Louisville: Westminster John Knox, 2005.

Letham, Robert. *The Holy Trinity: In Scripture, History, Theology, and Worship*. Phillipsburg, NJ: P&R, 2004.

Macleod, Donald. *The Person of Christ.* Downers Grove, IL: InterVarsity Press, 1998.

Reeves, Michael. *Delighting in the Trinity: An Introduction to the Christian Faith*. Downers Grove, IL: InterVarsity Press, 2012.

Sanders, Fred. *The Triune God.* Grand Rapids: Zondervan, 2016.

Wellum, Stephen J. *God the Son Incarnate: The Doctrine of Christ.* Wheaton, IL: Crossway, 2016.

Questions for Study or Discussion

1. In what ways did the epistemological shift of the Enlightenment relocate the essence of the person and work of Christ?
2. What is the difference between the immanent ontological Trinity and the economic Trinity?
3. If the word *trinity* is never used in the Bible, what is the connection between the doctrine of Scripture and the doctrine of the Trinity?

14

THE HOLY SPIRIT AND SALVATION

By Owen Strachan

Introduction

> People seemed to be put by it upon inquiring, with concern and engagedness of mind, what was the way of salvation, and what were the terms of our acceptance with God; and what was said publicly on that occasion, however found fault with by many else-where, and ridiculed by some, was most evidently attended with a very remarkable blessing of heaven, to the souls of the people in this town, to the giving of them an universal satisfaction and engaging their minds with respect to the thing in question, the more earnestly to seek salvation in the way that had been made evident to them.
>
> —Jonathan Edwards, 1735

Religious groups sometimes get the reputation of being dry and dusty, stale and fusty. In truth, the opposite is often the case. The modern era was a wild and rollicking time, a period of great upheaval that left the church and world changed through developments in the church's conception of salvation, revival, and the work of the Spirit (1700–2000). Much that was settled became unsettled; much that was established was uprooted; much that was believed was rethought. In what follows, we will examine the doctrines of salvation and the Spirit in three distinct contexts: the eighteenth, nineteenth, and twentieth centuries, respectively. In the interest of concision, we will, in several cases, track the thinking of a key thinker and leader (or two), which will allow us to understand how different paradigms developed in these periods. By undertaking this ambitious survey, we shall see twists and turns, recoveries and confusion, and explosive growth and splintering factions as we observe the passing of these eras.

Historical Overview with Case Studies

An Edwardsean Doctrine of Salvation and the Spirit: Explosive Piety in the Eighteenth Century

Jonathan Edwards (1703–1758) is known for many reasons: ranking as a masterly theologian, serving as a president of present-day Princeton University, and being very tall. Among Edwards's other significant accomplishments, he served at the burning center of the First Great Awakening. Edwards and George Whitefield (1714–1770) believed in preaching for conversions and turned New England upside down as they did so. When Edwards preached on justification by faith alone in Northampton, Massachusetts, (in colonial form) in 1734, God opened blind eyes to the glory of the gospel. Edwards was no shy pulpiteer; he preached long, dense, intricate sermons chock-full of rich biblical doctrine. He did not dumb things down; he did not seek to entertain anyone; his pulpit presence was minimalist, yet Edwards's congregation listened to him nonetheless. The Spirit quickened hearts.

The same happened in 1741 in the area surrounding Northampton. Edwards preached a sermon on Deuteronomy that registered not at all in his home congregation, the First Church of Northampton. Then, on July 8, he filled the pulpit in a tiny church in nearby Enfield. Once again, revival struck. As Edwards depicted the fires of damnation that awaited unrepentant sinners, his audience cried out with such intensity that the pastor could not finish his message. Edwards went on to preach the later-titled "Sinners in the Hands of an Angry God" many more times, and a second burst of gospel conversion broke out once more in the region.

Whitefield did not hold back, either. He also loved to preach on justification by faith alone, the doctrine of doctrines for the Protestant Reformers (one superintended, guarded, and promoted by *sola scriptura*). Whitefield, like Edwards, was a doctrinal preacher. These great revivalists did not execute extreme psychological maneuvers; they did not harass their hearers or use tricks to produce results. They preached stout and staunch biblical doctrine, and they preached to both the mind and the heart.

Whitefield and Edwards alike believed that God alone could save. Standing behind their theology of conversion, therefore, was a rock-ribbed theology of God. God was illustrious in holiness; fallen man had lost his birthright. Sinners faced not merely a less-than-optimal daily existence, but the very fires of eternal judgment, fires stoked by the hand of God himself. Whitefield and Edwards preached God as judge because they believed that God was holy. But here each man brought in the kicker: the same God is infinitely loving. This God made a way for the salvation of sinners by giving his only Son as a guilt offering for the wicked. The Son drank the Father's wrath in full on the cross and destroyed the devil's power to accuse the beloved in doing so (Rom 8:33). This same Son rose from the grave and ascended to the Father's right hand, living in union with his covenant people through the Spirit.

In their preaching, Whitefield and Edwards first laid out the "bad news" of man's hellish condition, a move that made the "good news" of Christ all the sweeter and all the more needful. Salvation for each man was all of God, just as every aspect of life was all from God. Man's will could not choose the Lord, for man was and is dead in sins and trespasses (Rom 3:10–18). In this,

Whitefield and Edwards differed theologically from another titanic figure of the eighteenth century, John Wesley (1703–1791). Like Whitefield, Wesley hailed from an Anglican background but found himself ill at ease in the high church atmosphere due to its seemingly deficient interest in genuine conversion. Whitefield and Wesley shared a deep and world-changing passion for Jesus (and were in fact each a member of the "Holy Club" at Oxford). In time, both men (and the pack of Edwardsean revivalists that formed around the Northampton pastor-theologian) came to be called *enthusiasts*. This was not a term of endearment but one of derision.

Wesley and Whitefield believed that unenthusiastic Christianity was a counterfeit. Wesley and Whitefield launched a spiritual rebellion in response, fostering a new wave of the Reformation in their time. As in the sixteenth century, the eighteenth-century awakening featured evangelical upstarts against the established church. In New England, this conflict was publicized as the "New Lights" of the Edwardsean kind against the "Old Lights" of Charles Chauncy (1705–1787) and his Bostonian peers. In truth, the lines surrounding gospel conviction were a little blurrier than some antagonists made them, but the fight over soteriology and ecclesiology was real.

The doctrine that these three figures championed clashed sharply with the paedobaptist practice that all three affirmed. This is a pregnant irony of the First Great Awakening: the figures most associated with a believer's church (at least in substantial measure) each held to paedobaptist convictions. Though historians debate just how far Edwards's proto-believer's church views might have gone had he lived longer, the point stands: Edwards and his revivalist peers came to understand that a mixed church membership bore potentially tremendous implications for the reception of the gospel. Said differently, if professing believers viewed themselves as Christians because of their infant baptism—including people who bore not an ounce of true spiritual fruit—then what need did they have of a message of judgment and repentance and hard-won salvation? The answer was plain in social terms: nominal Christianity had largely carried the day in England and the American colonies. Many people simply assumed they were truly saved. After all, their baptism signaled their entrance into the covenant community.

The eighteenth-century revivalists shook up this nominal quiescence with impunity. We have mentioned three already; we should also name the names of evangelist-preachers James Davenport (1716–1757), Gilbert Tennent (1703–1764), and William Tennent Jr. (1705–1777). They preached anywhere they could. They evangelized directly, calling people on the spot to flee to Christ. They forged a new evangelical order, one—as we have already observed—that mirrored the upstart revolution of the sixteenth-century Reformers (both magisterial and radical). A key part of their preaching and teaching was the doctrine of the Spirit. This is particularly true of Edwards, who featured the Spirit in a major way in his ministry and theological program. In his landmark text *Religious Affections*, Edwards lined out exactly what it meant to be spiritual. As we can plainly see, Edwards did not believe that a spiritual person was generically interested in the afterlife or the possible existence of a benevolent divine being. Edwards used the term *spiritual* to refer to a person indwelt and possessed in full by the Holy Spirit (*WJE* in quotations refers to *The Reader's Guide to the Major Writings of Jonathan Edwards*):

> Another reason why the saints and their virtues are called spiritual (which is the principal thing), is that the Spirit of God, dwelling as a vital principle in their souls, there produces those effects wherein he exerts and communicates himself in his own proper nature. Holiness is the nature of the Spirit of God, therefore he is called in Scripture the Holy Ghost. Holiness, which is as it were the beauty and sweetness of the divine nature, is as much the proper nature of the Holy Spirit, as heat is the nature of fire. (*WJE 2:201*)

The Spirit was not a lone ranger for Edwards. Instead, the Spirit's presence gave the believer access to nothing less than a taste of trinitarian delight:

> The Spirit of God so dwells in the hearts of the saints, that he there, as a seed or spring of life, exerts and communicates himself, in this his sweet and divine nature, making the soul a partaker of God's beauty and Christ's joy, so that the saint has truly fellowship with the Father, and with his Son Jesus Christ, in thus having the communion or participation of the Holy Ghost (*WJE* 2:201).

These quotations matter greatly for our broader discussion. They reveal that having a high conception of God, and thus a high view of salvation as the very work of God, in no way closed off space for a high view of the Spirit. Jonathan Edwards had as big a vision of God as any theologian in the Christian tradition, and yet his Reformed theology included a major place for the role, function, and importance of the Spirit. In his thinking, we partake of spiritual life only because the Spirit dwells in us "as a vital principle" in our souls. The Spirit enables us to drink of "God's beauty" and thus become more beautiful—in other words, holier—ourselves. The Spirit also allows us to take in "Christ's joy" and thus become more joyful—more righteous—in the Son. There is no category here for a Christian who is not fully indwelt by the Spirit; he is in us, "in the hearts of the saints," and no one can wrest him out, nor anyone take him away.

In this material, Edwards makes room for the believer to participate in the holiness of God through the Spirit, but always *as a believer*. This is a crucial, if fine, point. Our holiness is "infinitely less in degree" than God's, the pastor makes clear, yet it is not fake holiness, a sheen of brightness that cracks, chips, and fades with time. It is real, Spirit-wrought holiness. We reflect something of the character of God himself through conversion, for the Spirit comes to live in us.

There are numerous other figures to mention in the eighteenth-century context. We can only scratch the surface of this era's soteriological and pneumatological developments. Yet we have lingered on the theology of Edwards for one very clear reason: for him, these doctrinal areas are not and cannot be dissociated or separated. In truth, they are one. Rarely in the Christian tradition have these two areas of theology run together in such vigorous fashion. Edwardsean theology is conversionist, seeking salvation always and everywhere; Edwardsean theology is spiritual, grounded in the Spirit who brings the dead to life and beautifies the believer.

For the church. Many pastors desire to see sinners saved. In our time, however, it has become relatively rare to warn sinners of judgment to unfold the glory of salvation. We have no money-back guarantee for our preaching, but we do know that if we will preach the whole gospel of God—and not only the parts that people instinctually like—the Lord will quicken hearts. If we would see true biblical revival in our time, we need preachers who emulate Edwards and his peers. We need the preaching of the law, the holiness of God, and the gospel.

In addition, we must make clear that the Spirit is not given only to some Christians. All who receive the gospel by faith know the forgiveness of God and will bear the fruits of the Spirit. Edwards was no perfect man or theologian, but gospel and growth are linked in his doctrine in a striking way. In fact, Edwardsean theology gives us a model of how we may link salvation and Spirit, or said differently, how we may (and must) connect conversion to Christ by the Spirit with conformity to Christ by the Spirit—all for the Father's glory.

The Finneyites and the Keswick Movement: Getting Anxious and Letting Go in the Nineteenth Century

The fervent revivalist spirit of the First Great Awakening swept into the nineteenth century. In this era, Edwardsean figures evangelized their peers, with leaders such as Timothy Dwight (1752–1817) at Yale preaching up a storm and winning many to Christ. In the South and Midwest, figures such as Barton Stone (1772–1844), Alexander Campbell (1788–1866), and James McGready (1763–1817) offered their hearers a rough and ready frontier gospel. At camp meetings, these preachers drew thousands of hearers, some of whom purportedly experienced vivid physical effects of the preaching.

Many of these leaders differed from the First Great Awakening's strongly providentialist view of salvation. In the 1820s, a lawyer named Charles Finney (1792–1875) drew considerable attention for his strength as an awakening preacher. Though ordained as a Presbyterian, Finney had little sympathy for reformational doctrine. He did, however, have great zeal for the revivalist cause, and he threw himself into the work with a passion that left a permanent mark on American evangelicalism. Finney offered no glancing challenge to the idea that God had to move for mass conversion to happen. The fiery orator argued to the contrary that revival depended on human effort. He said in the most direct terms possible:

> For a long time it was supposed by the Church that a revival was a miracle, an interposition of Divine power. It is only within a few years that ministers generally have supposed revivals were to be promoted by the use of means. . . . God has overthrown, generally, the theory that revivals are miracles.[1]

Clearly gifted at direct speech and simplified concepts, Finney famously summed up conversion in his *Lectures on Revivals of Religion* as "the result of using the right means." The old ways had gone; the new ways had come. Instead of praying and waiting for miraculous results to flow, Finney believed that ministers should get out and use the right "means" to make them happen. For too long, Christians had lain in a trap of their own making. They had talked about salvation and prayed for it, but they had done nothing about it. But in Finney's time, even through Finney's efforts, that hidebound "theory" was "overthrown." A new day had dawned.

Finney's gospel ambition knew no bounds. He clearly had great confidence in the methods he espoused, and he seemed to hit the target he aimed at. Reversing the earlier paradigm mentioned above, Finney laid the

---

[1] Charles Grandison Finney, *Lectures on Revivals of Religion,* ed. William G. McLoughlin (1835; repr., Cambridge, MA.: Harvard University Press, 1960), 19–20.

responsibility to save the world at the church's feet. Enough with pious feelings and precious thoughts; what was needed in the nineteenth century was action, not talk. "You see why you do not have a revival," Finney thundered as noted in his *Lectures*. "It is only because you do not want one." What would happen if the church did "want one"? Here Finney both prognosticated and hedged (a little). At one point, he predicted that "if the Church will do all her duty, the millennium may come in this country in three years." Then he took the parking brake off: "If the Church would do all her duty, she would soon complete the triumph of religion in the world."[2]

This theology of salvation seemed to lay the responsibility for global triumph squarely at the church's feet. The reason why the world lay unreached was not the pervasive corruption of the human heart thanks to Adam's fall. No, the world lay unreached because the church failed to "do all her duty." This was no trifling matter; the church's laziness in fact held the millennium back. Finney's revival-driven theology shifted the evangelical movement's theology and ecclesiology more broadly. His man-centered worldview made salvation a matter of human effort, human will, and human ingenuity.

In his eyes, the proof that Finney's theology was sound came not from its grounding in the biblical text, but from the professions of faith he elicited. He reflected on the disagreement his new methods drew later in life: "After I had preached some time, and the Lord had everywhere added his blessing, I used to say to ministers, whenever they contended with me . . . 'Show me the fruits of your ministry.'"[3] This competitive rejoinder reveals much about Finney's conception of ministerial soundness. A given exercise was good not because it was biblical; it was good because it occasioned "fruits" according to Finney. People could argue text, chapter, and verse; they could not—in the mind of the successful evangelist—argue with results. Results spoke for

---

[2] Charles Grandison Finney, *Lectures on Revivals of Religion* (New York: Leavitt, Lord, 1835), 32, 282, 283.

[3] Charles Grandison Finney, *Memoirs of Charles G. Finney* (New York: Revell, n.d.), 83.

themselves and provided their own justification. This conviction came to be hugely influential in the post-Finney evangelical movement.

What exactly accounted for the results? In Finney's eyes, his "new measures" drove the data. In his *Memoirs*, Finney recounted the steps he introduced to his revivals to make revival less of a miracle and more of a method (the enumeration is mine):

1. I called upon any who would give their hearts to God, to come forward and take a front seat [the anxious bench, as he called it].
2. We insisted on immediate submission.
3. I called upon them to kneel down and then and there commit themselves forever to the Lord.
4. I called on those only to kneel down who were willing to do what God required of them, and what I presented to them.
5. I called for those whose minds were made up, to come forward, publicly renounce their sins, and give themselves to Christ.[4]

Many pastors and Christians with a heart for evangelism would commend the evident desire for the saving of sinners in Finney's outline of his methods. His otherworldly directness, his uncompromising boldness, and his zeal for the kingdom of heaven were conspicuous. Yet his innovations matter as well. The "anxious bench" ensured that those under conviction felt great pressure in a public setting to convert to Christ. They came under the fierce gaze of the revivalist preacher, who used psychological pressure to try to edge them to renunciation of sin. It is noteworthy that Finney mentioned Christ here, for his view of the atonement centered in the balancing of the moral government of the universe by Jesus's death. In other words, Jesus died to demonstrate the righteousness and benevolence of God. His atonement does not cleanse us, nor does it take the wrath of the Father that we deserve to bear. Rather, Christ's crucifixion draws us back to God as God shows his displeasure with sin while calling us to receive his love.

---

[4] Finney, 116, 190, 255, 261, 304.

Finneyite salvation tinkered with the mechanics of the cross, and thus tinkered with the reality of salvation more broadly. God did not have to rescue a sinner by reaching out of the darkness to them through his sin-bearing Son; sinners needed to do what Finney required of them to make plain their submission to God. This new conception of personal redemption swept over the American scene and beyond. It had a major effect on the burgeoning Baptist movement and sparked many new revivalist efforts anchored in the use of the anxious bench, psychological pressure, and a doctrine of conversion driven by the will of man. In large measure, Finney's thinking won his generation, as many churches came to see revival as something a church could schedule rather than a miracle only God could effect.

The miraculous came back to the fore later in the nineteenth century when Keswick theology burst on the scene. Keswick theology grew out of the theology of D. L. Moody (1837–1899) and John Wesley, and Moody drew influence in certain ways from Finney. Keswick theology taught a "victorious higher life" theology that came when a Christian took decisive steps against indwelling sin. In the nineteenth century, the rise of Darwinism, the explosion of social problems in overcrowded cities, and the displacement of traditional Christianity in certain sectors of the West led to an agitated evangelicalism. Many Christians felt defeated and marginalized. In England the influence of the evangelical empire seemed to wane in different respects. Some responded to these trends—which are merely a sampling of the experience of the Western Church—with a great passion for a deeper personal knowledge of God.

The Keswick conference began meeting in 1875 in the elegant Lake District of England. William Boardman (1810–1866) served as one of the leading lights of the early movement. Boardman's book *The Higher Christian Life* advocated for a richer, more explosive conception of sanctification than prior views as Boardman's acolytes believed. Boardman's position represented a tweak of the "Christian perfectionism" promoted by John Wesley. The stress in Keswick theology was not generally on absolute moral perfection *per se* but rather on a consistently victorious Christian life.

"Higher life" doctrine depended on the Spirit for its power. When a Christian desired a greater pursuit of holiness, and a more regular pattern of victory over the flesh, they needed to take decisive action. Though Keswick teachers varied in their individual presentations, they tended to emphasize the following: First, the believer should abandon all known sin on the spot. Second, the believer should surrender their whole being to Christ, in effect embracing his lordship. Following several elements of personal transformation, including the mortification of the "self-life," the believer should consecrate themselves unto God. Here is the "let go and let God" dimension of Spirit-driven Keswick teaching. When one offered oneself up to the Lord for spiritual use, the Lord would then fill the believer, allowing a later inrushing of the Pentecost blessing in the believer's life.

Keswick theology spread rapidly around England from 1875–1920, influencing many and creating a new evangelical movement where one had not previously existed. The "higher life" experience seemed to many to solve the vexing problem of Christian holiness. Out was the slow, gradual, difficult, plodding progress of traditional Reformed sanctification. In was the explosive, climactic, on-the-spot nature of a Spirit-filling convulsion. Believers did not need to fight daily, even hour by hour or minute by minute, to grow in godliness. Instead, the God-desiring Christian needed to make a radical commitment to God, break with all known wickedness, and give up on personally driven effort to change spiritually. Consecration formed the key to Christlikeness. Give up trying to be holy, Keswick effectively said. Let the Spirit lift you higher.

As with other systems of thought we have examined, Keswick began as a ground-level phenomenon. No troupe of dandified theologians approved its arguments; no ecclesial council green-lighted its contributions. Keswick bubbled from the soil up, and seemed all the more popular due to its out-of-the-box nature. Yet Keswick was distinctly and unmistakably theological. Instead of arduous battling with sin, it subbed in the consecration experience solemnized by the filling of the Spirit. This implied—for those with eyes to see—that the glad embrace of God's lordship came not through

God's action in conversion, but through an act of the will. This implied—pressing in still further—that one could know Christ as Savior but not as Lord. In effect, then, Keswick and its theological cousins made Christ the agent of salvation and the Spirit the agent of received lordship. This view counted as a sea change from the historic Reformed vision of conversion, in which the sinner who confessed Christ as Savior came at the same moment under his gracious rule.

Along with Boardman, Robert Pearsall Smith (1827–1898), Hannah Whitall Smith (1832–1911), and F. B. Meyer (1847–1929) spread the influence of the higher life theology. In America "Holiness" Christianity grew out of this teaching and surged in popularity at the turn of the century. Holiness Christians took their Spirit-empowerment seriously. They created a flurry of social programs and devoted much energy to abolition, activism, temperance, and women's suffrage. They believed that they could achieve victory over the flesh, and they believed that they could find victory over the forces of darkness in broader society.

The higher life and Holiness movements crossed numerous cultural boundaries, presented a positive and change-oriented spiritual agenda to the world, and effected real change in difficult places. The pneumatology promoted by Keswick and other camps drew real and deserved challenge from various evangelical voices; many called attention to the portrait of progressive holiness in various books of the New Testament. Nonetheless, higher life theology led many to "let go and let God," even if this teaching—anchored in the euphoria of consecration—struggled to handle subsequent struggles common to the experience of many Christians navigating life in a fallen world.

For the Church

The zeal of Charles Finney for the revivalist cause stands out. Even those who would disagree with Finney about some aspects of theology would nonetheless find his attention to evangelism noteworthy. Although never commending uncritical appreciation of any movement, we do well to avoid mere repudiation of historic voices while allowing our own hearts to grow cold for unbelievers. With this noted, we do well today to evaluate whether it is a good idea to put pressure on sinners to repent. The "pressure" of the biblical call to repentance is and should be sufficient for our witness. Perhaps we should think more about Jesus calling his hearers not to cross the line of salvation at the earliest possible instant, but to count the cost before leaving all and following him (Luke 14:28).

In a similar vein, while many believers would take biblical issue with a victorious consecration experience, we do well to remember how powerful the Spirit truly is. Instead of grumpily dismissing a desire for growth in godliness, we do well to disciple people in the faith, helping men and women to understand that we might indeed make real gains in short periods of time by God's aid. Nevertheless, we must also show that the Christian life includes many peaks and valleys, and that as one example, Job had to walk through terribly difficult circumstances that did not resolve with a momentary resolution of will. Many believers will hear God's call to weather trials, perhaps bitterly difficult trials, to give God glory not only in times of strength but also in times of weakness.

Clashing Camps and the New Wave: Salvation and Spirit in the Twentieth Century

Many American evangelicals attended churches in established denominations heading into the twentieth century. Baptists and Presbyterians came from doctrinally conservative roots, and many shared agreement on the "fundamentals" of the faith. How shocking, then, when seismic shifts rattled the Northern Baptists and Presbyterians in the early twentieth century. The fundamentalist-modernist controversy of the first three decades of the twentieth century altered the church landscape in America permanently and exposed major division over the nature of salvation among once-unified churches.

The conflict took shape shortly after World War I. In January 1919, a well-heeled Protestant pastor named Harry Emerson Fosdick (1878–1969) preached a fascinating message on the men returning from war. Hailing their courage, Fosdick did much more than celebrate the soldiers who overcame the German war machine. He slipped in a new understanding of salvation that he believed characterized many warriors:

> Many men, returning, will bless America with a heft and range of character that they did not have before. But they did not go to France to save their souls. They forgot themselves, and went to France to save the world. They are learning that innermost salvation that never comes except through social sacrifice; they have found their lives by losing them in a cause.[5]

The rhetoric here is largely anodyne, of the sort one would expect at a commemoration of honorable sacrifice. Yet among noncontroversial statements, Fosdick said something major: "innermost salvation," in his view, "never comes except through social sacrifice." This was a quintessential articulation of the "social gospel," as it was called. In Fosdick's understanding, the gospel centered not in a message of salvation from hell through Christ's atonement, but in throwing oneself into a cause of great meaning and purpose. This and this alone constituted "innermost salvation." In Fosdick's conception, one could suppose that any soldier (or any person besides) who invested their life in a cause bigger than their own small existence laid hold of salvation.

Fosdick continued the point. The church at its best was "the organized force of militant righteousness, fighting the evil of the world—how fair a picture!" He saw no strong dichotomy between church members who had professed faith in Christ, however, and strong, noble soldiers. The latter group formed the "highest" of earth, and the church's goal was to "gather up humanity's best." Alas, according to Fosdick "the church is failing just there. The best is escaping her." Initially, Fosdick argued that finding a great

---

[5] Harry Emerson Fosdick, "The Trenches and the Church at Home," *Atlantic Monthly* 123 (January 1919): 22–33.

cause rendered one "saved"; in the succeeding section of his postwar valediction, the New York City pastor concluded that the church needed to be a place where impressive people wished to gather. The "best" of humanity—including many soldiers—wanted nothing to do with the church, and that was the church's fault. Or, more accurately, it was the fault of those who resisted the soteriological changes proposed by Fosdick and others. This resistance kept the church from winning the "best."

Fosdick, a massively influential figure, was not the only liberal Protestant to offer a new conception of the gospel. Theologian Walter Rauschenbusch (1861–1918) had published a major book in 1917 titled *A Theology for the Social Gospel* that stated the following: "We have a social gospel. We need a systematic theology large enough to match it and vital enough to back it."[6] The order matters greatly here. Rauschenbusch already had his convictions lined out; he needed a theology to back them up. His text attempted no small task and sought to accomplish a "readjustment and expansion of theology" such that the vision of the social gospel emerged as grounded in the text.

For Rauschenbusch, the leading social gospel thinker of this era, sin took the form of selfishness. Although this sounds orthodox, the theologian identified sin primarily as a problem of society. The state had suffered penetration by systemic evil and as such needed redemption. The church existed to champion the need for love in all things, which would bring about the reign of the kingdom of God. The church's objection to unjust economic conditions was crucial to this promotion of the kingdom. As the message of God advanced, men and women would grow conscious of the suprapersonal problems endemic to the economic, political, and social order. They would know solidarity, which for Rauschenbusch was the essence of religion.

While not dismissing personal salvation, Rauschenbusch continually urged the church to effect real change in the social order. Looking to Jesus fired this burden. The liberal Protestant movement in no way negated the

---

[6] Walter Rauschenbusch, *A Theology for the Social Gospel* (Louisville: Westminster John Knox, 1917), 1.

work of Christ, but rather reinterpreted it. The cross served as a moral example or influence on the church. In the face of tremendous suffering caused by unjust powers and evil influences, Jesus died to show solidarity with the lowly. His atonement reveals that Christ himself suffered under the weight of oppression, but the resurrection inspires us to fresh action (although the resurrection was for many not a historical event but a spiritual one). The doctrine of salvation thus celebrated and preached by Protestant liberals was transformational but focused on social strengthening rather than "soul salvation."

We venture back to Fosdick once more. The change in soteriology just mentioned did not occur by accident. Fosdick, Rauschenbusch, and their peers held a different vision of God than their "fundamentalist" opponents. In a famous 1922 sermon, Fosdick scorched the following views:

> It is interesting to note where the Fundamentalists are driving in their stakes to mark out the deadline of doctrine around the church, across which no one is to pass except on terms of agreement. They insist that we must all believe in the historicity of certain special miracles, preeminently the virgin birth of our Lord; that we must believe in a special theory of inspiration—that the original documents of the Scripture, which of course we no longer possess, were inerrantly dictated to men a good deal as a man might dictate to a stenographer; that we must believe in a special theory of the Atonement—that the blood of our Lord, shed in a substitutionary death, placates an alienated Deity and makes possible welcome for the returning sinner; and that we must believe in the second coming of our Lord upon the clouds of heaven to set up a millennium here, as the only way in which God can bring history to a worthy denouement.[7]

[7] Harry Emerson Fosdick, "Shall the Fundamentalists Win?" *Christian Work* 102 (June 10, 1922), 716–22.

For our purposes, the comments about God and wrath have great weight. Fosdick called a "special theory" what the orthodox church had proclaimed for centuries. That a holy God might have wrath against sin, just wrath necessitating the "blood of our Lord" dying in our place, proved unthinkable for Fosdick. The concept of a God angry at man's rebellion repelled the preacher. This was exactly the kind of material that drove intelligent, cultured folks away from the church. In terms that sound positively postmodern, Fosdick bewailed such doctrine: "Now, the worst kind of church that can possibly be offered to the allegiance of the new generation is an intolerant church." This was why many "young people turn from religion to science for the regulative ideas of their lives"—this kind of noxious theology. People came to religion for uplift and betterment, Fosdick avowed. When they heard judgment, blood atonement, and repentant faith, they turned away, never to return.

Fosdick's cutting words drew many responses, none more incisive than that of J. Gresham Machen (1881–1937). Machen taught New Testament at Princeton Theological Seminary and held a theology familiar to that of the heirs of the Protestant Reformation. In his book *Christianity and Liberalism*, Machen brooked no compromise with Fosdickian religion. In his judgment, "The church of Rome may represent a perversion of the Christian religion; but naturalistic liberalism is not Christianity at all."[8] "Naturalistic liberalism" in Machen's handling equated to liberal Protestantism. Though Machen's concise formulation drew much protest, he succeeded in reframing the entire conversation. It was not that his Christianity was better than Fosdick's; it was that Fosdick knew nothing of true Christianity.

Machen had many prongs in his argument. He made very clear that liberal Protestantism had, among many other serious failings, opted not to preach the cross of Christ. In a speech he gave before his book came out, Machen indicted deficient theologies of the atonement:

---

[8] J. Gresham Machen, *Christianity and Liberalism* (1923; repr., Grand Rapids: Eerdmans, 2001), 52.

> Fortunately, if the church has failed, it is at least perfectly clear why she has failed. She has failed because men have been unwilling to receive, and the church has been unwilling to preach, the gospel of Christ crucified. Men have trusted for their own salvation and for the hope of the world in the merit of their own self-sacrifice rather than in the one act of sacrifice which was accomplished some nineteen hundred years ago by Jesus Christ. That does not mean that men are opposed to Jesus. On the contrary, they are perfectly ready to admit Him into the noble company of those who have sacrificed themselves in a righteous cause. But such condescension is as far removed as possible from the Christian attitude. People used to say, "There was no other good enough to pay the price of sin." They say so no longer. On the contrary, any man, if only he goes bravely over the top, is now regarded as plenty good enough to pay the price of sin.[9]

As is evident, Machen responded here directly to Fosdick. The cross did not happen in history in order for Christ to gather a "noble company" of brave individuals. The "gospel of Christ crucified" alone would save the guilty sinner, for it announced the truth that Christ gave himself up for sinners "in the one act of sacrifice" at Calvary. The gospel message proclaimed something greater than the power of moral emulation, important as that is. No, "For us he has done a greater thing—for us he died," Machen argued in *Christianity and Liberalism*. The cross purchased our salvation and made a way back to God.

The problem is not society's unkindness or a lack of noble souls; instead, the problem is the human heart itself. Machen made this clear: "Our dreadful guilt, the condemnation of God's law—it was wiped out by an act of grace. That is the message which brings Jesus near to us, and makes Him not

---

[9] J. Gresham Machen, "The Church in the War," *Presbyterian*, May 29, 1919.

merely the Saviour of the men of Galilee long ago, but the Saviour of you and me."[10] You could not simply admire Jesus, Machen argued. You could not only trust in him. Instead, you needed salvation, salvation of the soul:

> The truth is that when men speak of trust in Jesus' Person, as being possible without acceptance of the message of His death and resurrection, they do not really mean trust at all. What they designate as trust is really admiration or reverence. They reverence Jesus as the supreme Person of all history and the supreme revealer of God. But trust can come only when the supreme Person extends his saving power *to us*.[11]

The line of argument here resonates with Machen's formulation mentioned earlier. Mere admiration and reverence do not count as actual saving faith. Instead, admiration and reverence are distinct from saving faith. The difference between knowing about Jesus, and admiring him based on what one knows, and knowing Jesus as Savior, is infinite. This is the difference between eternal life and eternal death; this is the difference between salvation and damnation.

The fundamentalist-modern controversy died out but never really went away. Conservative Protestants and liberal Protestants continued to battle one another in the second half of the twentieth century, but never at the same pitch as in the 1920s, when the liberal side won control of both the Northern Baptist Convention and the Presbyterian Church in the USA. In the conservative evangelical world, leaders such as Billy Graham (1918–2018), Carl F. H. Henry (1913–2003), and Harold Ockenga (1905–1984) championed the gospel of a crucified Savior. In time, Graham became a bellwether for debates over first-order issues such as salvation and second-order matters regarding separation (and no small number of third- or fourth-order issues regarding legalism).

In the Baptist world, Southern Baptists avoided the split that characterized the northern denominations, although debates over the free will of man and the sovereignty of God in soteriology waxed hot throughout the second

[10] Machen, *Christianity and Liberalism*, 43–44.

[11] Machen, 44.

half of the twentieth century. Adrian Rogers (1931–2005) and Charles Stanley (1932–) were two of the best-known advocates of the "revivalist" side, while R. Albert Mohler Jr. (1959–) and Mark Dever (1960–) became two of the best-known advocates of the "God's will" side. Despite their differences, Southern Baptists held the convention together.

The stakes over salvation—and the doctrine of salvation—got very high indeed in the church in the twentieth century. Though discussion of pneumatology did not normally get quite so hot, nevertheless, evangelicals broke into different camps regarding the gifts of the Spirit during this era. The rise of "charismatic theology" came in three distinct waves over the course of the twentieth century. We shall treat them each in kind, offering the major idea of each aspect of the new wave. The first iteration, the rise of Pentecostalism, came in April 1906, when William Seymour (1870–1922) apparently spoke in an unknown "tongue" during a revival meeting at the Azusa Street Mission in Los Angeles. Not long afterward, many people reported they did the same. The tongues phenomenon traveled across America accompanied by numerous other manifestations of the Spirit, according to participants: prophesying, healing, and more.

Initially, onlookers argued that this Pentecostal outpouring marked the advent of a new movement of God that would bring the second coming of Christ. That expectation faded with time (though it still surfaces in literature), but the interest in this pneumatological development did not. In time, Pentecostalism took institutional form, as new denominations formed, new schools took shape, and a new emphasis on the "second baptism" of the Spirit took hold. This last idea had some historical precedent, but Pentecostalism made it an essential second major experience of the Christian life. When the believer undergoes the baptism of the Spirit, they acquire the ability to speak in tongues, according to Pentecostal doctrine.

The second wave of Spirit-interested evangelicals is called the Charismatic stage. This iteration is similar to the previous stage, but the doctrine of some members of the second wave downplayed the role of tongues. There is a range of belief on this among charismatics; though they disagree about tongues, they agree that a second baptism of the Spirit should happen for all who follow Christ, and they tie this Spirit baptism to conversion. The Spirit's infilling allows the believer to make use of the spiritual gifts of 1 Cor 12:8–10, commonly known as the word of wisdom, word of knowledge, faith, healing, miraculous powers, prophecy, distinguishing between spirits, speaking in tongues, and interpreting tongues. Against cessationists, charismatics emphasize that the church has access to these gifts today, and that local churches should encourage the use of these gifts in the life of the church.

The final major iteration of Spirit-driven theology in the twentieth century is called the "Third Wave." It debuted in the 1980s on the campus of Fuller Seminary and other schools. The Third Wave emphasizes the need for the filling of the Holy Spirit over a second baptism of the Spirit. The Third Wave has taken pains to separate itself from the "prosperity theology" taught by Word-Faith leaders such as Benny Hinn (1952–), Kenneth Copeland (1936–), Creflo Dollar (1962–), and T. D. Jakes (1957–). This slice of the charismatic world emphasizes that the death of Christ purchased not only individual salvation for the lost, but health, wealth, and general prosperity for those who follow Christ. Prosperity theology has long existed outside of the mainstream of evangelicalism, but it has drawn a tremendous following all over the world. It is a major challenge to biblical fidelity—equivalent to a modern heresy—and should be taken with the utmost seriousness.

Prosperity theology aside, the Third Wave is not denominational in character. It continues to promote the spiritual gifts mentioned above, though adherents disagree over the extent of gifting that each believer may experience. In general, it has a more consciously theological character than earlier iterations of the charismatic movement, and different groups within the broader movement have made vibrant contributions to the church's flourishing. Nonetheless, Third Wave doctrine calls for careful thinking and testing. As one example of this imperative, if apostolic sign gifts like tongues and prophecy are still in operation, then raising the dead must be as well. Though some will disagree here, perhaps the cessation of the apostolic line is a sign to us of the cessation of the sign gifts.

For the Church

The Machen-Fosdick battle reminds us of the importance of two things: first, we need to champion sound doctrine because it is true and glorifying to God, and second, we should remember just how much unsound thinking has come into Christ's church due to a missiological or evangelistic motive. Fosdick's stated concern was the lack of the "best" men of the world. Although Christians should want all men to be saved, we must never allow our missiology to rework our theology. Our theology, by contrast, *is* our missiology. Just because we have a good motive—wanting the salvation of sinners—does not mean that we have a blank check to draw people by any means we see fit. Our methods and models of ministry must be biblical.

With regard to the Spirit, we should always rejoice in the indwelling reality of the third person of the Trinity in our heart. Whether we affirm cessationism or charismatic theology, the joy of every Christian is to walk in the Spirit and take power over the flesh. We must all bear the fruit of the Spirit; this is not optional, only for emotionally attuned evangelicals. We should take care as well that we understand all the implications of affirming the extraordinary spiritual gifts as a part of the contemporary church's life. If tongues are operative, so is healing, meaning that some among us should have the gift of healing as the apostles did. This will take careful parsing. Whatever the believer concludes, the Spirit is our inheritance, our possession, and the guarantee—the down payment—of our redemption.

For Further Reading

Dorrien, Gary. *The Making of American Liberal Theology: Idealism, Realism, and Modernity, 1900–1950*. Louisville: Westminster John Knox, 2003.

Ferguson, Sinclair. *The Holy Spirit*. Contours of Christian Theology. Downers Grove, IL: InterVarsity Press, 1997.

Finn, Nathan A., and Jeremy Kimble. *A Reader's Guide to the Major Writings of Jonathan Edwards*. Wheaton, IL: Crossway, 2017.

Hansen, Collin, and John Woodbridge. *A God-Sized Vision: Revival Stories That Stretch and Stir*. Grand Rapids: Zondervan, 2010.

Hart, D. G. *Defending the Faith: J. Gresham Machen and the Crisis of Conservative Protestantism in Modern America.* Phillipsburg, NJ: P&R, 2003.

Kidd, Thomas. *The First Great Awakening: The Roots of Evangelical Christianity in Colonial America.* New Haven, CT: Yale University Press, 2009.

Marsden, George. *Jonathan Edwards: A Life*. New Haven, CT: Yale University Press, 2003.

Murray, Iain. *Revivals and Revivalism: The Making and Marring of American Evangelicalism, 1750–1858*. Edinburgh: Banner of Truth, 1994.

Murray, John. *Redemption Accomplished and Applied*. 1955. Reprint, Grand Rapids: Eerdmans, 2015.

Naselli, Andrew David. *Let Go and Let God? A Survey and Analysis of Keswick Theology*. Bellingham, WA: Lexham, 2010.

Storms, Sam. *Signs of the Spirit: An Interpretation of Jonathan Edward's Religious Affections*. Wheaton, IL: Crossway, 2007.

Stott, John. *The Cross of Christ*. 1986. Reprint, Downers Grove, IL: InterVarsity Press, 2006.

Strachan, Owen, and Douglas Sweeney. *The Essential Jonathan Edwards: An Introduction to the Life and Teaching of America's Greatest Theologian*. Chicago: Moody, 2018.

Straub, Jeffrey Paul. *The Making of a Battle Royal: The Rise of Liberalism in Northern Baptist Life, 1870–1920*. Monographs in Baptist History 8. Eugene, OR: Pickwick, 2018.

Wills, Gregory A. *Southern Baptist Theological Seminary, 1859–2009*. Oxford: Oxford University Press, 2009.

Questions for Study or Discussion

1. What should happen when both the word of judgment and word of salvation are preached?
2. What effect should the Holy Spirit's indwelling of every believer have in the Christian life?
3. Is revival a miracle, or can it be scheduled?
4. What does Spirit-driven sanctification—growth in godliness—actually look like as presented in the Bible?
5. How do we know when our missiology (our desire to reach people) is overcoming our theology (the doctrine the Bible teaches)?

15

THE CHURCH

By Jeremy M. Kimble

Introduction

The Reformation brought about great doctrinal changes in the church, especially as it related to the doctrine of Scripture. God's Word was now seen as our ultimate authority and not merely equal to tradition, and the doctrine of salvation was emphasized, particularly justification by faith alone in Christ alone. Reformation churches established their own identity by becoming strongly united around the *solas* of the Reformation and in their continued distancing from the Roman Catholic Church.

Beginning in the Reformation period, and becoming even more distinct in the modern era (1750–), ecclesiological differences became more pronounced, while unity around the doctrines of grace was evident. Variances among the Reformers regarding church life became entrenched doctrinal convictions and ecclesial distinctives, which brought about agreement in certain core theological areas (e.g., justification by faith alone) but disagreement over other matters (e.g., baptism, Lord's Supper, church government, forms of church worship). As a result, the modern era is a critical period in the history of the church regarding church doctrine. In many ways it called into question how the church was to cooperate and work together while also maintaining doctrinal distinctives often dealing with matters of ecclesiological importance.

Historical Overview

The First Great Awakening

By the mid-eighteenth century, Christianity—particularly in the West—found itself in the throes of particular ideologies, such as the Enlightenment (emphasis on the individual, objective reality, and reason) and Romanticism (emphasis on the subjective and emotions). Each of these philosophies would have their effect on culture at large and call into question many of the major tenets of Christianity, such as the possibility of miracles, original sin, status of Scripture, and identity of Jesus.

The First Great Awakening came about within this particular cultural milieu. In England, ecclesiological movements abounded, likely influenced by the strength of the Roman Catholic Church in Spain and Portugal; Lutheranism and Pietism in Germany; the Dutch Reformed Church; and Anglicanism in England. Puritanism had made an impression especially in England and other parts of Europe, calling for further reform, particularly in ecclesiological matters. The likes of John Wesley (1703–1791) and George Whitefield (1714–1770) were among key players in the First Great Awakening, preaching to thousands in open fields—unheard-of at that time—and bringing about institutional change within the Anglican Church as well as a new denominational identity, at least in Wesley's case (Methodism). Likely inadvertently, these individuals encouraged an individualistic piety that sought genuine salvation and holiness, became impatient with the relatively fixed forms of institutional church life, and believed evangelism and discipleship could occur outside of the local church.

Contemporary with these movements in Europe, revival in early America also had its effect. Some pastors in the seventeenth and eighteenth centuries—Solomon Stoddard (1643–1729) among the most notable—had adopted what came to be known as the HalfWay Covenant. In this arrangement, unconverted adults were allowed partial membership in a church. While they could not vote, they agreed to the church's confession, submitted to the church's discipline, and were able to have their children baptized. Nevertheless, due to the tenets adopted by advocates of the First Great Awakening, by the eighteenth and nineteenth centuries, there was increasing emphasis on conversion and the new birth as prerequisite to full church membership. Under the preaching and influence of men such as Jonathan Edwards (1703–1758), Wesley, Howell Harris (1714–1773), and Whitefield, the Great Awakening solidified a belief in individual conversion for membership among many branches of Protestantism, shaping church life in profound ways.

The Modern Missions Movement

By the late eighteenth century, the beginnings of the modern missions movement became evident. This movement came to fruition in large measure thanks to the work of William Carey (1761–1834), a missionary to India, particularly through his work *Enquiry into the Obligation of Christians to Use Means for the Conversion of the Heathen* (1791). Carey was deeply influenced by the theology of Andrew Fuller; both stood in opposition to hyper-Calvinistic tendencies that made their way, especially, into Baptist churches.

In 1792 the Particular Baptist Missionary Society was formed. The long-term effects of Carey's efforts and the society's presence would launch innumerable missionaries to the ends of the earth, while increasing the understanding and application of the church's role in missions. In present day, many Protestant churches and denominations are still characterized by their commitment to making disciples of all the nations.

The Second Great Awakening

The Second Great Awakening (1800–1840s), a movement seen mainly in the United States, brought an increased emphasis on the new birth, spiritual awakening, and evangelism. The methods by which these things were accomplished were often done outside of local church contexts in various revival meetings. This posed potential threats to a robust doctrine of the church and allowed parachurch organizations to increase in importance, even as an ecclesial reality for some. Nevertheless, the Awakening certainly has had an influence on the life of the church and the approach to such matters. In many ways, church worship itself became primarily concerned with evangelism, baptism, and membership. By the mid-twentieth century, many evangelical churches had shifted in viewing themselves preeminently as baptized, covenanted, local assemblies, to functioning primarily as outreach centers and corporate worship services as catalysts for revival. This perspective made the process for joining a church generally much quicker and more accessible.

This development's main proponent was a Presbyterian pastor from New York named Charles Finney (1792–1875). Finney was known for his promotion of personal religious experience as initially experienced by means such as the altar call, the anxious seat, and the mourner's bench—techniques designed to elicit a response in the revival meetings. These methods spread rapidly across the western and southern frontiers, making their way from revival meetings to local church practices. This trend spawned ongoing debate in the nineteenth century and beyond regarding the purpose and method of preaching, the rapidity with which members are brought into a church, and how one conceives of salvation along Arminian and Calvinist lines.

One response to the Second Great Awakening became known as "restorationism," which was the attempt to structure church life in the way of the church in the apostolic age. Proponents such as Alexander Campbell (1788–1866), Walter Scott (1796–1861), and Barton Stone

(1772–1844) eventually formed a denomination that coalesced under the name of Disciples of Christ. This group attempted to displace denominational divides with an emphasis on Christian unity based on New Testament teaching, leaving creeds and confessions aside. They rejected the lengthy, overly emotional conversion narratives of the Awakening and opted for a straightforward soteriology that they deemed understandable: conviction through the gospel, belief in Jesus, repentance, baptism, regeneration. In Baptist life, restorationist James Robinson Graves (1820–1893) repudiated the idea of the universal church. He argued that Baptist churches were the only true church and could mark their heritage as a succession dating back to the first century. Graves exhorted Baptists to recover key marks, such as restricting the Lord's Supper to members of a specific church only, and rejecting any form of baptism other than immersion performed within a Baptist church.

Covenant Theology and Dispensationalism

Although various details of ecclesiology met with debate in these latter centuries, a particular theological discussion emerged within the doctrine of the church as articulated by dispensationalists. This approach—in many ways considered an approach to biblical theology—gained traction through the writings of John Nelson Darby (1800–1882), Cyrus Scofield (1843–1921), and Lewis Sperry Chafer (1871–1952), each affirming strong amounts of discontinuity between the Old and New Testaments and, consequently, Israel and the church. Darby, for example, insisted on a complete separation between the Jews and the church, each having their own history, covenants, and destiny. Specific differences between Israel and the church included the church being a Spirit-indwelt people, earthly promises to Israel versus heavenly promises to the church, law as the rule of life for Jews versus grace for Christians, and incorporation for the church into the body of Christ. These authors further argued that the church began at Pentecost and was a mystery in that it was not revealed until the New Testament era, particularly in the events of Acts and the writings of the apostle Paul. As such, Old Testament teachings apply to Israel, while the New Testament dictates the way the church will approach doctrine, worship, ministry, the ordinances, and polity.

This theological system stands in contradistinction to what is known as "covenant theology." Articulated beginning in the seventeenth century by theologians such as Johannes Cocceius (1603–1669), covenant theology posits continuity between the people of God as seen in Israel and the church. Thus, they believe the church begins in the Old Testament and see great similarities due to the overarching covenant of grace between God's people throughout the Testaments. In more recent years—particularly the late twentieth and early twenty-first centuries—some dispensationalists have shown greater affinity for areas of continuity (i.e., progressive dispensationalism), and some in the covenant theology camp have recognized the need to nuance certain aspects of discontinuity concerning the people of God (i.e., progressive covenantalism).

Roman Catholic Ecclesiological Developments

This time period saw ecclesiological development not only in Protestant churches, but also in the Roman Catholic Church. From the Council of Trent (1545–1563) to the early twentieth century, the Catholic Church continued to define itself as the infallible one true church in concert with its classic marks: one, holy, catholic, apostolic. By the nineteenth century there was an overt emphasis on the authority of the church as it increasingly operated in ways counter to its culture, denouncing various contrary ideologies. Vatican I (1869–1870) cemented this view of the church as authoritarian and hierarchical, with particular emphasis on the infallibility of the pope. The bishop of Rome was declared to have power "both episcopal and immediate," "the supreme judge of the faithful," and infallible when "he defines a doctrine concerning faith or morals to be held by the whole church."[1]

The Second Vatican Council (1962–1965) stood in definite continuity with received Catholic tradition but also updated the church's theology. Due largely to the influence of Catholic theologian Johann Adam Möhler (1796–1838), Vatican II not only affirmed papal authority and traditional hierarchy, but also placed greater emphasis on the church as both mystical and organizational. This meant focus on Christological and pneumatological elements of the church, recognizing the organization and hierarchy in the body of Christ, and the dynamic participation of Spirit-indwelt laity. During the era of Vatican II, Catholic theologians such as Karl Rahner (1904–1984) and Hans Küng (1928–), through documents such as *Lumen Gentium*, spoke of the church as a "mystery" founded by the trinitarian God, comprised of the people of God—including clergy and laity—and as a hierarchical pilgrim church, existing sacramentally as a sign and instrument of communion with God. Vatican II further affirmed and qualified the powers of the pope, asserting further ecclesial authority, and recognized the possibility of salvation outside of the Roman Catholic Church, certainly a deviation from previous teachings.

The Ecumenical Movement

In the midst of significant change within the Roman Catholic Church, the twentieth century also saw a push toward greater unity among churches, crossing lines of denomination and tradition. One result of this concern came to be known as the ecumenical movement, begun initially at the World Missionary Conference (1910) and culminating as the World Council of Churches (WCC; 1948). The WCC began as a Protestant effort, centered

---

[1] See "First Dogmatic Constitution on the Church of Christ," 3.2, 3.8, 4.9.

on common confession of the trinitarian God and Jesus as Savior, and later came to include Orthodox and Catholic affiliates.

Due to the minimization of doctrine and a decreasing emphasis on world evangelization, evangelicals largely opted not to participate in the WCC, instead forming their own consortiums. In the United States this group came to be known as the National Association of Evangelicals (1942), and on a more global scale, the World Evangelical Fellowship came to fruition (1951). In these early days, evangelical unification efforts focused predominantly on local evangelism and global missions (e.g., World Congress on Evangelism, Berlin, 1966; International Congress on World Evangelization, Lausanne, 1974; Lausanne II, 1989; Lausanne III, 2010). However, one example of theological unity came in the document titled "Evangelicals and Catholics Together" (1994). The statement was written to spell out the need for Protestants and Catholics to deliver a common witness to the modern world at the dawn of a new millennium. Endorsers included Chuck Colson, J. I. Packer, Mark Noll, and Bill Bright on the evangelical side, as well as Avery Dulles, Richard John Neuhaus, George Weigel, and Peter Kreeft on the Roman Catholic side. The document was heavily criticized, particularly by evangelicals, noting agreement for social efforts to be unified but denouncing theological compromise they saw particularly in the doctrine of *sola fide*, which was condemned by Roman Catholics at the Council of Trent.

Pentecostalism

One of the most impactful movements relating to ecclesiology in the early twentieth century was the genesis and expansion of Pentecostalism and the Charismatic movement. Figures such as Charles Parham (1873–1929) and William Seymour (1870–1922) taught in their respective churches that their experience of the Holy Spirit should be the same as that seen at Pentecost in Acts 2. This included signs accompanying the baptism of the

Spirit (which they interpreted to be a post-conversion experience), particularly the ability to speak in tongues. The Pentecostal movement began in large measure at the Azusa Street Revival (1906) under Seymour's leadership, and it became worldwide, forming new churches and denominations (e.g., Assemblies of God, Church of God [Cleveland], Foursquare). The Charismatic movement, which permeated already existing churches and denominations, began in earnest in the 1960s under teachers such as Dennis Bennett (1917–1991). The "third wave" of the Charismatic movement, tied to Vineyard churches, Peter Wagner (1930–2016), and John Wimber (1934–1997), was seen largely in the 1980s. It was also principally independent in nature but showcased enthusiastic devotion to Christ and a tireless evangelistic energy.

Due to the denominational variety that encompasses charismatic theology, these churches have exhibited all manner of diversity in church structure and governance. Both Pentecostal and charismatic churches placed a stronger emphasis on personal, dynamic, spiritual experience as opposed to deep theological reflection. They also placed a distinct emphasis on the spiritual gifts of all believers, not just vocational ministers, to exercise their gifts by the Spirit's power for the good of the church. In all of this, there was a seeming desire to embody the ideals of the early New Testament church, as they understood it, from the book of Acts. In terms of its ecclesiology, these churches and denominations integrated the sign gifts into varying parts of their worship services, claiming that such things as tongues, healing, and prophecy were normative for the modern church.

The Church Growth Movement

Pentecostal and charismatic churches were not the only ones experiencing rapid growth. By the mid- to late twentieth century, church growth strategies were spoken of often in the West, and megachurches (usually defined as churches with more than 2,000 in attendance) increased in popularity.

Much of what came to be known as the church growth movement had its origins in the teachings of Donald McGavran (1897–1990). McGavran was a missiologist and founding dean of the School of World Mission at Fuller Seminary. Born in India, he went back there in 1923 as a missionary, working predominantly as an educator. He also spent seventeen years trying to start a movement of indigenous church planting among the Satnamis caste. In that time, many people were won to Christ, and fifteen small village churches were planted. McGavran's *The Bridges of God* (1955) explains more fully his approach to missions as an indigenous church-planting movement.

In 1958, McGavran returned to the United States and proposed to begin work training pastors on church growth. He eventually came to Fuller in 1965 and subsequently wrote works such as *Understanding Church Growth* (1970) and *Ten Steps for Church Growth* (1977), both of which expounded various principles, particularly the homogenous unit principle (i.e., individuals are more likely to convert to Christianity en masse when they share similar demographics), that would lead to the growth of local churches. Although McGavran likely applied this to indigenous efforts in missions, especially in terms of long-term leadership, others expanded the principle to think of local churches in terms of things such as socio-economic status and age. The church growth movement in the West, which subsequently was exported elsewhere globally, began in earnest in the 1980s. There was no doctrinal consensus within the movement, as one saw figures as diverse as Robert Schuller (1926–2015) and Jerry Falwell (1933–2007). Nevertheless, there were methodological similarities, such as stress on effective evangelism, empirical research on the community, homogeneity, marketing, mission statements, and sensitivity in church services to "seekers" (i.e., those coming to church who did not yet believe in Jesus). Many megachurches exist around the world today, but it is likely that around the 1990s the two best known would have been Saddleback Church and Willow Creek Church, founded by Rick Warren (1954–) and Bill Hybels (1951–) respectively.

The Emerging Church and Evangelical Responses

In response to megachurch and church growth trends, as well as shifting ideological realities in the West (i.e., modernism to postmodernism), the "emerging church movement" made its way into many ecclesiological discussions at the beginning of the twenty-first century. Ryan Bolger and Eddie Gibbs define this reality as "communities that practice the way of Jesus within postmodern cultures."[2] Academic theologians who were most influential within the movement included Stanley Grenz (1950–2005) and John Franke; its ecclesial leaders seen in speaking and writing included Brian McLaren, Doug Pagitt, Rob Bell, and Dan Kimball. Though varying widely, churches described as "emerging" generally included ideological elements, such as a focus on contextualization to the postmodern mind, antifoundational epistemology, a preference for truth to be conveyed as narrative rather than argumentation, and experientialism, as well as issues that focused more on church practice, such as authenticity, emphasis on the arts, and a reaching back to ancient church traditions. Although difficult to lump all proponents of the emerging church together, doctrinally there was seemingly ample drift toward theological liberalism as seen in various publications that sought to defend a "generous orthodoxy."

Although not in direct response to the emerging church movement, other organizations, such as the Gospel Coalition (TGC; 2005) and Together for the Gospel (T4G; 2006), came together around the same time period. Both of these groups are comprised of conservative evangelicals, mainly in the Reformed tradition, and are committed to understanding denominational differences and yet also committed to unity around the gospel. T4G has focused primarily on doctrinal issues at their biannual conferences, looking at topics such as expositional preaching, the gospel, conversion, and the Reformation. TGC has a more expanded vision, providing resources

---

[2] Eddie Gibbs and Ryan K. Bolger, *Emerging Churches: Creating Christian Communities in Postmodern Culture* (Grand Rapids: Baker, 2005), 44–45.

on their website (thegospelcoalition.org) and holding a biannual conference. They also have drawn up both a doctrinal statement and a theological vision for ministry. These kinds of evangelical groups express diversity and disagreement on certain topics, but the vision has been a broad theological unity. This has certainly had an effect on churches' attitudes toward one another in terms of cooperation and co-laboring for the sake of the gospel. These groups have encouraged one another, shared some of the same main speakers, and worked with other organizations at their conferences, such as the Acts 29 church-planting network.

In recent years, it is likely that no ministry has thought and produced more and had greater effect on the topic of ecclesiology than 9Marks Ministries. Founded in 1998 by Mark Dever (1960–), pastor of Capitol Hill Baptist Church, 9Marks is a ministry dedicated to helping pastors and church members understand the components needed to become a healthy, biblical church. They do so through an e-journal, website, books, curriculum, and conferences. Although Baptist by conviction, 9Marks has had an impact across denominational lines as people continue to think about topics such as conversion, church membership, church discipline, expositional preaching, discipleship, and church leadership. Ministries such as 9Marks, along with the continued concentration of books and conferences dedicated in some way to the doctrine of the church, ensure that this is a theological topic that will continue to gain attention.

The church continues to grow globally, and most predominantly in the global South and East. For example, the growth of the church in China over the twentieth century is staggering, with some estimates, amid severe persecution, a movement of mainly house churches that comprise more than 50 million believers. As churches continue to grow in places that have experienced and are experiencing persecution for their faith (e.g., the Middle East, parts of Africa), this has often resulted in ecclesiological models that look different than their American and European counterparts. These developments will greatly influence the doctrine of the church over the coming decades, signifying the importance of continued discussion of the doctrine's importance, speaking to the church's ontology and functionality.

Case Studies

Case Study 1: Nature and Polity of the Church

In viewing the narrative concerning the doctrine of the church in the modern era, some aspects of the doctrine are worthy of further attention. First, the nature of the church received ample attention, particularly in defining what is meant by different New Testament metaphors used to describe the church, such as the people of God, the body of Christ, and the temple of the Spirit. Keeping these images in mind, the Roman Catholic and Orthodox traditions focus on the universality of the church, looking to the Trinity as a model to emphasize unity in diversity, understanding the church as sacrament, relegating those who belong to the church as those who are baptized into the church and celebrate its sacraments. The free church tradition is broader in nature, recognizing differing ecclesiologies, often adopting a more minimalist approach to the nature of the church (Baptists would be the exception, holding more stringent convictions concerning the nature of the church).

The outworking of church governance structures is strongly tied to doctrinal understandings of the nature of the church. Typically, church polity is understood in terms of episcopal, Presbyterian, and congregational models. Episcopal polity emphasizes hierarchy within the governmental structure of the church. This results, in the case of Roman Catholicism, for example, in churches coming under rectors, then bishops, then archbishops, then cardinals, and, finally, the pope. Presbyterian polity affirms a degree of hierarchy but vests authority in elders of local churches. These elders gather in regional synods, as well as in an annual assembly. Finally, congregational church governance values church autonomy—although many churches governed in this fashion are part of associations—and allows members to have authority and a say in various church issues (e.g., doctrine, hiring a pastor, bringing in new members, church discipline).

One's understanding of the nature of the church certainly plays a role within these varying models of polity. In Catholic and Orthodox traditions, a bishop who stands in apostolic succession dating back to the days of Peter is constitutive to the church's function and existence. The bishop ensures the presence of Christ in the celebration of the Eucharist, which is an essential part of their worship. On the other hand, Presbyterian and congregational polities do not look to an authoritative bishop who constitutes the church by means of sacraments. Instead, while leadership structures do differ, the focus is on the assembling together of a people who have made a personal response of faith in Christ. In these models, Christ's presence is not mediated through a bishop in apostolic succession, but it is available to all through the finished work of Christ.

Specifically, within congregational models of polity, several iterations are seen in the modern era. Although two churches may affirm congregationalism, one might have a solo pastor and a board of deacons, while another might have a vocational pastor serving alongside a plurality of elders. In either one of these models, the congregation might have more or less say on different church matters. Some opt for votes on virtually every decision made in the church, others entrust certain decisions to committees, and still others give most of the decisions to the governing board. Megachurches and multisite churches also brought new questions to church polity. They focus more on business models and who makes decisions when a church claims to be one church but in multiple locations and, potentially, with different layers of leadership structures.

Finally, as it relates to polity, the modern era has witnessed numerous discussions pertaining to women serving in a church's senior leadership. Churches and denominations have discussed this at length, each falling into one of two camps: egalitarian (women can serve in any leadership role because God created them equal to men) or complementarian (men and women are equal in value and dignity but also created by God to fulfill different roles and functions). Although egalitarians and complementarians differ over this issue, there are ongoing discussions within the two camps themselves. For example, complementarians continue to discuss what kinds of classes a woman can teach within the church (such as middle and high school students); whether she can lead musical worship on a Sunday morning; or if it is permissible for a woman to preach on Sunday if done under the authority of church elders.

Case Study 2: The Ordinances of the Church

Another area of ecclesiological consideration in the modern era is the celebration of the ordinances or sacraments. The Roman Catholic view of baptism that held dominant in the medieval era was for infants a means of cleansing from original sin. As such, this sacrament held significance in that it was the starting point of the process of justification. Within the Reformation era, various views on baptism emerged, with varying versions of paedobaptism as well as the viewpoint of believer's baptism. In the modern era, with the exception of certain views (e.g., Quakers affirming Spirit baptism only, with no need for water baptism; World Council of Churches publishing the text *Baptism, Eucharist, and Ministry*, calling for unity wherever possible across denominational lines), the historic positions of Roman Catholics, Lutherans, the Reformed tradition, and Baptists still largely frame the discussion.

Rejecting the Roman Catholic view of baptismal regeneration, many Protestant denominations—including Lutherans, Presbyterians, Methodists, Episcopals, and Anglicans—continue to practice infant baptism. Some of these denominations affirm a more sacramental approach to baptism, while others believe in paedobaptism as a kind of dedication of the child to the Lord. Among those with Baptistic views, this practice is reserved for those who consciously understand and embrace the gospel, repent of their sins, and place their faith in Jesus as their Lord, Savior, and Treasure. These distinctives are historical and part of the confessional basis of each of the respective churches.

The Lord's Supper stands as the other sacrament/ordinance that is still practiced by churches. Once again, the Reformation questioned the belief of Roman Catholicism known as transubstantiation. Luther held to a view known as consubstantiation, and Calvin to a spiritual presence view, while Zwingli and later Baptists held to a memorial view of the Supper. These varying viewpoints are the typical starting points for discussion on the significance and meaning of this particular ordinance.

One detail that has been discussed in Baptist circles is the relationship between baptism and the Lord's Supper. Specifically, can one receive the Lord's Supper if they have not been baptized by immersion? As Landmarkism continued to gain traction in the nineteenth century, closed communion—the view restricting participation in the Lord's Supper to those who had been baptized by immersion—came to be more accepted. Paedobaptists were thus excluded, as were nonmembers. Other Baptist churches disagreed with such a view, some affirming participation by all who have been baptized by immersion (closed communion), and some welcoming all believers to join in celebrating the Lord's Supper regardless of baptismal status (open communion). Discussions of this kind, while still held in some circles, seem to be decreasing. Efforts within and outside of evangelicalism continue to be made in the modern era to focus on unity to minimize differences over the ordinances, opting for a more "mere ecclesiology."

Case Study 3: The Mission of the Church

The mission of the church also has received a great deal of attention in the last fifty years, with discussion focused on its responsibility within the world. Some recent pastor-theologians, such as Kevin DeYoung, Greg Gilbert, and Jonathan Leeman, want to emphasize the church's mission as making disciples of Jesus Christ, while also noting these disciples live and work as Christians, doing good deeds. Others, such as Christopher Wright, advocate for a fuller-orbed church mission that includes evangelism and disciple making, as well as caring for creation, social justice, and compassion.

Debate continues as people seek to understand the contours of the entire story line of Scripture and how to navigate the relationship of Israel and the church as well as the continuities and discontinuities that exist between the Old and New Testaments. Although the church can and should do good for all people, they should do so especially for "the household of faith" (Gal 6:10) while never forgetting that the central commission of the church is to make disciples of all nations (Matt 28:18–20).

Case Study 4: The Worship of the Church

One final area to explore is that of the worship of the church and how such worship is being contextualized in today's global church. Although *worship* can be used in a broad sense, we are thinking here of the corporate weekly gathering of believers to praise God and receive truth from his Word. Throughout the history of the church, this has been done in both liturgical and nonliturgical formats. Regardless, churches typically follow particular patterns as they engage in song, prayers, preaching, and the ordinances.

Early within the modern era many churches still approached worship from a high church perspective, incorporating liturgy that had been practiced for centuries (e.g., Roman Catholicism, Eastern Orthodoxy). The Anglican Church, largely influenced by Thomas Cranmer (1489–1556), initially had a similar liturgy to that of Roman Catholicism, while subsequent iterations began to speak to various elements of worship more generally. Lutheranism and the Reformed tradition held to their own forms of liturgy, each looking to particular books to guide them regarding the order and elements of services, whether the Book of Common Prayer or the Westminster Confession.

Protestant churches were thus historically focused on the worship of God by means of specific liturgy. In nineteenth-century America, however, a shift occurred within churches caught up in the Second Great Awakening, where the focus became evangelism and personal renewal. This mindset also contributed to the "altar call" becoming a predominant part of church services, where people were invited to repent and believe in Jesus. As such, an individualist mindset began to pervade churches. People seemingly looked more to their own personal need for conversion and growth in a moment at church service than to corporate conceptions of worship of God. This was also seen in the rise of Pentecostalism and the Charismatic movement. A conscious awareness of and sensitivity to the Holy Spirit was a key component to churches of this type, often paving the way for spontaneity in worship services as people expressed various gifts (e.g., tongues, prophecy) at various moments within the service. Freedom of expression was thus a key factor in such churches, even in mainline churches that practiced liturgical elements and wanted to embrace being open to the leading of the Spirit.

Although Roman Catholicism held to a particular liturgy for centuries, significant changes came about as a result of Vatican II. Catholic churches, for example, began to celebrate the Mass in native languages of the people as opposed to the traditional Latin. There was also an increase of Bible readings during a service, increased lay participation, and greater emphasis placed on the homily. Some saw this as tangible ways the Roman Catholic Church sought to engage with culture more effectively; others viewed the changes as a compromise, merely a means of modernizing the church in unnecessary and even dangerous ways.

In more recent years among evangelical circles, an increase in understanding worship as a lifestyle and a pointed emphasis on the role of music in worship has been evident. Modern authors such as Daniel Block, D. A. Carson, David Peterson, and Allen Ross have written extensively about worship as a response to our sovereign, covenant-keeping God in terms of personal fellowship and practical holiness in every sphere of life. These and other authors and preachers challenged the church to think in precise biblical and theological categories in relation to the worship of the church. Concurrently, in the late twentieth and early twenty-first century, contemporary Christian music was ushered into worship services, putting much of the emphasis on praising God through song. This led to what became known as the "worship wars," with traditional worship approaches vying against more contemporary forms. This has led to a rise in conversation among certain evangelical circles regarding whether churches should adhere to the normative principle (freedom to incorporate new worship elements if not prohibited by Scripture) or the regulative principle (elements of worship should only be comprised of that which is prescribed in Scripture).

This is one example of how churches must think about contextualization, a term for the process of making the gospel and the church as accommodating as possible in a given cultural context. Studies are demonstrating that the center of Christianity is moving away from the West to the global South and East. As one thinks of the gospel in varying global, cultural, and religious contexts, there has typically been a desire to avoid two extremes: colonialism and syncretism. The first tries to bring not only the gospel, but also particular cultural accoutrements to differing contexts as items that must be normative in church life. The latter seeks to accommodate existing cultural and religious beliefs and values, while bringing them into the same system as a new kind of amalgamation. Missiologists and theologians continue to think through these matters carefully for the sake of gospel fidelity in making disciples of all nations.

For the Church

Ecclesiology has often taken a back seat as a doctrine to theological topics such as the Trinity, atonement, and the person of Christ. This is understandable, but it does not render the doctrine as unimportant. The triune God by means of redemption is gathering a people dedicated to glorifying his name. And God has called these people to live as a kingdom of priests set apart for his purposes. As such, the more recent move toward a "mere ecclesiology" does not do justice to all that God wants the church to be. Instead, the church must hold to convictions in every doctrinal area, including the nature and functionality of the church.

Although the universal church certainly has a valid understanding of the term *church*, namely, believers across the world throughout history, the New Testament most often speaks of local churches, which are gatherings of believers to hear the Word preached and celebrate the ordinances, functioning as autonomous entities while also cooperating in ministry endeavors. This is true in the early church, as one can observe local churches being planted (Acts 2:42–47; 13:1–3; 14:21–27; 15:1–30; 16:5; 20:17, 28), as well as read the letters that were written to distinct local churches (Rom 1:7; 1 Cor 1:2; 5:1–13; Phil 1:1; Rev 2–3). Local churches should operate under the lordship of Christ (1 Pet 5:4), be led by qualified men (1 Tim 2:12–14) who work as pastors/elders (Acts 20:17–28; 1 Tim 3:1–7; Titus 1:5–9; 1 Pet 5:1–4), served by deacons (1 Tim 3:8–13), and governed by the congregation (Matt 18:15–20; Acts 15:1–30; 1 Cor 5:1–13). The church is on a mission to make disciples such that we will see followers of Jesus from every tribe, tongue, nation, and language (Rev 5:9–10).

In terms of the ordinances, debate has gone on for centuries, and there is no sign of abatement. Baptism, by its very meaning, is a symbolic act that should be done by immersion to signify our death to the old self and being raised to life with Jesus Christ (Rom 6:3–5; cf. John 3:23; Acts 8:35–39). Because this ordinance symbolizes salvation, it should be reserved for believers, as is the pattern in the New Testament (Acts 2:41–42; 16:30–33). Not only does it signify the beauty of conversion, but it is also the means by which someone enters into membership of a local church. This is crucial to mark out because a church *is* its membership.

Church membership is the reality of a people who gather regularly and are committed to overseeing and being overseen in their discipleship (Matt 16:16–19; Heb 3:12–13; 10:25–27). Church members in local churches regularly celebrate the Lord's Supper, doing so to remember and proclaim Christ's death and resurrection until he returns (1 Cor 11:23–29; cf. Matt 26:26–30). All views would agree that the Lord's Supper symbolizes this reality, but some go beyond the memorial view to articulate how it should be conceived beyond mere remembrance (e.g., consubstantiation, spiritual presence). Nevertheless, the focus of the church's preaching, worship, prayers, and celebration of the ordinances all comes back to a focus on the gospel. It reminds the people of their need for a Savior, pointing us toward repentance, building in us great joy as a result of God's grace.

A recent study shows that while there are gains in Western Christianity regarding the seriousness with which people take their faith and the means they will take to grow in godliness, the need they see for fellowship within a church context to grow as a disciple has decreased.[3] More people today than in previous years believe they can grow in godliness on their own without the assistance of others within the church. This can be discouraging news, but we also should not ignore what God is doing in and through the church throughout the world. It is likely that a robust view of our ecclesiology will further help all of us to see the beauty of Christ's bride and the need we have for one another as we continue to grow as his disciples.

For Further Reading

Ahlstrom, Sydney E. *A Religious History of the American People.* 2nd ed. New Haven, CT: Yale University Press, 2004.

Allison, Gregg. *Historical Theology: An Introduction to Christian Doctrine.* Grand Rapids: Zondervan, 2011.

Basden, Paul, and David S. Dockery. *The People of God: Essays on the Believer's Church.* Nashville: Broadman, 1991.

Chute, Anthony L., Nathan A. Finn, and Michael A. G. Haykin, *The Baptist Story: From English Sect to Global Movement.* Nashville: B&H Academic, 2015.

Dever, Mark. *Polity: Biblical Arguments on How to Conduct Church Life.* Washington, DC: 9Marks Ministries, 2001.

[3] Megan Fowler, "In Christ, Alone: Most Believers Say They Don't Need Others for Discipleship," *Christianity Today*, August 22, 2019.

Jenkins, Philip. *The Next Christendom: The Coming of Global Christianity.* Oxford: Oxford University Press 2001.

Kärkkäinen, Veli-Matti. "Ecclesiology." In *Mapping Modern Theology: A Thematic and Historical Introduction*, edited by Kelly M. Kapic and Bruce L. McCormick, 345–75. Grand Rapids: Baker Academic, 2012.

McGrath, Alister. *Historical Theology: An Introduction to the History of Christian Thought.* Malden, MA: Blackwell, 1998.

Questions for Study or Discussion

1. Does the doctrine of the church receive less attention than other Christian doctrines? If so, why do you think that is? Why should we as Christians think more intently about ecclesiology?
2. Within the history of the church, doctrinal fidelity and a call for unity across denominations have been two constant themes. How do we faithfully work for unity but maintain convictions regarding ecclesial matters?
3. What is the mission of the church? How is this being worked out in your local church? What could change? What more could be done?
4. What is the role of the ordinances in the local church? What are we celebrating? Why should we observe these ordinances within a local church?
5. How do different parachurch organizations (e.g., Cru, T4G, TGC, a Christian university or seminary) relate to the local church? What is their value? What can they not do that only the local church can do?

16

ESCHATOLOGY

By Malcolm B. Yarnell III

Eschatology literally means "the doctrine of the last." In the modern era, however, eschatology has become known as the doctrine of "last things." This is unfortunate, for Scripture never uses that terminology. Scripture speaks rather of God or Christ as the One who is "the last" (Hebrew *'acharon*; Greek *eschatos*), just as he is also "the first" (Isa 44:6; 48:12; Rev 1:17; 2:8; 22:13.) With a similar focus on God in Christ, the New Testament refers to the "last day" or "last days" as beginning with the first coming of Jesus Christ (Acts 2:17; 2 Tim 3:1; Heb 1:2; Jas 5:3) and concluding with Christ's resurrection of the dead and final judgment of unbelievers and scoffers (John 6:39–40, 44, 54; 11:24; 12:48; 1 Pet 1:5, 20; 2 Pet 3:3; Jude 18). As we shall see, the shift from an emphasis on God in Christ to an emphasis on the things of this world has resulted in significant controversy regarding the order of events that accompany Christ's second coming.

Historical Overview with Case Studies

Eschatology has become a subject of intense interest to modern Christians across the theological spectrum, from liberal to conservative. This intensity has manifested itself in various controversies, some of which have detracted from the primary aspects of eschatology. Nevertheless, eschatology is not the preserve of modernity but can be found throughout Christian history. One may find important eschatological themes within the writings of the early church fathers, within the ruminations of the medieval theologians, and within the Reformation.

Tertullian, a theologian in ancient Carthage, taught a form of premillennialism, the belief that Christ would return before establishing his reign over the earth for 1,000 years. During the high Middle Ages, Joachim of Fiore arranged world history in an eschatological way. His followers, such as the Spiritual Franciscans, developed speculative themes on the basis of Joachim's teaching that the Old Testament was the age of the Father, that the New Testament began the age of the Son, and that a coming age of the Spirit would be characterized by monastic triumph. Martin Luther published an early Wycliffite work on eschatology and personally concluded the papacy was Antichrist. Eschatology helped Luther visualize the church as requiring a thorough reformation. Although earlier eschatological movements are worthy of consideration, we must focus on the modern period.

Primary Eschatology and Debated Eschatology

The modern doctrine of "the Last" may be classified according to various essential doctrines as well as various debated doctrines that have occasioned controversy in recent centuries. Some doctrines of eschatology may be considered primary or essential or necessary, while other teachings within eschatology have generated vigorous disagreement within contemporary Protestant evangelicalism. Those doctrines of eschatology that may be considered primary include the person of Jesus Christ as "the Last," death, the bodily resurrection, the second coming of Jesus Christ, the final judgment, eternal life, eternal condemnation, universal renewal, and the beatific vision of God the Trinity. The doctrines within the field of eschatology that have offered grounds for dispute include, especially, the timing of the millennial reign of Christ and the timing of the Great Tribulation. There have also been disputes about the intermediate state, the meanings of hell, and the end of the world.

I have classified the doctrines of the Last according to these two categories, primary eschatology and debated eschatology, to highlight the general range of agreement and disagreement among evangelical Protestants. Unlike the evangelicals, however, liberal Protestants called into question most of the primary doctrines of eschatology. More recently, however, mainline theologians have recovered orthodox eschatology while dwelling on a theology of hope that makes much of Christ and the Trinity. To understand where eschatology is today, however, we must recall the backdrop provided by the Protestant Reformation.

The Reformation Diminution of Eschatology

The development of eschatology among modern Protestant theologians must take into account that it was downplayed to a great extent after the initial excitement that accompanied the genesis of the Reformation. For instance, the leading second-generation Reformer, John Calvin, only cursorily treated the doctrine within his highly influential *Institutes of the Christian Religion*. Calvin included a chapter on eschatology titled "Meditation on the Future Life" in book 3 of that influential work. However, it was a very short chapter and was primarily concerned with advancing the individual's thoughtful existence within contemporary life. Although Calvin famously issued extensive commentaries on nearly every book of the Bible, the Apocalypse of John is notable in its absence from his published body of works.

The diminishing of eschatology among orthodox Protestant scholars arose due to concerns about significant eschatological errors manifested among both Roman Catholics and Anabaptists. To the right of the Reformers, the medieval church had developed a whole economy of priesthood and sacrament centered on the idea that the Mass and good works helped to alleviate the suffering of Christians in purgatory. The core Protestant belief that one is justified by faith alone negated this medieval economy of sacerdotal salvation. The very fabric of Christian worship was upended as the Reformers rejected purgatory, the eschatological place where, following death and before entering heaven, Christians must atone for certain sins.

To the left of the magisterial Reformers, the Anabaptist teacher Melchior Hoffmann convinced many of his followers that the kingdom of God would be established in 1533. Jan Matthys recalculated the date as 1534. Matthys invited the Anabaptists, who were exploding in number but suffering persecution, to join him in taking over the German city of Münster. The polygamy, barbarity, and ultimate overthrow of the Kingdom of Münster under Jan of Leiden, the successor of Matthys, ensured that millennial enthusiasm would leave a bad taste in the mouth of every respectable theologian, whether Roman Catholic or Protestant, for at least a century. The confessions of the mainline Protestant churches still reflect a bias against Roman Catholic purgative eschatology and Anabaptist millennial eschatology.

Among the Lutherans, the Augsburg Confession condemned purgatory as an extrabiblical innovation, defined annihilationism as an Anabaptist peculiarity, and rejected eschatological "Chiliasm" (i.e., millennialism) as a product of Judaism (article 17). Among the Reformed, similar eschatological definitions appeared in their major confessions. The highly influential Second Helvetic Confession, for example, censured millennialism as "Jewish dreams that there will be a golden age on earth before the Day of Judgment, and that the pious, having subdued all their godless enemies, will possess all the kingdoms of the earth" (article 11). The Forty-Two Articles of the Church of England dismissed the millennium as a "fable of heretics." Scholastic Protestant systematic theologies continued to treat the doctrine of "Last Things," but it was reduced to a series of basic facts that should not elicit undue passion. Eschatology was, therefore, basically confined to four subjects: death, judgment, heaven, and hell.

Signs of an Early Modern Recovery of Futurist Eschatology

In spite of the confessional and systematic diminution of eschatology, there were signs at the popular level of continuing concern for the biblical picture of the future. For example, the wildly popular Geneva Bible contained numerous footnotes that reinforced a futurist and literalist historical reading of eschatological passages such as Romans 11. Moreover, some Reformed theologians, such as James Ussher of Armagh (1581–1656) and Johannes Cocceius of Bremen (1603–1669), argued that the millennia of Revelation 20 should be taken literally. Cocceius opposed the rigid confessionalism of the Voetian school of Calvinists in the Netherlands. Remaining orthodox Calvinists, Cocceians also embraced a philological study of the Bible and respected the historical development of doctrine. Coccieus, an expert in Hebrew and the classics, proposed a seven-tier eschatological scheme for salvation history.

There were positive and negative aspects to the recovery of eschatology in the British Isles. In the late seventeenth century, both independent and Baptist theologians, among others, concerned themselves with eschatology. In a positive vein, they advocated respect for the Jewish people as future Christians, and they encouraged Oliver Cromwell to invite their return to England. In a negative vein, the Fifth Monarchists in London believed they could welcome the kingdom through force of arms. Most of the independent and Baptist congregations separated themselves from the leaders of that eschatological revolutionary movement.

After the restoration of the British monarchy, the leading eighteenth-century Baptist theologian John Gill (1697–1771) encouraged Baptists and evangelicals in general to recover a more detailed eschatology. Gill has been labeled a High Calvinist, but he diverged from Calvin's legacy of diminished eschatology. Unlike Calvin, Gill wrote a commentary on the book of Revelation. And unlike many Calvinist theologians, Gill included a fairly comprehensive eschatology in his systematic theology. For example, in the seventh, final, and lengthy book of his *Body of Doctrinal Divinity*, Gill affirmed that "Christ will have a special, peculiar, glorious, and visible kingdom, in which he will reign personally on earth." This personal reign of Christ will be "with the saints" and for "a thousand years." Gill's recovery of a robust eschatology foreshadowed an eschatological renaissance. Gill did not remain alone, for Jonathan Edwards added his influential voice (see Case Study 1).

Case Study 1: Jonathan Edwards

The American theologian Jonathan Edwards (1703–1758) was instrumental in the development of the "Great Awakening" that shaped England and its American colonies. The Awakening was initiated in some sense through the literalist preaching of Edwards on the doctrine of hell in his famous 1841 sermon "Sinners in the Hands of an Angry God." Hell, for Edwards, was a necessary result of moral justice and represented his studied rejection of the moral optimism of the Enlightenment. Nevertheless, while warnings regarding the eternality of hell were an important part of his teaching, this was only one aspect of a monumental eschatology that included a postmillennial outlook.

The only biblical book for which Edwards left a full commentary was the Apocalypse of John. Edwards believed there would be an approximately 150-year process in which first Protestantism, second Rome, and third Islam would be won through great difficulty to Christ. After the theistic religions, the numerous heathens around the world would embrace the faith over the next century. After this approximately 250-year period, Christ would establish his spiritual reign on the earth for 1,000 years. Edwards argued the millennium constituted the third coming of Christ, a spiritual one. The

Lord's first coming had been at his birth, while his second coming occurred with the conversion of the Roman Empire. Edwards believed Christ's fourth coming, a physical one, would occur after a short rebellion by Satan had concluded the millennium. Then would follow the final judgment and either eternal life or eternal punishment.

Three Eschatological Tendencies within Protestant Liberalism

Protestant liberalism, which was prominent in the eighteenth and nineteenth centuries but continued well into the twentieth century, was marked by three tendencies in its own eschatology, which diverged from the Reformation's basic eschatology. Some liberals pursued an internal eschatology, while other liberals pursued a cultural eschatology; still others dismissed eschatology altogether. Initiating the first tendency, Friedrich Schleiermacher (1768–1834), the father of modern theological liberalism, radicalized orthodox Pietism's interiorizing treatment of end things by reducing eschatology to a process of personal and communal spiritual growth. Liberal eschatology could, therefore, move in an entirely internal direction.

In a second tendency, the German philosopher Georg Wilhelm Friedrich Hegel (1770–1831) developed an influential view of history that perceived human civilization as progressing through a historical dialectic of various cultures. Within Protestant liberalism, historicism thus issued forth in a concern for matching the Bible's message with *Heilsgeschichte*, the history of human salvation. Enlightenment philosophy and theology, moreover, became generally optimistic about the future progress of enlightened humanity. Following Hegel, many German philosophers and theologians traced the progress of humanity through various societies to its height in modern German culture.

In a third tendency, many Protestant liberals also became quite pessimistic regarding the credal dogmas of Christianity. Adolf von Harnack

(1851–1930) derided the traditional doctrinal focus on the deity and humanity of Jesus Christ as a Hellenistic innovation. Christianity, according to Harnack, is not about the God-man dying on the cross for the sins of humanity, arising from the dead, and ascending to the right hand of the Father, from whence he will return to judge the living and the dead. Rather, Harnack believed that the essence of Jesus's message was that God is the Father of all, all human beings are brothers, and we must love one another. The kingdom of God comes as human beings pursue love.

Among the last of the great liberal theologians, Ernst Troeltsch (1865–1923) dismissed the traditional Protestant treatment of last things, including the doctrines of death, resurrection, and the final judgment. Harnack and Troeltsch were instrumental in convincing many liberal Protestants to eject orthodox Christology and eschatology as irrelevant. Moreover, higher critical Bible scholars lent their support to this third direction within Protestant liberalism.

The Destructive Legacy of Historical Criticism

Some modern biblical scholars have been deeply affected by higher critical methods of Bible study. New Testament academics, for instance, have pursued various "quests" for the historical Jesus. These quests typically assumed the "Jesus of history" is not the same person as the "Christ of faith," for the New Testament documents were deemed neither contemporary with Jesus nor entirely reliable. Higher criticism thus undermined not only biblical eschatology but Christianity itself.

The New Testament had made much of the Old Testament prophecies that a descendant of David would come to establish an eternal kingdom on the earth (2 Sam 7:12–16; cf. Matt 1:1; Rom 1:3). Jesus and the apostolic writers also emphasized the ancient prophets' description of a "son of man" coming to the divine throne and being given the kingdom by God (Daniel 7; cf. Matt 25:31–32). Jesus argued prominently that David himself spoke of the Messiah as one who would sit on the throne of God (Psalms 110; cf. Mark 12:35–37). However, biblical critics in the modern period torpedoed the New Testament's claims that such prophecies regarding the Messiah and the "kingdom of God" were fulfilled historically and eschatologically in the person and ministry of Jesus Christ.

Immanuel Kant (1704–1824) prepared the way for a critical reevaluation of the eschatology of Jesus by calling for a rationally moral rather than a literally historical kingdom of God. In his *Religion within the Limits of Reason Alone* (1793), Kant argued that the kingdom should not be expected from above but pursued by human beings from below as they construct an ameliorating society. Following Kant, one of the first and most influential critics was David Friedrich Strauss (1808–1874). Strauss's *The Life of Jesus* (1835) distinguished between strict history and religious myth. Myth can be taken in either a positive sense as helpful poetic truth or a negative sense as an untrue story. Strauss and subsequent Protestant scholars replaced the eschatology that the New Testament ascribed to Jesus with a platitudinous desire for a liberated humanity. Protestant liberalism thus settled for a Jesus without a literal eschatology.

In his famous work, *Quest for the Historical Jesus* (1906), Albert Schweitzer (1875–1965) in turn undermined the liberal project by reminding his readers that Jesus really did believe in the imminent coming of the kingdom of God (see case study). The second quest for the historical Jesus began with the work of the leading New Testament theologian, Rudolf Bultmann (1884–1976). Bultmann and his school replaced eschatology, not with moralism but with existentialism. The historical, social, and ethical aspects of the expected kingdom of God were all downplayed, and a personal encounter with a Jesus acceptable to the modern moralistic academic was elevated. In the recent third quest for the historical Jesus, scholars such as Marcus Borg (1942–2015) have replaced the judgmental eschatology of the Jesus of the Gospels with the select words of a gentle sage who does not demand repentance.

Case Study 2: Albert Schweitzer

Albert Schweitzer (1875–1965) represents the culmination of the Protestant liberal eschatological tradition. Schweitzer brought together all three of the liberal eschatological tendencies as well as the historical-critical method in his own works on eschatology and in the ethical virtues he intentionally cultivated in his life. His life and thought were characterized by tension—between eschatology and ethics, philosophy and missions, academy and religion. An Alsatian, Schweitzer was simultaneously and precariously French and German during both murderous world wars. Appointed to his great work by the Paris Missionary Society, he nonetheless wrote theology and philosophy in German. He was subsequently honored with the 1952 Nobel Peace Prize and was universally feted for his lifelong medical career as a missionary in Africa.

Schweitzer's theological development began, continued, and ended with influential books on New Testament eschatology. His idiosyncratic *Quest for the Historical Jesus* furthered the historical-critical method even while it paradoxically contradicted the first quest's conclusions. Against his own liberal tradition, he concluded that Jesus truly believed the kingdom of God would come with his death. He said that Jesus erred historically in his eschatology, yet his ethics have remained true. Major writings on Jesus, Paul, and the apostolic fathers advanced his thesis that eschatology was central to early Christianity.

Advancing the first tendency in liberal theology, Schweitzer appealed to the encounter of "the inner person" (*Lebensanschauung*) with Christ as the locus for action. Incorporating the second tendency in liberal theology, Schweitzer also developed a worldview (*Weltanschauung*) characterized by a "reverence for life" rooted in Jesus's own call for personal love. Finally, he also maintained the third tendency within liberal theology by downplaying the central doctrines of the Trinity and Christology, remaining personally agnostic about the resurrection. Although Karl Barth (1886–1968) built his own career on a thorough critique of Protestant liberalism, the leading systematic theologian of the twentieth century admitted in his final university lecture that Schweitzer's theology was wrong, but his life was right.

Mainline Contributions to the Revival of Eschatology

The early and mid-twentieth century saw a debate among mainline theologians who were recovering eschatology from its liberal dilution. One group of theologians emphasized the fundamental difference between time and eternity; a second group emphasized realized eschatology; and a third focused on a futurist interpretation of the eschatological texts of Scripture.

First, various forms of "dialectical eschatology" were advocated by German-speaking theologians such as Rudolf Karl Bultmann (1884–1986), Paul Tillich (1886–1965), and the early Karl Barth, as expressed in his commentary on Romans (1st ed., 1919). Although dialectical theologians might vaguely mention the temporal terminals of the passion of Christ in the past and the parousia of Christ in the future, they dwelt on the transcendence of God versus the existence of humanity. Rudolf Bultmann made the sharpest separation between eternity and time, resulting in the trading of historical eschatology for a timeless experience of crisis. The reality of eternity existentially encounters the human being looking for God. Paul Tillich held to a milder form of this view, picturing Christ as the center of history. The full realization of the kingdom of Christ in history will bring timeless reality into history itself, but for now we live in an oscillation between the "already" and "not yet."

Second, the Welsh theologian Charles Harold Dodd (1884–1974) extended his well-received research on the development of the Christian *kerygma* toward a more controversial "realized eschatology." Relying on a form-critical dismissal of various statements within the Gospels, Dodd interpreted the New Testament statement with regard to the kingdom of God as having already occurred. Dodd argued that Jesus taught that "the kingdom has arrived" in its fullness. Any statements regarding the future of the kingdom were negated by Dodd as due to the early church's misapprehension.

Some have concluded that this innovative reading was nonetheless a denial of eschatology itself, because there was no longer any tension between the "already" and "not yet" aspects of the New Testament teaching.

Third, "futuristic eschatology" received a scholarly boost in the writings of Oscar Cullmann (1902–1999). If Bultmann qualitatively divided eternity from time, then Cullmann defined eternity as merely the extension of time. "Eternity," he said, "is the endless succession of the ages." The basic concern of Christian eschatology is with the passing away of the "present age" and the arrival of the "coming age." The parousia, or second coming, of Jesus Christ is the climax of the New Testament view of history. The later Karl Barth moved in the direction of Cullmann's historical understanding of eschatology as culminating in the real return of Jesus to raise humanity and judge them. Assisted by these three searching investigations of the biblical data, mainline scholars pointed toward a revival of biblical eschatology.

The Origin of Modern Millennialism

Although the recovery of eschatology among mainline Protestants came to the fore in the early twentieth century, the recovery of eschatology among evangelical Protestants had already begun in the mid-nineteenth century with a fringe group in England. Through the talented advocacy of itinerant ministers, publishers, and illustrators, this fringe eschatology subsequently became part and parcel of conservative evangelicalism around the world. Indeed, by the middle of the twentieth century, large swaths of evangelicalism considered a certain type of premillennial eschatology definitive for orthodoxy. Evangelical millennialism is widely embraced today, but in permutating forms.

Critical historians have identified the dynamic preaching and biblical ruminations of the controversial Scottish minister Edward Irving (1792–1834) not only as influential for Pentecostalism but also as the historical root of premillennial dispensationalism (see Case Study 3 below). Irving led a group that met at Albury Park in Surrey, England, between 1826 and

1830 to reconsider biblical prophecy. The mature convictions of that group gained a wide readership through Irving's fame and their popular journal, *The Morning Watch*. Irving was subsequently accused of Christological heresy, but that claim has been deemed overwrought.

Dissatisfied with the state of the churches of his day, Irving and the Albury circle began to read the eschatological portions of Scripture anew. They sensed the futuristic prophecies of Scripture were moving toward fulfillment. One of their most important conclusions was that Scripture showed God working differently with Israel than with the church. The Jews failed to receive Christ when he first came, so the kingdom was temporarily denied to Israel. The church, alas, with the advent of the papacy also failed. In spite of the Reformation, the contemporary churches were deemed largely apostate, especially after the French Revolution. God was preparing to have the seventh trumpet blown to bring in the kingdom.

Although the Albury circle did not use the language of "rapture," they did develop the concept of a pretribulation "translation," whereby true Christians would be removed from the coming great tribulation. Irving elaborated on "our unspeakable comfort" before his rapt audience. Unlike the fallen churches, true believers have "a promise of escape out of the awful judgment with which the Gentile church is to be consumed."[1] The Albury theologians believed that the approaching translation would be the next part of the divine plan to be fulfilled and that it would occur without warning.

Compelled by an ecclesiology of disillusionment, the Albury hermeneutic was characterized by a literal, historical, and futurist reading of biblical prophecy. They made a differentiation between the church and Israel, forecast the return of the Jews to Palestine under the Messiah, and perceived a pretribulation rapture before the return of Christ. The Albury hermeneutic was influential on a number of people similarly dissatisfied with the state of the existing churches, whether established or dissenting churches. One

[1] Edward Irving, "Signs of the Times in the Church," *Morning Watch* 2 (1830): 156.

Albury devotee was Theodosia, Lady Powerscourt, who organized a series of prophecy conferences in Dublin beginning in 1831. John Nelson Darby's (1800–1882) regular participation in these conferences developed into one of the first Brethren congregations by 1833.

Case Study 3: Three Classic Dispensationalists

John Nelson Darby, Cyrus Ingerson Scofield (1843–1921), and Clarence Larkin (1850–1924) were three of the earliest and most influential premillennial dispensationalists. Their teachings are still revered today among dispensationalists. As a vocational lawyer, Darby lacked theological education, but this did not keep him from exercising great influence wherever he ministered. He has often been identified as the founder of dispensationalism. His eschatology paralleled that of the Albury circle, but he modified it within his own comprehensive system of dispensations. Through an itinerant ministry that took him to Germany, Switzerland, and Italy beginning in the 1850s and stretching through the 1870s to include New Zealand, Canada, and the United States, he had a profound impact on the subsequent development of evangelical eschatology.

Although Darby disseminated classic dispensationalism through itineracy, C. I. Scofield deepened it dogmatically through his study Bible. There is no record of Scofield's education, but after a stint in the Confederate Army, he worked in law and politics. Although he suppressed information regarding his early life, it appears he was an alcoholic. He abandoned his first wife and children but remarried after a conversion experience in 1879 under the ministry of a Presbyterian leader of the fundamentalist and dispensationalist Niagara Bible Conference movement. He became a prominent defender of premillennial dispensationalism following the 1888 publication of *Rightly Dividing the Word of Truth*. Although serving as a pastor and Bible teacher at various churches and parachurch organizations in Texas, Massachusetts, New York, and Pennsylvania, Scofield continued to edit his personal notes on Scripture. The *Scofield Reference Bible*, first published by

Oxford University Press in 1909, became the doctrinal benchmark for the dispensational movement. Nevertheless, critics noted a recurrent tendency for adherents to grant Scofield's notes an authority best reserved for the canonical text alone.

If Darby was the evangelist of dispensationalism and Scofield provided its dogmatic standard, Clarence Larkin adorned dispensationalism with an attractive visual system. At first, Larkin worked in banking and pursued a college degree in mechanical engineering. He then served as a professional draftsman and teacher of the blind before his conversion in 1882 as an Episcopalian. After studying baptism for two years, he became a Baptist and was soon ordained. He served for decades as a pastor in Pennsylvania churches. He then studied dispensationalism and prepared colored wall charts to help his congregation envision the divine plan. Collecting these charts into a book, the first and second printings of his *Dispensational Truth: God's Plan and Purpose in the Ages* sold quickly. Describing that first experiment as a "feeler," he expanded the charts and completed a third and final edition for publication in 1920. Larkin's charts appealed to the modern layman's eye in ways a medieval layperson might appreciate, except perhaps for its mathematical and mechanical approach.

Premillennial Dispensationalism

There are various types of premillennial dispensationalism, but what unites them all is the maintenance of a strong distinction between national Israel and the church. There are three major forms, the earliest of which is "classic dispensationalism" and is our primary concern here. The classical form was altered by Charles Caldwell Ryrie (1925–2016) in the mid-twentieth century and has become known as "revised dispensationalism." "Progressive dispensationalism" is the latest major variant and received its programmatic statement in a book with that title written by two Dallas Theological Seminary professors, Darrell Bock and Craig Blaising. Later forms of dispensationalism retain the necessity of incorporating God's promises to national Israel in eschatology. They also retain the rapture as an invisible coming of Jesus Christ for his church before the great tribulation, although some now believe the rapture will not occur until the second half of the great tribulation begins. The second half of the great tribulation contains the most intense period of divine judgment on the earth. The later forms also intentionally reconnect dispensationalism with orthodox Christian dogma and method.

In explicit reaction against the higher critical method, dispensationalism advocates the utter truthfulness of the Bible. The Bible, as the true Word of God, must be interpreted through a hermeneutic of literalism, but recourse is also had to the illumination of the Spirit on the modern theologian's mind. With utmost epistemological confidence, Clarence Larkin replaced "the opinions of men" with what he claimed was "the teaching of the Word of God." Although denying he was infallible, Larkin nonetheless described an exultant process wherein his theology was "thought out and developed under the direction and guidance of the Holy Spirit." Recognizing that the Bible contains "figurative, symbolic, and literal" language, he still considered the latter typical and normative. Dispensationalists decry various attempts to spiritualize away the historical promises to the nation of Israel.

Adopting modernism's self-assured certainty, Larkin argued that "the Bible is to be interpreted according to the customary rules of grammar and rhetoric. That is, we are to read the Bible as we would any other book, letting it say what it wants to say, and not allegorize or spiritualize its meaning." Larkin deemed his first chart particularly trustworthy due to its having been tested by the application of the experimental method to his own spiritual experience of "literal" readings of the Bible.[2] In that first chart, Larkin compared the relationship of the biblical ages as construed from various intellectual standpoints. The Jewish standpoint and the postmillennial standpoint are merely developmental precursors to what "Pre-Millennialists

[2] Clarence Larkin, *Dispensational Truth, or God's Plan and Purpose in the Ages*, enlarged and rev. ed. (Glenside, PA: Larkin, 1918), preface and chap. 1.

See" now. Indeed, the premillennial dispensationalist standpoint is exactly "As God Sees," except that God views the matter from the perspective of the "Ages of the Ages."[3]

Dispensationalism identifies each dispensation in the divine economy with particular portions of Scripture. God is said to deal with people in different ways within each dispensation. The dispensations are often correlated with covenants and are divided into innocence (Genesis 1–2), conscience (Genesis 3–8), civil government (Genesis 9–11), promise (Genesis 12–Exodus 18), law (Exodus 19–Acts 1), grace (Acts 2–Revelation 19), and the millennial kingdom (Revelation 20). The Jews failed to fulfill the law. Moreover, when Christ Jesus came to redeem them and establish his kingdom, they rejected him. Therefore, God chose to establish the church as an interim institution before Christ comes again. The church age is a parenthesis in the divine plan for the world. Christ will come secretly to remove the church from the world before the great tribulation. Israel will be purified and come to faith during that tribulation. After this tribulation, Christ will return visibly to rule for a literal 1,000 years.

Other Forms of Modern Millennialism

Although dispensationalism remains a major proponent of millennial eschatology, three other influential versions of millennialism have vied for modern acceptance. In the early Middle Ages, premillennialism went into severe decline after Augustine of Hippo (354–430) set forth his understanding of future history. Augustine's view has become known as "amillennialism." For Augustine, the first resurrection of Revelation 20 occurs with one's baptism and regeneration. This indeterminate millennium is manifest in the church today. Augustine's view of the millennium dominated medieval and Reformation theological systems. Many evangelical theologians, especially

---

[3] Larkin, "The 'Ages' as Viewed from Different Standpoints" (chart) in *Dispensational Truth*, 3½.

among the Reformed, still embrace amillennialism. Although Augustine spiritualized the millennium, he taught a future bodily resurrection, an intermediate state for the dead, a future physical return of Christ, a future universal judgment, and either eternal heaven for believers or eternal punishment for unbelievers.

A third major view of the millennium held sway within American evangelicalism until the first world war dampened previously high expectations for the progress of Christian culture. "Postmillennialists" followed Jonathan Edwards in forecasting an advance in the Christian mission among unbelievers around the world. The hope of witnessing the coming of Christ as the nations turn to faith gave postmillennialist evangelicals a strong incentive to support or to engage in missionary endeavors. Although it is no longer a popular position and is somewhat difficult to support exegetically, there continue to be advocates of the postmillennial position.

A fourth major view of the millennium came into prominence with the work of George Eldon Ladd. A large contingent of evangelical scholars now concur with Ladd's millennial position, which is technically known as "historic premillennialism." Taking into account the biblical context for terms such as *parousia*, *apokalypsis*, and *epiphaneia*, Ladd placed the second coming of Christ after the great tribulation but before the millennium. His millennial position was buttressed by an argument for a comprehensive "inaugurated eschatology" that accounted for the sayings of Jesus, noting that the Lord gave evidence for the contemporary existence of the kingdom as well as its future fulfillment (see Case Study 4 below).

Case Study 4: George Eldon Ladd

George Eldon Ladd (1911–1982) was without doubt the most important evangelical theologian writing on eschatology in the twentieth century. Born a Canadian, he grew up in poverty and abuse by his father in New England. His difficult childhood prompted a lifelong sense of inadequacy. After an evangelical conversion and unaccredited education at Gordon-Conwell

Theological Seminary, he served as an American Baptist pastor. Nevertheless, Ladd also earned a PhD at Harvard University for a critical dissertation on early Christian eschatology. He was elected professor of New Testament at the new Fuller Theological Seminary in 1950, serving there until his retirement in 1982. Ladd's evangelical faith and higher critical education coupled with his yearning character generated a desire to convince the academy that the evangelical faith was intellectually defensible.

His first major book, *Jesus and the Kingdom*, took him ten years to write. Although published by a liberal press, a single negative review by Norman Perrin of the University of Chicago drove him into unremitting depression. Although unable to earn "a place at the table" in the liberal academy, Ladd had a profound impact on evangelical scholarship, particularly in its eschatology. An unquestioning adherence to dispensationalism was previously required among American fundamentalists, but Ladd's works led to the academic humbling of that dominance.

Alongside his popular general work *A Theology of the New Testament*, which itself had an eschatological frame, Ladd's writings were largely devoted to eschatology. In *Jesus and the Kingdom*, Ladd followed a hermeneutic of "biblical realism." Employing the best tools of modern biblical scholarship according to his evangelical convictions, he concluded that the tired battle between realized eschatology and radical futurism was misplaced. In his earthly ministry, Jesus had inaugurated his reign, but it awaited his second coming for fulfillment. Alongside his overarching "inaugurated eschatology," he dismantled the pretribulation rapture from a biblical perspective. Ladd's book *The Blessed Hope* and his contribution to a four-views book on the millennium established "historic premillennialism," that Christ will return after the great tribulation to bring in a literal 1,000-year reign.

Although Ladd has been credited with singlehandedly turning the tide against dispensationalist dominance, his failure to reach the broader academy fed his depression. Alas, a failing marriage and a struggle with alcoholism marred his later life. However, his own words demonstrate he was not without hope. He understood the "gospel of the kingdom" as the "good news" that "death has been defeated; our conqueror has been conquered. In the face of the power of the kingdom of God in Christ, death was helpless."[4] Many evangelicals, including the present writer, have been aided by Ladd's biblicist evangelical eschatology even as his life proved the danger of undue fascination with academic acceptance.

Positive Developments in Contemporary Eschatology

Although George Eldon Ladd was leading evangelicals to wield critical tools to deepen their eschatology, a number of mainline theologians were employing orthodox eschatological categories to resurrect liberal theology. Protestant evangelicalism and Protestant liberalism have thus been drawn closer together as both seek to foster an eschatological renewal. The recovery of a concern for the future in the present should be seen as a positive development for the entire Christian tradition.

Karl Barth's new Protestant orthodoxy has been met with profound appreciation by many mainline theologians. Gerhard Sauter (1935–), himself a major contributor to a renewal of eschatology, recently lauded Barth for calling Christian theologians to bring eschatology along with Trinity and Christology back to the center of theology. Barth argued, "A Christianity that is not wholly and utterly and irreducibly eschatology has absolutely nothing to do with Christ" (*Church Dogmatics*, 2/1, 634–35). Sauter, along with fellow Lutheran Wolfhart Pannenberg (1928–2014) and the Roman Catholic Johannes Baptist Metz (1928–2019), have been instrumental in creating what Douglas Meeks calls "a new eschatological mode of theology." The towering figure of Jürgen Moltmann (1926–), who is by far the most well-known person in the movement, should not be seen as standing alone (see Case Study 5 below). For example, Pannenberg's eschatology, expressed through his influential works on history, Christology, and systematic

---

[4] George Eldon Ladd, *The Gospel of the Kingdom: Scriptural Studies in the Kingdom of God* (Grand Rapids: Eerdmans, 1959), 128.

theology, has been instrumental in reconnecting "the Jesus of history" with "the Christ of faith."

Both Sauter at the University of Bonn and Adrio König (1936–) at the University of South Africa have called for the recovery of a Christological center in eschatology. Sauter laments that "strangely, the Christ predicate *eschatos* is rarely taken into account sufficiently. Jesus Christ announced himself as 'the first and the last [*eschatos*], and the living one' [Rev 1:17–18]. The *eschatos* is 'the coming one,' the Messiah."[5] The reconnection of eschatology to the center of the Christian faith received a boost when Hans Boersma's *Seeing God: The Beatific Vision in Christian Tradition* received the 2019 *Christianity Today* Book Award in Theology. Boersma (1961–), who teaches at a mainline Anglo-Catholic school, thus garnered evangelicalism's acclaim for demonstrating that the primary concern in Christian eschatology should be returned to the Christian tradition's vitalizing conclusion that "seeing God is the purpose of our life."[6]

Case Study 5: Jürgen Moltmann

Jürgen Moltmann (b. 1926) is one of the most respected theologians living today. He was converted when held as a German prisoner of war and suffering the trauma of defeat and the witness of death. Handed a Bible by a chaplain, he read in Psalm 139, "If I make my bed in hell, you are there." He ascribed to this unexpected personal encounter with God, when he was at his lowest, "the power of hope to which I owed my life."[7] The author of a dozen major texts and a multitude of minor ones, his first book,

---

[5] Gerhard Sauter, "Protestant Theology," in *The Oxford Handbook of Eschatology*, ed. Jerry L. Walls (New York: Oxford University Press, 2008), 258. Cf. Adrio König, *The Eclipse of Christ in Eschatology: Toward a Christ-Centered Approach* (Grand Rapids: Eerdmans, 1989).

[6] Hans Boersma, *Seeing God: The Beatific Vision in Christian Tradition* (Grand Rapids: Eerdmans, 2018), 1.

[7] Jürgen Moltmann, *History of the Triune God* (London: SCM, 1991), 166.

Theology of Hope (1967), is a widely recognized eschatological masterpiece. (Although Moltmann's writings on eschatology have garnered appreciation, his writings on divine passibility, panentheism, and the social Trinity have occasioned rebuttal.)

Moltmann interacted with Christian and Jewish writers to construct a dynamic picture of God, not as "One who was, who is, and who will be," but as "One who is, who was, and who is to come" (Rev 1:8). Moltmann's careful historical reading of Revelation prompted him to reject Bultmann's abstract separation of time and eternity. It also led him toward an immanent view of God, who is continually involved with the creation toward which he is rushing from the future. From the time he was a young pastor, Moltmann engaged wholeheartedly with people and tried to bring his eschatology into practice.

In *The Way of Jesus Christ* (1989), Moltmann framed the Christian life as an eschatological journey from the "already" of Christ's triumph to the "not yet" of the resurrection. In *The Coming of God* (1995), he criticized the traditional focus on *futurum* for being defined by the past and preferred to speak of *novum*, the expectation that God is doing a new work. He affirmed the intermediate state, the resurrection of the whole person, the transformation of the world, and God's goal of bringing humanity to see his glory. In his final major work, *Experiences in Theology* (2000), Moltmann explored the biblical theme of "promise," wherein God assures us he will make the future present to us.

Negative Developments in Contemporary Eschatology

In spite of such positive eschatological advances within evangelical and mainline denominations, there have been excesses in speculative eschatology. Unfortunately, contrary to New Testament warnings against doing so (Matt 24:42, 44; Mark 13:31–33; 14:32–37; Acts 1:7; 1 Thess 5:1–2), modern efforts to set dates have led to embarrassments, doctrinal innovations, hasty recalculations, and worse. William Miller (1782–1849), a popular Baptist preacher interested in Daniel's numerology, set the return of Christ for October 22, 1844. The Millerites' "great disappointment" led some to fall away, while others formed new denominations, such as the Seventh-day Adventists. The Jehovah's Witnesses likewise set dates for eschatological events to occur in 1874, 1914, 1918, and 1925, though these failures were redefined through doctrinal innovation.

The founding of the modern nation of Israel in 1948 and its astounding victory in a 1967 war encouraged preachers and publishers to stoke excitement for an immediate eschatology. Hal Lindsey's *The Late Great Planet Earth* proved a phenomenal bestseller in the 1970s, while Tim LaHaye's fictional Left Behind book series sold well in the 1990s and prompted a movie series. At best, date-setting millennialists, such as Harold Camping (1921–2013) and Hal Lindsey (1929–), have become adept at readjusting failed dates. At worst, enthusiastic millenarianism has not only occasioned departure from Christian orthodoxy but has also resulted in mass deaths, including the deaths of the eighty Branch Davidians who died during a siege in Texas in 1993 and the thirty-nine members of Heaven's Gate who committed suicide in California in 1997. These aberrant modern phenomena remind us that, as in Münster, enthusiastic eschatology may veer not only into the bizarre but also the dangerous.

Alongside the problem of date setting have been less significant but meaningful efforts to test the boundaries of eschatological orthodoxy. For instance, some British and American evangelicals have adopted the doctrine of annihilationism. One advocate, Clark Pinnock (1937–2010), defined the doctrine as "that the finally impenitent wicked will cease to exist after (or soon after) the last judgment."[8] Evangelicals such as John Robert Walmsley Stott (1921–2011) and E. Earle Ellis (1926–2010) argued that Augustine imported the doctrine of the immortality of the soul from platonic philosophy into theology, but that has been contested by historical theologians. Moreover, passages such as Matt 24:46 use the identical term, "eternal"

[8] Clark H. Pinnock, "Annihilationism," in *The Oxford Handbook of Eschatology*, 462.

(*aiōnios*), to correlate the longevity of life for the righteous with the longevity of punishment for the unrighteous.

FOR THE CHURCH

Christian attitudes to eschatology can err in two directions. On the one hand, some exhibit an "eschatomania," where they become entirely consumed with creating charts, setting dates, or judging others through their own imposed paradigm. On the other hand, often in reaction to the previous error, some develop an "eschatophobia," preferring to live in the here and now, focusing exclusively on the Christian mission, and neglecting to teach the Bible's many important teachings regarding eschatology. The best attitude may be found in a third stance, that of "eschatophilia," which expresses an appreciation for the doctrine of "the Last" as it remembers its proper Christological center and Trinitarian end.

Although discussions regarding the millennium remain important, for it is an explicit biblical teaching, it is not the only aspect of eschatology worth discussing. Next to the recovery of Christ as "the Last" and the beatific vision of the triune God as the goal of redeemed humanity, Christians should also be careful to affirm the severity of death, the certainty of the bodily resurrection, the intermediate state, the second coming of Jesus Christ, the final judgment, the new creation, and the eternal states of heaven and hell. We have much to learn about what God has done, is doing, and will do. May God build up an undiminishing hope within you as you hear his promises.

FOR FURTHER READING

Bauckham, Richard. *The Theology of the Book of Revelation*. New York: Cambridge University Press, 1993.

Blaising, Craig A., and Darrell L. Bock. *Progressive Dispensationalism*. Wheaton, IL: Victor Books, 1993.

Boersma, Hans. *Seeing God: The Beatific Vision in Christian Tradition*. Grand Rapids: Eerdmans, 2018.

Clouse, Robert G., ed. *The Meaning of the Millennium: Four Views*. Downers Grove, IL: InterVarsity Press, 1977.

Ladd, George Eldon. *The Blessed Hope*. Grand Rapids: Eerdmans, 1956.

Moltmann, Jürgen. *Theology of Hope: On the Ground and the Implications of a Christian Eschatology*. New York: Harper & Row, 1967.

Walls, Jerry L., ed. *The Oxford Handbook of Eschatology*. New York: Oxford University Press, 2008.

Questions for Study or Discussion

1. What were two major reasons why the Protestant Reformers diminished eschatology?
2. What did the historical-critical method of Protestant liberalism do to orthodox eschatology?
3. What were the eschatological beliefs of the leading evangelical scholar of the twentieth century, George Eldon Ladd?
4. How did mainline Protestants and evangelical Protestants foster a renewal of eschatology?
5. What would you say is the most exciting positive development in recent eschatology? And what is the most concerning negative development?

CONCLUSION

Nathan A. Finn

Today's theology is tomorrow's historical theology. Should the Lord tarry his return, the insights of contemporary theologians will shape the future of what is sometimes called the "Great Tradition" or the "Christian intellectual tradition"—the best of Christian theological and ethical reflection from the second century to the present day.[1] Our prayer is that we will be found faithful as theologians, and that *Historical Theology for the Church* will be a means the Lord uses to contribute to equip pastors, theologians, and other ministry leaders "to contend for the faith that was delivered to the saints once for all" (Jude 3). To that end, we want to close this book by offering a few final thoughts about the ministerial value of historical theology.

First, historical theology should inform the devotional lives of believers and the liturgical lives of churches. It should shape our prayers. When we pray to the Father in the name of the Son by the power of the Spirit, we

---

[1] See David S. Dockery and Timothy George, *The Great Tradition of Christian Thinking: A Student's Guide*, Reclaiming the Christian Intellectual Tradition (Wheaton, IL: Crossway, 2012), and Robert Louis Wilken, "The Christian Intellectual Tradition," *First Things*, June 1991, https://www.firstthings.com/article/1991/06/the-christian-intellectual-tradition.

are echoing the trinitarian reflections of believers from past centuries who have helped to clarify what Scripture teaches about our triune Lord. We are praying with the church, even as we are praying to the Lord, and in doing so we are standing on the shoulders of those who came before us.[2] Historical theology reminds us to whom we are praying—not just a generic deity but the triune Lord of all creation.

The same principle applies to our hymnody. The great Methodist minister and hymn writer Charles Wesley (1707–1788) wrote:

> He left His Father's throne above,
> So free, so infinite His grace;
> Emptied Himself of all but love,
> And bled for Adam's helpless race.

When we sing these lyrics to the famous hymn "And Can It Be," we are affirming truths about the person of Christ and his saving work that are taught in Scripture (especially Phil 2:5–11) and clarified by numerous ecumenical creeds, confessional standards, theological treatises, and published catechisms. Historical theology reminds us to write hymns that are richly biblical and deeply informed by orthodox theology, since our singing is not only an act of worship but also a key means of theological formation and spiritual encouragement among believers.

Second, historical theology should inform the preaching of the Word. At this point, we should lay our own cards on the table. We are committed to the principle that sermons should be text driven, which means they will necessarily include appropriate doctrinal content and not just moral exhortations and practical application.[3] At times, pastors might consider sermons

---

[2] Fred Sanders, *The Deep Things of God: How the Trinity Changes Everything* (Wheaton, IL: Crossway, 2010), 219–28.

[3] See Daniel L. Akin, David L. Allen, and Ned L. Mathews, eds., *Text-Driven Preaching: God's Word at the Heart of Every Sermon* (Nashville: B&H Academic, 2010); and Robby Gallaty and Steven Smith, *Preaching for the Rest of Us: Essentials for Text-Driven Preaching* (Nashville: B&H Academic, 2018).

or even sermon series on explicitly theological topics.[4] But anytime a pastor is preaching a text that touches on a doctrine, he can bless his congregation with insights from historical theology.

For example, if a pastor is preaching a sermon series on the book of 1 Samuel, he will eventually come to this much-debated verse: "Furthermore, the Eternal One of Israel does not lie or change his mind, for he is not man who changes his mind" (15:29). Does God ever change his mind? Historically, theologians have discussed this question when considering God's attributes of *omniscience* (he knows all things), *impassibility* (he does not suffer), and *aseity* (he is absolutely independent). Although there are many other biblical texts that address these attributes, and they should be considered, the pastor should also learn from the insights of theologians throughout history who have reflected deeply on this theme, nearly all of whom agree that God does not change his mind. On this question, the pastor could consult with the writings of Augustine from the patristic era, Anselm and Aquinas from the medieval era, the Puritan theologian Stephen Charnock (1620–1680), and the Dutch Reformed theologian Herman Bavinck (1854–1921)—among many others—in working through this question for the sake of his congregation.[5]

Third, historical theology should inform systematic theology. We will not say too much about this topic, since the relationship between historical and systematic theology is often covered in the introductory sections of systematic theology textbooks.[6] For our purposes, it is enough to note that

---

[4] For a helpful introduction to doctrinal preaching, see Millard J. Erickson and James L. Heflin, *Old Wine in New Wineskins: Doctrinal Preaching in a Changing World* (Grand Rapids: Baker, 1997).

[5] For a helpful introduction to God's attributes that interacts extensively with historical theology, see Matthew Barrett, *None Greater: The Undomesticated Attributes of God* (Grand Rapids: Baker, 2019).

[6] For example, see Bruce Riley Ashford and Keith Whitfield, "Theological Method: An Introduction to the Task of Theology," in *A Theology for the Church*, ed. Daniel L. Akin, 2nd ed. (Nashville: B&H Academic, 2013), 17–39. Each

there is a natural progression from studying individual texts that treat a doctrine (exegetical theology), to looking at how the doctrine is developed across Scripture (biblical theology), to engagement with historical reflections on the doctrine (historical theology), to synthesizing all of this material into a systematic presentation of the doctrine (systematic theology), to applying the doctrine to practical and pastoral considerations (pastoral/applied theology). Historical theology answers the question of what the church has said about a doctrine, and as such, it is a natural bridge from the text of Scripture to our own theological articulations and applications.

Finally, historical theology should inform ongoing debates about faith and practice. Topics such as the doctrine of election and the nature of baptism have evoked controversy off and on throughout church history, and especially since the time of the Reformation. Historical theology cannot and should not "settle" either debate, because Scripture alone is our ultimate authority for faith and practice. Nevertheless, we believe it is helpful to know the historical pedigree of various views, be aware of the cultural factors and philosophical presuppositions that have shaped the debates at times, and be familiar with the confessional assumptions (or lack thereof) that have informed how different ecclesial traditions have defined and defended their respective positions.

More recently, voices from outside the church—and increasingly from within—have called on Christians to revise their traditional understanding of human sexuality. Revisionists believe that Christianity should be "welcoming and affirming" of individuals who are homosexual or bisexual. Many also believe that gender is a fluid rather than fixed concept, and thus Christians should embrace transgenderism and similar phenomena. A growing number of congregations and even denominations have embraced revisionist views of sexuality, while others have continued to affirm traditional views. The former is accommodating their doctrine and ethics to wider

---

of the chapters in *A Theology for the Church* addresses a particular doctrine and follows the general progression we outline above.

trends in Western culture, while the latter have opted for an increasingly countercultural approach to these issues. The contributors to this volume agree that the traditional view is correct because it reflects the teaching of Scripture. God creates his human creatures male or female, and sex is a gift reserved for marriage between one man and one woman. Revisionist views are sinful distortions of God's design that do not reflect Scripture and do not contribute to authentic human flourishing.

Typically with theological debates, this is a topic for which historical theology can be useful. Revisionist sexualities, though seemingly new, actually have roots in ancient history. Homosexuality has an ancient pedigree, and throughout history there have been individuals who have chosen to identify as the opposite gender. Christian theologians have often reflected on these matters, and the near unanimous consensus from the early church until very recently is the biblical/traditional view.[7] Furthermore, historical reflections on the nature of theological anthropology (the doctrine of humanity) are helpful in framing the context for a faithful understanding of gender and sexuality.[8]

Historical theology is no mere academic discipline but is a gift to the body of Christ. May we receive this gift from the Lord, from whom every good and perfect gift comes (Jas 1:17). And may we use this gift for his glory, for the health of his church, and for the sake of those who do not yet worship him.

---

[7] Rollin Grams and S. Donald Fortson, *Unchanging Witness: The Consistent Christian Teaching on Homosexuality in Scripture and Tradition* (Nashville: B&H Academic, 2016).

[8] A good starting place is Gregg R. Allison, *Historical Theology: An Introduction to Christian Doctrine* (Grand Rapids: Zondervan, 2011), chaps. 15–16.

CONTRIBUTORS

Matthew Barrett serves as associate professor of Christian theology at Midwestern Baptist Theological Seminary and executive editor of *Credo Magazine*.

Zachary M. Bowden serves as executive assistant to the president and assistant professor of theological studies at Cedarville University.

Jason G. Duesing serves as provost and professor of historical theology at Midwestern Baptist Theological Seminary and Spurgeon College.

Stephen Brett Eccher serves as assistant professor of church history and Reformation studies at Southeastern Baptist Theological Seminary.

Nathan A. Finn serves as provost/dean of the university faculty and professor of Christian studies and history at North Greenville University.

Colman M. Ford serves as assistant professor of Christian formation and director of professional doctoral studies at Southwestern Baptist Theological Seminary.

W. Madison Grace II serves as associate professor of Baptist heritage and director of the Oxford Study Program at Southwestern Baptist Theological Seminary.

Matthew J. Hall serves as provost and senior vice president for academic administration and associate professor of church history at Southern Baptist Theological Seminary.

Jeremy M. Kimble serves as director for the Center for Biblical Integration and associate professor of theology at Cedarville University.

William M. Marsh serves as director of the master of divinity program and assistant professor of theology at Cedarville University.

Steven A. McKinion serves as professor of theology and patristic studies at Southeastern Baptist Theological Seminary.

Stephen O. Presley serves as associate professor of church history at Southern Baptist Theological Seminary.

R. Lucas Stamps serves as associate professor of Christian studies at Anderson University.

Owen Strachan serves as director of the Center for Public Theology and associate professor of Christian theology at Midwestern Baptist Theological Seminary.

Malcolm B. Yarnell III serves as research professor of systematic theology at Southwestern Baptist Theological Seminary.

John Mark Yeats serves as dean of students and student success and as professor of church history at Midwestern Baptist Theological Seminary and Spurgeon College.

NAME INDEX

L

M

N

O

P

SUBJECT INDEX

G

H

I

J

K

L

T

U

V

W